THE POLITICAL WORLD OF
THOMAS WENTWORTH,
EARL OF STRAFFORD,
1621–1641

THE POLITICAL WORLD OF THOMAS WENTWORTH, EARL OF STRAFFORD, 1621–1641

EDITED BY

J. F. MERRITT

The University of Sheffield

CAMBRIDGE
UNIVERSITY PRESS

PUBLISHED BY THE PRESS SYNDICATE OF THE UNIVERSITY OF CAMBRIDGE
The Pitt Building, Trumpington Street, Cambridge, United Kingdom

CAMBRIDGE UNIVERSITY PRESS
The Edinburgh Building, Cambridge CB2 2RU, UK
40 West 20th Street, New York NY 10011–4211, USA
477 Williamstown Road, Port Melbourne, VIC 3207, Australia
Ruiz de Alarcón 13, 28014 Madrid, Spain
Dock House, The Waterfront, Cape Town 8001, South Africa

http://www.cambridge.org

© Cambridge University Press 1996

First published 1996
First paperback edition 2002

A catalogue record for this book is available from the British Library

Library of Congress Cataloguing in Publication data
The political world of Thomas Wentworth, earl of Strafford, 1621–1641 / edited by
J. F. Merritt.
p.   cm.
ISBN 0 521 56041 1
1. Strafford, Thomas Wentworth, earl of, 1593–1691 – Congresses.   2. Great Britain – History
– Charles I, 1625–1649 – Biography – Congresses.   3. Great Britain – Politics and government
– 1603–1649 – Congresses.   4. Ireland – Politics and government – 1625–1649 – Congresses.
5. Statesmen – Great Britain – Biography – Congresses.   6. Trials (Treason) – Great Britain –
Congresses.
I. Merritt, J. F.   II. Strafford Papers Project (Sheffield, England)
DA396.S8P65   1996
941.06'2'092–dc20   95-40702   CIP

ISBN 0 521 56041 1 hardback
ISBN 0 521 52199 8 paperback

Contents

Contributors

NICHOLAS CANNY is author of *The Elizabethan Conquest of Ireland* (New York, 1976), *The Upstart Earl: A Study of the Social and Mental World of Richard Boyle, First Earl of Cork, 1566–1643* (Cambridge, 1982) and *Kingdom and Colony: Ireland in the Atlantic World, 1560–1800* (Baltimore, 1988) together with numerous articles on the history of early modern Ireland and colonial America. Dr Canny, who is Professor of Modern History at University College, Galway, is currently completing a comprehensive study of British settlement in Ireland and the Irish response to that presence which will be published by Oxford University Press under the title *Ireland in the English Colonial System, 1550–1650*.

THOMAS COGSWELL teaches history at the University of Kentucky and has written *The Blessed Revolution: English Politics and the Coming of War, 1621–1624* (Cambridge, 1989). He is currently completing a book on Whitehall and Leicestershire, 1618–1642 and another on Crown and Parliament in the 1620s.

RICHARD CUST is Senior Lecturer in Modern History at the University of Birmingham. He has published a book and articles on early Stuart political history, including *The Forced Loan and English Politics, 1626–1628* (Oxford, 1987).

TERENCE KILBURN studied history and social sciences at Birmingham University and obtained his M.A. at Leicester University's Department of English Local History. He has published articles on a variety of subjects. His book *Joseph Whitworth: Toolmaker* was published in 1989. His research into the public context of Strafford's trial was undertaken at Sheffield University.

PETER LAKE is Professor of History at Princeton University. The author of numerous studies on politics and religion under Elizabeth and the early Stuarts, he is currently working on English Conformist thought from Hooker to Laud, and the rise of the funeral sermon and godly life in the period up to 1660.

JOHN MCCAFFERTY is a Research Fellow of St John's College, Cambridge and Assistant Lecturer in Medieval History at University College, Dublin. He has published articles on the late medieval church in Ireland and on the Church of Ireland. His edition of the *Act Book of the Diocese of Armagh, 1518–22* is to be published by the Irish Manuscripts Commission and he is currently working on a book based on his Cambridge Ph.D. about the Church of Ireland in the 1630s.

J. F. MERRITT is Director of the Strafford Papers Project at the University of Sheffield, where she teaches history and is a Research Associate of the Humanities Research Institute. She has written on religion and society in early modern London and is the author of *A Courtly Community? The Transformation of Early Modern Westminster, 1525–1642*, to be published by Manchester University Press in 1996.

ANTHONY MILTON is Lecturer in History at the University of Sheffield. He is the author of *Catholic and Reformed: The Roman and Protestant Churches in English Protestant Thought, 1600–1640* (Cambridge, 1995) and *The British Delegation and the Synod of Dort* (1996). He is currently working on aspects of religious polemic in the early seventeenth century in England and the Netherlands, and is completing a biography of Peter Heylyn.

JANE H. OHLMEYER has authored *Civil War and Restoration in the Three Stuart Kingdoms: The Career of Randal MacDonnell, Marquis of Antrim, 1609–83* (Cambridge, 1993), has edited *Ireland from Independence to Occupation, 1641–1660* (Cambridge, 1995) and has contributed articles on the marquis of Antrim, Irish privateers and the Irish Civil War of the 1640s to *History Ireland, Historical Journal, History Today, Mariner's Mirror* and *A Military History of Ireland*. She teaches Irish history at Yale University and is currently working on a study of the landed elites in early modern Ireland.

BRIAN QUINTRELL is Senior Lecturer at the University of Liverpool. His publications include *Charles I, 1625–1640* (1993) and an edition of *The Maynard Lieutenancy Book 1608–1639* (1993). He is currently working on politics and government in the early Stuart period.

CONRAD RUSSELL is Professor of British History at King's College, London. His publications include *The Fall of the British Monarchies, 1637–1642* (Oxford, 1991), and most recently he has delivered the Trevelyan Lectures in Cambridge on the theme 'King James VI and I and his English parliaments'.

Acknowledgements

Many of the papers in this volume are derived from an international conference, 'The earl of Strafford and British politics, c.1621–1641', sponsored by the Strafford Papers Project and held at the University of Sheffield in July 1994. I am particularly grateful to the staff at Sheffield City Archives, especially Ruth Harman, for their many kindnesses in facilitating access to the Strafford Papers, and enabling conference guests to examine the papers at first hand. I would like to thank Olive, Countess Fitzwilliam, and the Trustees of the Wentworth Woodhouse Settled Estates for giving permission to quote from the Strafford Papers in the essays in this book.

I must thank all the contributors to this volume for the exemplary speed and efficiency they displayed in completing their chapters – and the good grace with which they have yielded to occasional editorial interference. I am especially grateful to Professor Nicholas Canny for agreeing to include his essay at very short notice. I would also like to thank William Davies of Cambridge University Press for all his help and advice in bringing the volume to fruition.

I am grateful to Nigel Williamson for his technical assistance in preparing the typescript, and Maveen Smallman for her emergency typing skills. Finally, I must thank my husband, Anthony Milton, who has offered advice, encouragement and cups of tea. His skill in judging when each of these was required deserves special recognition.

Abbreviations

BL   British Library
CJ   *Commons' Journals*
Cooper   *Wentworth Papers, 1597–1628*, ed. J. P. Cooper (Camden
            Society, 4th ser., xii, 1973)
CSPD   *Calendar of State Papers, Domestic*
CSPIre   *Calendar of State Papers, Ireland*
DNB   *Dictionary of National Biography*
Gardiner   S. R. Gardiner, *History of England, 1603–1642*, 10 vols.
            (1893)
HJ   *Historical Journal*
HMC   Historical Manuscripts Commission
Knowler   *The Earl of Strafforde's Letters and Dispatches*, ed.
            W. Knowler, 2 vols. (1739)
Laud   *The Works of William Laud*, ed. W. Scott and J. Bliss,
            7 vols. (Oxford, 1847–60)
LJ   *Lords' Journals*
NHI   *New History of Ireland*, ed. T. W. Moody, F. X. Martin
            and F. J. Byrne (1976, reprint 1991)
PRO   Public Record Office, London
RO   Record Office
Str P   Strafford Papers, Wentworth Woodhouse Muniments,
            Sheffield City Archives
TRHS   *Transactions of the Royal Historical Society*
Wedgwood   C. V. Wedgwood, *Thomas Wentworth, First Earl of Straf-
            ford: a Revaluation* (1961, reprint 1964)

Note

The place of publication for works cited in the footnotes is London, unless otherwise specified.

The historical reputation of Thomas Wentworth

J. F. Merritt

The name of Thomas Wentworth has always loomed large in accounts of seventeenth-century England. He was a controversial man in his own time, and in the work of subsequent historians his reputation has proved similarly controversial. The basic facts of his career are well known and undisputed. Born in 1593, the eldest son of a leading Yorkshire gentry family, privileges and responsibilities were swiftly loaded upon him. Knighted at the age of eighteen, he went on the Grand Tour immediately afterwards, and sat in his first parliament at the age of twenty-one, becoming second baronet and head of the family in the same year. In the 1620s he regularly attended Parliament, but his political career did not make further progress. In 1627 he was imprisoned in the Marshalsea for six weeks after refusing to pay the Forced Loan, and was dismissed from his offices of Justice of the Peace and Custos Rotulorum. In 1628 he played a major role in Parliament and encouraged the Petition of Right, but later in the same year he was appointed President of the Council in the North, and was appointed a privy councillor in the following year. In 1632 his political star rose still further when he was appointed Lord Deputy of Ireland, in which position he embarked upon a vigorous policy of building up his power. With the outbreak of war with the Scots, Wentworth became the king's most valued minister, summoned back to England, created earl of Strafford, and entrusted with a prominent role in the conduct of the so-called Bishops' Wars. After the collapse of the Second Bishops' War and the calling of the Long Parliament, Strafford soon found himself impeached for high treason. His trial dominated the political events of the early months of 1641 and led to tumultuous picketing of the House of Lords, which finally voted in favour of a bill of attainder. King Charles, despite earlier promises to Strafford that he would protect him, succumbed under pressure and gave his assent to the bill. On 12 May 1641, in the presence of a vast crowd, the earl of Strafford was executed on Tower Hill.

Beyond the broad outlines of Wentworth's career, however, historians have found little area for agreement. At Wentworth's trial, the prosecution and defence fought over the interpretation of every aspect of his troubled career. Not surprisingly, then, these arguments gave rise to sharply polarised views of the combative Lord Deputy. They were also a necessary by-product of the legal process, although much subsequent historical scholarship has tended to adopt a similar approach. Inevitably, later political divisions, formed in the aftermath of the Civil War, also meant that Whig and Tory commentators lined up for or against Strafford, as they did with regard to Charles I or Cromwell. In most interpretations of Strafford's life, then, writers have sought to understand his career by asking a series of either/or questions. On his conduct in the 1620s, they have asked if Wentworth was a man of principle, seeking to establish effective government. Or was he instead a political apostate, deserting his erstwhile parliamentary colleagues and the principles of the Petition of Right in return for the lure of office and power within what was to become an increasingly authoritarian government? Was there, in other words, a 'change of sides'? Wentworth's role in the politics of the 1630s has been construed in similarly polarised terms. Was he the king's chief minister, urging him along absolutist and unparliamentary courses? Or was he a dedicated and effective administrator, unappreciated by intriguing courtiers, working selflessly to safeguard the king's power, but still cherishing his earlier hopes for a peaceful and consensualist political nation?

Strafford's government in Ireland has similarly served as a battlefield for Whig and Tory historians. Was it, as his opponents claimed, a laboratory for absolutist ideas that would then be implemented in England? Or were these unique policies for what was by tradition a uniquely governed country? Was Strafford's government a potential success that was rudely cut short by the Scottish troubles? Or was it doomed from the beginning – a set of misguided policies which hastened rather than delayed the Irish Rebellion that erupted in 1641? The pathos of Strafford's final trial and execution has also prompted historians to investigate the validity of the charges against him and to ask just what it was that Strafford died for.

Undoubtedly, Wentworth's legacy has been a complex and ambiguous one. For Whigs seeking to emphasise the power of parliaments, the figure of Wentworth looms large in parliamentary debates during which some of the most cherished principles of constitutional liberty were supposedly proclaimed. But is his later association with the government of the Personal Rule to be conceived as a desertion of his principles, or as evidence that he had never been sincere in holding them? For royalists and later Tories, Wentworth represented a similarly ambiguous inheritance. After all, to the minds of the so-called 'constitutional royalists', Strafford stood for many of the most hated and arbitrary aspects of the Personal Rule – the patron saints of the later 'Tory' tradition, such as Hyde and Falkland, were determined in their condemnation of Wentworth in 1641. But the apparent injustice of Wentworth's attainder and execution made it particularly tempting for later royalists to portray this as the first crime of a parliamentary absolutism that would lead in natural progression to the execution of the king. In addition, Wentworth's exemplary conduct at his trial and his honourable behaviour on the scaffold have all endeared him to royalist opinion in subsequent ages as a martyr – not of royal absolutism – but of honest service to the crown in the face of popular radicalism and puritan fanaticism.

This essay explores how writers and historians have constructed the set of questions brought to bear on Strafford's career, and how other factors, particularly the varying availability of primary sources, have contributed to changing interpretations of Strafford's career, and of the political world in which he lived.[1]

I

The first assessments that were made of Strafford after his death were understandably most preoccupied with his death on the scaffold. These tragic circumstances were not lost on observers, the

I am grateful to Anthony Milton for his comments on a draft of this chapter.
[1] A number of brief surveys of the historiography of aspects of Strafford's career have been published: see, for example, Hugh Kearney, *Strafford in Ireland: A Study in Absolutism* (2nd edn, Cambridge, 1989), pp. xi–xxviii and *ibid.* (1st edn, Manchester, (1959), pp. xxxiii–xxxviii, on Strafford's Irish policies, or P. Zagorin, 'Did Strafford change sides?', *English Historical Review* 101 (1986), pp. 152–5, on his career in the later 1620s. The present essay does not attempt a comprehensive survey, but concentrates on some of the lesser-known but often most influential interpretations of Strafford's career. I am currently working on a more detailed analysis of perceptions of Strafford in the period 1641–89.

conventions of classical tragedy shaping how contemporaries regarded him. During his own lifetime, even Wentworth had compared
himself to Caesar, assassinated by his enemies, and his conduct at his
trial and execution bore not a little trace of his attachment to
Stoicism.[2] This was recognised even by his opponents. Lady Brilliana
Harley, commenting on Strafford's noble bearing at his execution,
noted that he 'dyed like a Senneca', but could not resist the
qualification that this conduct was 'not like one that had tasted the
mistery of godlyness'.[3] Early accounts of Strafford's fall were quick to
identify classical parallels. Sir Richard Fanshawe's 'On the Earle of
Straffords Tryall' followed Wentworth in comparing his trial to the
assassination of Caesar, and the Interregnum playwright, Cosmo
Manuche, wrote an English translation of Plautus' *The Captives*
relating to the fall of Strafford. Abraham Wright's more favourable
account of Strafford's trial and execution rendered the events in
Tacitean Latin, reflecting that, while Strafford's fall was not inferior
to that of the admired old Romans, his surviving fame and glory
were in every way superior and more noble still. Strafford also
appeared, inevitably, in the role of Coriolanus in the 'playlet'
Mercurius Britannicus.[4]

Obviously, Strafford could be clothed in the garb of a range of
classical models: if Wright saw him as a classical hero, then Thomas
May could compare him with the dictator Sulla.[5] But classical
writings were not simply a supermarket of stereotypes to be
plundered; the conventions of classical tragedy also exercised an
important influence over the ways in which Strafford's contemporaries described and assessed his character and interpreted his fate.
Just like Elizabeth's favourite, the earl of Essex, Strafford could be

---

2   T. Ranger, 'Strafford in Ireland: a revaluation', in T. Aston (ed.), *Crisis in Europe 1560–1660*
    (1965), pp. 281–2. On Wentworth's Stoicism, see Knowler, II, 39; K. Sharpe, *The Personal
    Rule of Charles I* (1992), p. 235. See also Richard Cust's reflections in chapter 3 below. The
    latter part of Wentworth's travel diary (Str P 30) contains many extracts from works
    discussing the figure of Cato.
3   *Letters of the Lady Brilliana Harley*, ed. T. Lewis (Camden Society 1st ser., vol. 58, 1854),
    p. 131. Note also Richard Brathwaite's later description of Strafford reading Seneca 'on
    the tranquillity of the mind' when told of the king's assent to his execution: Wedgwood,
    p. 398.
4   N. Smith, *Literature and Revolution in England, 1640–1660* (New Haven, 1994), pp. 278, 86,
    341; Abraham Wright, 'Novissima Straffordii', ed. and trans. J. Wright, *Roxburghe Club
    Historical Papers* (1846), p. 58; [Richard Brathwaite], *Mercurius Britannicus* (1641). See also
    M. Butler, 'A case study of Caroline political theatre: Brathwaite's "Mercurius Britan-
    nicus" (1641)', *HJ* 27 (1984), pp. 947–53.
5   Smith, *Literature*, p. 343.

made to fit the classical model of a tragic hero who overreaches himself and falls due to his own ambition. The fact that Strafford's friends and contemporaries, such as Sir George Radcliffe, Clarendon and Sir Philip Warwick, reached instinctively for such classical models in their accounts of his character and failings has meant that these models have exercised a strong (though often unacknowledged) influence over later historians' depictions of him.[6]

The outbreak of the Civil War so soon after Strafford's own execution inevitably polarised depictions of the earl. Parliamentarian writers were eager to sustain the justice of the charges made against Strafford at his trial. However, it is interesting to note that, while anti-Strafford pamphleteers might seek to depict Laud and Wentworth as partners in crime, there were few attempts to depict Wentworth's threat in religious form. There was no real equivalent in anti-Strafford materials of the anti-papal satire aimed at Laud in countless popular pamphlets. But if charges of crypto-popery were few, Strafford's posthumous opponents did not hesitate to charge him with another form of religious heterodoxy – that of atheism. Several parliamentarian writers asserted that Wentworth was an avid student of Machiavelli.[7]

Pamphlets that directly attacked Wentworth after the outbreak of the war were infrequent. After his execution Wentworth no longer constituted a personal threat, and his usefulness as a scapegoat for Charles's policies inevitably diminished. The continued parliamentarian attacks on Wentworth that did emerge were prompted in part by royalist championing of him as the first royalist martyr. The publication in 1647 of a royalist account of Strafford's trial and execution, the *Briefe and Perfect Relation of the Answers . . . of the Earl of Strafford,* placed the trial again at the centre of royalist/parliamentarian polemical exchanges. The need to vindicate the proceedings against Strafford therefore required that he be painted in the blackest possible colours. Thus when Milton went on the attack and described Wentworth as 'a man whom all men look'd upon as one of the boldest and most impetuous instruments that the King had to

---

[6] Many examples could be cited here. But for striking examples of how rhetorically constructed accounts have been treated by historians as objective historical evidence, see C. V. Wedgwood's comments on the *historical* value of Wright's *Novissima Straffordii* and Richard Brathwaite's *Panthalia*: Wedgwood, pp. 353, 398.

[7] F. Raab, *The English Face of Machiavelli* (1964), pp. 121, 131n, 167. Similarly, satirical woodcuts of Wentworth are scarce, whereas the figure of Laud could tap into a rich seam of anti-clerical feeling.

advance any violent or illegal designe', he was directly responding to the canonisation of Strafford in Charles's *Eikon Basilike*.

Even in the *Eikon Basilike*, however, the royalist view of Wentworth was not an unambiguous one. While Charles's remorse for yielding to the attainder of Strafford was a central preoccupation of his later years, it is interesting however to note that the discussion of Strafford in the *Eikon Basilike* is not a uniformly approving one. Charles was famously made to say that he had looked upon Strafford 'as a Gentleman, whose great abilities might make a Prince rather afraid, then ashamed to employ him, in the greatest affairs of State', and continued in reserved fashion that 'I cannot in My judgement approve all he did, driven (it may be) by the necessities of times, and the Temper of that People, more then led by his own disposition to any height and rigor of actions.'[8] As we have seen, the most important point in the royalist account of Strafford was not the defence of his ideas or policies, which seemed so out of harmony with the ideals of the *Answer to the Nineteen Propositions*. Instead they emphasised the manifest injustice that had been done to him by those who had subsequently sought the ruin of the king and his followers. His trial portentously marked the beginning of a ruinous parliamentary tyranny, of which Strafford had been the first of many victims.

Wentworth's role as martyr and emblem of the royalist cause was given an added lustre at the Restoration, when, alongside the restoration of the king, the Cavalier Parliament reversed Strafford's attainder and directed that all records and proceedings of Parliament relating to it should be 'wholly cancelled and taken out of the Fyle, or otherwayes defaced and obliterated'.[9] It was entirely fitting, then, that when Civil War memories and divisions were revived during the Exclusion Crisis, Strafford's status as royalist martyr was again prominent, encapsulated in the publication in 1679 of an account of his trial and execution. The battle over the trial continued with a vengeance during the following years. The ex-civil servant of the Protectorate, John Rushworth, published his enormous documentary account of Strafford's trial in 1680, basing it in part on notes that he

---

[8] Kearney, *Strafford*, 2nd edn, p. xii (quoting from Milton's *Eikonoklastes*); *Eikon Basilike* (Wing E311: 1649), pp. 5–6.

[9] However, while the relevant passages in the Lords Journal were defaced, they were not wholly erased: P. Christianson, 'The "obliterated" portions of the House of Lords Journals dealing with the attainder of Strafford, 1641', *English Historical Review* 95 (1980), pp. 339–53.

himself had taken at the trial. Where Rushworth claimed to reserve judgement on where justice lay in the trial, John Nalson's *Impartial Collection of the Great Affairs of State*, published in 1682, had no such qualms. This was a work given explicit royal patronage, and it included a very detailed and highly partisan account of Strafford's trial which was intended to join battle directly with the account given by Rushworth.[10]

Rushworth himself was surprisingly charitable in his comments on Wentworth, but Nalson provided the most effusive and uncritical account of Wentworth's career that had so far appeared in print.[11] Other royalist accounts of Wentworth that appeared towards the end of the seventeenth century were rather more qualified in their praise. Clarendon's *History of the Rebellion* presented him as a flawed individual: 'a man of great parts, and extraordinary endowments of nature', but spoiled in part by his early success, which 'applied to a nature too elate and arrogant of himself' made him proud and disdainful towards other men. Like so many other writers, Clarendon ultimately had recourse to a classical author – in this case Plutarch – to provide the epitaph to his sketch of a man notorious 'in doing good to his friends... [and] in doing evil to his enemies'.

Sir Philip Warwick's *Memoires*, published in 1701, presented a similar portrait. Again, Strafford's political failure rested on personal shortcomings. He was a man of high abilities, but tainted by 'a sowre and haughty temper' and 'a roughnes in his nature'. He had himself to blame in generating so many implacable enemies, especially at court: 'It was a great infirmity in him, that he seem'd to overlooke so many, as he did; since every where, much more in Court, the numerous or lesser sort of attendants can obstruct, create jealousies, spread ill reports, and do harme... there a little friendlines and opennes of carriage begets hope, and lessens envy.' Warwick also repeated contemporary rumour that Strafford's quarrel with Lord

---

[10] *An impartial account of the arraignment, trial and condemnation of Thomas late Earle of Strafford* (1679); R. C. Richardson, *The Debate on the English Revolution* (1977), p. 17; John Rushworth, *The Tryal of Thomas Earl of Strafford* (1680); John Nalson, *Impartial Collection of the Great Affairs of State from the Beginning of the Scotch Rebellion in the Year 1639 to the Murder of King Charles I* (2 vols., 1682–3), II, 1–210. On the importance of reflections on the 1640s during the Exclusion Crisis, see J. Scott, 'England's troubles: exhuming the Popish plot' in T. Harris, P. Seaward and M. Goldie (eds.), *The Politics of Religion in Restoration England* (Oxford, 1990).

[11] Rushworth, *Tryal*, ep. ded. Rushworth's charitable words here and elsewhere in the work are to be explained mostly by the fact that the book is dedicated to the marquis of Halifax, who was a nephew of Strafford.

Loftus 'was sullyed by an amour... betwixt him and his daughter'.
This was a libel repeated by Clarendon, and not finally rejected by
scholars until subjected to the meticulous attention of S. R. Gardiner
in the later nineteenth century. Warwick was approving of Strafford's
rule in Ireland, stressing his justice, although again reflecting that 'his
haughtines to amplifie his authority' had undone some of this good
work. More generally, he saw and approved a policy of Anglicisation:
Strafford had successfully attempted 'to regulate the Irish Church
unto the English', and more generally, 'like a good English-man' he
had sought to keep Ireland dependent on England.[12]

II

The following century was to see further hot dispute among historians over Strafford's career, but for the first time Strafford's own
descendants began to play a more determined role in acting to
safeguard their illustrious forebear's reputation. Wentworth's son
and heir, William, seems to have been obsessively concerned with
preserving his father's memory, putting up one monument to him
and leaving £1,000 in his will for another in York Minster.
Strafford's eighteenth-century descendants would appear to have
shared these concerns. Rushworth's volume on Strafford's trial, and
the character sketches in Clarendon and Warwick's works were
carefully tracked down and noted by family members when they
emerged from the press, while Warwick's references to 'my Lord
Straffords amours' drew hostile comment from the family as 'a
lessening to his memory'.[13]

But it was Strafford's great-grandson, the earl of Malton (later
first marquis of Rockingham) who was most of all preoccupied with
the memory of the first earl of Strafford, perhaps as a way of
boosting his own political career by this association. The revival of
Strafford's reputation was intended to be achieved in part by the
final publication of material from Strafford's surviving collection of
correspondence.

The survival of Strafford's papers is one of the most fortunate

---

[12] G. Huehns (ed.), *Clarendon. Selections from the 'History of the Rebellion' & 'The Life by Himself'*
(Oxford, 1978), pp. 146–7; Sir Philip Warwick, *Memoires* (1701), pp. 109–17; Gardiner, IX,
71.

[13] Wedgwood, p. 395; J. J. Cartwright (ed.), *The Wentworth Papers, 1705–1739* (1883),
pp. 100–1.

accidents for historians of the seventeenth century. Strafford's son, William, apparently preserved the Strafford papers in the stone tower of the family seat of Wentworth Woodhouse in Yorkshire, where they later, particularly fortunately came to the attention of the famous eighteenth-century antiquary, William Oldys. Oldys seems to have spent the period 1724–30 in Yorkshire, mostly at Wentworth Woodhouse, the seat of Strafford's descendant the earl of Malton 'with whom he had been intimate in his youth'. It is quite possible that Oldys may have overseen the organisation of Strafford's correspondence into the form in which it now survives. In 1729 Oldys wrote an 'Essay on Epistolary Writings, with respect to the Grand Collection of Thomas, earl of Strafford' dedicated to the earl of Malton, and it has been plausibly suggested that Oldys assisted Malton's chaplain, William Knowler, in preparing the latter's much-cited edition of Strafford's correspondence.[14]   *Read*

It is Knowler's two-volume collection of materials from the Strafford papers which has remained the single most important published source for Strafford's life down to very recent times. But this was not intended to be a dispassionate historical selection. It was Malton's intention that extracts from Strafford's papers should be published according to certain specified criteria. Knowler's dedicatory epistle spelled out Malton's involvement in the enterprise in unambiguous terms. The published letters had been 'selected from a vast Treasure of curious Manuscripts by Your Self, and published according to your Lordship's own Directions and Instructions, to vindicate his [Strafford's] Memory from those Aspersions, which it is grown too fashionable to cast upon him, of acting upon Arbitrary Principles, and being a Friend to Roman Catholicks'. Knowler's references to Malton's involvement were no polite fiction. When one Henry Goddard sent Knowler a number of transcribed letters by Strafford for possible inclusion in the forthcoming edition, Knowler duly presented a list of them to Malton. The earl, 'upon consulting his books over again found every one of them, & told me [Knowler], He had passed them over by design, & did not think them proper to be made publick at present'. Malton was certainly very jealous of his forebear's reputation. Indeed, Oldys suggested that one possible reason for Malton's deliberate burning of the papers of the antiquary Richard Gascoigne (who had laboriously composed pedigrees of the

[14]   J. Yeowell (ed.), *A Literary Antiquary. Memoir of William Oldys, Esq.* (1862), pp. vii, viii–x; *DNB*, s.n. 'William Oldys' and 'William Knowler'.

Wentworth family) was that the papers might contain something derogatory to the first earl of Strafford.[15]

Nevertheless, despite Malton's anxieties and interference, it is important to emphasise that Knowler's selection does not simply present a sanitised, pro-Strafford account. While Knowler undoubtedly did omit many letters that cast Wentworth in a bad light, there is still a good deal of potentially 'incriminating' material in what remains. Indeed, one of Strafford's most violent nineteenth-century critics declared that 'the family of Lord Strafford have done his Lordship's memory a most irreparable injury, by the publication of his letters, which afford such a mass of evidence of his rapacity, rancour, utter disregard of the ties of honour and justice, inhumanity, hypocrisy, and Machiavellianism, as has rarely been bequeathed to posterity'.[16] The fact that parts of the Knowler edition have been read in this light has tended to give historians the impression that Knowler's volumes represent a virtually complete edition of the important materials among the papers.

However, not only were some inflammatory letters dropped altogether, but Knowler often omitted significant sections from other letters without warning, especially if they took the form of indiscreet postscripts and endpapers. In the case of Laud's correspondence with Wentworth, this could seriously mar understandings of what was written. The main body of their letters was sometimes deliberately bland so as to mislead anyone who might intercept the correspondence. More pungent observations were kept for endpapers, which could be treated separately and burned if necessary. Some of these endpapers may also have been omitted because Knowler generally seems to have avoided letters containing large amounts of cipher. The tendency to avoid passages in cipher may also explain the omission of many of the letters detailing Strafford's remorseless hunting down of the earl of Cork, although Knowler later confessed

---

[15]   Knowler, I, dedicatory epistle; C. H. Firth (ed.), 'Papers relating to Thomas Wentworth, First Earl of Strafford, from the MSS of Dr William Knowler', *Camden Miscellany* 9 (1895), pp. vi, xi; *DNB*, s.n. 'Richard Gascoigne'. For a few useful details of the career and activities of Malton, later the first marquis of Rockingham, see M. Bloy, 'Rockingham and Yorkshire. The political, economic and social role of Charles Watson-Wentworth, the second Marquess of Rockingham' (unpublished Ph.D. thesis, University of Sheffield, 1986), ch. 1. Note also Malton's notes on aspects of Strafford's life and letters in Str P 40/67, 70, 85. Knowler describes in a later letter to the second marquis how, having copied out the letters, he used to present them to Malton 'who read every one of them over to his Lady & me, when he had an Evening at Leisure and without Company': Str P 40/74.

[16]   M. Carey, *Vindiciae Hibernicae* (3rd edn, Philadelphia, 1837), p. 177.

that in his edition 'there was a Tenderness shown to the Howards and the Boyles'.[17]

That much significant material was missed out of the Knowler volume was recognised by the editor himself. Thirty years after the original publication, Knowler, now an old man of seventy, wrote to the second marquis of Rockingham urging that an edition of Strafford's full correspondence should be considered. He stated frankly that the earlier collection had been intended to be only a 'Specimen', and that rich collections of sources, particularly the correspondence of Strafford with Laud, deserved to be published as part of a full edition which 'would be the greatest Honour to your noble Ancestor'. Nothing further seems to have come of these proposals. The prohibitive cost of the proposed enterprise, together with the death of Knowler a few years later, presumably helped to stifle the plans, although the Rockinghams may also have entertained some misgivings about allowing the full collection into the public domain.[18]

Whatever the shortcomings of the Knowler edition, however, it rapidly became and has remained the standard historical source for Strafford's career, and an important resource for broader studies of the Personal Rule. It was therefore consulted by later eighteenth-century historians such as Hume, Oldmixon and Carte, although both Carte in his *Life of Ormond* (1735) and the author of the article on Strafford printed in the 1766 *Biographia Britannica* also published a number of other minor surviving letters by Strafford.[19]

It was David Hume, however, who first used the Knowler letters as part of a more sympathetic portrait of Strafford and his policies. Hume's *History of Great Britain* was a deeply unfashionable work, propelled in part by a distaste for 'enthusiasm' and many of the traditional parliamentary heroes, and a desire to understand and forgive the policies of Charles I. Self-confessedly 'Tory as to persons and Whig as to things', Hume praised Strafford as 'one of the most eminent persons that has appeared in England'. As a consequence, Hume found himself assailed by all sides: 'English, Scotch and Irish;

---

[17] Knowler to the 2nd marquis of Rockingham (n.d.), Str P 40/74. On the Laud–Wentworth correspondence see my discussion in chapter 5 below. Some useful examples of omitted endpapers can be studied by comparing versions of Laud's letters in the nineteenth-century edition of his *Works* in volume VI (transcribed from Knowler) and volume VII (transcribed from the originals).

[18] Str P 40/72–6.

[19] Robert Browning, *Prose Life of Strafford* (1892), p. lxxi.

Whig and Tory; churchman and sectary, freethinker and religionist; patriot and courtier, united in their rage against the man who had presumed to shed a generous tear for the fate of Charles I and the Earl of Strafford'. But Hume was not quite as solitary a figure as he chose to present himself, on this matter at any rate. Carte, in his *Life of Ormond*, had also sounded a highly positive note in his treatment of Strafford.

With the coming of the French Revolution, there was an increasing vogue for Strafford in royalist circles on both sides of the Channel. Inevitably, parallels began to be drawn between events in France and the advent of the English Civil War. Indeed an extraordinary Strafford cult seems to have developed among French conservatives both before and in the wake of the Revolution. In particular, they seized on the stern warnings that Strafford's story offered of the self-destructive perils to be incurred by yielding to popular pressure. Remarkably enough, it was from this group of French exiles that the first ever full-length biography of Strafford emerged. Its author was the comte de Lally Tollendal, who had already composed a tragedy *Le Comte de Strafford*, containing explicit reference to its parallel with the royal sacrifice of the comte's own father. The play was printed in London in 1795, and was followed by a full biography of Strafford in French by the same author. This made copious use of Knowler's edition of Strafford's letters and was published by the subscription of a number of those prominent in English political life as well as exiled French ex-ministers. This 'rehabilitation' of Strafford was opposed by both French and English historians alike, including Catherine Macaulay and Jacques-Pierre Brissot de Warville, all of them conscious of the strong resonance that these historical interpretations had for contemporary political conflicts.[20]

III

The nineteenth century saw a notable expansion, both in available materials for the study of Strafford's career, and in the acuity of the

---

[20] Richardson, *Debate*, pp. 45–8; Kearney, *Strafford*, 2nd edn, p. xiii; Trophime Gerard de Lally Tollendal, *Le Comte de Strafford: tragedie en cinq actes* (1795); Trophime Gerard de Lally Tollendal, *Essai sur la vie de Thomas Wentworth, Comte de Strafford* (1796; 2nd edn, 1814); L. L. Bongie, *David Hume, Prophet of Counter-Revolution* (Oxford, 1965), esp. pp. xiii, 13–14, 104–5 n.4, 108–9. I am grateful to Dr Linda Kirk for drawing Bongie's work to my attention. For a vehement attack on Lally Tollendal's work by a later poet who was similarly drawn to compose both a tragedy and a biography of Strafford, see Browning, *Life*, p. 5n.

historical scholarship that was brought to bear on them. Whitaker's edition of the *Life and Correspondence of Sir George Radcliffe* made available several important letters by Wentworth that were not in Knowler's volumes. The opening of the Public Record Office and the greater availability of the state papers, together with the compilation of the Calendars of State Papers Domestic, also brought important new evidence into the public domain. Ironically, however, as the century progressed and new generations of historians sought to exploit unpublished manuscript collections, increasing problems began to emerge concerning scholarly access to the Strafford papers at Wentworth Woodhouse. The historian of South Yorkshire, Joseph Hunter, seems to have been one of the first scholars since Knowler to study the papers. Hunter described how 'a vast mass of Strafford's correspondence remains behind, in what is called the Earl of Strafford's chest, in the archives at Wentworth House, well arranged and bound in volumes'.[21] James Bliss, the editor of Laud's *Works* for the Library of Anglo-Catholic Theology, seeking initially one presumes to verify Knowler's transcriptions of Laud's letters to Wentworth, also applied for and was granted access to the collection. He thereby came across the enormous unpublished collection of their correspondence. The result was another full volume of Laud's correspondence, including the archbishop's newly discovered letters to Wentworth. Only restrictions of space prevented Bliss from publishing Wentworth's side of the correspondence – a decision which historians had bitter reason to regret for the next century, as the family seems henceforth to have prevented access to the papers. Not even the great S. R. Gardiner could secure admission. In the preface to the ninth volume of his celebrated *History of England*, Gardiner described with barely concealed fury how he had scoured the country for pertinent manuscript collections, and was frustrated 'in one quarter only', as 'I regret that the Lord Fitzwilliam has not considered it to be consistent with his duty to allow me to see the Strafford correspondence preserved at Wentworth Woodhouse'. Reading Bliss's thanks to the Earl Fitzwilliam 'for the unhesitating manner in which the use of these papers was most obligingly conceded' just a few decades earlier must only have increased Gardiner's frustration.[22]

This renewed sensitivity to outside readership of the Strafford

---

[21] Joseph Hunter, *South Yorkshire* (2 vols., 1828–31), II, 84, quoted in Browning, *Life*, p. lxxiii.
[22] Laud, VII, v–vi; Gardiner, IX, viii.

collection – perhaps prompted by some of the revelations provided
by the edition of Laud's *Works* – drove Gardiner and his colleague
C. H. Firth to track down whatever traces they could find of those
who had dealt with the forbidden papers. The result was the
publication by the Camden Society of several unpublished transcriptions of Strafford letters found among a collection of Knowler's
papers which Firth purchased.[23]

Even with the closure of the archive at Wentworth Woodhouse,
new Wentworth material continued to appear and challenge received
orthodoxies. The growing accessibility of the State Papers Domestic
revealed materials that illuminated Wentworth's earlier career, and
were used in studies of his early electoral activities in Yorkshire, as
well as in Charles's first parliaments. The new accessibility of private
archives in Ireland also allowed aspects of his Irish administration to
be studied from the perspective of Strafford's enemies, Cork and
Lord Chancellor Loftus, to supplement Wentworth's self-presentation.[24] For most of the century, however, Strafford's biographers
were essentially restricted to Knowler's volumes and Rushworth's
Tryal.

While the nineteenth century for the first time saw the publication
of full-length biographies of Strafford, they mostly told a familiar
tale. The traditional Whig view of Strafford reigned supreme,
whether couched in Macaulay's memorable prose or in a popular if
curious life of Strafford that was published in 1836 in the series 'Lives
of Eminent British Statesmen' under the name of John Forster. From
America came a most virulent attack from the Irish Catholic lobby.
One Matthew Carey complained of how 'Clarendon, Nalson, Carte,
Hume, and all the long train of monarchical writers whine and
lament over his grave'. His own account, bristling with capital letters
and exclamation marks, maintained of Strafford that 'those who take
a correct view of his career, must acknowledge that he was a bloated
mass of almost every species of vice and crime of which a public
officer is capable'.[25]

By the later nineteenth century, however, a rather more subtle
portrait of Wentworth was emerging from the researches of S. R.
Gardiner and C. H. Firth. Gardiner denied that Wentworth had
been guilty of any political 'apostasy' in 1628, declaring imperiously

---

[23] Firth, 'Papers'.   [24] Browning, *Life*, lxxii–lxxiii.
[25] *Ibid., passim*; Lord Macaulay, *The History of England* (6 vols., 1913), I, 76–7; Carey, *Vindiciae*,
      p. 177.

'that there was no real or pretended change of principles is obvious'. While his change of circumstances brought with it a change of view, Wentworth still sought only 'to return the kingship in the position it had acquired under the Tudors'. Charles Firth echoed Gardiner's sentiments in a substantial but often neglected portrait that was commissioned as an introduction to a re-publication of the life of Strafford – one published under Forster's name, but apparently written in part by the poet, Robert Browning. Firth's was a notably balanced account. On Wentworth's supposed 'apostasy', Firth commented, in language that anticipated the thrust of the later twentieth-century 'revisionist' school, that

> it [cannot] fairly be said that Wentworth left the side of the people and adopted the side of the King. Nothing misleads so much as the application of the ideas of modern politics to the times before party government was born or dreamt of. The first axiom of Wentworth's political creed was that there were not and could not be two sides. – Charles Firth

Firth made the telling addition, however, that 'he never saw that what had once been a truth was rapidly becoming a mere phrase'.[26] Firth's Wentworth was a man sincerely committed to an ideal of constitutional harmony in which the rights of king and people were equally preserved. But this is an ideal rooted 'in the traditions of the past rather than the necessities of the present'. By 1630, the difference between king and people 'was too great to be healed; whichever prevailed, the harmonious balance of the constitution must be destroyed'. Seeing the necessity that one side must rise at the expense of another, Wentworth chose to back the power of the crown.[27]

If Gardiner and Firth brought a new historical rigour into depictions of Wentworth, it would however be wrong to distinguish too firmly between these sober exponents of the new 'scientific' history and the romantic spirit that Wentworth's career inspired in a man such as Browning. John Adamson has recently reminded us of just how far the historical vision of the famously 'objective' Gardiner was shaped by late Victorian values, and specifically by his Gladstonian politics.[28] Nor was Gardiner immune to poetical insight. Just as Firth

---

[26] *DNB*, s.n. 'Thomas Wentworth, first Earl of Strafford' (by S. R. Gardiner); Gardiner, VI, 335–8, VII, 24–8, IX, 370–1; Browning, *Life*, pp. xxiii–xxiv.
[27] Browning, *Life*, pp. xxiii–xxxv.
[28] J. S. A. Adamson, 'Eminent Victorians: S. R. Gardiner and the Liberal as Hero', *HJ* 33 (1990), pp. 641–57.

wrote a tactful introduction to Browning's *Life* of Strafford, so the supposedly austere Gardiner corresponded with Browning, and was happy to write an introduction to an edition of Browning's play, *Strafford*. Indeed, Gardiner opined that 'every time that I read the play, I feel more certain that Mr. Browning has seized the real Strafford'. When it came to his own treatment of Strafford's execution in the *History of England*, Gardiner found it impossible to restrict himself to the sober tones of the historian, and resorted instead to direct quotation from Browning's play. This took the form of a fanciful meditation by Pym on Strafford's execution, though Gardiner felt compelled to qualify it as being 'an imaginary Pym, recalling an imaginary friendship'.[29]

From the late nineteenth century onwards, a new charity seems to have entered into many accounts of Strafford's career. Right-wing authors of the late nineteenth century found Strafford's ideals – as they saw them – much to their taste. The most widely read late-Victorian account of Strafford's career was not that of Gardiner or Firth, but the biography composed by the newspaper editor H. D. Traill for Macmillan's 'English Men of Action' series. First published in 1889, this work was the first genuinely popular study of Strafford to be published, going through three editions in thirteen years. Traill saw Strafford in straightforward terms as 'the historical representative of the Absolutist cause'. On Wentworth's political 'apostasy', Traill emphasised Wentworth's consistency, specifically dissenting from Gardiner's recently published portrayal of Wentworth as the sincere and disinterested patriot. Denying alike suggestions that Wentworth either underwent an honest conversion or was politically seduced, Traill maintained that Wentworth 'was from the first an adherent of those absolutist principles of government of which he afterwards became so firm a champion'. There was, then, no change of sides – Wentworth was merely guilty of 'making use of a political party for his own ends' by seeking to convince Buckingham 'that it was better to have him for a friend than an enemy'.

The 'Absolutist cause' of which Traill saw Wentworth as a distinguished representative was, moreover, a cause which Traill considered to be well worth fighting for. He rejected the assumption that this was a course that was somehow doomed, and that Strafford's victory could only have briefly delayed the irresistible

<hr/>

[29] Browning, *Life*, introduction; Robert Browning, *Strafford: A Tragedy* (1884), introduction, p. xiii; Gardiner, IX, 371.

'advance of triumphant Democracy'. For the right-wing Traill, confident that 'the once imposing train of believers in the divine right of Democracy is diminishing every day', the victory of Strafford's ideals might still lie in the future.[30]

Strafford's other defenders in the early twentieth century had less of an ideological agenda, but were more impressed by the pathos of the man and his failed cause. The 1930s saw no less than three biographies appear, the most famous of them the life written by C. V. Wedgwood. This was her first book, and, as she later admitted, was written when she was 'still very young in the ways of the world', with the result that 'I took him altogether too much at his own valuation'.[31] For all of its firmly pro-Strafford tone, Wedgwood's was a scholarly work, but she was hampered, like Strafford's earlier biographers Elizabeth Cooper, Browning and Traill, by lack of access to the unpublished papers at Wentworth Woodhouse. She was not alone. The librarian of the new Central Library in Sheffield received a 'dusty answer' when he wrote to the Earl Fitzwilliam suggesting that the collection might be moved to the new library, and an 'even dustier' answer from his heir when he repeated the request on a later occasion. But the selective nature of this restriction became all the more clear in these years as the papers were made available to two amateur biographers, Lady Burghclere and Lord Birkenhead. Access to the papers would appear to have been granted because of family connections.[32] Clearly, this was a rare privilege. It might well have been felt that professional historians could not be expected to be discreet in dealing with some of the papers' contents – an attitude with which Lord Malton would certainly have agreed. Nevertheless, it should not be supposed that access was only given to these biographers so that simple hagiographies could be composed. Both authors were talented amateurs with a serious interest in tracking down other surviving manuscript collections, including those at Broughton Castle, the Jervoise of Herriard manuscripts, and those of the duke of Rutland at Belvoir

---

[30] H. D. Traill, *Lord Strafford* (3rd edn, 1902), pp. 1–2, 32–42, 61, 200–6. Among other works, Traill also composed a biography of William III: *Who Was Who 1897–1916* (1920), s.n. 'Henry Duff Traill'.

[31] Wedgwood, p. 14.

[32] Lady Burghclere's brief first marriage had been to the son of the second earl of Strafford: *Who Was Who 1929–40* (1941), s.n. 'Lady Winifred Burghclere'. The comments of Sheffield's Central Librarian (J. P. Lamb) are extracted from the typescript of a paper which he delivered to the National Register of Archives in December 1949, currently in possession of the Strafford Papers Project.

Castle.[33] Whatever the deficiencies of the books that emerged, they did not represent simple whitewashes of Strafford's career. Indeed, Lady Burghclere's is a substantial two-volume work which at times is surprisingly shrewd and balanced in its judgements, containing lengthy and revealing extracts from unpublished Strafford correspondence.

Obviously, however, these books represented missed opportunities which professional historians could have hoped to exploit more thoroughly. Historians finally got their opportunity after the Second World War, when the combined persuasive talents of G. R. Potter of Sheffield University and one Colonel Malet finally secured the Strafford papers for Sheffield Central Library, along with a vast collection of other historical papers of major importance among the Wentworth Woodhouse muniments.

It was, however, historians of Ireland rather than England that were the first to make effective use of the newly available papers. A number of scholars now undertook searching inquiries into the nature and success of Wentworth's Irish policies using the papers. Nineteenth-century historians had been chiefly hostile towards Strafford on this topic, following the accusations made by Strafford's prosecutors in 1641 that his Irish record had been a blueprint for absolutism in England, and had made the Irish Rebellion inevitable. The early twentieth century, however, had been as kind in its interpretation of Strafford's Irish career as we have already seen in relation to his English career. Hugh O'Grady's *Strafford and Ireland* provided an enormously detailed and lavish apologia for Strafford's policies, and one that was generally followed by Strafford's English biographers.[34]

With the assistance of the Strafford papers, however, a series of historians set about demolishing Strafford's Irish career with a vengeance. Hugh Kearney contributed a learned and devastating account. In his *Strafford in Ireland*, subtitled ominously 'A Study in Absolutism', Kearney was partly concerned to re-establish Wentworth's absolutist credentials. But he also sought as never before to place Strafford's policies in their full historical context, and argued as a result that there was little that was new or distinctive in Strafford's policies. Terence Ranger, in the course of work on Strafford's arch-enemy, the earl of Cork, constructed a similarly

---

[33] Earl of Birkenhead, *Strafford* (1938); Lady Burghclere, *Strafford* (2 vols., 1931).
[34] Kearney, *Strafford*, 2nd edn, p. xxxvii; W. H. A. O'Grady, *Strafford and Ireland* (2 vols., Dublin, 1923).

damning picture of Strafford, but reverted to earlier Whig traditions by emphasising the distinctiveness of his policies. With extra evidence from the newly released papers, as well as further research in the Lismore papers kept at nearby Chatsworth House, Ranger offered an unqualified endorsement of the traditional Whig view of Strafford's 'absolutism', and also sought to diminish O'Grady's picture of the heroic reformer by emphasising Strafford's avid pursuit of his own personal fortune.[35] J. P. Cooper offered a more balanced approach. While he rejected Strafford's self-image of the selfless administrator indifferent to personal wealth, Cooper still emphasised that Strafford 'had principles and loyalties', that he made substantial gains for the crown as well as himself, and that his staking everything on Charles's regime compared favourably with the behaviour of most of his contemporaries at court.[36] If Strafford's self-valuation could not simply be accepted as accurate, it still had much to tell historians about how Strafford understood himself and shaped his actions.

This was all scholarship that was understandably most focused on Strafford in Ireland. But the emergence of the Strafford papers was also leading to re-evaluations of his English career. This partly took the form of a new edition of C. V. Wedgwood's famous biography, which offered a more complex picture of a decidedly flawed and self-deluding figure. But the Strafford papers, and the figure of Strafford himself, were destined to play a larger role in the shifting scholarly interpretations of early Stuart politics. For Perez Zagorin, working through some of the materials in the early 1960s, the figure of Thomas Wentworth was central to the thesis of his book *The Court and the Country*. The letter written to Wentworth by Sir Edward Stanhope in 1631 on the subject of his 'change of sides' in 1628 provided allegedly crucial evidence for the argument that there were indeed sides to change – and for Zagorin the personal breach between Wentworth and the Holles family was 'an emblem of the formation of sides and of the political polarisation between the Court and the Country from which the English Revolution took its origin'.[37]

---

[35] Ranger, 'Strafford', pp. 271–93. Cf. Carey, *Vindiciae Hibernicae*, pp. 190–1.

[36] J. P. Cooper, 'The fortune of Thomas Wentworth, Earl of Strafford', *Economic History Review* 2nd ser., 11 (1958), pp. 227–48; reprinted in G. E. Aylmer and J. S. Morrill (eds.), *Land, Men and Beliefs* (1983), pp. 148–75. Cooper also responded to some of Ranger's use of evidence in 'Strafford and the Byrnes' Country', reprinted in *ibid.*, pp. 176–91.

[37] P. Zagorin, 'Sir Edward Stanhope's advice to Thomas Wentworth... An Unpublished Letter of 1631', *HJ* 7 (1964), pp. 298–320; P. Zagorin, *The Court and the Country* (1969); P. Zagorin, 'Did Strafford change sides?', p. 163.

However, Zagorin's interpretation of the period was soon to be challenged, and once again the figure of Thomas Wentworth, and the contents of the Strafford papers, were seen as holding the key. An important stage in the development of early Stuart 'revisionism' came with the publication by J. P. Cooper in 1973 of an edition of hitherto unpublished Wentworth correspondence from the 1620s. As a result, new Strafford materials emerged in time to play a significant role in the important re-thinking of the early Stuart period then underway. In his editorial introduction, Cooper urged that the papers bore witness to several themes that were to become prominent in revisionist historiography: the importance of the role of the court in the parliamentary politics of the period, the interdependence of 'court' and 'country', and the significance of religious change in the 1620s. Cooper denied any political 'apostasy' on Wentworth's part, but identified instead a significant change in 'churchmanship' in the late 1620s as Wentworth switched his allegiance from Archbishop Abbot to Bishop Laud. Cooper's assessment was echoed in Conrad Russell's *Parliaments and English Politics, 1621–1629*, where Wentworth's parliamentary career was taken to encapsulate the close relationship of court and country. In the same book, Wentworth's parliamentary speeches from 1625 and 1628 provided important evidence for the revisionist emphasis on the strength of 'localism', rather than constitutional issues, in the conflicts of the period. Similarly, in an important article on Wentworth's early political career, Peter Salt emphasised the 'localism' of the Yorkshire electorate which Wentworth struggled to court, and downplayed the value of Parliament either as an institution which truly sought to represent local concerns, or as a mechanism whereby aspiring politicians such as Wentworth might draw themselves to the attention of courtly patrons.[38]

In the ensuing debates between revisionists and other historians, Wentworth was made to don a variety of Whiggish and post-revisionist garments. Zagorin's answer to the precepts of revisionism concentrated entirely on Strafford's 'change of sides' as the pivotal event for his interpretation of early Stuart politics. The figure of Wentworth also loomed large in the arguments of the so-called 'post-

---

[38] Cooper, pp. 5–8; C. S. R. Russell, *Parliaments and English Politics, 1621–1629* (Oxford, 1979), pp. xxi, 6, 9–10, 18, 19, 79, 121, 145, 258–9, 332–3, 427; S. P. Salt, 'Sir Thomas Wentworth and the parliamentary representation of Yorkshire, 1614–1628', *Northern History* 16 (1980), pp. 130–68.

revisionist' school of historians. Richard Cust returned once more to
Wentworth's electoral activities in the 1620s in order to argue against
the revisionist emphasis on 'localism'. Cust used Wentworth's contested elections in Yorkshire in the 1620s, and the evidence provided
in Cooper's edition of letters in particular, to argue that England in
this period had an active, independent and politically informed
electorate, with local and national issues being blended in the minds
of both MPs and their constitutents. The terminology of 'court' and
'country' was revived, not to describe concrete, monolithic political
factions, but rather to denote ideological polarities through which
contemporaries viewed their political world.[39]

The historiographical successor to post-revisionism has yet to
emerge, but the debate on the nature of early Stuart politics, and the
challenge that Strafford's career presents to each interpretation of
the period, shows no sign of abating.

*   *   *

In various ways the essays in this volume contribute to a range of
long-standing debates which have attached to Wentworth and his
career and they seek to borrow him (or the evidence of his papers) to
re-evaluate current debates over the nature of English and Irish
politics in the 1620s and 1630s. Thomas Cogswell and Conrad
Russell exchange revisionist and post-revisionist views on the parliaments of the early 1620s and the motivation of the different elements
within them, with the question of the typicality of Wentworth's views
on the Spanish war emerging as pertinent as ever. Richard Cust
addresses the age-old question of Wentworth's 'change of sides', but
places the debate within the new post-revisionist sensitivity to
rhetoric and discourse. Brian Quintrell uses the Strafford papers to
cast significant doubt on the traditional view of the grip that Laud
and Strafford were able to exercise at court, following recent scholarship in emphasising the fluidity of court politics and the decisive role
played by the king. My own essay looks at the character of Strafford's
correspondence in the context of a broader discussion of how
Strafford sought to maintain lines of influence and communication in
the first few years of his Irish administration. Anthony Milton seeks
to use Wentworth's political behaviour and ideas to comment on the

[39] Zagorin, 'Did Strafford change sides?'; R. Cust 'Politics and the electorate in the 1620s,' in
R. Cust and A. Hughes (eds.), *Conflict in Early Stuart England* (1989), pp. 134–62.

recent historiographical controversies over the extent to which early Stuart political thought was 'consensualist' or riven by constitutional conflict prompted by new forms of absolutist thought. The essays by Nicholas Canny, John McCafferty and Jane Ohlmeyer tackle Irish affairs and Wentworth's role in them – always significant issues in Wentworth's career, but now studied in dialogue with questions thrown up by the consideration of the 'British problem'. Strafford's trial, a subject for historical debate from the day that it began, is considered by Terence Kilburn and Anthony Milton, informed by the more recent historiographical interest in the formation and working of public opinion in the early Stuart period. Finally, Peter Lake offers a broader overview of post-war developments in the scholarly analysis of Wentworth's political world, and locates this volume and its contributors among the recent historiographical trends of post-revisionism and the 'New British History'.

The need to re-evaluate the career of Thomas Wentworth has been a task passed down through successive generations of early Stuart historians. Whigs, Tories, revisionists, post-revisionists, cultural historians – each new current in historical thinking has returned to the extraordinary career and voluminous letters of Wentworth for evidence and scholarly ammunition. If many of these pictures of Wentworth have resulted from privileging some types of evidence over others, they have cumulatively helped to draw attention to the rich and multi-faceted nature, both of Wentworth's own career and of the collection of materials he left behind. Historians, the better to examine their sources, compulsively divide up their period of study – chronologically, geographically and thematically – but the varied career of a man such as Wentworth should challenge them to attempt a more holistic view. Until historians can put forward an explanation that can encompass the extraordinarily complex and varied career of Wentworth, they cannot hope to explain the broader structures of British political life in the early Stuart period. He will continue, then, to be at the centre of early Stuart historiography, a figure who puzzles and intrigues.

Tempting new avenues of inquiry are certainly open for exploration. The Strafford papers still remain seriously under-exploited by historians. If Cooper's edition has made Wentworth's 1620s' career better studied, there has still been less of an attempt by English historians to make systematic use of the sprawling collection of unpublished correspondence from the 1630s. While Irish historians have indeed made use of materials from the Personal Rule, they have been generally most concerned to study their contents from an Irish perspective. But for the English history of the Personal Rule, the papers remain almost as untouched as when S. R. Gardiner seethed in annoyance at finding the doors of Wentworth Woodhouse closed to him in the 1880s. It is to be hoped that this collection of essays may help to remind early Stuart historians of the unexploited glories of the collection and promote a more sustained research effort. It is unlikely that a definitive picture of Sir Thomas Wentworth will emerge, but on past evidence we may expect that the search will do a great deal to expand our knowledge of, and reshape the categories that we use to explore, the political world in which he lived and died.

CHAPTER I

Phaeton's chariot:
The Parliament-men and the continental crisis in 1621

Thomas Cogswell

Scarcely had the second session of the 1621 parliament begun before matters went awry. The alarming situation brought Sir Edward Sackville to his feet, warning his colleagues against proceeding 'as Phaeton did, [and] take in Hand the Rule of a Chariot which appertaines not us'. Such boldness, he cautioned, would only lead to 'as great a Confusion here, as the other is said [to have been] an Inflammation of the whole World'.[1] His prediction proved all too correct. A majority persisted in their effort to control a political chariot, which their royal father regarded as his own. The conclusion was acrimonious debate over freedom of speech, followed shortly by a thunderbolt from Zeus, a hasty dissolution. Contemporaries could hardly have missed the spectacle of Phaeton's chariot lighting up the winter sky, a scene which fascinates scholars. Later attention understandably has focused on the legal and constitutional implications of the celebrated confrontation. Yet what generated much of the heat late in 1621 was the Commons' attitude to the continental war. After all, the brief second session began with the Lord Keeper announcing that 'Janus Temple must be opened' and that 'the voice of Bellona' replace that of the turtle. Seconding Williams's appeal was Lord Digby, James's ambassador extraordinary, who announced that the Commons had to help the king to draw his sword since the involved pursuit of a negotiated settlement had failed. In the event, the most that the government could extract from the House was a single subsidy. Even that was only approved in principle, for emotional

---

I would like to thank the NEH for a fellowship in 1990–91 when I drafted this chapter and to the Folger Shakespeare Library for providing a delightful haven in which to write.

[1] Edward Nicholas, *Proceedings and Debates in the House of Commons in 1620 and 1621* (2 vols., Oxford, 1766) 'hereafter *PD*', ii, 269. Although the 1621 parliament technically was one session with an extended adjournment, I have followed contemporary practice and divided it into two distinct sessions. For more on this point, see G. A. Harrison, 'Parliaments and sessions: the case of 1621', *Parliamentary History* 12 (1993), pp. 19–28.

pleas from the government bench could not persuade a majority to
give the bill even one reading.

The urgency of the government's pleas and the coolness of the
House's response has made some scholars wonder about the depth of
the Commons' commitment to anything other than rhetorical
flourishes on behalf of Frederick and Elizabeth of the Palatinate, to
say nothing of the hard-pressed continental brethren. Close analysis
of these debates, Professor Russell has argued, 'does not give the
impression that either desire to seize the initiative in foreign affairs
or desire for war with Spain was a very deep seated emotion in the
Commons'. Indeed aside from a few prominent MPs, it was clear
that 'the anti-Spanish brigade in the Commons were neither large,
powerful nor determined'. Such a conclusion naturally followed
from the first meeting. Then the House's reticence to support the
nascent war effort was so obvious that 'if James observed the first
session... carefully, his reluctance to go to war can only have been
increased'.[2] Such a judgement is far from novel. In a dialogue which
Sir Robert Phelips composed in 1623, a country gentleman and a
councillor of state sparred over recent events, and the sharpest
exchange took place over the 1621 parliament. 'Let me tell yow in
plaine English,' the councillor maintained, that all of the Parliament-
men's devotion to Elizabeth's cause 'were but flourishes for when the
overture for her assistaunce was propounded unto them, they then
shrunke back and fell upon other distastefull digressions.' Russell's
judgement therefore merely elaborates on this point.

The distinguished origins of this position rightly demands careful
scholarly attention. Yet Phelips's councillor notwithstanding, this
essay will caution against allowing serious consideration to slide into
blind acceptance. This is not to maintain that the Parliament-men
were all fire-breathing interventionists. Plainly a few of them were
dead set against any military involvement, and just as plainly, more
than a few were apprehensive about where intervention might lead
the country. Nevertheless, to focus exclusively on these apprehensions is to miss the full significance of what actually happened. In
fact, a compelling case can be made that a majority of the
Commons, notwithstanding their apprehensions, were quite interested in war. For it, they were willing to offer up the most precious
commodity in early Stuart England – new parliamentary taxation.

[2] Conrad Russell, *Parliaments and English Politics, 1621–9* (Oxford, 1979), pp. 130–1, 121. For a
different and still useful analysis see Robert Zaller, *The Parliament of 1621* (Berkeley, 1971).

Indeed, a careful examination reveals that the search for 'little Englanders' in the Commons is misdirected. To be sure, a case can be fashioned, highlighting the few Parliament-men opposed to war. Yet this eminently debatable case should not overshadow another, almost ironclad one; for serious, principled opposition to involvement, scholars should look, not in the Chapel of St Stephen, but rather in the Palace of Whitehall, among the leading crown officials and in the royal bedchamber itself.

Given the existing scholarship, such a statement is provocative in the extreme. Yet before abandoning the task as hopelessly audacious, it is worth recalling that in response to Phelips's councillor, the country gentleman delivered the lie direct. If the 'proceedings of that assembly... be dewly and without passion considered', only one conclusion emerges: 'if ever men were resolved to lay downe their lives and fortunes in any imployment yt was that assembly for the recovery of her estate'.[3] Quite simply, this essay will argue that, after a due and dispassionate consideration, Phelips's gentleman had it right.

I

While the attention of modern scholars has been riveted on the dramatic confrontations of the second session, the Parliament-men at the end of 1621 had their eyes fixed just as steadily on the first session. Hence, in order to understand the logic of their arguments then, we must appreciate the significance of what had happened earlier in the year.

Behind all the parliamentary rhetoric about the Palatinate and the Protestant cause were about two thousand men and one woman. Chief among them was James I's only daughter, Elizabeth, and her husband, Frederick V of the Palatinate. On the death of Prince Henry, all those disgusted with the Jacobean regime looked to her as the paragon of virtue, and her involvement in the Thirty Years War only confirmed this sentiment. Surrounding Frederick and Elizabeth in the popular imagination were General Vere and two thousand English volunteers, who were grimly defending the only three towns which Frederick retained in the Palatinate. Early in 1621, those men were isolated, low on food and even lower on money. Steady reports

---

[3]   [Sir Robert Phelips], 'A Discourse by way of dialogue', Somerset RO, Phelips MSS DD/ Ph 227/17.

from men penning variations on the complaint that 'wee are so dishartned' left the English ambassador in The Hague constantly fearful of some 'mutination', either from the local residents upset with the unpaid soldiers or from the troopers themselves. If the government sometimes appeared indifferent to their plight, the Parliament-men simply could not be so blasé. Heidelberg, Mannheim and Frankenthal held the largest assembly of the prominent younger sons outside of the Inns of Court. A Parliament-man glancing over the list of Vere's officers, which included last names like Herbert, Sackville, Rich, Holles, Fairfax, Harrington, Wentworth and Devereux, could scarcely fail to find a friend, if not a relative.[4]

Opposing them was a bewildering constellation of enemies. Contemporaries raised during the long Elizabethan war naturally assumed that most Catholic states and all Habsburg princes operated under the direction of the King of Spain. Yet Frederick's actual opponent was Emperor Ferdinand II whose military muscle came from both the Catholic League and the even more formidable Spanish Army of Flanders, which had been temporarily seconded to Imperial control. Spain itself, at least outwardly, supported James's search for a negotiated settlement. His preferred solution was Prince Charles's marriage to the Infanta, and their dowry would be the restoration of the Palatinate. If this goal remained elusive, precisely what James would do was most unclear.[5]

Against this confused backdrop, Parliament opened early in 1621 and eventually approved two subsidies. 'As a grant towards a war which might have cost a million pounds,' Russell has argued, '£140,000 would not have gone very far.' Therefore, 'if, as is possible, James was allowing the decision for peace or war to be influenced by the size of the grant he got from the Commons, the influence would be against war'.[6] Appealing though such an analysis might be, several factors severely undercut its persuasiveness.

[4] Morgan to Trumbull, 18 Nov. 1620; Carleton to Trumbull, 12 Aug. 1621, BL, Trumbull MSS Misc. x/unfol., xvi/98; and 'A Generall Accompt for the Palatinate', 1621, PRO, SP 81/23/16. (Since the BL's recataloguing of the Trumbull MSS is unfinished, I have used the volume references from the Berkshire RO.)

[5] For the diplomatic background to this parliament, see R. Zaller, 'Interest of State: James I and the Palatinate', *Albion* 6 (1974), pp. 144–75; S. L. Adams, 'Foreign policy and the parliaments of 1621 and 1624', in K. Sharpe (ed.), *Faction and Parliament*, (Oxford, 1978), pp. 139–71; and Adams's magisterial essay, 'Spain or the Netherlands? The dilemmas of early Stuart foreign policy', in H. Tominson, (ed.), *Before the Civil War*, (1983), pp. 79–102.

[6] Russell, *Parliaments*, p. 91.

Contemporaries knew all too well, if later scholars have forgotten, that this grant was not the first contribution to the war effort. Early in 1620, James I permitted Palatine representatives to organise a benevolence in support of Vere's men. Because this money was not paid into the Exchequer, no record of the total amount survives. Nevertheless scattered local evidence reveals impressive returns. Leicestershire, where a single subsidy netted about £750, gathered £1,558, easily equal to two parliamentary subsidies. Likewise Hampshire collected another £2,717 pounds, and Essex £2,000.[7] The best indication of the success was James's envy; at the end of year, he launched his own benevolence for the same purpose, which soon netted almost £35,000.[8] Since Frederick and Elizabeth on their own must have gathered more than this amount, the realm voluntarily offered up somewhere around £80,000 to £90,000. 'The People', Sir Benjamin Rudyard concluded, 'weare never soe forward in any as this Action.' The dubious legality of such benevolences made the popular response all the more remarkable. That so much came in so easily in an appeal which many regarded as 'not legal', Phelips remarked, can only be taken as evidence of 'our love to the party'.[9] Hence when the Parliament-men began their deliberations over supply, they and their constituents had already given handsomely to the Protestant cause.

The House eventually approved two subsidies, which together with three clerical subsidies netted the Exchequer £199,851. Yet even if we add the benevolences to the parliamentary grants, the grand total of almost £300,000 is still well short of a million pounds. On the other hand, no one so much as whispered the larger figure. Granted the Council of War had prepared a military proposal calling for £838,105 in the first year and £579,735 in subsequent ones. But this was for a truly massive army of 25,000 infantry, 5,000 horse, 20 cannon and a staggering logistical tail which required 10,112 draught-horses and 5,000 cavalry mounts. Little wonder that the main purpose of this awesome plan seems to have been to shock James out of any illusions about marching into

[7]   Huntingdon to Dohna, 1 June and 30 Oct. 1620, Huntington Library, HAM 53/6, ff.60, 60v–61; receipt from Williams and Dohna, 26 Nov. 1620, Hampshire RO, Wroithesley MSS 5M53/971; and Warwick to Dohna, [1620], PRO, SP 81/91/305.
[8]   PRO, E 405/273, f. 6v.
[9]   Rudyard to Nethersole, 2 Oct. 1620, PRO, SP 81/19/17–7v; W. Notestein, F. H. Relf and H. Simpson (eds.), *Commons' Debates in 1621* (7 vols., New Haven, 1935) (hereafter *CD 1621*), III, 404–5; V, 393–4.

central Europe. It certainly ended further discussion of the idea in Whitehall.[10]

In Parliament itself, there was no mention of £800,000, to say nothing of an even million, because the government presented no military plan *at all* to the first meeting. In his discussion of the second session, Russell rightly emphasised that much of the confusion stemmed from the lack of 'any clear lead' from the king and his ministers. Secretary Calvert conceded as much: while he could count on a number of members, 'they are no Speakers for the most part.'[11] In fact, this was a crippling problem throughout the entire parliament, and it may account for the profound mystery which surrounded the government's military plans. Only Calvert and Sir Edward Sackville, a member of the Council of War, ever mentioned the Council's report, and then they did nothing except to insist that the price tag for this massive force of 30,000 men would be merely £300,000. Their insistence makes more understandable the fact that of all of the members on the government bench, only Sir Julius Caesar objected to the idea of a grant of two subsidies, and then he only wanted to add two fifteenths, which would have netted less than £60,000. If Caesar managed to sow any doubts about the size of the grant, then the Chancellor of the Exchequer himself dispelled them: two subsidies, Lionel Cranfield insisted, would be just fine.[12] Given the government's lame presentation, it was nothing short of miraculous that James received anything at all from the Commons.

Even more remarkable was the speed with which the House offered supply. The importance of this fact, which has often eluded modern scholars, certainly astonished contemporaries. Consider Bishop Ussher's confusion when he preached to the Commons three weeks after the opening. Then an elaborately prepared sermon on the need for generosity suddenly gave way to 'but a drie sermon'. In his defence, Ussher explained that there was no need 'to be earnest in exciting you to put your helping hands to the making up of these breaches; your forwardnesse herein hath prevented mee, and instead of petitioning (for which I had prepared my selfe) hath ministered

---

[10] 'A Collection of Subsidies and Fifteenths', Centre for Kentish Studies (hereafter CKS), Cranfield MSS u269/1, OE 1375; Council of War's report, 13 Feb. 1621, Folger Shakespeare Library, Vb 151, ff. 79v–89v.

[11] Russell, *Parliaments*, p. 125; *CD 1621*, VII, 625.

[12] *CD 1621*, II, 19, 88, 90, 95.

unto mee matter of thanksgiving'.[13] Thanksgiving was in order because less than a month after the opening the House voted two subsidies, and in less than two months presented them to the king.

The long intermission between sessions accounts for much of the uncertainty about all things parliamentary. Otherwise canny operators in North Wales were consumed with anxiety since they had forgotten whether boroughs could return non-residents. Likewise it is hard to know which was more embarrassing: the uncertain clerks in the Petty Bag Office who sent out defective summons to the entire peerage or the peers themselves who took so long to spot the error.[14] In all the confusion, one certainty concerned the subsidies. 'It hath bene no parliamentary custome', John Woodford noted, 'to proceede to subsidies before the end of the parliament.' And yet that is precisely what the Commons did. Secretary Calvert acknowledged 'the like precedent was never in the house before', and even the Clerk of the House of Lords noted in the Journals' margin, 'not usual to grant subsidies in the Beginning of a Parliament'.[15] Eagerness to get the money into the Exchequer led the members to another extraordinary measure. Although the subsidy bill was customarily presented with the other bills at the end of the session, William Hakewell and William Noy produced some obscure precedents, the most recent from Mary's reign, which allowed the monarch to issue a special commission to receive an early subsidy without concluding the session. No one had any illusions about the risks. Such ignorance was impossible with members like Edward Alford loudly protesting he 'Never saw Parliament so out of Order.' The danger with reversing the traditional order of redress and supply was that once the money reached the Exchequer, the monarch might prorogue or dissolve the session at any time. To be sure, James vowed that he would not, since 'never a Lower howse shewed more respect unto their kinge, than the Common Howse this Parliament have done unto me'.[16] Eventually the House agreed to trust him, although not without serious misgivings about the potential for disaster.

[13] Chamberlain to Carleton, 27 Feb. 1621, *The Letters of John Chamberlain*, ed. N. E. McClure (2 vols., Philadelphia, 1939), II, 347; James Ussher, *The Substance of that which was delivered... before the Commons House* (1621), p. 10.

[14] Locke to Carleton, 5 Feb. 1621, PRO, SP 14/119/67; R. Wynn to J. Wynn, 25 Dec. 1620, National Library of Wales (hereafter NLW), Wynn of Gwethyr Papers, MS 9057E/933.

[15] Woodford to Nethersole, 17 Feb. 1621, PRO, SP 14/119/102; Calvert to Carleton, 17 Feb. 1621, PRO, SP 84/99/179; *LJ* III, 51.

[16] *CJ*, I, 523; 'The effect of the Kinge's Majestie's speach', 10 March, *The Hastings Journal of the Parliament of 1621*, ed. Lady De Villiers (1953), p. 25.

Once we fully appreciate these circumstances, then the logic becomes almost impossible to follow which holds that the Parliament-men were uninterested in war. Russell suggested that the members were resigned to voting two subsidies just as tenants were to paying ground rent. But in 1621, for the privilege of sitting in Westminster, the members paid a hefty price, in contemporary terms at least a stiff entry fine *and* a rack rent. The delighted noises from along the government bench suggest that none of them expected such extravagance; an ordinary subsidy bill presented at the end of the session would have been quite sufficient. The best explanation for these irregular actions therefore is that the majority of members wanted to do what they could for the Palatine cause, even if it meant that they had to 'innovate ancyent proceedings'.[17]

II

The same judgement applies to the rest of the first session. Exhilarated by the early supply, James had encouraged the Parliament-men to search out abuses in the state, a task which they found wholly congenial. The reports which York's burgesses sent back to the Corporation illustrate the widely shared excitement, as Askwith and Brooke breathlessly listed all the local and national issues which Parliament was tackling. For them there was only one conclusion: 'ther was never like to be a happie Parliament'.[18]

For the otherwise delighted Parliament-men, the anxiety which most troubled them concerned the exact date of the prorogation, and this growing apprehension soon became entangled with the issue of war. Fair warning of the end came in late April when James in the guise of Baron-Tell-Clock urged the members to begin wrapping up their deliberations. At the same time he also lodged an appeal for additional funding. All but half of a subsidy, he announced, had been spent, and meanwhile Vere's men were 'left so destitute as their throats are like to be cut every day'.[19] Although James assured the Palatine agent that he had formally requested 'further ayde', the Parliament-men can be forgiven if they failed to recognise it as such. Earlier in the excitement over the Commons' swift grant of supply,

[17] Sir Edward Sackville's speech, 15 Feb. 1621, Hatfield House, Salisbury MSS 130/52.
[18] Askwith and Brooke to the Corporation, 24 March 1621, York City Archive, House Book, vol. 34, ff. 217v–218. On this period, see Zaller, *Parliament of 1621*, pp. 37–141.
[19] *CD 1621*, II, 303–6.

well-placed observers had confidently predicted that James would raise a massive army. Yet in James's address there was neither a faint sign of any plan of action nor even a passing allusion to the Council of War's earlier proposal. Those curious about how the last grant had been expended were equally mystified. All that could be gleaned was that aside from £18,000 spent on new arms, the rest had gone to underwrite impressive efforts to apply Jacobean standards of conspicuous consumption to diplomacy. Even more thoroughly confused were those who might have interpreted James's speech as the beginning of a major campaign for additional supply; from the government bench came only a studied silence.[20] As flat-footed as this overture was, it was not entirely hopeless. Archbishop Abbot had earlier noted that James's encouragement of 'the reformings of anie abuses' would eventually 'produce good Effects for the further supplyinge of his Maiesties wants'. Success, however, depended on reciprocation from the crown. Although James had permitted the repeated mauling of royal officials, the long list of projects which Brooke and Askwith had sent back to York gave place of honour to an extended list of planned legislation.[21] Until much of this was ready – and almost none of it was – it was going to take a much more impressive appeal to get the Commons' attention. Hence, when confronted with a scarcely audible request, the House merely followed the lead of the government bench and sat in silence.

From this episode in late April arose a sense that if anyone was uninterested in military action, it was James. Suspicion abruptly hardened into belief a month later, when the king suddenly announced that the adjournment was six days away. Pandemonium greeted the news in the Commons, and a few days later, the Speaker had to lock the members in the chamber to restore order. Their despair arose from a feeling of betrayal. Having cast tradition to the winds, the members had voted supply early in the meeting, and then confident in James's promise to permit substantial redress, they had started over a hundred bills. James had of course encouraged Parliament to present all the legislation which could be finished in a week. Yet since only a handful of bills could be completed, the members resolved to present none rather than a few 'rattles'. Wags

[20] Nethersole to Carleton, 2 May 1621, PRO, SP (Holland) 84/101/11; Murray to Trumbull, 19 March 1621, BL, Trumbull MSS Misc. XII/unfol.; *CD 1621*, II, 305.
[21] Abbot to Edmondes, March 1621, BL Stowe MSS 176, f. 228; and Colin Tite, *Impeachment and Parliamentary Judicature in Early Stuart England* (1974), pp. 83–148.

consequently were able to quip that in that parliament 'nothing is passed but 18 or 20 weeks.' Indeed, the 1621 parliament had even surpassed the lamentable record of its predecessor, for while the Addled Parliament of 1614 'brought fort nothing', at least 'it parted with nothing'. Not surprisingly, the Parliament-men were profoundly agitated. Sir Richard Grosvenor was physically afraid of his constituents; Sir Samuel Sandys wanted to leave the country; and Mr Delbridge this life.[22]

Equally alarming was James's attitude towards Parliament and the Palatine cause. James's steps towards war had been so tentative as to be scarcely perceptible. Earlier in March, the vote of supply prompted him to plunge £18,000 into the Dutch arms market and to ask Prince Maurice's comments on a plan to march an English army to Heidelberg. This enthusiasm did not survive the Dutch leader's patient review of the idea's madness and his advocacy of a diversionary strike in Flanders.[23] Likewise when Elizabeth offered to come over to encourage Parliament, James firmly blocked the idea. Lest he be perceived as heartless, he thoughtfully sent her a good bedstead from Whitehall.[24]

Ironically the session's greatest diplomatic success moved James closer to the Habsburgs, not further away. No one in the metropolis could have missed this development. After apprentices in April attacked the Spanish ambassador's entourage, James ordered the rioters flogged – only to have the crowd free the prisoners. This outrage brought James to Guildhall to berate the mayor and aldermen for their 'misgovernment'. In the end the sentence was carried out, even though one of the prisoners died, and afterwards the aldermen lectured all masters on the necessity of controlling their apprentices. Just to be on the safe side, the Corporation also banned football matches.[25] Reports of Gondomar's power were not news to the Parliament-men. His influence had blocked the House's attempt to enforce the penal laws and to cut off the flow of English cannons to the Spanish army. These frustrating reverses, however, were nothing compared to Gondomar's great project, the English match,

---

22   Savile to Carleton, 7 June 1621, PRO, SP 14/121/85; *CD 1621*, II, 407; V, 182; III, 334.
23   Calvert to Carleton, 17 Feb. 1621; Carleton to Calvert, 26 Feb. 1621, PRO, SP (Holland) 84/99/178–9 and 201–3.
24   Calvert to Carleton, 16 March 1621; James to same, 13 March 1621, PRO, SP (Holland) 84/100/66 and 51; 'An Inventory of such stuff', [1621], PRO, SP 14/121/45.
25   Gondomar's complaint, 4 April 1621, Corporation of London RO, Rep. 35, ff. 141–2v; 'An Act of Reformation', [April 1621], Journal 31/317–7v.

which increasingly seemed imminent. The king had not hidden his desire for a negotiated settlement and an Anglo-Spanish marriage alliance. For him, Parliament was simply a noisy sabre, whose rattling might well bring on better terms from Madrid. By May it seemed to have done the trick; hence James had no need to humour Parliament. The House begged James to reconsider the adjournment, since it would not be useful in 'Encouradging the people to a newe supplye when we meete againe'. On the other hand, if he delayed the adjournment, then 'we will be as farr more willing to doe him service as wee have been allready'. Such a delay, Sir Edward Coke broadly hinted, would be worth at least four subsidies. Yet James was in no mood to haggle, rounding on them for daring to defy his authority. The only possible deduction from his response, Alford observed, was that 'we shall have no wars'.[26]

If a majority had been looking for an opportunity to evade any foreign involvement, this development should have delighted them. Yet it did not. In his frustration Phelips blurted out that 'I came with a resolution to have had somewhat donn for ther restablishment and that we might not spend summer upon summer in speculation of ther miseries withoute redress.' Since 'it hath been the Honour of this kingdom, not to bear an ill Word,' he asked, 'shall we now take such a Blow as that which hath been given to the King of Bohemia and our Kings children?' James's inactivity was doubly galling since 'we want not men, money, harts for this'. After Phelips struck the keynote, his colleague pondered 'what we shall do'.[27] Others echoed Phelips's concern. England's response to 'the poore Pallatinat' appalled Mr Wrenham. As for the Spanish match, 'lett us never thinke', he boldly exclaimed, 'that ther open enemies [are] our frends'. He too thought that the House should do something. Even Edward Alford concurred, although James's cowardice distressed him: 'We all sawe how forward the King was at the beginning [of the meeting] but I have seene a greate quailing since Easter.'[28] James's mood thus made it difficult to think of a solution which did not invade the *arcana imperii*.

Confused and depressed, the Parliament-men sat on 4 June, waiting for adjournment, when Sir James Perrott rose. Since James in his opening address had already pledged to expend his own 'blood

---

[26]   *CD 1621*, II, 403; and IV, 387.
[27]   *PD*, II, 124; *CD 1621*, II, 347–9.
[28]   *CD 1621*, III, 350–3.

and life' in the defence of the Palatinate, then they too could go on record about their eagerness to 'adventure the lives and estates... for the maynetenance of the cause of God and of his Maiesties yssue'. That way the members could gently remind James 'to performe the princely promise which he made'. A few were leery of *any* commitment; Alford characteristically argued against formally registering the Declaration. But significantly his idea never found a seconder. Instead the House followed the logic of Sir Nathaniel Rich: the Declaration would 'show the World that we are not insensible of the Sufferance of those of our Religion, nor of the Wrong done to the Count Palatine'. Thus Perrott's proposal

was entertained with much joy and general consent of the whole House and sounded forth with the Voices of them all, withall lifting up their hats in their Hands as high as they could hold them, as a visible testimony of their unanimous Consent, in such a sort, that the like had scarcce ever been seen in Parliament.

The final flourish came from Sir Edward Coke. With tears in his eyes he led a recitation of the prayer for the king's children. They petitioned the Lord

to blesse our noble Prince Charles, Fredericke the Prince Elector Palatine and the Lady Elizabeth his wife; enduw them with the Holy Spirit, enrich them with thy heavenly grace, prosper them with all happinesse, and bring them to thine everlasting kingdome.

To this customary prayer, Coke added his own touch: 'and defend them from their cruel enemies'. To this the House roared a hearty 'Amen.'[29]

As political theatre, this scene certainly had few equals. But what did it mean? Russell has argued that the Hispanophobia and anti-Catholicism was merely ritualistic and that the actual bellicosity was at best lukewarm.[30] But since James was then in hot pursuit of an Anglo-Spanish *entente*, the little Englanders certainly had an odd way of exhibiting their lack of interest. By all rights they should have dropped the topic altogether just as the king and his ministers had. Likewise, if 4 June was simply an elaborate anti-popery display, the Parliament-men could have selected a less awkward declaration. Alford had warned all who would listen that Perrott's text created an obligation to support further military intervention. An overwhelming

[29] 'The motion of Sir John Parret', 4 June 1621, PRO SP 14/121/79; *PD*, II, 169; *The Book of Common Prayer* (1619), [sig. b].29.
[30] Russell, *Parliaments*, pp. 119–20.

majority of his colleagues agreed, and precisely for that reason they voted for it. Yet the oddest thing about Russell's interpretation is that it has no recorded contemporary support. Far from dejecting William Trumbull, the declaration thrilled him. Hitherto the agent in Brussels had found it impossible to shake the 'constant beleefe' there that 'wee will not upon any condition engage our selves in a warre'. His powers of persuasion changed dramatically with 'the vigorous and masculyne Declaration of the Commons'. Likewise Sir Edward Herbert, the envoy in Paris, was similarly delighted: 'it is a greate while since I heard any so good newes as the Declaration of our Parliament dated 4 June'.[31] Admittedly these developments did depress one member, that smooth courtier, Sir Richard Wynn. James's policy, he confessed to his father, was 'to the great dishonor of our nation'. While war devastated the continent, 'only we sleepe secure seing the fyre in our naibours hoses'. All he could do was to beg the Lord to 'keepe us for we never had more need of his helpe'. Oddly enough for Wynn, the problem was James, not the Parliament-men. Little wonder then that the scene on 4 June made Sir Dubley Digges earnestly pray that 'god incline the kings hart to make use of his people's forwardnesse in tyme'.[32]

III

In the interval between meetings, the distance between James and many of the Parliament-men only widened. By then, it had become apparent that all of James's senior appointments in 1621 argued against military intervention. Earlier in the year, James had suspended Secretary of State Naunton for merely suggesting an alternative to the Spanish Match, and sporadic rumours of his rehabilitation never moved him out of the category of the 'deade alive'. His eclipse left Sir George Calvert, a crypto-Catholic, in control of the bureaucracy. The same pattern held true with the prince's secretary. An attempt to woo Charles away from a Spanish bride disgraced Sir Thomas Murray. His replacement, Francis Cottington, was another crypto-Catholic who had no qualification

---

[31] Trumbull to Carleton, 16 June 1621, PRO, SP (Flanders) 77/14/350; Herbert to Calvert, 25 June 1621, PRO, Powis MSS, 30/53/4, f. 214. I am grateful to Malcolm Smuts and Simon Thursley for invaluable discussions of the Trumbull letter.

[32] R. Wynn to J. Wynn, 15 June 1621, NLW, Wynn of Gwethyr Papers, MS 9057E/959; Digges to Carleton, 28 July 1621, PRO, SP 14/122/47.

for the post, one commentator noted, 'save only the spanishe tongue', and that 'he speakes better then English'. In the same year Lionel Cranfield rose to be Lord Treasurer and Lord Cranfield. While no Catholic, his attitude to the war can be divined from his response to an alarming report on England's crumbling coastal defences; rather than repair them, he proposed pulling them down. Into the Exchequer went Sir Richard Weston, another crypto-Catholic. On his appointment, Calvert praised, not Weston's financial skill, but rather his standing 'as one well affected to the peace'.[33]

The rise of conformable men, while unsettling enough in the bureaucracy, was positively hair-raising in the Church, and for that reason, many watched John Williams's ascent with anxiety. Affable and talented, he was also notorious for his conformity to James's wishes. So apprehensive were the members about Williams that in the first session they shifted their communion service from the Abbey to St Margaret's, 'because they did not like to receive the communion at the Deane of Westminster's hands'.[34] Unfortunately for them, the members could not stop Williams's rise. In fact, their impeachment of Bacon simply vaulted Williams into office as Lord Keeper and Bishop of Lincoln. Archbishop Abbot's inadvertent killing of a gamekeeper later in the year nearly signalled an even greater potential disaster, for in the event of his retirement, Williams was touted as his successor. Mercifully Abbott eventually retained his post, but not without enduring Williams's loud protests about being consecrated by 'a man of blood'.[35] This clerical jostling assumed more sombre hues, as it coincided with new Catholic concessions. Immediately after the adjournment, James ordered the judges to proceed with 'all Moderation and Clemency' towards the recusants. Catholics not only could pray as they pleased, but fight whom they would as well; he also suspended the statute which made foreign military service a felony if not preceded by the oath of allegiance. Thus troops whom Trumbull dubbed his 'unnaturall Countrymen', together with English cannons, could be employed against Vere and his men. For Catholics these developments were

---

[33] 'Mortalletys of Great Men', CKS, Sackville MSS u269, f37 (misc.); Castle to Trumbull, 1621, BL, Trumbull MSS xviii/85; Calvert to Trumbull, 22 March 1622, BL, Trumbull MSS, xiv/80; Mainwaring to Zouche, 9 July 1621, PRO, SP 14/122/8.
[34] Beaulieu to Trumbull, 15 Feb. 1621, BL, Trumbull MSS vii/7.
[35] Beaulieu to Trumbull, [Sept. 1621], BL, Trumbull MSS xviii/25. See also Kenneth Fincham, 'Prelacy and politics: Archbishop Abbot's defence of Protestant orthodoxy', *Bulletin of the Institute of Historical Research* 61 (1988), pp. 36–64.

increasingly ordinary in a year when James tolerated Lancelot Andrewes 'seeming to say Mass' and when he placed a gold crucifix in his own chapel. One priest's judgement on these events was a miracle of understatement; 'our kings proceedings of late... give me hope'.[36]

This became all even more chilling with the persecution of Protestant militants. By the end of the year, the earl of Pembroke's standing had come into such doubt that politic preachers in Oxford omitted the customary prayers for the university Chancellor. The erosion of his position was simply another manifestation of the anti-interventionist tide which swept away the earl of Southampton. Scarcely had the meeting ended before he found himself subjected to house arrest and then to a particularly painful torture – James cut off his pension. Without that £3,200, the earl protested, 'I know not how I shall subsist'; 'it is my meat and drinke'. Along with Southampton went a Parliament-man, Sir Edwin Sandys, who was also confined and interrogated. Although the government insisted that the adjournment and their arrest were unrelated, contemporaries widely believed the two were connected. If so, then it represented a direct violation of parliamentary freedom of speech, a privilege which James himself had confirmed in February.[37]

These developments had the cumulative effect of poisoning the political atmosphere on the eve of the second session. On one hand Father Bishop excitedly told a friend at Douai that the king had 'disgraced them that are hottest against us, canterbury, nanton, southampton', and in their place 'promoted to the chief offices men better affected to our religion, the Lord Treasurer Cranfield, the lord keeper Williams, [and] the great Secretarie [Calvert]'. On the other extreme, the summons to the second session found Mr Spencer vowing that the Parliament-men first 'shall fall upon Sir Edwin Sandys his imprisonment'. For him, it was a simple choice: either 'to maintain the libertyes of parlement or to live quietly in our countryes'.[38] Many of Spencer's colleagues did not hold such an

---

[36]   Calvert to Aston, 26 June 1621, BL, Add. MSS 36,445, ff. 151–1v; and Bishop to Burnet, 14 Dec. 1621, Westminster Diocesan Archives (hereafter WDA), A16, p. 248.

[37]   M. Nicholas to E. Nicholas, 5 Nov. 1621, PRO, SP 14/123/88; Southampton to [Buckingham?], 20 Oct. [1621], Nottingham University Library, Portland MSS, NeC 4. See also Christopher Thompson, *The Debate on Freedom of Speech in the House of Commons* (Orsett, 1985).

[38]   Bishop to Burnet, 14 Dec. 1621, WDA, A16, p. 248; Spencer to Isham, 20 Nov. 1621, Northants. RO, Isham MSS IC 155.

extreme position. Nevertheless his stark choice between 'libertyes' and retirement represented a striking contrast with the buoyant mood at the beginning of the year.

In this less than propitious atmosphere, James suddenly recalled the Parliament-men. In preceding months he had operated on the assumption that a negotiated settlement was within reach. Yet by October even Digby appreciated that further discussion would only ensure the slaughter of Vere's men. Shuttle diplomacy between Vienna, Munich and Brussels, he discovered, increasingly resembled a shell game; agreements made at one place were promptly abrogated in the next. Meanwhile the pressure on Vere mounted. Although abundantly furnished with envoys, the English general prayed nonetheless that God would 'moove some affectionate and powerful persons to cast their thoughts... uppon this place which notwithstanding the mediation by treaty lyes gasping for other kind of succour'. A few weeks later he reported that 'our misery is great, [since] things grow into great confusion by reason of want of pay'.[39] Vere's deteriorating situation brought Digby hurrying back to London, convinced that the only means of recovering the Palatinate was 'a vigorous war'.

Hastily summoned back into session, the Parliament-men confronted the news that the Temple of Janus must be opened. Instead of delighting them, it led them to lay hands on James's prerogative chariot. The mystery of their response vanishes once we remember exactly what James was asking of them. The temple doors in fact were not swung wide open; they were just cracked a bit. Although the armies threatening Vere were Spanish, James carefully focused his hostility onto Ferdinand II. The best means of thwarting his designs, government spokesmen maintained, was to retain Mansfelt's mercenaries, who would assist Vere over the winter. With Ferdinand's Spanish cousins, however, James intended to remain at peace and to pursue a marriage alliance. To finance this initiative, the government requested an emergency vote of supply; afterwards James would adjourn the session until February 1622 when he promised to summon it for a full session.[40]

[39] Vere to Carleton, 21 Sept. and 11 Oct. 1621, PRO, SP (German States) 81/22/43v and PRO, SP (Holland) 84/102/59. See also A. W. White, 'Suspension of arms: Anglo-Spanish mediation in the Thirty Years War, 1621–1625', (unpublished Ph.D. thesis, Tulane, 1978), pp. 172–268.
[40] *CD 1621*, III, 414–26.

Most members found this a most peculiar brief. First of all, it brought into the open the haunting question about what exactly had happened to the previous grant, to say nothing of the nearly £70,000 which various impeachments had netted the crown. Vere's difficulties were largely financial, and yet the first vote of supply should have underwritten the garrison for years. Diplomacy of course was expensive, but even in the style to which Doncaster was accustomed, all ambassadorial bills only came to roughly £50,000. Indeed for James's subjects, the only visible sign of his belligerence was his decision to deck the Gentlemen Pensioners with new summer uniforms replete with jaunty spangles. Such queries exposed the basic fact that when James should have been taking his role as Defender of the Faith seriously, he was acting more like a lucky punter whose horse had just come in. Late in 1621, when economy measures might have seemed in order, the royal painter, Juan de Critz, was gilding James's barge; royal estate agents, far from selling manors, were buying £4,354 of new land; and the marquis of Hamilton was collecting a free gift of £5,000. James himself was thoughtfully keeping the metropolitan jewellers happy. First there was a set of new gold medals, worth £2,500; then the matter of re-mounting some old jewels, another £2,000; and finally £15,356 of new gems which James found he could not live without. To no one's great surprise, James found it impossible to choose between guns or butter. Yet his indecision left the members understandably 'afraid their monie will not be employed' towards the war effort.[41]

Even more alarming was the crown's apparent blithe indifference to parliamentary custom and military logic. While the government in the first session asked for supply before redress, it requested in the second that redress be deferred altogether until a subsequent meeting. Sir Thomas Edmondes, the Treasurer of the Household, sought to set the best possible face on the extraordinary demand: 'we must create presidents in urgent causes'. Most others, however, stuck at this 'preiudious president'. Sir George More spoke quite bluntly: 'we may not be returned into our Country with empty Hands'. And no one, Glanville maintained, had any time for the idea of 'adiourning and calling and adiourning one upon an other withoute

---

[41] PRO, E 405/274; 'An abstract of such moneyes... [for] the Palatinate', 21 Nov. 1621, CKS, U269/1, OE 1409; and Beaulieu to Trumbull, 29 Nov. 1621, BL, Trumbull MSS VII/ 34. On the impeachment fines, see Mandeville to Buckingham, 1 Aug. 1621, Hartley-Russell MSS (formerly deposited as the Packer Add. MSS in the Berkshire RO).

any thing donn'.[42] Equally distressing was the precision with which James had defined his enemies. Military pundits had unanimously argued against limited action in the Palatinate. 'It wilbe a tedious warre', one analyst observed, and while the English troops will be 'infested on every side', their opponents will be 'there amidst many friends'.[43] Thus, as Sir Richard Grosvenor protested, 'To have an army maintayned in the Palatinate is the desire of the enemie.' Furthermore, James's rejection of a diversionary strategy allowed the Habsburgs to mass against Vere. Sir Edward Giles was disgusted with the idea that 'we must fight with the Spanyards in the Pallatinate And be freinds with them Every where else'. Finally, some balked at the idea of retaining mercenaries when England had soldiers aplenty. 'I would have an armie', Mr Mallet grumbled, 'not of auxiliaries onelie but of our owne.' In essence, Pym protested, James had insisted on a limited conflict where 'the Enemy [was] strongest and we weakest'.[44]

A lack of enthusiasm for James's plan should not be confused with disinterest in war. The Parliament-men, Russell suggested, 'had not been eager to offer advice'. Yet in these long debates, the government speakers could scarcely shut them up. Those raised to believe that the King of Spain was aiming at a Universal Monarchy naturally found James's willingness to fight some Habsburgs while marrying others incomprehensible. Phelips openly pointed to James's erstwhile ally as the enemy; Philip 'is the President of the Council of War... against the Palatinate; and... war moveth not but by the Wheel of Spain, who payeth all the souldiers there'. Likewise Mr Wilde denounced the notion of trusting Habsburgs, who 'hath the ambition to subiugate all kingdomes to themselves'.[45] This assumption led naturally to a war of diversion, which would divide the Habsburg forces and so would increase the odds of success. Practically everyone, including those on the government bench, concurred; even Alford called for 'a diversion of war'. The only real question concerned the enemy's most vulnerable area. Grosvenor and Sir John Jephson thought it was Flanders, where Sir George Hastings envisioned 30,000 English soldiers.[46] Many more cast their eyes

---

[42] *PD*, II, 214; *CD 1621*, II, 456, 460.
[43] 'The Road to Hedelburg', BL, Egerton MSS 2651, ff. 78v–79.
[44] *CD 1621*, IV, 438; V, 214, 216; *CJ*, I, 647.
[45] Russell, *Parliaments*, p. 141; *CD 1621*, V, 214; *PD*, II, 211.
[46] *PD*, II, 458, 464; *CD 1621*, III, 454; V, 216.

further afield. Giles wished that James 'would rather thinke of Queene Elizabeths course and the West Indyes'. If 'wee maye have such a warr as will inritch us and imploy our Navie', he was convinced that England would become 'one of the greatest and richest kingdoms in the world'.[47] This transformation, Sir Dudley Digges predicted, only required two years of open war. Even novices like Mr Shilleto called for James 'to strike at the Root' and 'to take away his West Indian Treasure'. This chorus made Sir Thomas Crewe confident that for a western design 'everyone would give with a swift and open hand'.[48]

Calls for 'a Thorough War' also had a distinct domestic component. Even in a limited conflict, the recusants were a threat, and the recent quasi-toleration only increased the danger. Hence speaker after speaker echoed Pym: 'we are not secure enough at home in respect of the enemy at home which growes by the suspence of the lawes at home'. From these complaints it was only a short leap to 'the politic blazing star', who had caused all of these problems. The wives of Ahab and Ahaziah, Crewe reminded the House, had lead their husbands into idolatry. Consequently he could only pray that 'wee might see him [Charles] tymely marryed to one of our owne Religion'.[49]

In this long three-day debate, the government's problem was not prodding the House to discuss a war; rather it was struggling to hold the debate exclusively to Mansfelt's men. Scholars confused about the House's attitude to the continental crisis need look no further than Sir Edward Sackville. He quickly put his finger on 'our desires' – 'a general War against him [Philip IV]'. But first his colleagues had to humour the king and to fund a limited war; anything more ambitious would 'enforce him to make Peace with those with whome hee would have war'. Likewise Weston sympathised with the House's frustration, but he warned that 'we do not by precipitated course run headlong' into disaster. Instead, as Edmondes stressed, the House must 'leave the choyce of the Enemye and direction of the Warr to the Kinge'.[50] Such pleas at last sank in, and on 28 November the House approved one subsidy to be collected on 1 February.

Secretary Calvert immediately relayed the happy news abroad,

---

[47] CD 1621, III, 453; VI, 438.
[48] PD, II, 216–17; CD 1621, II, 451; CJ, I, 648.
[49] PD, II, 213; CD 1621, III, 461; IV, 440.
[50] PD, II, 220; CD 1621, IV, 441, 443. See also Russell, Parliaments, pp. 123, 126, 130–1.

but he might have been more cautious, for the bill had yet to pass the House. In the meanwhile, the members resolved to petition James about 'the State of Religion', and this time an anodyne response was not likely to soothe the members who were, as Mr Lister reported back to Hull, determined to 'remedy some grevances'.[51] It was becoming equally apparent that some numbers were not prepared to pass over in silence Sandys's case and the question of freedom of speech. Thus nervous anxiety swept over the government bench on 1 December when the House resolved to send two members to see about Sir Edwin's alleged ill health.[52] Just as the Sandys case reached centre stage, so too the Petition on Religion left committee to illustrate that the government speakers had not quashed enthusiasm for a wider war. Arguably the best evidence for the government's delight with the 4 June Declaration was its attempt to orchestrate another one. On 29 November, Sir George Goring, a close Buckingham protégé, suddenly proposed an addition to the petition: *if* Philip failed either to support a ceasefire or to withdraw assistance from Ferdinand, *then* the House agreed to assist James in a Spanish war. In essence, it was a modification of the earlier Declaration. The clear involvement of prominent courtiers in this motion has rightly attracted considerable attention.[53] Yet it should not overshadow another equally remarkable fact: when the petition left committee, Goring's motion was not in it. Instead it was full of the controversial points which the government had struggled to suppress a few days earlier.

The explanation for the omission is quite simple. After having fumbled for months in comparative darkness, the Parliament-men at last received what appeared to be a clear lead from the court. Their reaction was remarkably unambiguous. Russell rightly stressed the curious fact that the members failed to appreciate the conditional nature of Goring's motion.[54] Yet he in turn failed to consider what this fact said about the House's bellicosity. Far from having to be coaxed and cajoled into discussing foreign affairs, the members, once they received the green light, were off like a shot, and a cursory reading of the petition gives a fair indication of the House's velocity.

[51] Calvert to Carleton, 3 Dec. 1621, PRO, SP (Holland) 84/105/23; Lister to the Corporation, 29 Nov. 1621, Hull RO, L149.

[52] *CD 1621*, v, 411; Goring to Buckingham, 3 Dec. 1621, BL, Harl. MSS 1580, f. 430.

[53] Russell, 'The foreign policy debate in the House of Commons in 1621', *HJ* 20 (1977), pp. 302–9; and Zaller, *Parliament of 1621*, p. 152.

[54] Russell, *Parliaments*, p. 134.

The basic point of the petition, Ignatius Jordan reported back to Exeter, was to ask James 'to have war with our common enemy... the Spaniard'. Although they approved a subsidy for Vere's men, they urged James 'not to rest upon a war in those parts only, which will consume your treasure and discourage the hearts of your Subiects'. Instead, 'the best advantage', they recommended, was to 'manage this war... by a diversion'. Not surprisingly they had no time for the niceties of Jacobean diplomacy; 'the point of your sword', they advised James, should be 'against that prince... who first diverted and hath since maintained the War in the Palatinate'. Nor were they coy about naming names; the enemy should be 'the Pope of Rome and his dearest son, the one aiming at as large a Temporal Monarchy, as the other at a Spiritual Supremacy'. In this struggle, James had to close ranks with the continental brethren and assist 'those of our religion in foreign parts'. Needless to say, the penal laws had to be enforced, and of course, there was no more room for a Spanish Princess of Wales; Charles, they recommended, should 'be timely and happily married to one of our own religion'.[55]

This document made the government spokesmen sputter in amazement. Weston dubbed it 'presumptious' and above all begged the House not to 'meddle with the marriage'. For his part Sir Humphry May announced, 'he never knew the like within the Compass of these walls'. Hakewell, however, disagreed; the House was simply following distinguished medieval precedents of advising the king. And a host of members – Perrott, More, Phelips, Crewe, Coke and Mr Wentworth – seconded him. At this point Sackville summoned up his best classical learning and rose to deliver his warning about Phaeton's chariot. For his pains, he 'was hemmed at'.[56] Moving swiftly his colleagues downgraded the petition to a remonstrance and were fussing about the details when the first thunderbolt arrived from Newmarket.

IV

From this point on, the meeting came to an impasse over the Commons' freedom of speech. While the details of this dispute are outside the bounds of the present essay, it is vital to remember that what lay at bottom of this confrontation was not simply a thorny

[55] Jordan to the Corporation, 30 Nov. 1621, Devon RO, EC/XI 600/210; and PD, II, 264–6.
[56] PD, II, 267–79; CD 1621, VII, 220.

issue of constitutional law; it also involved the House's freedom to speak about foreign policy. About the majority's views on war and peace, James at least had no doubt. 'What Inference can be made upon this,' the king lectured the Parliament-men, only than that 'we must presently denounce War against the King of Spain'. Instead of thanking him for maintaining 'a settled Peace in all Our Dominions, whenas all our Neighbours about are in a miserable Combustion of War', the members pressed for 'a Public War of Religion, through all the World at once'. Far from thinking that the Parliament-men merely wanted to avoid the burden of war, the king lectured them on the sombre fact that 'dulce bellum inexpertis'.[57]

Unfortunately for all involved, James's dogged defence of the prerogative only confirmed the House's doubts about *his* bellicosity. James's effort, his French secretary noted, 'so grieved' the members, for it revealed that he was 'not so thoroughly resolved as yet to a warre'. Consequently the members 'grew therby the slacker in the affording of their assistance', and indeed until James gave 'them better satisfaction to their mynds, they wil not so much as make good the subsidie'. On the floor of the House, Christopher Brooke neatly described the confrontation. On one hand, 'we were asked for supply', and on the other, 'we desire the money may be imployed as it may do most good'.[58] In the end, the inability to resolve this issue brought Phaeton's chariot, and the parliament, crashing to the ground. With a clearer understanding of the background to the 1621 parliamentary debacle, a sharply different interpretation of the Commons' attitude to the continental crisis emerges. To be sure, a case can be constructed, as Phelips's councillor did, for arguing that the Parliament-men's enthusiasm was largely rhetorical. Yet the persuasive power of this contention markedly diminishes once this parliament is set in context. 'No mortal historian', Professor Russell has rightly observed,

is ever likely to become equally familiar with the misdeeds of the saltpetre men at Chipping Sodbury, the fortunes of the Dartmouth fishing industry, the limits of King James I's confidence in the Duke of Buckingham, and the day-to-day fluctuations in Richelieu's relations with Marie de Medici.[59]

Mercifully it is a much easier task comprehending the political and financial background to the parliament. The benevolences of 1620,

57 'His Majesties Answer', 11 Dec. 1621, *PD*, 11, 318–27.
58 Beaulieu to Trumbull, [Dec. 1621], BL, Trumbull MSS v11/37; *CD*, 11, 494.
59 Russell, *Parliaments*, p. 2.

the House's determination to dispense with precedent and to offer James an early subsidy bill, and the unnecessary Declaration of 4 June all cast doubt on the members' purported pacifism. These suspicions harden when we remember the patronage moves within Whitehall and the Exchequer's dispersals, together with the government's refusal in the first session to explain to itself, and its extremely peculiar brief in the second. Nor can the majority's stubborn refusal to yield in the contest over freedom of speech be held as a tacit sign of their aversion to war. Immediately following the dissolution, James launched another Palatine benevolence, and in the subsequent two years, almost £90,000 poured into the Exchequer. Leading the way in their appeal were a host of Parliament-men ranging from Sir Edwin Sandys, John Hampden and Christopher Brooke to Sir Thomas Wentworth, John Glanville and William Hakewill. Even James's decision to place John Pym under house arrest did not stop him from opening his purse for the Protestant cause.[60]

From all of this, it follows that the fundamental problem bedevilling both sessions was the king, not the Commons. James's French Secretary stated the central difficulty with admirable brevity: since the king 'hath not gott a resolute mynde to make warre', the Parliament-men were understandably 'afraid their monie will not be employed in that use'.[61] Thus, with enough care it is indeed possible to construct a political temperature gauge which produces lukewarm readings on the Parliament-men's bellicosity in 1621. But the results from this one thermometer should not obscure the fact that any such device which a scholar might employ would report that conditions in Whitehall for the same period were positively polar.

[60] PRO, E 401/2434; and 'Moneyes paid into the... Exchequer', 8 March 1624, CKS, u269/
i, OE 1376
[61] Beaulieu to Trumbull, 29 Nov. 1621, BL, Trumbull MSS vii/34.

Sir Thomas Wentworth and anti-Spanish sentiment, 1621–1624

Conrad Russell

Sir Thomas Wentworth was Justice of the Peace, Member of Parliament, Custos Rotulorum, Lord President of the North, Lord Lieutenant of Ireland, and executed on Tower Hill. Inevitably, in such a career, the question of consistency has become the underlying theme. I grew up with the picture of him as 'that grand apostate of the common wealth, whoe cannot have his pardon in this life, till he come to another'.[1] I am now more impressed by the fact that George Digby, the author of this judgement, was of the next generation, and full of the next generation's questions, values and judgements: he was a man who was to enjoy the peak of his career under Charles II, and who cannot necessarily be assumed to have understood the political values and objectives of a man born in the reign of Elizabeth I.

A politician who is always consistent in all details is like a batsman who plays forward to every ball: he must be wrong at least half the time. The consistency for which historians are entitled to look is on a deeper level: it is a consistency in underlying values and objectives, the sort of views which can only be changed on the road to Damascus. It is this journey to Damascus which is so hard to find in the career of Sir Thomas Wentworth. I am inclined to put down the desire to search for it to the imposition on him of a later generation's code of values.

Much depends on our formulation of what we take Wentworth to have opposed during the 1620s. Is it, or is it not, a coincidence that he first began to be seen as a real nuisance to the king and the duke during the parliament of 1625, when war with Spain was becoming a serious practical fact, and that his peace with the king was made after the session of 1628, when war with Spain was ceasing to be part of

---

[1] BL, Harleian MSS 163, f. 183a.

47

the practical agenda, and through the good offices of the reputedly
pro-Spanish Sir Richard Weston?

Later in his career, Wentworth was clearly a Spanish sympathiser.
He was described by Necolalde in the 1630s as 'as Spanish as if he
were born in Old Castile', and in 1640 caused deep alarm both to
Richelieu and to Pym by his attempts to organise a Spanish rescue
for Charles in the Bishops' Wars. Does this represent a selling out to
royal interests, or had he always belonged to an older English
political tradition, going back to Paget and beyond, which saw no
essential English interest demanding any conflict with Spain?[2]

If, as Professor Cogswell claims, in 1624 'the political nation fell
into line behind the king in the European conflict', it would seem
that Wentworth was always an exception.[3] We do not find in him
any of the blood-curdling tales told by Coke about Spaniards
bringing the pox, or papal assassins searching out the queen's life.
His attitude to recusants was not entirely sympathetic, but was
encapsulated by his remark that it was 'only civil' to ask recusants to
stay to dinner after fixing their fines.[4] In fact, cradle Calvinist though
he may have been, he seems never to have absorbed that passionate
anti-popish and anti-Spanish hatred which, for Pym, Harley or Sir
Francis Drake, was the hallmark of English nationality. In this, he
may have been typical of a larger part of English opinion than is
sometimes supposed. Pauline Croft's article on 'Trading with the
enemy' during the Elizabethan war with Spain suggests that, all the
way through the war itself, there were Englishmen willing to treat
Spaniards as friends if granted a sufficiently compelling motive to do
so.[5] The case of Sir Robert Phelips, who regularly made confidential
annotations on his papers in Spanish, suggests that even among anti-
Spaniards there may have been a reluctant admiration like that
which took so many anti-Americans to the States in the 1960s. Anti-
Spanish feeling, like the plague, was a virulent infection, but like the
plague, it seems to have left some people immune.

All this is highly relevant to the biggest open question of the

[2] A. J. Loomie, 'The spanish faction at the court of Charles I', *Bulletin of the Institute of
Historical Research* 59 (1986), p. 42; J. H. Elliott, 'The year of the three ambassadors', in
H. Lloyd-Jones, V. Pearl and B. Worden (eds.), *History and Imagination: Essays in Honour of
H.R. Trevor-Roper*, (1981), pp. 170, 173–81.
[3] T. Cogswell, 'England and the Spanish Match', Richard Cust and Ann Hughes, (eds.),
Conflict in Early Stuart England (1989), p. 130.
[4] J. C. H. Aveling, *Northern Catholics* (1966), p. 223.
[5] Pauline Croft, 'Trading with the enemy, 1585–1604', *HJ* 32, (1989), pp. 281–302.

political history of the 1620s: why did the war with Spain, entered into with so much apparent enthusiasm, so rapidly go sour? Those who believe with Professor Cogswell that in 1624 'a new consensus emerged' have a great struggle to explain why, by 1626, it had been entirely dissipated.[6] That analysis requires the placing of a vast amount of blame on the Stuart monarchy for incompetent and arbitrary management of the war. For some members, such as Pym and Rich, such an analysis may hold some water, especially when we throw in the drift, crucial to Eliot and Pembroke, towards war with France. For many of Buckingham's other opponents of 1626, of whom Wentworth is undoubtedly one, such an analysis will hold no water at all. They had never been enthusiastic supporters of war with Spain, and their growing resistance to the war is only the reaction we would expect to an unsuccessful war into which they had been dragged against their better judgement. No one, for example, has ever accused Thomas Howard, earl of Arundel of seeing popery as a form of 'egyptian darkness', or Spanish power as an agent of the devil, yet the Duke seems to have been right, in 1626, in seeing Arundel as being as important an opponent as Pembroke. Explanations which rely, Gardiner-style, on looking for the opinions of 'the nation' risk writing people like Wentworth and Arundel out of the story, and thereby making it incomprehensible. We will have no hope of understanding the attack on the duke in 1626 until we can get away from a two-dimensional invocation of 'they', and start asking who, in 1621–4, hailed the drift towards war with Spain with enthusiasm, and who did not. As always in parliamentary history, what we need is names. There is no such thing as 'the attitude of the House' – 'they' is always a wrong classification.

When I was a postgraduate, Sir Richard Southern, in a friendly word of advice, warned me that there was nothing more difficult to do than broad conceptual and fine technical work both at once. He was quite right, yet unfortunately the debate on the proposed revision of the political history of the 1620s demands that combination on every page. We disagree about our concepts, our terminology and our basic causation. We disagree, even, about the language in which we should describe these issues. Yet we cannot tackle these disagreements on a broad conceptual level, because, underneath these disagreements, we disagree with equal passion about the

---

[6] Cogswell, 'England and the Spanish Match', p. 126.

factual details of the story: what happened on 26 November 1621 or 5 March 1624. We disagree, in fact, about the textual reading of some of the most crucial speeches.

My case is, and has always been, that we cannot tackle this difficulty from the top down. We cannot decide on the correct conceptual apparatus, and then hope that the right spectacles will make the debates of 5 March properly legible. We must begin from the bottom up, with the comparatively, though not absolutely, value-free disciplines of textual scholarship. We must establish what Seymour, Mallory or Alford actually said, and use these discoveries as the building blocks from which we arrive at our newly re-created terminology and concepts. Like Sir Edward Montague, we should hold that correct resolution of a conflict is the result of following the proper procedure. Otherwise, our critics may end up saying, with Jane Austen, that it is odd history should be so dull, since a great deal of it must be invention.

It is, however, legitimate, and I think necessary, to interpret some of these speeches in the light of an understanding of how a debating assembly actually works, and in particular of how members set out to oppose a current whose strength looks dangerous. The calls for war with Spain in 1621 appeared to enjoy official approval, first because of the hasty recall of Parliament before it had been expected, second because of the speeches of the Lord Keeper and Digby in favour of war on 20 November, and third, because of Goring's motion on 29 November. In 1624, war was well known to enjoy the support of the reversionary interest of Charles and Buckingham, and in no age have skilled politicians been addicted to the worshipping of the setting sun. In any age, people are reluctant to indulge in head-on opposition to the clear wishes of authority, and in the 1620s it was a foolhardy activity. Sir Thomas Wentworth, who was kept away by illness from the beginning of the session in 1624, wrote to Wandesford: 'I pray yow that I maie understand by your letteres the effect of the king's speech, for upon perusall of that, togeather with your advice, I shall ground my resolucon what to doe'.[7] Many others may have done likewise. Real enthusiasts such as Pym and Wilde did not, but they were not necessarily typical of the House. In any parliament, those who oppose the wishes of authority often do it obliquely and indirectly.

[7]   Cooper, p. 205. He also asked Wandesford to get advice from Sir Arthur Ingram and Secretary Calvert.

Calls for war with Spain were not merely suspected to enjoy the support of authority: they were also politically correct, in an age which had a far stronger notion of political correctitude than our own. It is the definition of a politically correct view that it is much easier not to share it than to argue against it. When we hear someone saying: 'of course I'm in favour of increasing the proportion of women among the membership, but are these ladies' claims made out on grounds of merit?', I am tempted to ignore all the words before the 'but'. Those who oppose political correctitude head-on tend to get their heads bitten off. Doubters will often instead take refuge in appeals to follow the proper procedure.

The view that the Dutch, rather than the Spaniards, were England's natural enemy had been expressed by Lord Burghley as early as 1596, but Burghley had been writing a memorandum to himself.[8] It was not an easy view to express in public. Anyone who was tempted to call Pym a water-buffalo would have been much wiser to take refuge in diversionary or obstructive questions. The ease of these questions to the speakers, and their difficulty for us, arise from the fact that most of them could be asked, with perfect goodwill, by those who were nevertheless in favour of war with Spain. That is why they were an effective camouflage.

The force of political correctitude, as Edward Floyd learnt to his cost, meant that doubts about anti-Spanish fever were not always safe to express outside Parliament. There was often someone around ready to report the unwary for seditious words. That is why I have not found it useful to search for dissent for anti-Spanish views outside Parliament. Those opposing a politically correct view often find it the most sensible course to keep their heads down and rely on the force of inertia to make the storm blow over. Those who had recently lived through 1618 could see the force of that argument.

Similarly, I am not persuaded of the point at issue by Professor Cogswell's ability to collect a vast amount of literature in favour of war against Spain, recusants, the pope and so forth. He is, in *The Blessed Revolution*, making a tremendous effort to prove what was not at issue. He lists a vast amount of anti-Spanish material, but it has never been disputed that there was a large amount of passionate anti-Spanish feeling. What is at issue is how many people did not share this approach. This is a question he has not addressed.[9] In a

8 Conyers Read, *Lord Burghley and Queen Elizabeth* (1960), p. 544.
9 Thomas Cogswell, *The Blessed Revolution* (Cambridge, 1989), pp. 3–4.

cause where people might be afraid of coming into the open, the only way to tackle the question is the method of Ralph Davis's famous paper on 'How to be a mediaeval king'. Describing the ceremonial crown-wearings, he said: 'if you were a bad king, you thought how nice it was they were all singing nice songs about you. If you were a good king, you looked around to see who wasn't there, and said: "come on, chaps: we're going to fight him" '.[10] We must look round Professor Cogwell's list of anti-Spaniards, and see who isn't there. The answer is rather a lot of people. There is the whole of the not insubstantial Catholic and church papist community, for a start. There is a considerable section of the episcopate, and whatever body of the church may have followed them. Almost everyone Professor Cogswell has found is on the hotter Protestant side of the divide which separates Bishop Morton from Bishop Harsnet. That is a substantial body of respectable opinion, but it is not 'the nation', nor anything remotely resembling it.

However, I am reluctant to place weight on the *argumentum ex silentio* where the survival of evidence is so patchy. That is why I have preferred, and still prefer, to look at the reactions of members of Parliament, who were forced to take a line, and therefore had to conduct their equivocation within hearing of the Parliamentary diarists. I have sometimes heard it suggested that the hotter Protestants and anti-Spaniards were over-represented in Parliament, but I have never heard any suggestion that their opponents were over-represented in Parliament. If, then, I conclude that a substantial proportion of Parliament did not join in the rush to war with Spain, I will entertain the hypothesis that a corresponding proportion of the country may have agreed with them. It is in any case the members of Parliament who need to be understood, since it is their behaviour over the next two to three years which cries out for explanation.

For a member of Parliament who wished to divert the drive to war with Spain, there were a number of suitable options. It was, for example, possible to introduce another, and highly contentious issue, which might lead the debate to break up in disorder. The imprisonment of Sandys in 1621, and the matter of the 1621 imprisonments in 1624, provided such an issue. The chance that it might produce a big enough row to bring the moves to war to a stop must be regarded as substantial. When, on 20 November 1621, William Mallory moved

[10] Oral history: communicated by R. I. Moore, Merton College, Oxford, 1959.

Sir Edwin Sandys be sent for, Barrington noted in his diary: 'quaere, quare?' He was asking the same question as I am. It was easy to divert calls for war into attacks on domestic recusants, and all the easier for the fact that such genuine anti-Spaniards as Pym would come along with the process. It was particularly easy to divert the issue with calls to return to the passage of bills in order to satisfy the country. Again, Wentworth has provided a paradigm case. In his speech written for delivery on 11 or 12 December 1621, he asked 'I desire we may be furnished with sum fitting answer to such obiections, as they, being men wise in their own generations, they may bluntly and shrewdly make; as thus, you have given three subsidies to be paide all in a yeare, which was never before, what is the reason we have not our pardon, our lawes, and greevances removed? Do you delight your selfs to heare one another talk, to give away our money and bring home nothing?' Like the famous story of Spenlow and Jorkins, this put the blame for diversion elsewhere, and has the even greater advantage of being true. Indeed, the argument is one which war supporters might even raise because they thought the difficulty needed a solution. It is worth noting Wentworth's assumption that to his voters, a war would be 'nothing'.[11]

Similarly, the argument that they should not rush ahead before the king had committed himself could be deployed from both sides of the divide, either by Coke and Phelips, wanting not to wreck their plans by appearing to force the king's hand, or by Seymour and Alford wanting to shunt the business aside. Speeches about cost could be designed to get the money, or they could be designed to play on James's very deep fear of finding himself committed to war without any means of covering his costs.[12] Since all these techniques depended for their effectiveness on the fact that others as well as opponents of war could use them, it is not easy for us now to distinguish who was really trying to be obstructive. It is only by placing a single intervention within a member's whole record that we can sometimes progress from suspicion, through vehement suspicion, to something near certainty.[13] The rule we should apply is Goldfinger's: 'once is happenstance, twice is coincidence. The third time

---

[11] W. Notestein, F. H. Relf and H. Simpson, (eds.), *Commons' Debates in 1621* (7 vols., New Haven, 1935) (hereafter, *CD 1621*) III, 410; Cooper, p. 167.

[12] On James's fears on this point in 1624, see Robert E. Ruigh, *The Parliament of 1624* (Cambridge, Mass., 1971), pp. 200–2, 230–1, 242.

[13] See Sir Francis Seymour's speech of 5 March 1624 (BL, Add. MSS 46,191, f. 10v) as an example of the sort of speech to which this rule must be applied.

it's enemy action.' By applying that rule, we can come to something
very near a list of opponents of the war, and they are a powerful part
of the Parliament. In the absence of a division list, it is impossible to
tell whether it was a majority or not. Even in the most fully reported
debate, the speakers are a tiny fraction of those present in the House.
I can only say that, whatever side of the question I was on, I would
have advised against a division, because success was uncertain, unless
it were possible to rely on the weight of certain royal authority to
gather in the votes.

In the remainder of this essay, I will test some of these questions
against the debates of six days: 26, 27 and 28 November 1621 and 1, 5
and 11 March 1624. These, of course, are not the only days against
which such questions should be tested, but they are a sample which
is not chosen to my advantage, and as big a sample as can be
disposed of in the space available. In November 1621, it cannot be
stressed too strongly that members were debating a war because they
had been ordered to do so. The House had been recalled at short
notice, and told by the Lord Keeper, at the conference of 21
November, that 'the cause was for the maintenance of a war'. Digby,
who made the foreign policy speech at the conference, made clear
that the occasion of war was the need to sustain the forces of Vere
and Mansfeld in the Palatinate, and that they were facing defeat at
the hands of armies in the pay of the King of Spain. He did not
make clear, and made no attempt to make clear, whether the war
against armies sustained by the King of Spain was to be confined to
the Palatinate.[14] Members could not be blamed for discussing one
type of war rather than another, since this was a question on which
they had been given no official guidance. It has always been an
ambiguity in the theory that kings decide on wars and parliaments
pay for them that parliaments cannot know what to pay until they
know what war is intended. They cannot therefore discuss financing
a war without discussing the nature and theatre of the war. This was
well enough understood by Edward III and Henry V, and there is no
reason to suppose that James and his advisors understood it any less.
Moreover, it is impossible to be too restrictive about the theatre of a
war for the simple reason that once war is begun, the choice of
theatre is 50 per cent in the hands of the enemy, and it is impossible
to predict what choices he will make.

[14] C. S. R. Russell, *Parliaments and English Politics, 1621–9* (Oxford, 1979), pp. 125–6.

When debate on these questions began, on 26 November, Secretary Calvert, who waited to speak until late in the debate, did not reprove anyone for meddling in matters which were not their business. He reproved Sir Robert Phelips, for arguing that 'I would not presently give too much until our next meeting because our own kingdom may have some content in lieu of their subsidies already given'.[15] This was probably not obstructionist, but it did not indicate excessive enthusiasm. On the first day of debate, the supporters of war seem to have been organised with a list of ready speakers. The opening list of Digges, Rudyerd, Fleetwood and Perrott would seem to indicate that the patronage networks of Pembroke, Abbot and Buckingham were all in line, and would suggest a widely, if not unanimously, concerted conciliar line in favour of war. It was certainly a green light to bring out other supporters of war. Sir Edward Giles, the first supporter of a war of diversion, argued for war in the Indies, asking ironically whether 'we must fight with the Spaniards in the Palatinate and be friends with them everywhere else'.[16]

On that first day, only two speakers came out of the closet. The first is Glanville, and his exact words are worth hearing:

That we should in a Parliamentary course go to a sudden supply before Christmas. First the bills that concern religion may be finished. Secondly, the trade of the kingdom and the bill of monopolies; we dare without blushing demand and present these things that concern the commonwealth. Thirdly, concerning justices, the bill of continuance and repeal of statutes and the bill of informers. That a subsidy be called in May. And that now we would grant a subsidy and a fifteen and a committee to be chosen for these.

There is nothing in this speech which is necessarily the speech of an opponent of war, but Glanville was too experienced a legislator not to know that he had set out a time-consuming and controversial programme, and that the chance of failure to reach agreement with the Lords over, for example, the bill of monopolies was far from negligible. The Barrington diary reports him saying 'we have a subsidy to gather yet, and the soldiers will not be payed without the granting of a new'.[17] This at least hinted at the familiar objection to granting subsidies in reversion, while the previous ones were still being collected. Moreover, he was able to appreciate, as Seymour

---

[15] *CD 1621*, II, 448–9.
[16] *Ibid.*, IV, 438.
[17] *Ibid.*, II, 450; III, 456.

did in 1625, that one of the best ways to prevent a war was to grant a subsidy which was too small for the purpose, and then argue that it was impossible to grant another in the same session. There is nothing certain in the interpretation of this speech, but for Glanville, it must be noted as 'happenstance'.

The other doubting Thomas was Wentworth, who argued to put off the supply till Saturday 'and tomorrow patiently to fitt ourselves for the eand of a session, and not to loose the fruit of a Parliament'. 'Adiournement upon adiournement, subsidie upon subsidie and nothing done will make us ridiculous.'[18] It is interesting to note that Wentworth thought his voters would classify a declaration of war as 'nothing done'. If there was a massive demand for war around the country, Wentworth did not seem to think it had reached Yorkshire. He seems to have been in no doubt that what the country wanted was not wars, but bills. Taken together with his speech of 12 December, already quoted, this should count as 'coincidence'. It is not direct opposition to war, but it makes two occasions in which he behaved in way unhelpful to it.

On the second day, 27 November, the supporters of an ideological foreign policy fielded their second eleven. Wilde, Neale, Pym, Grosvenor and Sir William Strode were all clearly in favour of war. So was Mr Shellito, whom Professor Cogswell rightly reproved me for confusing with Solicitor-General Heath. My only excuse is that in doing so I was following two usually reliable sources. The first shadow was again cast by Sir Thomas Wentworth, calling for a return to bills, and arguing, in words he repeated in a more polished version in August 1625, that 'our affairs in Christendom are so clouded that the sharpest sight enters but obscurely into them'. Wentworth's interventions now pass the test for 'enemy action'.[19]

Edward Alford stood even more clearly against the current. He dissociated himself from the current anti-popery in a most politically incorrect manner, by arguing that there had been no practice of the papists against the king since the powder treason, and that they were much more dutiful to the king than they had been to the queen. He then said that 'I take it *pro concesso* that we must give, but lett us remember that England sent us. That must bee satisfied. We must

<hr />

[18] *Ibid.*, III, 457–8; V, 214; IV, 440.

[19] *Ibid.*, II, 454–5; III, 463–4; Cooper, p. 237. Seventeenth-century MPs, like their successors, had a weakness for recycling their best lines, and this weakness deserves more study than it has yet had.

not leave England miserable and looke only to the Palatinate.'[20] Again, these words just might have been spoken by a supporter of the war, but their claim to qualify as 'happenstance' is surely unquestionable. Behind him came Sir Guy Palmes, who argued both for return to bills and for deferring subsidy, Seymour, who wanted subsidy and back to bills, Mallory, who wanted to return to bills and defer a subsidy till after Christmas, and Poole, who followed Seymour. Sir William Cope argued that there could be no subsidies before June, since the last payment of the subsidy already voted was not due until May.[21] Taken together with Mallory's attempt, on 20 November, to raise the restraints of Sir Edwin Sandys (which had been reintroduced by Hayman on the morning of the 27th) this puts Mallory's action into the category of coincidence. The action of the others counts as 'happenstance'.

On 28 November, most of the morning was taken up with a speech by Pym which led Chamberlain to remark that he was 'somewhat long in the explanation of these particulers'.[22] The second part of the day went on debate on voting supply. Phelips, again showing himself less than red hot, moved for one subsidy, and had to be reminded by Sir Francis Fane to add a fifteenth with it. He assumed a new grant at another meeting in February. Again, James was being jockeyed into declaring himself before he had been granted any substantial supply – a proposal which, while sensible from Phelips's point of view, was highly inconvenient from the king's. Giles, an undoubted supporter of war, asked for the king to do something to encourage the House to give at their next meeting in February. Again, he seems to have assumed that war was not likely to be of itself pleasing to the country.[23] The resolution for one subsidy was not satisfactory. Calvert was moved to say the king had already borrowed one subsidy and £40,000 more, and Sackville to remark that one subsidy was not sufficient to maintain the army.[24] Alford asked that the necessity should be set down in the preamble of the subsidy, so that it would not be made a precedent, adding that the farmers would say that if you had three taxes in one year, you must have three harvests. Alford here achieved coincidence. Wentworth,

---

[20] *CD 1621*, II, 458; III, 469; V, 219; IV, 445; *CJ*, 649. This speech is a good illustration of how a small ellipsis in the reporting may shift the apparent emphasis of the whole speech.

[21] *CD 1621*, III, 472–3; II, 459; V, 408; VI, 203, 326.

[22] *Letters of John Chamberlain*, ed. N. E. McClure, (2 vols., Philadelphia, 1939), II, 412.

[23] *CD 1621*, II, 465; V, 223–4; VI, 207.

[24] *Ibid.*, VI, 208; V, 225.

continuing enemy action, said that if he did not believe there would
be a session, he would not give his voice for a subsidy. We should
perhaps see a barb in the remark by Nathaniel Rich: 'those that are
about the chair have not spoken to persuade a subsidy, but we have
done it freely'. The sum was so small that James did not bother to
secure it before dissolving the parliament, and it was capable of
having the same obstructive effect as Seymour's motion for one
subsidy in 1625.[25]

These three days, then, have supplied us with a list of seven
members whose views give rise to question, which is a substantial
number in the face of strong official encouragement to debate war.

In 1624, there was again strong encouragement to debate the
breach of the treaties with Spain, and the war 'likely to ensue'. This
time, the official vehicle of encouragement was Buckingham's Relation, describing the story of previous negotiation with Spain. Again,
James's attitude kept members guessing, and the official encouragement, though strong, was not overwhelming.

On 1 March 1624, when these issues were first debated, Professor
Cogswell has rightly pointed out that the issues were blurred by the
fact that the ostensible issue was only whether the treaties with
Spain, for the match and the Palatinate, should be broken off. Most,
but not all, of the House agreed with Rudyerd that war was 'likely to
ensue' if they were broken off, but the question was not formally on
the agenda, and it was risky for war supporters to put it there before
James did. This fact accounts for some of the apparent hesitations of,
for example, Sandys and Coke. It does not, in my opinion, account
for an undertow of opposition to war, and my complaint of Professor
Cogswell's account is that he ignored that undertow.[26]

On both sides, the names read remarkably like a rerun of 1621.
The anti-Spanish team was again organised, and the opening list of
Rudyerd, Phelips, Heath, Fleetwood, Eliot and Pym sounds remarkably like that of 1621. The list of other members backing them
approaches double figures, and since Cogswell and I can stipulate

[25] Ibid., II, 467; Russell, Parliaments, p. 225.
[26] Cogswell, Blessed Revolution, pp. 174ff. I have no argument with Professor Ruigh, who holds,
as I do, that in March 1624, 'the apparent unanimity of the Commons was deceptive', and
quotes a letter of 5 March from Dudley Carleton to Sir Dudley, referring to many 'that, by
the consideration of the whole charge of war like to rest upon their shoulders, were
wavering, and ready to advise the continuance of the treaty of restitution'. Professor Ruigh
and I are in broad agreement on the likely identity, as well as the existence, of these
people. Ruigh, Parliament of 1624, pp. 183–4.

that most of these supported war, there is no need to run through the list. The immediate purpose is to look at those who impeded the current, and that list again is mainly familiar. The first name, however, is new. It is Sir George More, taking a rather different line from that which he had taken in 1621, and perhaps influenced by the debacle at the end of the 1621 session. His formal position was simply the correct one, that they had only been asked to consider the breach of the treaties and no more. That something more was behind it might be guessed from Spring's note that he was interrupted by 'some that misliked his tediousness'. Since More was tedious, this may mean no more than it says, but it may also illustrate the intolerance of the politically correct. It is just enough to go down with a question mark as 'happenstance'.[27] A more interesting question arises from the speech of Sir Francis Seymour. He seems to have spoken for breach of the treaties and execution of laws against recusants, and to have left it there. Seymour, perhaps more than any other member, is capable of having seen the breach of the treaties in a purely isolationist, and not belligerent, sense. His speech of 1 March gives so vivid a suggestion of displacing aggression from foreign onto domestic enemies, that it promotes him from 'happenstance' to 'coincidence'.

Next comes Edward Alford. His opposition to having the great business expedited could have been for the perfectly good reason, advanced by some war supporters, that the matter was not yet ready for resolution. It is at least a coincidence, however, that he followed this up by opposing Secretary Calvert's message from the king, not to attack Lord Keeper Williams unless for corruption. He directly opposed acting on the message.[28] The taking of so potentially disruptive a stance by people already suspect of opposition to war with Spain perhaps elevates these two into the category of 'enemy action'. Almost immediately after them, Mallory and Hayman moved to stop the clerk recording the names of speakers. This more than oblique suggestion of reviving a privilege dispute over the imprisonments of 1621 was again liable to divert the House from the great business. It raises Mallory, who was suspected of church popery or worse, into the category of 'enemy action', and Hayman into that of 'coincidence'. The group gained one more new recruit that day,

---

[27] Northants. RO, Finch-Hatton MSS 50 (hereafter 'Pym'), f. 11v; Diary of Sir William Spring (hereafter 'Spring'), 1 March; BL, Add. MSS 18,597 (hereafter 'Earle'), f. 36r.
[28] Spring, 1 March; PRO, SP 14/166 (hereafter 'Nicholas'), ff. 34v–35r, 37; Earle, f. 38.

Dr Barnaby Gooch, Vice-Chancellor of Cambridge. He argued that
it was impossible to recover the Palatinate, that England did not
have the munitions for one day's good service, and that war was a
word pleasing to men without experience. He had offended political
correctitude, and was stopped by the noise.[29] It seems safe enough to
count Gooch as an opponent of war, and his experience shows why
the others chose to speak from behind cover.

The debate of 5 March arose on a report by Sir Edwin Sandys of a
conference with the Lords, at which Southampton, with the support
of Pembroke, had said the king might object that on breach of the
treaties, there would be a war, and ask what assistance he was likely
to get. They therefore asked the Commons to resolve 'that in the
pursuit of this advice, we will assist his Majesty with our persons and
fortunes, as becometh good and obedient subjects'.[30] This motion
touched on James's deepest and most rational fear, that he might
find himself committed to war, with insufficient supply to carry it
through. The Commons, of course, were entitled to their equally
rational fear that James, as in 1621, would take the money and run
away from the war. The whole story illustrates the difficulty of a
system in which one authority decided on foreign policy, and
another on finance.

There is perhaps nowhere where Professor Cogswell and I disagree more deeply than in our assessment of this motion. He says:
'most of the Commons made a distinction between Sandys' motion
and the war: Russell unfortunately did not'.[31] I might with equal
justice reply: 'James and Russell did not make a distinction between
Sandys' motion and the war: the Commons unfortunately did.' If
some members of the Commons made such a distinction, it was
unsustainable, and no distinction will help to explain the fact that
most of these who objected most vigorously to Sandys's motion were
already open to suspicion of opposing the war. What James needed
to know was not just whether he was going to get supply, it was
whether he was going to get *enough* supply to wage a war without a
serious risk of defeat. It was on precisely that point that the House's
later resolution of 12 March fell short of that for which it was asked
on 5 March.

The reservations of such men as Coke at a motion which, however

---

[29] Pym, f. 12v; BL, Harleian MSS 6383 (hereafter 'Holles'), f. 88r. For Gooch, Spring, 1
    March; Earle, f. 39v; Cogswell, *Blessed Revolution*, pp. 177–9.
[30] Earle, f. 52v.   [31] Cogswell, *Blessed Revolution*, p. 186.

necessary it might be, was in breach of Commons' privileges was to be expected, and could have been overcome. What was rather more serious is that the group who should be familiar by now as the anti-war brigade chose this issue as the chance to come out in force. The mere reminder of their existence reinforced the fear that the king might be committed to war and find himself without the supply to defend the kingdom: the threat of the crisis of 1626–7 is already visible in the debate of 5 March 1624.

The attack was begun by Edward Alford, who moved from the safe point that the Lords had broken the Commons' privileges to his familiar refrain that in the last parliament they had given two subsidies for nothing, and should do something for their country before they charged it with any new grant.[32] He was supported by Sir John Saville, saying, this will engage us 'to generalities, even to all our estates, for who shall be judge of our abilities?' He was objecting to entering into an open-ended commitment. This was fair enough, yet James was being asked to enter into an open-ended commitment, whose extent might be determined by the enemy but not by himself. If he was to undertake that commitment, he would need his subjects to undertake it with him.[33] Christopher Wandesford, who expressed the next misgivings, is likely to have had similar views to Wentworth.[34] Sir George More, raising the issue of privilege, might have meant no more than he said, but after his speech of 1 March, this raises him into the list of 'coincidence'. Mallory, extreme as usual, proposed that the committee who brought this proposal from the Lords should be expelled from the House, and added that in the last parliament, they had been told they should have good laws, and had had none.[35] Seymour asked for the paper to be suppressed 'lest it may be thought that the king did accept of our advice upon promise and contract'.[36] This is the sort of remark which makes ministers despair of back-benchers: there was no other sensible way in which a king who did not want to have England invaded could or should enter into a commitment to war. Glanville, asking whether the king

---

[32] Nicholas, f. 49r; BL, Add. MSS 46,191 (hereafter 'Rich'), f. 13v; Pym, f. 19r; Earle, f. 52v.

[33] Spring, 5 March; Nicholas, f. 50v. For a rather different report, see Rich, f. 12v. One possible resolution of the apparent conflict is that in the words reported by Rich, Saville was using the good political device of reproving the king for lack of trust in the Commons because he wanted a commitment from them. It is certainly the version of Spring and Nicholas which is consistent with Saville's record as a whole.

[34] Nicholas, f. 50v.

[35] Rich, f. 11v; Nicholas, f. 51; Holles, f. 92v; Spring, 5 March.

[36] Holles, f. 92v; Spring, 5 March; Rich, f. 10v.

should be thought so weak that he could not make war without contracting with his subjects, made exactly the same point.[37] His interventions rise to the level of 'coincidence'.

On 11 March, Alford appeared to support war, but in the light of his previous record, it is hard to miss his meaning when he 'mooved not to conclude too hastily'.[38] Glanville, appearing to do the same, perpetrated a misunderstanding so gross as to be brilliant. He asked the House to decide that the king might lawfully undertake a war, and that his conscience should be satisfied in it. It is hard to think of anything to which James was likely to take stronger exception than a parliamentary debate on whether his conscience should be satisfied. It is not surprising that Solicitor General Heath told him 'it is not fit for us to determine the king's conscience and honour'.[39] It was a good try, and raises Glanville to the status of 'enemy action'. It is a wonderful example of the oblique style of opposition.

It emerges from these debates that the opposition to war, just as much as its supporters, were a stage army: a limited number of people who keep running round the back and coming in from the other wing. They are not the House, but neither are their opponents. The supporters of war, in these debates, are a significantly larger stage army than their opponents, but this is no guide to whether they had more support in the House or not. The godly always made more row, and when they were fortified with official favour, they could easily appear the larger number. However, when the two sides together do not muster more than forty speakers with an identifiable line, it is rash to jump to conclusions about the opinion of the House, still less that of 'the nation'. I make no claim that 'the House' was against the war: I claim that the House was divided and we cannot *a priori* assume a majority for one side or the other. What we can assume is that defeat was likely to make the number of apparent opponents of the war grow, and that fact provides much of the explanation of what went wrong later in the decade.

---

[37] Pym, f. 19r; Rich, f. 9v.
[38] Holles, f. 96v; Earle, ff. 73–4.
[39] Pym, f. 26r; Nicholas, f. 70r; Earle, f. 70r; Bodleian Library, Tanner MSS 392, ff. 46r–v.

CHAPTER 3

Wentworth's 'change of sides' in the 1620s

Richard Cust

In 1986 Perez Zagorin published an article which revived the old debate about whether Sir Thomas Wentworth changed sides when he entered royal service in 1628. Taking issue with Conrad Russell's view that Wentworth could not have changed sides because there were 'no sides to change', Zagorin argued that, on the contrary, his actions were seen by friends and neighbours as a definitive shift from the 'country' to 'court', citing amongst other evidence the 'common opinion' in Yorkshire that Wentworth had taken on 'Sir John Savile's character and that there is a Thomas as well as a John for the king'.[1] In a sense, of course, both verdicts are correct, depending on which story line is adopted. If one accepts the seventeenth-century vision of England's political order as an organically united commonwealth, in which crown and people had to co-exist in harmony, then no change of sides was involved. If, on the other hand, one applies the theme of 'court' and 'country', in which a corrupt and tyrannical 'court' confronted a virtuous 'country', then Wentworth's accommodation with Buckingham so soon after leading the Commons' campaign for the Petition of Right was a monumental sell-out. Either interpretation would have made sense to contemporaries, and either would have made sense to Wentworth himself. In spite of this, however, I would argue that the debate – which has coloured interpretations of Wentworth's early career – is ultimately rather limiting. This is because it implies that Wentworth can be fitted into one simple narrative or another: whether it be a whig or revisionist narrative, built around themes of conflict or unity, or a traditional biographical

I am very grateful to Ann Hughes for reading and commenting on drafts of this chapter. I also wish to thank the participants in the Strafford conference at Sheffield for their comments, in particular Derek Hirst and Peter Lake.

[1] P. Zagorin, 'Did Strafford change sides?', *English Historical Review* 101 (1986), pp. 149–63; C. S. R. Russell, 'Parliamentary history in perspective, 1604–1629', *History*, 61 (1976), pp. 4, 20.

narrative which seeks to identify consistent patterns in an individual's life. Given that recent feminist and post-modernist approaches to biography have suggested that consistency in an individual is largely illusory,[2] we should perhaps be wary of being able to identify a straightforward integrated personality, particularly in a politician.

It has recently been argued that in the early modern period Englishmen displayed a new interest in the self-conscious fashioning of their identities through manipulating the narratives, symbols and rhetorics which formed contemporary culture.[3] This is my starting point for looking again at Wentworth's early political career. Leaving on one side the issue of whether or not it is possible to identify an authoritative 'self' in the case of Wentworth – a concept which anyway has been rendered problematic by recent critiques of the centred, Enlightenment view of personality – I want to investigate the ways in which he drew from contemporary cultural resources to construct positive images of himself. Arguably this should be one of the primary tasks of the political historian – to look at how political identities were constructed and maintained from the discourses and languages available to be appropriated in a given context.[4] In the process I hope to show that within a complex political culture, such as existed in England in the 1620s, it was open to political actors to present themselves in all sorts of different ways, according to the ends they sought and the circumstances in which they were operating. Much of the skill of an undoubtedly adroit politician like Wentworth lay in knowing which images and rhetorics to deploy with which audiences and how these could be combined and spliced together to construct a convincing whole.

Wentworth, I would suggest, lends himself well to this type of approach. He and his friends were very conscious of the 'public' nature of politics. They compared political involvement to ascending 'the stage', they reflected on the roles which were appropriate in a given set of circumstances, and they worried about the humiliation which could result from exposing themselves to the scrutiny of a

---

[2]   See, for example, 'Special issue: auto/biography in sociology', *Sociology* 27 (1993).
[3]   S. Greenblatt, *Renaissance Self-Fashioning* (1980).
[4]   K. Sharpe and P. G. Lake (eds.), *Culture and Politics in Early Stuart England* (Basingstoke, 1994), introduction, pp. 12–20. The arguments I advance in this chapter owe a good deal to ideas put forward in this seminal collection of essays. The introduction, in particular, sets out what is effectively a new agenda for the study of early Stuart political culture.

news-hungry public.[5] Wentworth's early letters and drafts of speeches enable us to reconstruct some of the processes which this involved. They show him trying out different rhetorics and experimenting with identities in an effort to fashion appropriate images. This was particularly apparent in the correspondence with his close friend, Christopher Wandesford. A favourite device in these letters was to play with different contemporary stereotypes. In one letter Wentworth would cast himself as a simple, impoverished northerner to Wandesford's 'southerne man', in another he was the plaine 'countryman' to Wandesford's sophisticated courtier and 'statesman'.[6] The main object here was to pass ironic comment on the contemporary political scene and their respective circumstances. Elsewhere, however, Wentworth's letters hinted at the more immediate applications of political images. When he dispensed patronage as sheriff to a client of his opponent Lord Scrope, he commented that 'I can make this use of it as that whatever I do hereafter shall not appear to come from any particular dislike of his person, but from the truth and duty I owe unto the safety and good government of my country.'[7] Here he was aware of the need to counteract any negative gloss on his future actions by establishing his image as a good magistrate. More intriguingly, when he faced the prospect of being shut out at court because of Buckingham's disfavour, he confided in Wandesford that

I will, to use Sir Edward Coke's phrase, quiet myself and, according to my fashion, keep on a Spanish march, expecting that happy night that the king shall cause his chronicles to be read wherein he shall find the faithfulness of Mardocheus, the treason of his eunuchs and then let Haman look to himself.[8]

The implicit self-identification with Mordechai, the honest courtier whose true worth was finally recognised, is as significant as the apparent association of Haman with Buckingham.

The same letter to Wandesford also illustrates another facet of Wentworth's make-up which is relevant here. He was a self-professed Stoic and like other neo-Stoic contemporaries he manifested a concern to 'make himself' in certain specified ways. The neo-Stoic set out to conquer his passions through the use of reason, to maintain his conscience and integrity in the face of fortune and to stand

[5] Knowler, I, 9, 36, 37; Cooper, p. 105.
[6] Cooper, pp. 204–5, 209–10, 213–16, 229–30; Knowler, I, 21–3.
[7] Knowler, I, 33.   [8] *Ibid.*

foursquare and serene against adversity.[9] Wentworth's letter was a classic expression of these aims. He was determined, he said, to

> fold myself up in a cold, silent forbearance [and] apply myself chearfully to the duties of my place... For my Rule, which I will not transgress, is never to contend with the prerogative out of a parliament, nor yet to contest with a king but when I am constrained thereunto, or else make shipwreck of my integrity and peace of conscience, which I trust God will ever bless me with, and with the courage too to preserve it.[10]

Here, then, we can see Wentworth aspiring to ideals which involved self-consciously shaping and forming oneself, whilst at the same time seeking to extract maximum advantage from difficult circumstances by presenting an image of Stoic forbearance. There is the complex mix of idealism and calculation which often appears to have accompanied political self-fashioning of this sort.

By investigating the processes through which Wentworth sought to construct and maintain his political identities, it should be possible to gain a clearer understanding not only of how an ambitious politician attempted to negotiate the challenges of the 1620s, but also of the cultural resources available to him. This will lead to a more fragmented account of Wentworth's early career, but ultimately, it is hoped, to a more convincing one.

*　　*　　*

I want to begin by looking at a couple of episodes in local politics which illustrate some of the themes which Wentworth deployed. The first of these resulted from Sir John Savile's attempt, in September 1617, to oust him from the post of Custos Rotulorum for Yorkshire. Savile had procured a letter from George Villiers telling Wentworth that it was the king's wish that he should resign.[11] Wentworth was determined not to go, but he had to tread carefully. Somehow he needed to persuade James and the royal favourite to back off without appearing undutiful or self-seeking. He achieved this by deploying

---

[9]　Knowler, ii, 40; K. Sharpe, *The Personal Rule of Charles I* (1992), p. 137. Among the works which Wentworth read whilst on his Grand Tour were the letters of Justus Lipsius, the leading neo-Stoic philosopher of the period; J. W. Stoye, *English Travellers Abroad 1604–1667* (1952), p. 65. I am grateful to Kevin Sharpe and Anthony Milton for these references. For an excellent discussion of Stoicism and what it meant for a leading political figure of the late sixteenth century, see E. McCutcheon, *Sir Nicholas Bacon's Great House Sententiae* (English Literary Renaissance, suppl. 3, 1976), pp. 21–58. For reference to the neo-Stoic's concern to 'make himself', p. 32.

[10]　Knowler, i, 33.　　[11]　*Ibid.*, i, 4.

the rhetoric of honour. In a long letter to Villiers he stressed his
gratitude to James for past favours, his willingness to obey him in all
things and his lack of personal ambition. But he then pointed out
forcefully that if 'Sir John should supply the roome in my place... itt
might justly be taken as the greatest disgrace that could be done unto
me'.[12] He reinforced this in a further letter which he drafted for his
father-in-law, the earl of Cumberland, to send to James, in which it
was stressed that Wentworth had fulfilled his duties as well as could
be expected of any royal servant and that 'being thus taken from him
without any cause of offence ytt would bee a great disgrace unto him
in the cuntrye'.[13] Infringing on a gentleman's honour in this way was
not something even the king could consider lightly, particularly if
that gentleman had performed good service. In these circumstances
Wentworth could legitimately refuse to yield, and within a few days
Villiers had backed off and apologised.[14]

The second episode, the Yorkshire election of 1620, presented a
more complex set of problems. Wentworth had to persuade the
Yorkshire gentry and freeholders to support not only his own
candidature, but also that of his running-mate Sir George Calvert,
Secretary of State, who came under widely publicised attack from Sir
John Savile as a courtier and a 'stranger', and 'therefore one not safe
to be trusted by the country'. Wentworth justified his own decision to
stand in conventional terms, arguing that it was to satisfy his friends
rather than out of personal ambition, and again pointing to the
disgrace involved if his old rival should carry the day. To legitimise
the extensive arm-twisting which was needed to get the gentry and
freeholders to turn out and vote, he resorted to frequent references
to the sense of neighbourliness and reciprocal obligation within the
gentry community of Yorkshire. At the same time, he also portrayed
his opponent as an alien divisive force, bent on stirring up the lower
orders to defy the gentry. 'Such a carriage of the commons', he
warned, 'might breed ill blood in the example and imbolden them
more then wer fit for this government.'[15] The most difficult of his
tasks – persuading the freeholders that Calvert would serve them

---

[12] S. R. Gardiner (ed.), *The Fortescue Papers* (Camden Soc., new ser., 1, 1871), pp. 23–7.
[13] Cooper, p. 101. See also drafts of letters to Lord Keeper Bacon and Lord Wooton; *ibid.*,
        p. 100.
[14] Knowler, 1, 4.
[15] Cooper, p. 144. This election is discussed in more detail in R. P. Cust, 'Politics and the
        electorate in the 1620s', in R. P. Cust and A. L. Hughes (eds.), *Conflict in Early Stuart
        England* (Harlow, 1989), pp. 143–6.

properly – he sought to accomplish by altering the frame of reference. Whereas Savile deployed images of 'court' and 'country' in which he presented Calvert as a grasping courtier and himself as their 'martyr' for having stood out against impositions in 1614, Wentworth discussed Calvert's candidature within a rhetoric of organic unity. In a circular letter to the high constables during the election, and an address to local subsidy assessors during a recess in the parliament, he set out to show that the commonwealth as a whole could only function where there was a 'most happy union betwixt the king and his people', with a king prepared to listen to their grievances and then provide laws and injunctions to remedy them. Within such a scenario, well-intentioned royal councillors such as Calvert played a vital role, informing the king of what was going on and executing orders which would benefit the people. And here Wentworth was able to make a good deal of Calvert's work early in the parliament in securing a comprehensive bill against informers, which 'as itt is more then any of your neibours could have been able to doe for you soe is itt better service then hath been dun by any of your knights in parlament thes twenty yeares'.[16] Calvert won the election with support from the leading gentry, but how far Wentworth was able to make this line stick with the freeholders is unclear. Nevertheless he evidently felt it was an appropriate theme for someone seeking to serve the king and at the same time retain credit with his neighbours.

This applied just as much to Wentworth himself early in his career. From his teens he had been groomed for public office, not just in the county but also in the service of the crown. His father first presented him at court in 1611 and soon after he departed on a Grand Tour with the blessing of the earl of Salisbury. The diary he kept on the tour shows him reading a wide range of historical works and drawing lessons from contemporary French politics which could be applied back in England.[17] In 1614, at the unusually young age of twenty-one, he was elected knight of the shire for Yorkshire. Although his involvement in the parliament's debates was minimal, he did draft two speeches on the vexed issue of undertakers. And here already one can see him presenting himself as a reconciler of divisions between 'court' and 'country', urging the Commons to

[16]   Cooper, pp. 152–7; A. Gooder, 'The parliamentary representation of the county of York', (2 vols., Yorkshire Archaeological Soc., XCVI, 1937), II, 167.

[17]   Cooper, pp. 48–9; Stoye, *English Travellers Abroad*, pp. 63–9.

satisfy James that 'our lib[erties] and loves went hand in hand, our
zeals to our cuntry and king kissed each other'.[18] From 1619 onwards
he made a determined bid to secure preferment at court. He moved
his household to London for long periods, assiduously cultivated his
two main court contacts, Calvert and Sir Arthur Ingram, and
appears to have attached himself to Lionel Cranfield by the time the
latter became Lord Treasurer in September 1621.[19] Cranfield offered
him the receivership of crown lands in Yorkshire with the assurance
that 'I reserve better busines for you then this to shewe my respect
unto you.'[20] For periods of the 1621 parliament Wentworth operated
not just as the representative for Yorkshire, but also as a supporter of
the court lobby of which Calvert and Cranfield were leading
spokesmen.

Reconciling these two roles was straightforward enough in the first
session, when he could align himself with reformers at court and
press for stern measures against patentees and bills to redress local
grievances. At the subsidy assessors' meeting in April he was able to
present the Commons' early grant of supply as a means of healing
the divisions opened up in 1614 and also to point to a series of
beneficial bills and the punishment of Mompesson, 'of more safety to
the commonwealth in the example then 6 of the best lawes that have
been made in 6 of the last parlementts'.[21] In the second session,
however, his task became rather more difficult. He was required to
back up the king's request for additional supply with no strings
attached in a House of Commons bent on discussing privilege
disputes and war against the Emperor. Again he sought to reconcile
what might be seen as conflicting concerns by deploying variants on
the theme of unity. He repeatedly urged the Commons to avoid
contentious matters and get back to passing bills, both to satisfy their
neighbours and encourage gratitude for 'his Majestie's piouse and
fatherly government over them'. He drafted a speech against
pursuing the matter of Sir Edward Sandys's exclusion from the
house, arguing that 'discourses of this nature betwixt the king and his
commons have heartofore been allwayes ill accompanied with

---

[18] Cooper, pp. 76–8. For this theme, see also Wentworth's speech in Yorkshire supporting
      the king's request for a free gift in 1614; *ibid.*, pp. 79–83.
[19] Cooper, pp. 126–9, 142, 148, 157–8; Knowler, I, 10; II, 430.
[20] Cooper, p. 168.
[21] W. Notestein, F. H. Relf and H. Simpson (eds.), *Commons' Debates in 1621* (7 vols., New
      Haven, 1935), (hereafter *CD 1621*) II, 163; III, 350; C. S. R. Russell, *Parliaments and English
      Politics, 1621–1629* (Oxford, 1979), pp. 104–5; Cooper, p. 155.

distrusts and jealousies'. In the subsidy debate of 26 and 27 November he also spoke against the mainstream in support of the councillors' request for providing subsidies, but leaving decisions about war and peace in the hands of the king. Additional supply would be 'the meanes' of 'uniteing us to the king' and continuing the 'joyfull incoation of an amyty betwixt us and the king' which 'all honest men must desyre'.[22] Language of this sort is so much in evidence in Wentworth's public addresses that it is tempting to see it as the bedrock of his political beliefs. It is, however, important to be sensitive to the context and recognise that many of the best examples of this rhetoric belong to the late 1610s and early 1620s, when he was seeking to reconcile ambitions to become a royal servant with retaining credit amongst his neighbours.

Wentworth's early efforts to enter the royal service appeared to be about to bear fruit in July 1622, when he was strongly tipped to become Controller of the King's Household. But this did not happen and soon after his prospects declined rapidly. The main cause was a series of bouts of tertian fever which struck in the summer of 1622, early 1623 and again early in 1624. The fever killed his first wife and left Wentworth himself close to death for long periods. He was forced to give up his London residence and return to Yorkshire.[23] At the same time he suffered his first serious political setbacks. In 1623, for reasons which are unclear, he was forced to resign the receiver-ship of crown lands;[24] then, in the 1624 parliament, his most powerful patron, Cranfield, was driven from office.

During this period Wentworth tended to adopt a much lower political profile. In part this was a response to the drift towards war with Spain, of which he strongly disapproved; but his disenchant-ment went much deeper. He carefully avoided any hint that he might contest the 1624 county election, which allowed his great rival, Savile, and his son to be returned unopposed; and he discussed the prospects for the coming parliament in uncharacteristically pessi-mistic terms, reflecting that 'services done there [are] coldly requited

---

22 Cooper, pp. 167, 163; *CD 1621*, III, 463–4.
23 *The Letters of John Chamberlain*, ed. N. E. McClure (2 vols., Philadelphia, 1939), II, 446; Knowler, I, 16–17; II, 430.
24 J. P. Cooper, *Land, Men and Beliefs* (1983), p. 153 has suggested that Wentworth sold the receivership because he was facing financial difficulties. However, the comment by Sir Arthur Ingram, that 'if there should be any chans[g] now itt mytt bee a tuch to your reputacion', and the tone of Wentworth's letter to Cranfield surrendering the office, suggest that he was pressured into this; Cooper, p. 185; Knowler, I, 16.

on all sides and which is worse many times misconstrued'.[25] He gave every indication of drawing in on himself and abandoning his earlier aspirations, and this was accompanied by an intriguing refashioning of his self-image, at least in his letters to Calvert and Wandesford. Deploying an extensive repertoire of pastoral imagery, he ranged over the renaissance themes of *otium* and *negotium*, advancing the classical arguments that retirement from public duty was essential to achieving the highest religious and philosophical understanding and that involvement with the court meant being tainted with corruption, deceit and superficiality. He depicted himself as the simple northerner or rustic swain, steeping himself in Ovid and the pleasures of gardening whilst his friends busied themselves with affairs of state.[26] Much of this, of course, was intended as a vehicle for ironic comment, but there was also a sense in which Wentworth was adjusting to the more attenuated political role that circumstances had forced on him. He may not have wanted retirement, but he seems to have been determined to fashion it into an acceptable role.

However, this was not to last. From the spring of 1624 his health started to recover and when he finally made it to the parliament in April he offered a spirited defence of his patron, Cranfield. By October he was lobbying to obtain the stewardship of the Honour of Pontefract and talking of coming down to court to promote his cause. And when he got news of Charles's accession, in April 1625, he immediately wrote off to Wandesford for 'advisement how to sett my cards upon this new shuffle of the packe'.[27] Wentworth's prospects of preferment had been seriously damaged by the removal of Cranfield and, soon after, Calvert as well, but he had clearly not abandoned his hopes. Now there was the possibility of cultivating a new connection with Lord Keeper Williams, or even gaining access to Buckingham through Sir Edward Conway and Sir Richard Weston.[28] This said, however, his main priority in 1625 appears to have been restoring his local power, and this involved positioning himself so that he was less closely identified with the court than in the

---

[25] Cooper, p. 202; Knowler, I, 19, 20–4.

[26] Cooper, pp. 205–6, 209, 214–15; Knowler, I, 16, 23–4. For a discussion of these themes, see R. Tuck, 'Humanism and political thought', in A. Goodman and A. MacKay (eds.), *The Impact of Humanism on Western Europe* (Harlow, 1990), pp. 43–65; F. Heal and C. Holmes, *The Gentry in England and Wales, 1500–1700* (Basingstoke, 1994), p. 277.

[27] Russell, *Parliaments*, p. 200; Cooper, pp. 211–15, 229.

[28] J. Hacket, *Scrinia Reserata : a Memorial Offered to the Great Deservings of John Williams D.D.* (1692), pt. II, 17; Knowler, I, 34–5.

early 1620s. Wentworth sought to reconcile these various aims by appropriating the theme of 'honesty', with all it implied. 'Honest' was most commonly used in contemporary political parlance to describe the 'honest patriot', willing to follow his conscience and speak out for the 'country' and the public interest. But it also had more general connotations which reached back to the Roman term *honestus*, used to describe a man who was virtuous and worthy of honour. In this sense, 'honesty' was also a quality sought in the service of the king, denoting the good councillor who could be relied on for loyal and conscientious advice without resorting to flattery or expediency.[29] It was therefore a theme which could legitimate the various different roles which Wentworth was seeking to sustain.

The first of these was in Yorkshire where he soon became embroiled in the 1625 county election. As in 1620, he based his strategy on getting out his gentry supporters and their freeholders, but in this campaign there was a much more marked stress on associating himself with 'the country'. Hardly a letter survives from this period which does not mention his desire 'to serve the country' or to do 'that which shall appear best to the country'. And this was explicitly coupled with the theme of 'honesty' when he urged his running-mate, Sir Thomas Fairfax, to tell the voters that they were being challenged 'by a faction for serving them honestly and boldly'. This rhetoric presumably helped Wentworth's cause, but it was double-edged in that it also implied an obligation to stand up against what one of his correspondents described as 'such insufferable oppressions as are not to be endured in a commonwealth'.[30]

One can see Wentworth experimenting with different ways of responding to this in two drafts of a speech which he prepared for the subsidy debate at the end of the 1625 parliament. His basic line was to oppose the king's request for an additional grant of supply, but suggest that a date be set for a new session in which the Commons would pledge itself to offer further subsidies. In the context of the debate this was a moderate stance. However, Wentworth set out to frame his argument with significantly different

[29] For a more extensive discussion of the contemporary usage of the term, see my introduction to *The Papers of Sir Richard Grosvenor (1585–1645)* (Lancashire and Cheshire Record Soc., 1995). For the Roman concept of *honestus*, see Cicero, *On Duties*, ed. M. T. Griffin and E. M. Atkins (Cambridge, 1991), xliv–xlv, *passim*.

[30] Cust, 'Politics and the electorate', pp. 147–8; *The Fairfax Correspondence*, ed. G. W. Johnson (2 vols., 1848), I, 8–10; Cooper, pp. 232–4.

rhetorics. One draft deployed the language of unity, but with a different slant from 1621 in that he now emphasised that harmony could best be ensured by not pressing the taxpayer too hard and waiting until there was a consensus in the Commons behind making the grant. The other, however, focused on the dangers of departing from precedent by making two grants of supply in the same parliament. It emphasised that innovation tended to disadvantage the subject in relation to the prince, producing 'such effects as weare neither forseen nor yett dreamed of', and that it would be difficult to justify to 'those that sent us'.[31] Which, if either, of these versions Wentworth actually delivered in the debate is unclear, but they provide an interesting insight into the choice of theme and language to create different impressions. The first draft fitted well with the image of someone emphasising his loyalty to the king and putting himself forward as a bridge-builder between crown and subject, whilst the second was the line of a 'patriot', seeking to prevent any slippage in the rights of the subject.

During the months which followed, Wentworth tended to hover between these two roles, keeping his options open as far as possible. If an opportunity was offered for gaining a foothold at court he pursued it, but generally in ways which could enhance a reputation for integrity. Thus when Buckingham approached him, via Weston, at the Oxford Parliament of 1625, he told him he would 'be ready to serve him in the quality of an honest man and a gentleman', and during the parliament carefully refrained from anything that might be construed as opposition to the duke.[32] In spite of this, in November 1625, at Buckingham's behest, he was pricked as a sheriff to exclude him from the following parliament. At this point he might have accepted that advancement at court was unlikely and thrown himself wholeheartedly into the role of 'honest patriot'. He was invited to join a scheme proposed by Sir Francis Seymour whereby those pricked as sheriffs would use their influence to secure seats for the others outside their home counties, thereby avoiding the prohibition on sheriffs sitting as MPs. This would have raised Wentworth to the status of one of the leading 'Parliament men' of the day, but almost certainly at the price of being branded a troublemaker by the court. So instead he chose to bide his time and discharge his shrieval duties as conscientiously

---

[31] Cooper, pp. 239, 236–9.
[32] Knowler, I, 34–5; *Scrinia Reserata*, pt. II, 17.

as possible.[33] It was in this context that he wrote to Wandesford about Mordechai and Haman, and his determination to maintain his 'integrity and peace of conscience'.

Wentworth, however, was not always consistent. On several occasions during the early months of 1626, he abandoned the moral high ground and showed he could fawn and flatter as well as the next man. His soliciting of Buckingham when it looked as if the presidency of the Council of the North might become available, and again during the parliament, were classic examples of the unctuous obsequiousness which had become *de rigeur* in circles around the duke.[34] But in spite of these efforts he suffered another rebuff in July when, on Buckingham's instructions, Savile finally took the place of Custos Rotulorum. The dismissal took place at the summer assizes and Wentworth squeezed what advantage he could from the occasion with an eloquent address to the gentry and jurymen. After describing the persecution he had suffered, he declared his steadfast determination not to 'overlive the opinion of an honest man amongst you', which meant that he had

never... declined forth of the open and plain ways of law and truth towardes their Majesties; never... falsifid in a tittle the precious and general trust of my county; never... injured or over born the meanest particular under the disguised mask of justice or power.[35]

Again the role of 'country martyr' beckoned, but again he held back and sought to retrieve his credit at court. Within a few days he was drafting a letter to Weston, begging for an audience with the king at which he might demonstrate that, in spite of everything, he remained 'an honest, well-affected, loyal subject'.[36]

The careful balancing act that Wentworth had performed during 1625 and 1626 was abandoned on the occasion of the Forced Loan in 1627 and it is instructive to consider why. Wentworth held off from committing himself for as long as possible, pleading illness as an excuse for staying away from the meetings of the local commissioners, but he was forced to make up his mind in May when a letter from the Privy Council arrived in Yorkshire ordering that all those who did not pay would have to answer in London. Wentworth faced a perplexing decision. On one side the king and the court were

[33] Knowler, I, 28–31, 33; Cooper, p. 243.
[34] PRO, SP 16/18/110; Knowler, I, 34–5.
[35] Knowler, I, 36.
[36] *Ibid.*, I, 35.

exerting enormous pressure to secure payment. Lord Clifford informed him that the king's heart 'is so inflamed in this business as he vows a perpetual remembrance' of refusers. On the other the example set by early opponents of the loan created a surge of expectation that those who stood for the 'country' would resist and his brother-in-law, Lord Haughton, warned that if he did pay, Savile expected this to damage his reputation locally.[37] Public interest was so high that it was almost impossible to keep a low profile as he had done previously. He was forced to choose one way or the other, and in the end, of course, he opted to resist. This decision was closely bound up with his efforts to present himself as 'honest'. During the period of the loan the term came to take on much more specific connotations than previously, being used to describe those like Wentworth's friend, George Radcliffe, who suffered imprisonment for standing up to what was perceived as a fundamental attack on the subject's liberties.[38] For Wentworth to do anything other than refuse would be to risk destroying an image that he had worked so hard to cultivate. As it was, his action triumphantly affirmed it. 'To bee committed in a causs of this nattur', his friend Sir Arthur Ingram told him, 'doth so much redown to your honor, and to the honor of your posteryty, thatt your friends [should] rather bee glad of itt then other wiss.'[39] However, although Wentworth had abandoned his earlier resolution 'never to contend with the prerogative outside parliament', he had not finally burnt his bridges with the court.

There were degrees of opposition to the loan. Some refusers, like William Coryton or Sir John Eliot, sought to obstruct the Privy Council at every turn, but others – including Wentworth – were willing to compromise. When he appeared at the council table in July to answer for his refusal he was said to have carried himself 'discreetly', unlike those who openly argued about the loan's legality. When the order went out for refusers to be confined in the counties away from London he obeyed it without question, telling the councillor Sir Humphrey May that he was 'naturally more delighting, more comforted, to serve my soveraigne his owne way then my owne'. If it was possible to extract any credit at court from

---

[37] R. P. Cust, *The Forced Loan and English Politics, 1626–1628* (Oxford, 1987), pp. 221–3; Knowler, I, 37–8.

[38] Cust, *Forced Loan*, pp. 219–20; R. C. Johnson, M. F. Keeler, M. J. Cole and W. B. Bidwell (eds.), *Commons' Debates in 1628* (4 vols., New Haven, 1977–8) (hereafter *CD 1628*), IV, 76.

[39] Cooper, p. 259.

refusing the loan, Wentworth did so. The result was apparent in November 1627 when he petitioned to be allowed out of confinement to attend to business. Senior councillors, like Weston and the earl of Dorset, queued up to endorse his request and even the king commented favourably when his petition was presented. Unlike the Eliots and Corytons, branded as 'factious spirits', Wentworth was apparently regarded as the acceptable face of loan resistance.[40]

His role in the 1628 parliament was calculated to draw maximum advantage from this. As a prominent resister, he had every opportunity to take a leading role in the debates which would consolidate his reputation as a 'patriot', both in Yorkshire and the country as a whole. But he was still mindful of what was needed to restore his prospects of preferment at court. Throughout the parliament, then, he sought to present himself as one of the more moderate critics of the crown. His most significant intervention came during the subsidy debate on the 22 March. This opened with council spokesmen warning of the dangers of a rerun of the 1626 parliament, to which Seymour and Eliot responded with speeches apparently intended to test the level of support for another assault on Buckingham. Wentworth was the first non-court spokesman to seek to steer the Commons away from this, towards securing their liberties through legislation.[41] For the remainder of the parliament he followed this line consistently, even in the latter stages when Buckingham was assailed on all sides. In the process he identified himself as somebody with whom the court could do business.

During 1628 Wentworth again deployed several of the rhetorics used in 1621 and 1625. The rhetoric of unity was much in evidence. When he was seeking to secure redress of grievances before supply, he used the familiar argument that it was impossible to relieve the king if the people were not secure in their liberties. On the other hand, when a speedy declaration of intent to grant subsidies was needed to keep up the momentum of negotiations with the crown, he talked of the need 'to proceed equally between king and people'.[42] His main effort in 1628 went into supporting the Petition of Right and in these circumstances he repeatedly used the arguments drafted in 1625, that they 'owed a duty to the country' and that they must

[40] Cust, *Forced Loan*, pp. 232–8; Cooper, pp. 261, 273, 279–80.
[41] R. P. Cust, 'Charles I, the Privy Council and the Parliament of 1628', *TRHS* 6th ser., 2 (1992), p. 32; *CD 1628*, II, 60–1.
[42] *CD 1628*, II, 250, 301.

not allow precedents which could damage the subject's liberties. And when it came to charging those responsible for abuses he was careful to blame unspecifed projectors, returning to the language he had used in 1621 :

this hath not been done by the king, under the pleasing shade of whose crown I hope we shall ever gather the fruits of justice, but by projectors who have extended the prerogative of the king beyond the just symmetry which maketh the sweet harmony of the whole.[43]

Wentworth's success in presenting himself as a moderate influence amongst the Commons' leaders was attested immediately after the parliament. Buckingham, looking for an effective, pro-Spanish spokesman in preparation for the next session, finally opened the way to the advancement he had craved so long. In July 1628 he was elevated to the peerage as Baron Wentworth and in December he became Lord President of the Council of the North.[44]

*   *   *

In the context of Wentworth's longstanding efforts to secure a foothold at court his preferment could hardly be seen as a change of sides. On the other hand, given his efforts in Yorkshire to present himself as a 'patriot', his elevation to the peerage amongst a batch of Buckingham nominees, at a time when public opinion was enormously hostile to the duke, could hardly be seen as other than a sell-out. This is why the debate about whether or not he changed sides is so limiting. It presumes that his political identity was somehow fixed, when in fact, as we have seen, it was subject to continual shifts and adjustments. There was not one Thomas Wentworth, but several. He changed his identities not only as his options and opportunities altered, but also as he sought to legitimise his actions before different audiences. The way he milked his pricking as sheriff and dismissal from the custoship to consolidate his image as a 'patriot', whilst at the same time continuing to cultivate Buckingham with all the obsequiousness of the most practised courtier, is a good example of this. Wentworth was also aware, however, that shifts could not be made too suddenly or pushed too far lest he strain his credibility. This was one of the reasons why he held off from joining Seymour's scheme in 1625. For much of this period Wentworth's skill enabled

[43] *Ibid.*, II, 250, 60.   [44] Wedgwood, pp. 68–74.

him to sustain a precarious balancing act and keep his various audiences in play. However, there were moments when his level of visibility was so high and the public's perception of the issues so polarised that this was more or less impossible. One of these was the occasion of the Forced Loan when, in spite of all the pressures, he just about managed to retain his credit in the eyes of the court. The other was the aftermath of the 1628 parliament when he threw in his lot with Buckingham and for the first time appears to have forfeited his reputation as a 'patriot'.

The balancing acts that Wentworth sought to perform were by no means exceptional. There are parallels in the careers of Sir John Savile, Sir Robert Phelips and Sir Dudley Digges, to name only three of the best documented examples from the 1620s.[45] Like Wentworth, these were politicians intensely ambitious for preferment at court, but also concerned to uphold their reputations in their various 'countries'. This led to them reshaping their political identities at different times for different audiences, and in the cases of Savile and Phelips suffering a comparable loss of local reputation when their closeness to Buckingham became apparent. In many respects Wentworth's early career can be seen as a paradigm of the choices and challenges faced by leading politicians in the 1620s. It is exceptional mainly in that it is so well documented.

Wentworth's early political career is also instructive for what it reveals about the political culture of the period. There has been a tendency in recent scholarship to stress the dominance of certain discourses, to present them almost as ideological templates which allowed little scope for individual initiative. The revisionist stress on ideas of consensus and unity is a case in point, so, to a lesser extent, is the post-revisionist gloss on the discourse of anti-popery.[46] Whilst acknowledging that these were powerful themes, it should be recognised that they were also relatively open-ended, and the ways in which they could be deployed were far from fixed. This suggests that we should allow more scope for the capacity of political actors to manipulate such themes to fit their circumstances and objectives. Wentworth was very adept at deploying the theme of unity between

---

[45] For Savile, see Cust, 'Politics and the electorate', pp. 143–51; for Phelips and Digges, see Russell, *Parliaments, passim*.

[46] See, for example, K. Sharpe, *Politics and Ideas in Early Stuart England* (1989), pp. 3–71; P. G. Lake, 'Anti-popery: the structure of a prejudice', in Cust and Hughes (eds.), *Conflict in Early Stuart England*, pp. 72–106.

crown and subject when he found himself trying to reconcile the
differing pressures that they exerted, but on other occasions – when
he was trying to hold on to the custosship or position himself as a
leading figure in the Commons – he could adopt much less compro-
mising rhetorics based on the defence of honour or the liberties of
the subject. It was open to him, to some extent, to pick and choose
the themes which fitted his circumstances, to engage in what Peter
Lake and Kevin Sharpe have called a process of 'creative bricolage'
as he sought to construct different identities.[47] There were, however,
limits to this.

This raises the vexed question of how far a political agent, such as
Wentworth, was being 'sincere' when he deployed a particular
rhetoric and how far he was simply seeking to justify self-interested
political manoeuvres. Ultimately this is an issue which is almost
impossible to resolve. However, it is feasible to point to some of the
constraints on rhetoric and action which appear to have been
operating in this particular instance.[48] One of these was the limitation imposed by the need to present images which were credible and
acceptable to his audiences. Much of Wentworth's skill lay in
knowing how far he could go in this. It is interesting, for example,
that unlike many leading 'patriot' politicians of the day he does not
seem to have deployed the rhetoric of anti-popery. Some rhetorics
were inherently more constraining than others and he seems to have
recognised that it would be hard to fit such powerful language to his
basic stance as a rational, secular-minded politician and supporter of
friendship with Spain.

Another limitation lay in the content of the languages he deployed.
Most political rhetorics are double-edged in that as well as allowing
politicians to legitimise their actions and persuade others, they
impose obligations on those who deploy them. An example of this is
the self-professed Stoicism which was so much admired in the early
Stuart period. This could help an aspiring politician to secure an
invaluable reputation for moderation, constancy, plain dealing and
'public' service. But there was a price to pay.[49] For Wentworth, who

[47] Sharpe and Lake (eds.), *Culture and Politics*, p. 15.
[48] For an illuminating discussion of the links between political rhetoric and motivation, see
Q. Skinner, 'The principles and practice of opposition: the case of Bolingbroke versus
Walpole', in N. McKendrick (ed.), *Historical Perspectives. Studies in English Thought and Society*
(1974), pp. 93–128.
[49] Some of these issues are tackled in a revealing study of Sir Nicholas Bacon: P. Collinson,
Godly People (1983), pp. 135–53.

was renowned for his wilful and 'cholericke' temperament, it surely involved considerable struggles to curb himself and – probably just as irksome – having to submit to being lectured to by his friends. Calvert voiced considerations which Wentworth must often have been forced to address when he tried to dissuade him from refusing the Forced Loan.

> The conquering way sometimes is yielding; and so is it, as I conceive, in this particular of yours, wherein you shall both conquer your own passions and vex your enemies who desire nothing more than your resistance.[50]

Perhaps the best example of the power of political languages in Wentworth's case, however, is the effect of his efforts to present himself as 'honest' – and here there is also an interesting example of how the changing meanings of language can subtly alter its impact. When Wentworth initially sought to present himself as 'honest' in 1625, the term still had relatively neutral connotations, applicable to royal councillors as well as 'country' MPs, however, when it was used to describe loan refusers in the highly charged context of 1627 it came to imply a particular course of action. If Wentworth wanted to go on being regarded as 'honest' he had little choice but to resist the loan.

The connection between political language and action, then, emerges as very much a two-way street. Political agents are capable of manipulating the rhetorics and discourses they deploy, but at the same time their aims, their actions, their responses – indeed, according to recent narrative theory, their very thought processes – are structured by the same rhetorics and discourses.[51] This is, perhaps, stating the obvious, but it is surely something to which early-Stuart historians need to pay more attention.

[50] Knowler, I, 37; II, 435; I, 39.
[51] P. Joyce, *Democratic Subjects: The Self and the Social in Nineteenth-Century England* (Cambridge, 1994), pp. 153–4.

CHAPTER 4

The Church triumphant?
The emergence of a spiritual Lord Treasurer, 1635–1636

Brian Quintrell

When Lord Treasurer Portland died in March 1635, the man many of his contemporaries thought was his obvious successor was over the water in Ireland. And there Wentworth was to remain, unmoved by the pleadings of his friends and proof against the clumsy early probing of his intentions by the Queen's Chamberlain, Dorset.[1] Even before he had left England, there had been unhelpful talk at court of Wentworth's ambitions to be Treasurer; and he had learned to be careful.[2] Besides, he still had work to do as Lord Deputy; and more to the point, Charles never showed any sign of wanting to call him home. Instead, he put the Treasury for the time being into commission, placing at its head Archbishop Laud and the current Chancellor of the Exchequer, Francis Lord Cottington, Portland's old associate, and newly appointed Master of the Court of Wards. While this commission lasted, speculation about a successor was continual, in no way discouraged by the firmness of the disclaimers from those thought to be in with a chance. For it did not do to offend a king so careful of his patronage, and as private in his thoughts, as Charles was. None of the possible candidates ever openly expressed an interest in the post, even to each other, or was so foolhardy as to suppose publicly that he might get it. From Dublin, Wentworth appeared to enjoy it all, writing encouraging letters to Cottington by one post, while assuring Laud by the next that Cottington did not

I am grateful to those present at the Strafford conference for their comments on an earlier version of this chapter. I owe a special debt of thanks to Fiona Pogson, who has generously provided expert guidance on the Strafford archive and on Wentworth's dealings with the English court during the 1630s. The title's phrasing reflects remarks made at the time by James Howell and Edward Hyde.

[1]   Knowler, I, 386–7.
[2]   Str P 3, pp. 81, 83; Knowler, I, 79–80, 85–7, 89; PRO, C 115/N3/8555; Perez Zagorin, 'Sir Edward Stanhope's advice to Thomas... Viscount Wentworth', *HJ* 7 (1964), pp. 298–329.

stand a chance.[3] Only after a year did Charles bring this tense, and rather unreal, period to an end; and then he did so abruptly one Sunday afternoon, shortly after the Lenten sermon, by announcing to the assembled Privy Council the appointment of a clerical Lord Treasurer, William Juxon, the bishop of London.

Few had anticipated such an outcome, even within the court. Although, since the Reformation, the senior clergy had continued to be associated with affairs of state, their roles had invariably been appropriate to their station. A select few sat at the council table, and Archbishop Abbot had headed the Treasury commission of 1618–20, set up after the disgrace of Suffolk; but James's views on the law of God and the importance of conscience in dispensing justice had inclined him to associate his bishops with Chancery, and after rumours of a episcopal successor in Ellesmere's last days, John Williams, bishop of Lincoln, did succeed Bacon in 1621.[4] But Juxon's elevation was different. Not for many generations had one of the princes of the Church been so closely associated with the engine of the state as Juxon was to be. It might be thought to be a triumphant moment for the Church, one not matched since the Reformation.

How this came about is the subject of this chapter. Traditionally, the key has always seemed to lie with the attitude and aspirations of William Laud, and his need to protect his interests, and those of Wentworth, at court. By the early 1630s he had developed a dislike, already on its way to becoming an obsession, with the lax and indulgent administration of Portland, epitomised in the code he and Wentworth used, as the Lady Mora, with Cottington cast as her waiting woman. Despite some lingering regard for past friendships, Wentworth joined Laud in deploring their activities which seemed to represent all that Thorough was intended to root out. Yet Charles had remained unswervingly loyal to Portland, for the Treasurer had done a little to fill the void left by Buckingham and, with his fellow hispanophiles, Cottington and Secretary Windebank, alone had some knowledge of the inner workings of his foreign policy. No minister was better informed than Portland about the king's purposes, or about the resources available to attempt them. It was Laud's intention, or so it is commonly argued, to fill the gap left by the Treasurer's death with a creature of his own, since Wentworth

[3]   Str P 3, pp. 219, 236; Str P 6, p. 263.
[4]   G. W. Thomas, 'James I, equity and Lord Keeper John Williams', *English Historical Review* 91 (1976), pp. 506–28.

was not available; and his chosen instrument was Juxon. Although relatively obscure, he was in some ways an obvious choice. He and Laud had known each other for many years and shared common interests, so much so that Juxon might appear to be his protégé. Laud by 1635 was already borne down by the burden of administration, and needed a trustworthy younger man to take on the responsibility for the Treasury, someone like Juxon who was competent but not overly ambitious. He was also unmarried, and, unlike Portland, had no family interests to which he might divert the king's revenues. If Juxon was appointed, Laud could stop the advance of Cottington; and he took advantage of his rival's lengthy absence from court through ill-health late in the year to hammer his argument home to Charles. The king's compliance secured Laud's own ascendancy in the affairs of both Church and State, and was a resounding acknowledgement of their indivisibility. It also emphasised the central role of the senior clergy in Charles's government. Cottington is held to have been so cast down at the outcome that he sought solace in the hunting-field, and began to neglect his duties. With his trusted lieutenant in place, Laud was thus able to exercise unrivalled influence under the king at court. As he put it in a celebrated entry in his diary, under 6 March 1636:

Sunday, William Juxon, Lord Bishop of London made Lord High Treasurer of England. No Churchman had it since Henry 7's time. I pray God bless him to carry it so, that the Church may have honour, and the King and the State service and contentment by it. And now if the Church will not hold up themselves under God, I can do no more.[5]

The Church did indeed seem to be triumphant, as James Howell remarked to Wentworth soon afterwards; and another of Wentworth's familiar informants, George Garrard, noted how the 'young fry' of the clergy were almost beside themselves with excited speculation about a clerical takeover of other offices of state.[6] Laud's influence with the king seemed truly unassailable.

*　　　*　　　*

So the story might rest, were it not for a privileged reporter much closer to events at the moment of Laud's supposed triumph than were Howell and Garrard, one whose testimony casts rather a

---

[5]　Laud, III, 226. No churchman had been Treasurer since 1470 (9 Edward IV).
[6]　Knowler, I, 522; II, 2.

different light on proceedings. In a hitherto unregarded letter, James, marquis of Hamilton recounted how the announcement of Juxon's appointment had been accompanied by

ane publyk declaration of his Majestie att the Consall tabill thatt he woold heaive med Choyes of Canterberi for that plase if itt had not beine out of the Consideration of over pressing his aged bodie with affaires, who[s]e fidelity and affection to his servis his Majesti did much Commend.[7]

At first sight, this seems so much at odds with the standard version that it might be thought to be garbled. Why on earth should the king make this apparently unnecessary statement about Laud – as though *proxime accessit* – at the moment of his protégé's triumph? Why, if Juxon was Laud's candidate, should Laud ever have come, even for a moment, under consideration? Surely Juxon had been put forward because Laud already knew he could not do everything himself? Can the report possibly be accurate?

On this occasion at least, Hamilton can claim to be a good witness. He was on close enough terms with Charles to have had foreknowledge of what was to come. He was present at the council table that Sunday afternoon, for the first time in seven weeks, along with Laud, Cottington and sixteen other councillors. He had a particular interest in the proceedings, for his brother-in-law, Basil Lord Fielding, to whom the king's words were reported, had married Portland's daughter Anne, who had died within days of her father, shortly after joining Fielding in his embassy at Venice. Any comment about Portland's old critic, Laud, was likely to have stuck in Hamilton's mind, especially if the remarks seemed have been prompted by a belief that Laud's standing with the king was thought in need of reaffirmation.[8] Yet, if Juxon had been Laud's successful candidate, and was known in the inner circles of royal government to be such, what call would there have been for such mollifying remarks? Laud's sense of his own importance could hardly have been slighted by the success of his own candidate. Why, too, was it necessary to make those remarks in front of the whole body of the council, unless Laud had himself been a contender for the treasurer's place – and perhaps was known, at least to some councillors, to have

---

[7] James 3rd marquis of Hamilton to Basil Lord Fielding, from Whitehall, 11 March 1636, Warwickshire RO, Fielding of Newnham Paddox Correspondence, CR 2017/C1 no. 59; transcription in HMC, *Fourth Report*, 257a.

[8] PRO, PC 2/46, p. 10. Fielding's mother, Susan, countess of Denbigh, and his sister, Margaret, countess of Hamilton, were both in the circle around the queen which was keen to check Laud's pretensions.

been so? The king's appreciation of the danger of 'over pressing his aged bodies with affaires' also strongly suggests that Laud had indeed thrown his mitre into the ring and had, in effect, been his own candidate. Even though Charles chose not to appoint him, it would be in keeping with Laud's estimation of his worth that he should nevertheless have sought a public affirmation of the king's continuing confidence in him. And Charles, who handled Wentworth relatively sensitively in not dissimilar circumstances, may well have been prepared to give it.[9]

In sum, since Juxon succeeded where Laud did not, it seems reasonable to suppose that Laud had stood on his own behalf, and far from putting Juxon forward, had in effect run against him; that Juxon may well have been successful by virtue of not being a client of Laud, especially since Cottington remained as Chancellor of the Exchequer; and that he had instead benefited from other, more compelling, patronage, not only from other courtiers but directly from the king himself.

It is thus worth taking a closer look, during the year which preceded it, at the circumstances which surrounded Laud's supposed moment of triumph in 1636. Four lines of inquiry seem to be worth following.

The position of Laud, customarily regarded as the principal promoter of Juxon, needs to be examined in order to see how far it is possible to reconcile the statement in his diary with that in Hamilton's letter. What grounds are there for supposing that he found himself drawn into contention? Was his position at court such that he felt impelled to assume more and more responsibility, heedless of his own physical limitations? Given his current dismay over the supposed defection of his old friend, Secretary Windebank, was he at all likely to have been disposed to trust a lieutenant? [10]

What, indeed, was the nature of the relationship between Laud and Juxon in the early 1630s? Were he and Juxon so close, and of a sufficiently common mind by 1635–6, for Laud to propose him, subordinate and apparently inexperienced as he was, for a post at the centre of government, apparently in the knowledge that Cottington might still retain his place as Chancellor of the Exchequer? A

---

[9] Charles to Wentworth, 23 Oct. 1634, Knowler I, 331–2.
[10] Laud gave a contrasting version of his part in Windebank's appointment as Secretary of State, in a letter to Sir Thomas Roe shortly afterwards, playing down the major role he had cast for himself in his diary entry; see Laud, VII, 74 and III, 215.

measure of their degree of closeness might be established by asking how Juxon, no outsider by now, had got as far as he had at court between 1632 and 1635. Was this also Laud's doing, or that of another hand?

Juxon's credentials for the Treasury are also germane. Despite his lack of experience of central government, might he nevertheless have possessed attributes and associations which made him, in other eyes, a credible candidate in his own right?

Finally, some attention must be paid to the role of Charles I, almost wholly neglected in conventional accounts of this business. He it was who had decided not to appoint a new Treasurer immediately, thus prompting continual speculation about the identity and character of an eventual successor. It would have been uncharacteristic of a king who placed a premium on loyalty to his person to have remained a bystander, or to have acted merely as a cipher, in a matter which concerned him so directly.

I

LAUD'S POSITION AT AND AFTER THE TREASURER'S DEATH

When Portland died at the age of fifty-eight, Laud was already sixty-one. Yet the gap left by Portland meant that the scope of his own activities widened substantially. 'I grow old', he told Wentworth, 'and yet now my business multiplies upon me, being now at once called unto three troublesome committees, that of Trade, the Foreign and the Exchequer. Ergo, give me leave [in writing to you] to make such haste as I can.'[11] He and Wentworth began to compete, almost like schoolboys, with their tales of which of them was working the harder, and Sir Thomas Roe, noting Laud's enthusiasm for his new responsibilities, was soon urging Elizabeth of Bohemia to encourage Laud to spread his wings in foreign affairs.[12] For all his burdens, he at times sounded almost light-hearted, remarking in June 1635, with a levity which seemed to surprise and gratify him, 'I have not leisure since I meddled with the Treasure', adding 'See how I am fallen into rhyme, and what I might do if I could give my mind to it.'[13] There is little doubt that responsibility

[11] Laud, VII, 116.
[12] PRO, SP 16/286/34, 287/13, 297/35.
[13] Laud, VII, 141.

fuelled his self-esteem, providing a measure of his importance, indeed of his near-indispensability. It is by no means clear that he ever felt he had too much of it and could not, at a pinch, take on another office.

Of the future, however, Laud was still in some doubt. A series of bitter clashes with Cottington over the late Treasurer's conduct of government and matters incidental to it, seldom ended to Laud's advantage, and suggested a damaging lack of compatibility between them. The Treasury might be in commission; but Cottington was still Chancellor of the Exchequer, and although he often maintained that his days were numbered, Charles showed no inclination to dismiss him.[14] On the contrary, the king seemed to Laud repeatedly to condone Cottington's attitudes and activities. Although he had managed to ensure that Charles at last received unvarnished figures about the state of his finances, he was not confident that they were appreciated. In foreign affairs, his clumsy interventions had got him nowhere; and over a whole series of vexed domestic issues, from the new soapers and the emparking at Richmond to the handling of the case against John Williams and the protection of the grafting Sir James Bagg, it was apparent to Laud that the king was still being misled.[15] For all Cottington's protestations that he commanded no favour at court, Laud came to believe that he had an ascendant interest there, bolstered by a closer understanding with the queen achieved during the summer of 1635.[16] In these dispiriting circumstances, Wentworth proved to be of little help. The treasurership might have seemed a matter on which the two proponents of Thorough would have been in close and continual correspondence. Yet one of the curiosities of their odd relationship is that, although they often discussed the vacant Treasury, they seldom did so with reference to themselves, but either in general terms or in relation to a third party, usually the late Treasurer or Cottington.[17] Wentworth had of course informed his relatives and close friends from the outset that he did not want to succeed Portland and, 'delivered from a mighty and determined malice', may well have been genuinely less interested in the succession than Laud, believing that, whoever was

---

[14] E.g. Str P 15/143, 15/173.
[15] He was also alarmed by the headway Cottington seemed to be making with the king in securing a settlement of John Williams's protracted prosecution by the crown.
[16] Laud, VII, 145.
[17] Str P 6, pp. 236, 240, 265-6; Laud, VI, 423; VII, 125, 129-30, 141, 159, 172.

appointed, Irish business was unlikely to be severely inconvenienced in future.[18] But much was always going to depend on the will of the king; and it may be significant that he did not tell his courtly associate Laud as much for several months; and by then, late in July, Laud was not at all sure whether he could believe him or not. He came close, at that point, to begging the Lord Deputy to return.[19]

The cumulative effect on Laud of the king's waywardness and Wentworth's self-restraint was to leave him, for all his recent accession of additional influence, lonely and isolated at court. He missed being able to talk freely to Windebank, whose failure to support him over the soap monopoly in July wounded him deeply, and told Wentworth that same month that he hoped the king would soon put an end to the troubled and unproductive life of the Treasury commission, and appoint a new Lord Treasurer. But he was prepared to soldier on 'till the king resolve of a good one; for certainly such a one he will need, and perhaps more an honest than a cunning one. I would write more at large to you in this argument, were I at leisure for my own hand, which at present I am not.'[20]

Here perhaps is the first sign that Laud was thinking of moving directly against Cottington, even while he was still uncertain of Wentworth's intentions. At no time then, or earlier or later, was there any mention of a combination with Juxon or any other 'honest' candidate; and the scale of the task of winning over the king and stopping Cottington, whose appointment as Treasurer was now regularly forecast by court observers, was such that he must have reckoned only he or Wentworth had, in their own persons, any chance of succeeding. A further straw in the wind is provided by Cottington's prediction, made a month later to the Lord Deputy, that Laud might himself become Lord Treasurer, apparently the first time that possibility had been raised.[21] By then, as he later confessed,

---

[18] E.g. Knowler, I, 391, 411, 420, letters to the Earl of Newcastle and Dorset, and to George Butler. See also Str P 6, p. 162, for his relief at Portland's death. Thereafter Laud was much the more likely to bring the subject up. Wentworth had little more contact with Juxon as Treasurer than before: their entire correspondence in the Strafford Papers consists of only five letters. I am indebted to Fiona Pogson for this point.

[19] Laud had prompted Wentworth's response by telling him, on 12 June, of a court rumour that he sought the treasurership through the queen and Laud. Wentworth's amused rejoinder, of 14 July, reached Croydon before the end of the month. It was Laud's first clear indication, at least on paper, of how his ally stood. Str P 6, p. 206; Laud, VII, 145, 155–67.

[20] Laud, VI, 423; Knowler, I, 438–9.

[21] Str P 3, p. 218; Str P 6, p. 206; Cottington to Wentworth, 4 Aug. 1635, Knowler, I, 449; the other candidate he mentioned was Wentworth himself.

Laud had also taken it upon himself to sound out Charles about Wentworth's own chances, should he be interested in them. Gamely he reported that the king 'did speak as much good as he could' of the Lord Deputy; and himself encouraged Wentworth to consider how things stood: he might be 'unwilling to dance', but 'little good will be done here if he dance not'. In return, Wentworth in September made it clearer than before that there was 'no possibility' of reconciling him with the Treasury: 'meet they will not together by any means. Soe I have layd it aside as a case desperate.'[22]

Although Laud did not entirely abandon the notion that Wentworth might yet come forward, his growing antipathy to Cottington, and his long-standing hostility to all that Portland had stood for, now drove him on. Betrayed he might be by friends; but no one could doubt his sense of personal commitment to what he believed was right. All summer he had found that Cottington's views and values carried so much weight with the king, that he was 'unable to open' Charles's eyes to Laud's own 'apparent and certain good through the mists which those jugglers [Portland and Cottington] have cast before them'.[23] Early in October, he told Charles 'he would give up all hope to see things mend' if Cottington became Treasurer; and, reflecting on his own position, concluded, 'I am alone in these things which draw not private profit after them.'[24] There were signs now that he was taking upon himself a personal mission to save the king's government from the effects of its folly.

By the end of that month, Cottington was prompted to inform Wentworth, with whom he was still regularly corresponding, that 'we conceive the King wyll shortly make' a Treasurer, 'and we can gues[s] at no man but the Archbishop, who without all doubt wyll be most unfitt; yet better he than none'; at least it would 'not tye me [Cottington] to soe much attendance and observance as I afforded the last man, who was my Frend'.[25] Given its source, Wentworth may have been tempted to discount much of this letter. But Cottington was doing more than spinning a yarn here; he was

---

22 Laud to Wentworth, 31 July/3 Aug. 1635, Laud, vii, 155–67; his reply, 12 Sept. 1635, Str P 6, p. 240.
23 Laud to Wentworth, 31 July/3 Aug. 1635, Laud, vii, 160.
24 Laud to Wentworth, 4 Oct. 1635, Laud, vii, 173.
25 Cottington to Wentworth, 30 Oct. 1635, Str P 15/324. Cottington here anticipates the leisure he allowed himself after Juxon's appointment. Compare his advice to Wentworth back in June, when he claimed to be expecting early dismissal: 'if I can doe you any more servis, speake quickly'. Str P 15/173.

relating Laud's anticipated elevation to his own particular circumstances, in the process revealing that, for the first time since Portland's death, he was feeling secure enough as Chancellor of the Exchequer to contemplate conditions of service under his successor. Wentworth did not pass this on to Laud, any more than Laud confirmed or denied his own heightened activity over the Treasury. Cottington's regained assurance followed a visit the queen made, at her own instigation, to Hanworth in mid-August, about which, Laud heard later, she was 'exceedingly well content'.[26] If the two circumstances were directly related, some candidate other than Cottington – and almost certainly other than Laud and Wentworth – must have been suggested for the Treasury. Even before Portland died, George Garrard had told Wentworth that opinion in city and court had marked Juxon out as a possible successor. The recollection may well have given him pause for thought, and confirmed the wisdom of his own stance.[27]

By November, he clearly sensed that Laud was getting into deeper waters, and was moved to warn him about the court's dangerous cross-currents, advising 'against expostulations of any kind' and stressing that the soap business should not be regarded as a difference between friends, which might be put right, but was factious, involving 'transgressions... willfull by Designe of Partys, and for Endes'. Laud must avoid further outbursts to the king against Cottington who, as Wentworth had repeatedly asserted, stood no chance of becoming Treasurer, 'least by often reiterating, what came from faith and Judg[e]ment might be interpreted [by Charles as] Anger and Spleen'.[28] Although he was careful not to say so, Wentworth in this last piece of advice was implying that Laud would otherwise wreck his own prospects in this matter, should he ever wish to test them, besides damaging his credibility as Wentworth's trusted friend at court. Laud made no direct response; and instead hotly denied a rumour Cottington had put about that he was trying to stop Wentworth from becoming Treasurer. 'Good God', he protested, 'What a fiction is here!'[29] Nevertheless, in the course of his denial, he revealed that there were those at court who believed that his support for

---

[26] Laud to Wentworth, 4 Oct. 1635, Laud, VII, 175. Hanworth, in Middlesex, across the Thames from Oatlands, was one of Cottington's two principal country houses.
[27] Knowler, I, 388.
[28] Str P 6, pp. 265-6.
[29] Laud, VII, 209. Cottington had also declared he would rather die than be made Treasurer.

Wentworth had indeed been damaging to the Lord Deputy's chances – which came to much the same thing. One way or another, this may well be intended by Laud to indicate that his enthusiasm for Wentworth's return had by now cooled. It needed saying, even obliquely; for as it happened, the Lord Deputy had become anxious to come over, in order to sort out his personal affairs following the unexpected death of his steward Richard Marris and also to put to the king his side of recent controversial dealings against Mountnorris. His presence at court might have proved an awkward distraction for Laud, embarked as he now was on the course of action necessary, as he supposed, to stop Cottington. He had waited too long on the Lord Deputy already. Wentworth's circumspection had made it hard to know exactly where he stood and what, if anything, he intended. At this late stage, Laud did not want him in the way. As far as he knew, there was still all to play for; and Cottington's timely illness either side of Christmas, gave him a chance.[30]

By the autumn of 1635 Laud thus gives a clear indication of having taken on the task of removing the sole remaining agent of the Lady Mora. He did so in his own interest and in his own person; and he does not appear ever to have told Wentworth explicitly what he was up to. At no time did he receive the Lord Deputy's endorsement, even though he seems for a long time to have been looking for it. His recent betrayal, as he saw it, at the hands of Windebank made him cautious about trusting deputies. His mission had become a personal one. Even his enthusiasm for the closer union of Church and State took second place.

II

LAUD'S RELATIONSHIP WITH JUXON IN THE 1630S

The notion that Juxon primarily owed his advancement to Laud's patronage is often assumed but not easily sustained. The two certainly had much in common. They both took an unemotional approach to doctrine, and, unlike Matthew Wren, preferred not to press too hard for religious conformity.[31] Their careers, too, took a similar course. There is a good deal of evidence over many years of association and co-operation between them in college, university and

---

[30] For Laud's continuing uncertainty about Wentworth's position, see Laud, VII, 209.
[31] Julian Davies, *The Caroline Captivity of the Church* (Oxford, 1992), p. 45.

church affairs. But Juxon may never have been Laud's man in the way the 6 March diary entry suggests. He was temperamentally quite different, preferring to keep his own counsel and seldom showing his hand until urged to do so. Laud does not seem to have used him at court as an intermediary with the king, except in routine matters. On the contrary, in the court politics of the mid-1630s, Laud had to take what satisfaction he could from standing alone. Juxon, after all, had no experience of matters of state, and did not even become a Privy Councillor until he was appointed Lord Treasurer.

Years before, Juxon had certainly played a helpful part in the electoral machinations which preceded Laud's appointment as President of St John's, Oxford; but he was not alone in this, and his role was not in itself decisive. His easy manner and lack of partisanship made it likely that his subsequent range of friendships would always be wider than Laud's, raising the possibility of alternative sources of patronage. Thus, while Laud's diary suggests that he had secured Juxon's appointment as Clerk of the Closet in July 1632, in order to have someone around the king that he could trust, it is not impossible that even at this early stage he was overstating the case. It should be remembered he had made a similar entry a few weeks before concerning the appointment of his 'old friend' Francis Windebank as Secretary of State, credit for which he was later to disclaim. By 1632, Juxon was already quite well known to Charles. He had entertained the king at Woodstock in July 1627, while Vice-Chancellor of Oxford, and shortly afterwards was made Dean of Worcester. At much the same time, and no less importantly, he became one of the king's chaplains; for Charles always took a close interest in their careers.[32] Given the king's concern for his chaplains, and his sensitivity to Laud's penchant for interfering in matters of state whenever they happened to involve churchmen, it is likely that thereafter the scope for Laud's patronage on Juxon's behalf was circumscribed. He would not find it easy to press the case for an episcopal Lord Treasurer, whoever he might be, unless Charles was already thinking along such lines himself. Nevertheless, any help he was able to give Juxon in securing posts about the person of the king was important to Laud, for his ascendancy within the Church was not beyond challenge. He might be able to trust Juxon; but there

---

[32] Laud's copy of Juxon's formal address, in praise of both Charles and his father, given in Latin at Woodstock is in PRO, SP 16/73/2. See also T. A. Mason, *Serving God and Mammon: William Juxon, 1582–1663* (1985), pp. 34–5.

were others he could not. Among the latter was Matthew Wren, who had become one of Charles's chaplains in 1622 and had gone to Madrid with him in 1623. Wren, who found Cottington more congenial than Laud, followed immediately in his old schoolfellow Juxon's footsteps during the 1630s as Clerk of the Closet and Dean of the Chapels Royal, and like Windebank evidently had other means of gaining the king's favour.[33]

Earlier that year, Juxon had been appointed first to the see of Hereford, and then in quick time translated to London; on both occasions the preferment was at the king's own pleasure, as the Privy Seal Office warrants and the Signet Office docquet books show, not by the patronage of his primate or any other bishop.[34] As Laud himself was fond of saying, the king always preferred to advance his own chaplains whenever he could; and Juxon was a case in point. Within six months of becoming Clerk of the Closet, he had resigned from the presidency of St John's and confirmed his entry into a courtly world where Laud was always ill at ease. In patronage terms, he had by 1633 become the king's man. Already there were clear signs that Charles felt comfortable with him.

Others at court were not slow to recognise the position. Juxon's circle soon extended well beyond Laud. He seems to have been on friendly terms with Weston, Cottington and Windebank, for example, and to have shared their worldly attitudes. That was evident during the close-run Star Chamber case of Pell *v.* Bagg, part of a wider attack on Portland's legacy, which concluded with a tied vote in November 1635. Juxon carefully aligned himself with Cottington and Windebank in favour of Sir James Bagg who, according to his lights, had served Buckingham and the late Treasurer in the West Country for many years, and who continued to enjoy the support of the king and queen. Laud, on the other hand, was so moved by the iniquities of the 'bottomless' Bagg, that he naively assumed that the king would be backing the less culpable Sir Anthony Pell.[35] Juxon needed no lessons in the ways of the court from Laud.

---

[33] From 7 March 1636, it is likely that neither the Clerk of the Closet (now almost certainly Richard Steward) nor the Dean of the Chapels Royal (now Wren) was close to Laud. W. H. Marah, *Memoirs of Archbishop Juxon* (1869), pp. 26–7; J. Bickersteth and R. W. Dunning, *Clerks of the Closet in the Royal Household* (1991), pp. 19–21; Davies, *Caroline Captivity*, p. 45.

[34] PRO, PSO 2/ 94; SO 3/10.

[35] PRO, SP 16/301/56; Knowler, I, 489; John Rushworth, *Historical Collections* (7 vols., 1659–1701), II ii, 303; Laud, VII, 206.

Indeed, once Juxon reached court, his relationship with Laud becomes quite difficult to establish. Their intermittent correspondence seems to have been almost entirely formal; and Laud seldom mentioned him elsewhere. His diary records Juxon's appointment as Clerk of the Closet in July 1632, but then falls silent until March 1636. Laud's correspondence with Wentworth while the Treasury was in commission seems to contain no reference to Juxon, and he does not even have a number assigned to him in the cipher which was by now regularly in use in their aptly named 'great letters'.[36] It is as though Juxon did not figure at all prominently in Laud's customary frame of reference, as one not obviously fitted to the in-fighting associated with politics at a factious court. Juxon's blandness put him, temperamentally, at an opposite pole to Laud. To the king, Juxon's amiability and unobtrusiveness were hardly a problem. He wanted a finance minister prepared to accommodate his chosen ways, as established under Portland, not an isolated and headstrong reformer. Laud found this a hard, and unpalatable, lesson to learn. Nevertheless, signs of divergence were quickly apparent in the spring of 1635. While Garrard was taking notice of Juxon, Laud was concentrating his attention – as he was long to do – on Wentworth, a much more vibrant figure. Garrard gave no sign of discerning a close relationship between the two bishops and, despite his ready access to Cottington, who might have known about such things, was no more inclined than other commentators to link the two in 1635–6. So slender is the evidence of effective patronage links between them by this time that it would be unwise to use it as the basis for accepting the oft-repeated but unsubstantiated assertion that Juxon not only remained on friendly terms with Laud during the 1630s but was also his protégé.

Moreover, after Garrard's early reference to him, Juxon seems to disappear entirely from public speculation about either Treasury or Exchequer for almost a year until February 1636, when that astute reader of the courtly tea leaves, John Holles, earl of Clare, got pretty close to the mark.[37] Could Laud possibly have been so discreet for so long, if Juxon had been his candidate? Such absence of comment, on the other hand, may well reflect close royal interest. Charles, as ever, was playing his cards very close to his chest. In state as in church, he

---

[36] After his appointment as Lord Treasurer, Juxon inherited Portland's old number (105).

[37] Str P 14/323; Knowler, I, 388; P. R. Seddon (ed.), *Letters of John Holles, 1587–1637* (3 vols., Thoroton Society, xxi, xxxv, xxxvi, 1975–86), p. 479, no. 631.

preferred to dispense his patronage to those of whom he had direct experience. He liked to have an immediate, personal relationship with his ministers of state. They were expected to abstain from combining amongst themselves, and to deal directly with him: he had once caught Laud off-guard by asking him about an annotation to a paper, referring to the Lady Mora, 'and would needs know what we [he and Wentworth] meant by it'. There was every reason why he should involve himself directly in the making of the new Lord Treasurer.[38] His criteria did not necessarily rule Laud out, for all his awkward high-mindedness; but they brought the accommodating Juxon firmly into consideration, despite his ostensible lack of experience of financial affairs.

III

JUXON AS A CREDIBLE CANDIDATE FOR THE TREASURY?

That Garrard had named Juxon so early among the leading candidates to succeed Portland seems at first sight curious; and yet it may also be illuminating, for it was not idly done. Juxon has customarily been regarded as a pale reflection of his supposed patron; and yet here Garrard brackets his name with those of Cottington, with whom he was himself frequently in touch, and Wentworth, whom he was currently striving to impress by his skill as a newsletter writer. He is thus unlikely to have been speaking carelessly. Despite his leisured existence in the houses of the great, Garrard himself came from a long and distinguished line of London merchants, including seven lord mayors, five in direct descent. He was sitting for Preston, a Duchy of Lancaster seat, during the 1620s when he first heard Wentworth speak; and his links with Cottington may have been strengthened by common financial interests.[39] In this respect his family background is not dissimilar to Juxon's own; for although Juxon's father had become a senior church court official in the diocese of Chichester, most of his family remained rooted in the mercantile community of London, and his brother John practised during the 1630s as a proctor in the Court of

---

38   Laud, VII, 102, 167.
39   Cottington was showing an active interest in the succession to Portland, then seriously ill, by April 1634; Garrard noted shortly afterwards how he had been taking him 'all summer' to see Sir Arthur Ingram, later talked of as a possible Chancellor of the Exchequer. Str P 3, p. 81; Knowler, I, 267.

Arches.[40] Juxon's uncles and cousins were members of City companies, notably the Salters and the Merchant Taylors, the former particularly receptive to new projects and ideas.[41] Through his uncle Thomas's marriage into the Ireland family, the Juxons were linked with the enterprising mercantile family of Crisp; and the bishop and the most successful of the younger generation of Crisps, the increasingly wealthy Guinea merchant Nicholas, had a Juxon aunt, born Elizabeth Ireland, in common.[42] By the early 1630s, Nicholas Crisp combined energetic service to the City as a trained band captain with substantial means; but his potential value to the crown was as yet untapped, and he was not a member of either of the syndicates, dominated by Sir Paul Pindar, which were entrusted with farm of the great customs in 1632 and 1635. Principally through the Crisps, a wider network of connection opened out, to include Abraham Reynardson, Thomas Cullum and George Stroud, as well as Sir Walter Pye, the attorney of the Court of Wards until his death late in 1635. Juxon's many years at Oxford should not be allowed to conceal his enduring mercantile associations, which were given new life once he had been translated to the see of London in 1633, even before he could be instituted to Hereford.[43] By this summary transfer, the consequence of a decision to which the king was as likely to have been prompted by the percipient Cottington as by Laud, Juxon became a possible future Lord Treasurer, although he may not then have known it.[44] It is true he already had a base at Court as Clerk of the Closet and then

---

[40] Juxon had been born at Chichester, and his father Richard and brother Thomas served there over many years as registrars of the bishop and the cathedral chapter. *The Acts of the Dean and Chapter of the Cathedral Church of Chichester, 1545–1642*, ed. W. D. Peckham (Sussex Record Society, LVIII, 1959), *passim*.

[41] Joan Thirsk, *Economic Policy and Projects* (1978), p. 102. Juxon, like Wren, had been a pupil at Merchant Taylors' School in the City.

[42] Crisp was a Salter, like his father Ellis and uncle Nicholas, as well as a Merchant Adventurer. See Robert Ashton, *The Crown and the Money Market, 1603–1640* (1960), pp. 104–5.

[43] C. M. Clode, *London during the Great Rebellion* (1892), p. 1; Alan Simpson, *The Wealth of the Gentry, 1540–1660* (1961), pp. 120, 127; G. E. Cokayne, *The Lord Mayors and Sheriffs of London, 1601–1625* (1897), p. 59; G. E. Cokayne, *The Complete Baronetage*, vol. IV (1904), p. 11; Valerie Pearl, *London and the Outbreak of The Puritan Revolution* (1961), pp. 169, 208n, 305, 315; M. F. Keeler, *The Long Parliament* (1954), p. 78; W. K. Jordan, *The Charities of London, 1480–1660* (1960), pp. 125, 303, 346 n.151; Richard Newcourt, *Repertorium Ecclesiasticum Parochiale Londinense* (2 vols., 1708–10), I, 610–11; *The Visitation of London 1633, 1634 and 1635*, ed. J. J. Howard and J. L. Chester (2 vols., 1880–3) II, 210, 202; II, 23, 198. Pye was Nicholas Crisp's step-father.

[44] Laud is sometimes said to have urged Juxon's move on the king, thereby excluding Matthew Wren, on the grounds that he needed a friendly face at Fulham; but the sole source for this appears to be John Hacket as recorded in *Parentalia*, which makes it plain

as Dean of the Chapels Royal; but his responsibilities as bishop of London allowed him more scope.[45]

Juxon's family background, combining rewarding practice in the church courts with commercial enterprise, gave him a wholly different attitude from Laud to the relationship between public service and private profit. Where Laud was a purist, Juxon was practical and flexible. Unlike Laud, he never seems to have doubted the value of having the customs put out to farm, for example, or failed to recognise the benefits which might thereby accrue to the crown on the side. He was to show none of Laud's reluctance to accept Sir Abraham Dawes's new book of rates, prepared under Portland's guidance. At some point before or during 1635 both Cottington and aspiring members of the queen's circle, perhaps prompted by the king's obvious favour towards him, came together in appreciating his suitability in terms of his family associations with commercial activity and his as yet under-employed business instincts.[46] Cottington, looking for new allies, needed no prompting. Around the queen, those anxious to exploit the opportunities offered by the loosening of Portland's grip were scarcely less alert to his prospects. This was especially true of her Master of Horse, George Lord Goring, a courtier of middling rank but large ambition.

The queen's visit to Cottington at Hanworth in August 1635, while Charles was away hunting, evidently finalised their understanding. She was in a privileged position to suggest a way forward to their mutual advantage. Laud, ever apprehensive, grimly noted how it had recently been his 'hap to see such smiles of dearness pass' between the queen, Holland, Jermyn and Cottington that he feared the worst. Once more he predicted that Cottington would become Lord Treasurer.[47] But Cottington himself, recognising he might lose his chancellorship of the Exchequer while vainly seeking the Treasury, seems to have settled for what he had, and, subsequently, consistently

Wren regarded Hacket's attempt to involve Laud as mischief-making. Stephen Wren, *Parentalia or Memoirs of the Family of Wrens* (1750), pp. 49–50. See also Marah, *Juxon*, p. 27.

[45] For early dealings with Crisp, see e.g. House of Lords RO, Original Act, 16 & 17 Car. I, no. 32. I am indebted to Professor Conrad Russell for drawing my attention to this evidence.

[46] Apart from Dorset's enquiry of Wentworth, and Garrard's hints, there are comments by Senneterre, 26 March/4 April 1635, and Panzani 19/29 Aug. 1635 on the queen's heightened activity, as well as much agonising by Laud about Cottington's liaison. PRO, PRO 31/3/68, 31/9/16.

[47] Laud, VII, 161.

gave every appearance of being contented with his lot. His ally
Garrard was soon reporting, apparently as the sole source, a rumour
of a further sign of the king's favour towards Juxon: a place at the
council board. If they had ever been in doubt, Cottington and the
queen could not have failed by this time to observe Juxon's standing
at court, while noting the appropriate nature of the qualities he
might bring to the Treasurer's office. But the newsletter writers and
other commentators seem to have had only limited awareness of
what was going on. Garrard himself still interpreted the signs from
court as indicating Cottington's imminent appointment as Treasurer,
even though as he conceded 'he will not confesse yt to mee. Yett I
have seene him often this Summer...'[48] The absence of any public
indication of how matters stood strongly suggests that the king had
every intention of exercising his patronage in his own way in his own
time. So does the careful reticence of all the rumoured candidates.
But as John Harrison, a farmer of petty customs later strongly critical
of the turn of events, observed, Goring's interest in royal concessions
had grown substantially during 1635, giving him a vested interest in
developing a more helpful relationship with any potential Treasurer
than the one he had had with Portland.[49] It is by no means clear how
well Goring knew Juxon before March 1636, despite their common
association with Chichester and the county of Sussex; but he was
surely aware of Crisp's growing substance and his lack of connection
with Portland and Pindar. Certainly, Goring had few equals in his
determination to make the most of Juxon's elevation, and quickly
showed his readiness to become close to the new Lord Treasurer.
With a shrewd eye for Juxon's welfare in unfamiliar surroundings, he
lost no time in persuading his self-confident young kinsman, Philip
Warwick, to leave his own service for Juxon's, and become his
secretary. It was not long before Sir Robert Pye, the Auditor of
Receipt, was moved to alert Secretary Coke against a damaging
combination developing between Cottington, Windebank and 'the
Lord Treasurer's secretary, who doth not understand and is very
forward'.[50]

---

[48] PRO, SP 16/298/10, Garrard to Conway, 18 Sept. 1635.
[49] Harrison's views are to be found in his various recollections of customs affairs, now in BL,
      Stowe MSS 326, the earlier of them written in 1641 when MP for Lancaster, in the shadow
      of possible parliamentary impeachment. Goring had by 1635 begun to establish his hold
      on the revenue-raising aspects of the tobacco trade. See, e.g., Stowe MSS 326, ff.62v, 63r.
[50] George Rawdon to Conway, 16 March 1636, PRO, SP 16/316/41; HMC, *Cowper*, II, 126.

IV

THE ROLE OF THE KING

The prominence accorded to Laud's supposed role in the choice of Juxon has served to obscure that of the king, who has seemed to behave with unaccustomed passivity in a matter of central concern to his administration. Yet it was because he recognised the importance of making the right choice of successor that he put the Treasury into commission on Portland's death, as he was widely expected to do. He had used such a device in difficult circumstances in the past. In 1627 Archbishop Abbot's powers had for some months been invested in an episcopal committee; and more appositely for the case of the Treasury, he had put, and left, the Admiralty in commission after Buckingham's murder. Now he had again lost the minister he trusted most, and needed time to settle on a successor who could match Portland's flexibility of approach.[51] Given the straitened nature of his finances, and the flimsiness of royal credit, a new Treasurer would need to have an appreciation both of the central place of the customs and of the importance of developing a fruitful relationship with the customs farmers. Harrison's proposal for the return of the customs to the direct control of the crown found no favour with Charles, despite Laud's sympathy towards it. Whatever its merits in administrative terms, it closed down his opportunities for raising loans from farmers. This was a vital consideration at a time when the king's foreign policy hung, as it now did, in the balance. His first ship-money fleet, to be launched in May 1635, had already been delayed a year, and had its impact muffled, by Spain's failure in 1634 to produce the subsidy it had seemed to promise. In the interval, Spain and France had finally gone to war; while the Peace of Prague was already fast diminishing whatever hopes Charles had of securing a remotely satisfactory settlement of the Palatinate for his sister's family.[52]

He must also have hoped to find a Treasurer who might help to

---

[51]   H. Trevor-Roper, *Archbishop Laud* (2nd edn, 1962), pp. 215, 225, suggested Laud won the delay in order to block Cottington and give him time to press the case for Juxon. It is possible he was performing this same service for Wentworth; but Charles's decision attracted little comment, and evidently was not widely thought to have fatally damaged Cottington's chances.

[52]   BL, Stowe MSS 326, ff.61v–62r; Ashton, *Crown and the Money Market*, p. 98; F. C. Dietz, *English Public Finance, 1558–1641* (1932), p. 335.

bind his factious court together, rather than act as a focal point for division as Portland had done. Laud and Coventry, as well as Henrietta Maria and her courtiers, had been joined in common cause against Charles's chief minister. With Portland gone, there was a possibility that Cottington might be able to resume his old, reasonably cordial, relationship with Laud; but the fractious year which the Treasury spent in commission emphatically ruled it out. Laud's obsession with raking over past Treasury proceedings so that he could show Charles how right he had been to oppose Portland as often as he did, meant that the commission was from the outset both quarrelsome and backward looking.[53] By the autumn of 1635 it was stuttering so badly that there was widespread expectancy that the appointment of a new Treasurer would not long be delayed.[54] With Laud beginning to press his own case, Charles's preference for Juxon may well have hardened. Not only were the queen and Cottington apparently favourably disposed; but Laud himself could hardly object to such a choice. Indeed, as Charles deliberated, Laud seems unwittingly to have given him one of his more persuasive arguments for appointing Juxon.

For it is to this period, late in 1635, that the well-known but undated and incomplete list of clerical Lord Treasurers from the time of the Conqueror to 1470 very probably belongs.[55] It has customarily been regarded as part of Laud's campaign on behalf of Juxon; but it may well have been intended by Laud for presentation to the king in his own interest. Internal evidence suggests as much. Two of its inaccuracies and omissions are revealing. One of them concerns the only archbishop of Canterbury listed: somehow the gap of three-and-a-half years between Simon Langham resigning his treasurership and becoming archbishop in the mid-fourteenth century is overlooked so that he appears to hold both positions simultaneously. The other concerns the only other archbishop of Canterbury who was also Lord Treasurer, Roger Walden, who is entirely omitted, perhaps because he resigned from the Treasury as soon as he was appointed to Canterbury in 1398. Neither example, if accurately presented, did anything to advance Laud's case. The most detailed entry in the entire document, moreover, may well reflect Laud's preoccupation with recent financial mismanagement. It concerns John Stratford, bishop of Winchester, who took over as

[53] See, e.g., Laud to Wentworth, 12 June 1635, Laud, VII, 143–5.
[54] Str P 3, pp. 219, 225–6.   [55] PRO, SP 16/315/61.

Treasurer in 1326 with less than £30 in hand, after gross maladministration by his lay predecessor, circumstances which might be thought to have a current application. Nothing in the paper links it directly with Juxon; and those who prepared the relevant *Calendar of State Papers* for publication were careful to avoid doing so, apart from assigning it rather too firmly, perhaps, to 6 March 1636, the day Juxon became Lord Treasurer.[56] Its endorsement, 'A Catalogue of such Bishops as have bine Lord Treasurer of England' is undoubtedly in Laud's hand; but neither its purpose nor the identity of its compiler is anywhere revealed. Charles seems to have been referring to the list in his comment on the advantages of a clerical Lord Treasurer when announcing Juxon's appointment, and consoling Laud, on 6 March; and it is possible that he had himself prompted Laud to have it drawn up, while making up his mind about Juxon, without telling him why he was interested in it.[57] If so, Laud's discomfiture must have been even more acute when he first learned the identity of Portland's successor.

Quite how and when Charles finally settled on the bishop of London remains unclear. He was not in the habit of revealing his thinking; and the restrained manoeuvring which took place within the tight confines of the court helped further to obscure the process, while encouraging misleading speculation. Juxon's appointment surprised many who knew only of his amiability. Yet to Charles that easy and biddable manner must have been important, holding out fresh hope of a more united administration than he had yet enjoyed. Afterwards, Charles was at pains to make it clear that Juxon had been his own choice, and that he had had him in mind for much of the life of the Treasury commission. He could hardly say otherwise; but although he does not appear to have explained his reasoning, it may well have been true.[58] The impediment that Laud had seemed to feel that he met with while still trying to block Cottington that January was thus in practice the king's preference for Juxon.[59] Although he surely cannot have known it, Laud was in effect striving

---

56   *CSPD, 1635–6*, p. 225, but see Preface, pp. xi–xii; E. B. Fryde *et al., Handbook of British Chronology* (3rd edn, 1986), pp. 103–7, 227–88.

57   *The Diary of Thomas Crosfield*, ed. F. S. Boas (1935), pp. 87–8.

58   *The Life and Letters of Sir Henry Wotton*, ed. Logan Pearsall Smith (2 vols., 1907), II, 363; HMC, *Denbigh*, v, 22.

59   Laud told Wentworth on 14 January 1636 that although he was convinced the king would appoint Cottington as Treasurer as soon as he was well again, 'yet I write [with] no certainty herein more than out of my own judgement'; six weeks earlier, though, his confidence had been unqualified. Str P 6, p. 312; Laud, VII, 203, 223. Cottington, by

to displace a fellow bishop. Within a month, however, there was a more general appreciation of the likely outcome, picked up by Clare in a letter to his son of 15 February 1636 from London: 'The tresorer's staff hangs in the ayre, and is thought generally to dropp at the last unto the Bishopp of London's feet, notwithstanding (as the story goes) Cottington must do the busines.'[60]

This need to establish a working relationship between Treasurer and Chancellor of the Exchequer was, of course, a key consideration in Charles's choice. Although he had put the Treasury in commission, and thereby denied Cottington immediate succession to his old master, he was reluctant to lose his services altogether. For Cottington not only had some understanding of the king's foreign policy but appreciated why royal finances were as they were, and felt no compulsion to attempt thorough-going reform. The queen may well have referred to these advantages during her visit to Hanworth. Thereafter Cottington became consistently cheerful; and while steadfastly denying all rumours of his impending appointment as Treasurer, even to Garrard, spent the rest of that summer bull-baiting, hawking and entertaining flocks of country people. Garrard predicted that, despite his uncertain health, he would be 'fit for business this winter; for he never enjoyed himself more since he came out of Spayne' (18 September 1635); three months earlier, he had been expecting dismissal from the Exchequer. The possibility of Juxon's advancement, with the prospect of Laud inadvertently struggling against one of his own bishops, must also have appealed to his sense of humour and lifted his spirits.[61]

For Cottington was shrewd enough to have appreciated that, if he retained the chancellorship of the Exchequer, Laud was unlikely ever to become Treasurer. That consequence must have been in the forefront of Charles's mind, and was implicit in Cottington's own dealings with the queen's party. For Charles needed not only a Treasurer he trusted and found agreeable, and who could work with Cottington, but one who was not unduly under the influence of

---

contrast, was still denying persistent rumours of his elevation, even to Garrard who noted afterwards, 'I am sure I saw him daily'. Knowler, 1, 510.

60 Seddon, *Holles Letters*, p. 479, no. 631. By 'the busines' Clare probably meant providing the expertise.

61 PRO, SP 16/298/10. Garrard confessed to Wentworth later in March that he would have preferred him or Cottington for the post, but admitted 'Your Friend and mine [Cottington] is much pleased with it', adding that he hoped he would live longer without the strain of a great office of state. Knowler, 1, 523. Cf. M. J. Havran, *Caroline Courtier: The Life of Lord Cottington* (1973), pp. 130–3.

Laud. He found one among his chaplains, whose preferment was always his particular concern. If Juxon had been closely associated with Laud, or had in any way been regarded as Laud's client or creature, the prospects for a successful working relationship with Cottington would have been fatally compromised. That it was not is suggested by Cottington's readiness, according to the French ambassador Senneterre, to claim the credit for Juxon's appointment well in advance of the formal announcement in March.[62] Cottington reportedly referred to Juxon as his friend, whom he had recommended for the post because his own health was too frail to bear it. When the proposition was in due course put to Laud, he had allegedly been prepared to accept it because, at least, it meant Cottington would not become Treasurer, even though he would have a continuing influence on royal finances. Senneterre, who was scarcely versed in the intricacies of English court politics, chose to doubt the story; and it is true Cottington could rarely resist making mischief. But the turn of events rarely left him at a loss, and his claims are by no means beyond all belief. He is as likely to have first mentioned Juxon to the queen and her friends as she is to have done so to him; Charles had probably settled finally on Juxon before he briefly left London for Newmarket on 20 January, as the 'general' rumour in circulation by early February suggests; and Cottington, restored to health, was back at court in good time to pick it up, if need be. His subsequent indulgence in hunting from Hanworth is much less likely to indicate sulking at Juxon's appointment, as is often supposed, than the fulfilment of the promise he had made to himself the previous autumn, not to work so hard for the next Lord Treasurer. Clare's well-tuned ear subsequently caught an echo of this interpretation on the evening of Juxon's appointment, noting that already 'sum say Cottington recommended him therunto, but I believe in God, for man doth nothing but juggle and beguyle himself in the conclusion'. The principals in the action did not necessarily find such restraint appropriate, however. For their own self-respect, and perhaps for the sake of posterity, they needed to reconcile the outcome with their role in bringing it about. This process of rationalisation had no set form. Cottington enjoyed being publicly expansive; Laud preferred his diary, in the privacy of which he may well have indulged in beguiling himself over Juxon, as he had already done

[62] PRO, PRO 31/3/69, at some date between 3 and 24 February, according to Gardiner, VIII, 141.

over Windebank. If each to some degree made a fiction of the facts, that was in keeping with an episode in which much that was said was intended to be misleading.

V

CONCLUSION

As he listened to the king at the council table on 6 March 1636, Laud might have been forgiven for reflecting that, of the principals, he had, despite much striving, achieved least. He had fought a belated and lonely fight, without genuine support from Wentworth, and apparently without a confidant of any kind at court. During its course he had even ranged himself, unwittingly, against a fellow bishop. If he had ever entertained the notion, with Sir Thomas Roe, that he might become the Richelieu of England, it was now an empty dream.[63] Lambeth and the Treasury remained as far apart as precedent suggested they habitually did. Worse, Cottington was still in post. The residuary legatee of the Lady Mora lived on to subvert the king's business when and where he would. The inexperienced Juxon could scarcely prevent him, for all his mercantile connections; besides, if Harrison is to be believed, he too had a keen eye for private profit.[64] Yet Juxon had supplanted Laud as the churchman closest to the heart of Charles's government. In future, there were to be finite limits to the archbishop's influence and areas of activity. Unlike Juxon, he was not destined to sit, *ex officio*, on all the council's committees. Nor would he have any more part in Treasury affairs, at least officially. In sum, he could no longer presume to be indispensable as an adviser to the king.

It is unclear when Laud first learned of Juxon's impending appointment, and it is thus uncertain whether he had any part in the preparation of Charles's mollifying comments on his behalf. Cottington's remarks to Senneterre suggest Laud had ample forewarning; and he had ceased to make predictions about the Chancellor's impending promotion after his noticeably vague one of 14 January, when he knew something was in the air, but was not quite sure what, although he still contemplated a bleak future in which he and the

---

[63] PRO, SP 16/286/34, Roe to Elizabeth of Bohemia, 5 April 1635.
[64] Laud, VII, 252. Within his own sphere of interest, Harrison deserves to be taken seriously: see Ashton, *Crown and the Money Market*, p. 102 and his *The City and the Court, 1603–1643* (1979), p. 148.

Lord Deputy would have to 'freely follow our own or other counsels'.[65] Of all the interested parties, he had most reason for feeling perturbed, for his experiences in 1635–6 had been sobering ones. He had failed to convince Charles of the error of Portland's financial practices. He had failed to penetrate the inner recesses of the king's foreign policy on Elizabeth's behalf. Now he had also failed to sway, or even to read, the king's mind in a matter of immediate concern to himself. He was entitled to feel despondent. The elevation of Juxon by other hands was hardly a consolation, particularly if, like Clare, he had doubts about the new Treasurer's suitability.

Thus, while the entry in his diary for 6 March 1636 may, as a whole, be viewed as a face-saver, its last line: 'And now if the Church will not hold up themselves under God, I can do no more', may also represent a feeling of resignation, a shrugging of primatial shoulders, the moment at which Laud, perhaps without knowing it, began to take a hard, detached, view of the king's government.[66] Like Wentworth in Ireland, he too had further cause to feel displaced and under-appreciated at court.[67] Within six months, he was dreaming 'that the King was offended with me, and would cast me off, and tell me no cause why. *Avertat Deus.* For cause I have given none.'[68] Charles's remarks on 6 March, as recorded by Hamilton, must have been intended to guard against that very possibility. Even so, Laud could hardly resist continuing to keep his eye on financial management, although he was looking now less for malpractice than for incompetence and faintheartedness. Early in 1637, he intervened at a late stage to have Coventry and Bankes's final draft of the king's case for ship money crucially amended, or so he claimed, before Charles put it to the judges, to save it from 'fall[ing] short'.[69] By contrast, Juxon was, according to talk in the City, already contemplating resort to Parliament as the answer to his financial problems, hardly

---

[65] Str P 6, pp. 339–40.
[66] There are signs of disillusion in Laud's letter to Wentworth of 30 November 1635, where he remarked that the king's attitude during the proceedings over the soap monopoly had 'discovered that to me which I would have been content not to have known'. Laud, vii, 205.
[67] Later in the same letter of 23 January, Laud seemed to doubt the constancy of Charles's word as a source of protection for his servants. Laud, vii, 234.
[68] 14 Oct. 1636, Laud, iii, 227.
[69] Laud to Wentworth, 5 April 1637, Laud, vii, 333. Laud thus credited himself and his unnamed legal adviser with ensuring Charles's continued freedom to determine his own foreign policy, outside Parliament.

what the king required.[70] By late 1638, Laud was openly telling
Charles that were he in Juxon's place he would have the determination to stand firm against all supplicants, and 'not a penny of money'
would be disbursed unnecessarily until the Scottish troubles were
settled. He found, of course, that once again he had done himself 'a
mighty ill office' with the king; but as he said, 'I cannot help it, and I
despair utterly of any thrift'.[71] It was not that Juxon was dishonest;
but he was weak.

From the outset, Juxon had gone his own way, one much more
in keeping with the king's preferences. Unlike Laud, he was happy
to endorse the advantages of the prevailing system, and once in
office did not hesitate to exploit the competition among syndicates
for the farm of the great customs, to the disadvantage of Sir Paul
Pindar's group, which had presided without serious challenge
under Portland and which had, before the late Treasurer's death,
effectively secured a further three-year term from December 1635.
By the summer of 1637, it was clear that Pindar's ascendancy was
for the moment coming to an end. In July of that year, he and his
partners learned that Charles wanted them to join with, among
others, the queen's favourite George Lord Goring, and Nicholas
Crisp, and by early August Goring was able to advise his friend
Conway, then at sea with the ship-money fleet, against 'landing so
much as a bottle of Smyrna water without custom, for a customer
I am, not for any virtue of my own, but by the folly of others
which gave me the opportunity to try my gracious master's
favour'.[72] Goring and Crisp duly headed the syndicate which took
over the great farm on its renewal on revised terms in December
1638.[73] Harrison was unhappy, but not surprised. It was the
predictable outcome of the king's preference, encouraged by the
queen, for an amenable Lord Treasurer most notable, in Sir John
Temple's words, for his 'moderacion... and serenitie'. But even by
the modest standards of Caroline financial management, Goring
was hardly a success as a customer. Pindar was soon back in
harness; and as the Bishops' Wars stretched the king's resources

[70] Anthony Lowe to the Earl of Middlesex, from London, 20 Dec. 1636. Centre for Kentish
Studies, U269/1 CB 137.

[71] Laud, VII, 51.

[72] The other newcomers were Sir Job Harby and [Sir] John Nulls, Say's son-in-law. See
C. S. R. Russell, *The Fall of the British Monarchies, 1637–1642* (1991), p. 257n. for Nulls.

[73] Ashton, *Crown and the Money Market*, p. 100.

close to breaking point, Laud had ever more ground for forthright criticism.[74]

At the time, in March 1636, shrewd commentators about the court had not been disposed to draw the all too obvious connection between Laud and Juxon; and the link probably only became common currency after Prynne had publicised Laud's diary just before his trial in 1644.[75] When, shortly after the event in 1636, James Howell wrote of 'the Church Triumphant', he managed to do so without any mention of Laud at all. So too did Clare, who missed little, and who was astute enough to pick up the possibility of an existing understanding of some kind between Juxon and Cottington. In this they confirm the burden of the strictly contemporary evidence available from those in the best position to know, very little of which even hints that Laud might have been busy promoting the candidacy of Juxon; only the entry in Laud's diary and the list of clerical Treasurers might make any sort of claim to do so, and neither offers a compelling case. Instead, the likelihood is that Juxon's elevation owed much more to the interests of Mammon than it did to any benediction on the Church. The religious association, although it has come to seem self-evident, is thus deceptive. For it played little or no part in determining which of his servants Charles chose to replace Portland, beyond providing an argument for honest, single men. Much more important was Charles's awareness that Juxon, with whom he already enjoyed a comfortable relationship, was unusually well placed to be able to work effectively with Cottington and the queen's friends without overtly antagonising Laud. Such an appreciation was no doubt encouraged by interested parties during 1635, but it may even predate Portland's death. Once appointed, Juxon became as much a senior civil servant as a triumphant prince of the Church, despite the splendour with which he, with Laud and six other bishops, rode in procession with councillors and lawyers to Westminster Hall for

---

[74] Str P 16/19; Mark Charles Fissel, *The Bishops' Wars* (1994), pp. 69, 112–14, 295.

[75] The most notable of those who did make an immediate connection were the Venetian ambassador, Correr, and the Vatican envoy, Panzani, neither of whom had been in England much more than a year. For Prynne and the diary, see Laud, III, 259–60; William Lamont, *Marginal Prynne* (1963), pp. 131–2. Laud annotated his diary entry for 6 March 1636, when printed in Prynne's *Breviate of the Life of William Laud*, with the remark: 'I hope it was no crime to pray for him [Juxon] in that slippery place [the Treasury], and that the Church might have no hurt by it.' Laud, III, 266. It provides an understandably cautious, but possibly revealing, gloss. He made no claim to patronage, but remembered his misgivings.

the opening of the Easter law term in 1636, and the temporary excitement felt by the junior clergy.[76]

It ought to have been a great moment for the Church when Juxon became the first clerical Treasurer for a century and a half; and it is undoubtedly tempting to see it as one of Laud's more successful attempts to get behind the Reformation. But it was not really so. What the choice of the bland and amenable Juxon demonstrates, above all, is the king's tight grip on patronage in the years after Buckingham, and his readiness, in England as in Scotland, to use his own judgement in picking men suitable to his purposes wherever he might find them. A wealth of feeling very probably lies behind Laud's celebrated words: 'now if the Church will not hold up themselves under God, I can do no more'. And it may well be more appropriate to see them, not as a boast, but as the reluctant admission of a disappointed man.

[76] PRO, C 115/N4/8607, Sir John Borough to Scudamore, 13 May 1636; Knowler, II, 2.

CHAPTER 5

Power and communication:
Thomas Wentworth and government at a distance during the Personal Rule, 1629–1635

J. F. Merritt

In recent years, political and cultural historians alike have turned their attention to the representation and delegation of authority in early modern England. Studies of the exercise of power in this period have increasingly focused on the role of the court rather than Parliament, as the crucial 'point of contact' through which power was mediated, with access to the person of the king seen as vital to the acquisition and maintenance of political influence.

In this context, the career of Thomas Wentworth during the Personal Rule offers a particularly fascinating case study in the politics of access and the delegation of authority. Here was someone for whom personal access to the monarch was theoretically impossible. He was absent from court, and indeed from England, throughout much of the 1630s, leading historians to cite him as an example of just why personal access to the sovereign was so crucial and absence so dangerous.[1] Nevertheless, this absence did not hold Wentworth back from embarking upon a range of ambitious, if controversial, policies in Ireland, while in 1639 he found himself summoned back to England as the only man who could solve the king's problems.

It is not the intention of this essay to deny the vital connection between personal access to the monarch and political influence – Wentworth suffered constant anxieties about what might be happening while he was away from court. Indeed, his enforced absence provides a richly documented case of how a seventeenth-century statesman dealt with the all-important problems of absence from court, and the maintenance of royal authority at a distance. But it is possible to delve deeper and to use Wentworth's dilemma to

---

[1] E.g. Kevin Sharpe, *Politics and Ideas in Early Stuart England* (1989), pp. 78–9, 166. For a general discussion of the importance of access to the monarch, see David Starkey (ed.), *The English Court from the War of the Roses to the Civil War* (1987), esp. pp. 1–24.

investigate the multiplicity of ways that influence could make itself felt at the early Stuart court.

As an active and interventionist Lord Deputy of Ireland, Wentworth's constant need for the king's support led him to develop a range of strategies to maintain his position at court. Among the most powerful of these was the influence that could be wielded through royal and courtly correspondence. This literary form of access could control the flow of information to the king, orchestrate the circulation of rumours and manipulate the reputations of friends and enemies alike. This chapter, then, examines how Wentworth turned a serious handicap – distance from the court – into a relative virtue. In doing so, it looks at Wentworth's own access to information, particularly the shadowy world of private secretaries, men of business and newsletter writers, and the ways in which Wentworth attempted to control rumour and disinformation.

It will also be argued that the essentially contrived and public nature of Wentworth's *private* correspondence with figures at court demands greater recognition. The rhetorical aspects of this correspondence have seldom been fully appreciated, yet they played an important role in allowing Wentworth to pursue controversial policies on behalf of the crown. As Charles I attempted to assert a more active supremacy over his three kingdoms, the mechanics of government at a distance and the exercise of royal authority by proxy assumed ever greater significance.

The very richness of Wentworth's surviving papers invites the question of how effectively he was able to govern at a distance, first as President of the Council in the North and later as Lord Deputy of Ireland. The letters also allow us to gain some impression of how Wentworth himself assessed the potential difficulties of ruling at a substantial remove from king and court. But distance was not the only issue here. It was also Wentworth's political style that raised questions about the nature of authority and its effective representation. In particular, Wentworth pursued strongly activist, high-risk policies, which at times threatened to expose the limits of his power. In these circumstances, as we shall see, effective networks of communication, and Wentworth's access to and control over the dissemination of information, were decisive factors in ensuring his political survival. This essay concentrates on the sometimes neglected period 1629–1635, when Wentworth first encountered the set of problems associated with government at a distance.

The outlines of Wentworth's early career are well known. His first major political appointment was that of President of the Council in the North in 1628. Wentworth was most concerned to raise the public profile and political clout of royal government in the North. In some ways this period of rule in the North acted as a dress rehearsal for Wentworth's later government in Ireland, even if he was acting on home territory. Wentworth was particularly sensitive to the need to accompany the legal strengthening of royal authority in the North by a public campaign which drew attention to the symbolic representation of royal power. Of course this was partly accomplished by emphasising the respect to be granted to him as the king's delegated representative. Wentworth built a palatial new wing on to the Manor House at York, as befitted the official residence of the king's deputy, and carefully maintained a formal distance from the local nobility. Although Wentworth undoubtedly felt such behaviour to be more than necessary, for some it symbolised only his own arrogance and love of power.[2]

Wentworth also devoted considerable time and relentless energy to the pursuit of those who were held to have offered personal affronts to him – and hence to the authority of the crown. In practice, this sometimes meant stretching to the limits the special powers vested in the Council in the North itself. Bitter court cases involving men such as Lord Fauconberg and his son, Sir Thomas Gower, and most notoriously of all, Sir David Foulis, obviously reflected rivalries inherent in local power politics.[3] But the grounds upon which Wentworth chose to fight these battles are significant. Slander, the slighting gesture, trespasses demeaning to the king's authority, were all seen as undermining the consolidation of royal power in the North, as well as threatening Wentworth's own political reputation. Regardless of the actual personal threat posed by an individual, Wentworth would also appear to have had a very developed sense of the importance of his popular reputation in the effective exercise of authority and the development of his own political career.[4]

That being said, Wentworth did discriminate between the different forms of slander to which he was subjected. Some he regarded

[2] Wedgwood, pp. 104–6; R. R. Reid, *The King's Council in the North* (1921), pp. 404–35.
[3] J. T. Cliffe, *The Yorkshire Gentry: From the Reformation to the Civil War* (1969), pp. 297–304; Wedgwood, pp. 107–12.
[4] See Cust, this volume, pp. 63–80.

as relatively harmless. During the levying of the unpopular knighthood fines in the early 1630s, Wentworth described how he was 'libelled all over that part of ye Kingdome, for one, hung up in effigie with Empson and Dudley, for another, my Lord Treasurer, that was, and myself painted upon Gibbets, our names underwritt with a great deale of poetry besides'. Not surprisingly, various individuals offered to search out the perpetrators. As Wentworth later explained, however, he did not feel it necessary to pursue those who challenged him anonymously (as opposed to the direct attacks of a Fauconberg). Apparently, this turned out to be quite a shrewd move and 'thus did I quite spoil their feast. There was no noyse of them at all went abroad, and once within a month ye humour was spent, so as I never heard more of them since.' Wentworth explained his behaviour thus: 'My distinction when these insolencies trench upon the public, I would have them sought after and driven to ye uttermost of discovery and Punishment. But when their venom is only cast out against particulars I would bring them as little upon the Stage as might be.'[5] As Wentworth had shown during the 1620s elections, he was himself an accomplished actor upon the local 'stage', to the extent that he was among those defaulters who were deliberately imprisoned away from their own county for refusal to pay the Forced Loan.[6] This evaluation of the relative threat posed by the different attacks on his reputation is therefore especially illuminating. Popular libels – which seem so striking to the modern reader, and about which his friend Laud developed an anxious obsession – he did not necessarily consider a problem. Their anonymous authorship and surreptitious distribution emphasised their marginal political status. It was the less lurid attacks that were made publicly by individuals such as Foulis, who identified themselves and appealed to the authorities, which constituted the real threat to Wentworth's power and authority in the region.

Once appointed Lord Deputy, Wentworth did not leave for Ireland immediately. Instead he had at least two major tasks before him. One was to consolidate his position in the North. The other was to establish the ground rules for his administration in Ireland and to familiarise himself with the Irish political scene.

Even as Wentworth plunged himself into preparations for his new

[5]   Wentworth to Laud, 18 Oct. 1637, Str P 7, pp. 55–6.
[6]   See Cust, this volume, pp. 63–80; Richard Cust, *The Forced Loan and English Politics 1626–28* (Oxford, 1987), pp. 221–3, 225–6, 234–6.

office, he kept one eye on his northern power base – as tempestuous as that might be. In particular, he was determined to retain his position of Lord President of the Council side-by-side with his new office of Lord Deputy. Once again, questions of delegated authority and government by proxy loomed large. Just as Wentworth had struggled to maintain his position as the personal embodiment of the king's authority in the North, he now needed to ensure that his Vice-President, Sir Edward Osborne, would also be able to command a similar level of support in his absence. This proved to be a serious problem. Indeed Vice-President Osborne's alternately exasperated and despairing letters to Wentworth in the months following the latter's removal to Ireland provide an ironic echo of the letters that Wentworth himself was writing at that time.[7] Wentworth lamented his lack of real power, the hostility facing him from jealous rivals and his fears over the level of support he could command from the king. Osborne also faced a range of petty and not so petty challenges to his authority as he attempted to govern in Wentworth's absence. His power of veto was challenged, for example, and his colleagues refused to accord him the honours due to the Deputy, particularly in matters of precedence. In November 1633, Osborne wrote in some anxiety to Wentworth concerning defective musters. Osborne actually requested that Wentworth send him a stern, formal order, imploring that 'I may receave a stricte letter from your Lordship commandinge me nott to forbeare any whatsoever, butt to certifye all defects and excuses as I will answer [for] it'. Osborne particularly found himself struggling to assert his symbolic authority, being instructed by Wentworth to take up the Deputy's seat in the church of St Michael-le-Belfry, despite the opposition of the Lord Mayor of York, among others.[8]

Osborne's problems were compounded by the fact that Wentworth still intended to keep control of policy in the North. In part this was because he wanted to ensure that he was in power to deal with the continued implementation and aftermath of controversial policies, such as those touching recusancy fines, as well as overseeing impending Star Chamber cases against 'slanderers' such as

---

[7]   E.g. Osborne to Wentworth, 28 March 1634, Str P 14/8; and especially Osborne to Wentworth, 9 Jan. 1634/5, Str P 8, pp. 123–4.

[8]   Osborne to Wentworth, n.d., received 7 Nov. 1633, Str P 13/88. For letters written to Wentworth criticising Osborne and his handling of authority, see Sir John Hotham to Wentworth, 5 May 1635, Str P 15/64 and Cottington to Wentworth, 20 May 1635, Str P 15/79.

Foulis.[9] As he prepared to move to Ireland, Wentworth assured Sir John Coke that the Vice-President and Secretary at York would never suffer from lack of advice and direction, 'but shall have it as often, and with as much speed from Dublin as if I were here in London, to which end I will lay a Foot-Post of my owne charge betwixt Chester and Yorke, which shall with safety and speed carry our letters to and fro'.[10] But government by letter in the North was also to be carried out in other ways. Wentworth not only corresponded with Osborne and other members of the Council in the North, he also bolstered his position in the North by the use of London contacts. When his case against Sir David Foulis was heard in Star Chamber, Wentworth sent out what was essentially a form letter to various members of the Privy Council. The letter, carried by one of Wentworth's secretaries, specially asked the recipient to attend the trial 'holding it indeed to concern me very deeply', mentioned that Foulis had 'indeavoured to wound his Ma[jes]ties Service through my sides' and requested the recipient to 'cast your Eye' upon a short brief of the cause.[11] Despite being in Ireland, Wentworth effectively monitored the London Star Chamber case, even down to his directions concerning the precise penalty to be exacted, and how the public recantations at York were to be delivered.[12]

But what of Wentworth's rule in Ireland? Just as in the North, Wentworth initially sought in Ireland to raise the profile of the crown, and particularly the dignity which he acquired as the king's representative. On one notable day, he made a special point of first visiting all the justices in their own houses in the morning, and then proceeded in the afternoon to take his oath as Lord Deputy and receive the sword from the justices in the Council Chamber 'with all the usual ceremonies'.[13] The intention was to draw the greatest possible distinction between Wentworth as a private individual and

---

9 Wentworth also ensured that appointments to the Council in the North remained with him and sought Laud's reassurance that the king would not interfere, Laud, VII, 146. See also Wentworth to Coke, 3 June 1635, Str P 15/93.

10 Wentworth to Coke, 17 June 1633, Str P 5, pp. 4–5.

11 Str P 8, pp. 46–51, include letters written on 3 and 4 November 1633 to Coventry and Arundel and a 'form' letter sent to the Lord Privy Seal, Carlisle, Pembroke, Dorset, Suffolk, Bridgewater, Danby, Exeter, Wimbledon, Chief Justice Heath and the two secretaries (p. 51).

12 E.g. Wentworth to Cottington, 4 Nov. 1633, Str P 3, pp. 32–3 (Knowler, I, 145–6); Wentworth to Laud, 31 Oct. 1633, Str P 8, p. 45.

13 Wentworth to Coke, 3 Aug. 1633, Str P 5, p. 8 (Knowler, I, 97).

the dignity and respect to be accorded him once he became the king's official representative. As in the North, Wentworth adopted ceremonies that underlined his vice-regal status. He planned a palatial country residence on a scale larger than Hatfield House, he restricted access to rooms of state, and demanded the attendance of the nobility upon the Deputy on his visits to church. He also enforced the codes of the English Privy Council upon the meetings of their Irish counterpart in the interests of greater 'Civility and Dignity', including the stipulation that no man should speak uncovered at the Council save the Lord Deputy.[14]

Wentworth also did his best to ensure his free hand on paper. He demanded (and received from Charles) specific confirmation of direct powers not exercised by his predecessors as Lord Deputy.[15] While he had his own private reasons for wanting to wield a completely free hand in the exercise of patronage, he also argued that he could not afford politically to be seen to be circumvented by others in appointments that were theoretically in his gift. He emphasised in a letter to Laud that it should be a basic rule of state that the Deputy should not, as he put it, be made 'vile and Cheape before this people' by intrusions into his patronage. If the people believed him to be weak, then he already was.[16]

Nevertheless, in trying to convert potential into actual power, Wentworth was especially hampered in Ireland by his lack of accurate information and what he felt to be the untrustworthy character of the Irish council. He complained to Carlisle soon after his arrival in Ireland that 'I see it is a Maxime amongst them to keepe the Deputy as ignorant as possibly they can that soe allbeit not in Place *yet he may be subordinate to them in knowledge*'.[17] During the long period between his appointment and his arrival in Ireland, Wentworth corresponded with a number of Irish statesmen (especially Lord Mountnorris) and began to gather a virtual archive of material relating to previous lord deputies.[18] Once in Ireland, this process

[14] Wedgwood, pp. 123, 135–6, 225–7; Wentworth to Coke, 31 Jan. 1633/4, Knowler, I, 200–1.
[15] Knowler, I, 65–7; Wedgwood, pp. 135–7.
[16] Wentworth to Laud, 1 Oct. 1634, Str P 6, p. 99. For a very strongly worded letter from Wentworth, arguing his need to control appointments, see Wentworth to Coke, 26 Oct. 1633, Str P 3, pp. 22–4 (Knowler, I, 138–40) and his fears that 'the empty Name or Ghost of a Deputy General to be only worn by me'.
[17] Wentworth to Coke, 27 Aug. 1633, Str P 8, p. 12, italics mine.
[18] Str P 1 contains correspondence with Mountnorris and other Irish political figures, plus instructions to previous lord deputies 1611–28; Str P 24–25/80–350 contains a variety of Irish state papers for the period before Wentworth's appointment, acquired at various

continued. Wentworth borrowed books of letters on Irish affairs
written by James I as well as those from the Jacobean House of
Lords, while on another occasion he obtained a lengthy account of
the Jacobean commission on fees in Ireland, from those who had
been involved.[19] But it was a slow process, and in October 1633,
Wentworth admitted to Carlisle that 'I am yet gathering with all
Circumspection my observances' about where and when to advise a
'Reformation' in Ireland.[20]

Given the limitations upon his knowledge and information in
Ireland, the only way that Wentworth could initially boost his
position was by restricting access to the only type of information that
he possessed but others were ignorant of: his own intentions. From
the start, Wentworth determined to keep Irish politicians off-
balance, deliberately planting contradictory rumours of his impending arrival in Ireland. Once there, he kept his own counsel
secret and revealed his intentions to virtually no one. In 1634, he
declared to Lord Treasurer Portland with some satisfaction that 'ther
is not a minister on this side, that knows any thing I either write or
intend, excepting the Maister of the Rolls & Sir George Radcliffe'.[21]
Such reticence was particularly necessary to his longer-term plans for
Ireland, as his basic strategy was to hold out the hope of the
confirmation of the Graces to the Old English until subsidies had
been voted in the planned parliament of 1634.[22]

Wentworth could build up his power base in Ireland, but ultimately his position was dependent on the support of the king. It is
here that distance from the court was potentially a significant
problem. Sir Edward Stanhope had warned him of the danger of
removing himself from court in this way, and the past history of lord
deputies of Ireland demonstrated how easily they could be undermined by covert appeals to the English court.[23] It was vital, then,

dates. Clarke suggests that it was as a member of the Irish committee of the English privy
council, investigating charges against Mountnorris, that Wentworth first gained familiarity
with the Irish political scene, *NHI*, p. 244.

19   Str P 14/245, 14/238.

20   Wentworth to Carlisle, 7 Oct. 1633, Str P 8, pp. 31–32 (Knowler, I, 120).

21   Wentworth to Laud, 16 Aug. 1633, Str P 8, p. 16; Wentworth to Portland, 31 Jan. 1633/4,
Str P 3, p. 46.

22   *NHI*, pp. 245–50; Aidan Clarke, *The Old English in Ireland, 1625–1642* (Cornell, 1966), p. 65.

23   P. Zagorin, 'Sir Edward Stanhope's advice to Thomas Wentworth, viscount Wentworth,
concerning the deputyship of Ireland: an important letter of 1631', *HJ* 7 (1964), p. 301;
Hugh Kearney, *Strafford in Ireland, 1633–41* (Manchester, 1959; 2nd edn, Cambridge, 1989),
pp. 10–14, 84.

that Wentworth retain and even extend his Whitehall connections. If he could not be there himself, then it would be through the management and manipulation of his correspondence that he would seek to maintain his position and influence. This correspondence repays careful study and reveals how Wentworth sought to strengthen his position at court while remaining in Ireland.

First of all was Wentworth's direct correspondence with leading members of the English court. Here it is worth emphasising that the most important of Wentworth's court correspondents was the king himself. Wentworth kept up a regular correspondence with Charles throughout the early years of his lord deputyship.[24] But this could never be enough. The king was often reticent and Wentworth was never certain of his master's full support. Given this situation, Wentworth needed to make use of carefully chosen intermediaries to ensure that his correspondence was favourably received and to advise him on the king's changing moods.

In the early 1630s, James Hay, earl of Carlisle, was one of Wentworth's most important contacts among those with intimate access to the king. In his early days in Ireland it was Carlisle to whom Wentworth wrote his most despairing letters, complaining of his isolation, and fearful of the king's unrealistic expectations.[25] He wrote these letters secure in the knowledge that Carlisle would be able to put his case directly to the king, and indeed ultimately he procured the letter he desired from Charles, assuring Wentworth of his support and his realisation of the many obstacles that his Lord Deputy faced. Carlisle was especially valuable to Wentworth as he clearly enjoyed open access to both the king and queen.[26] Wentworth's younger brother George, for example, memorably describes Carlisle trotting up the back-stairs of the king's lodgings at Newmarket to arrange a discreet and timely interview with Charles and later, Henrietta Maria. Carlisle was ideally placed to provide Wentworth with a general sense of what was said about him, and to interpret the behaviour of others at court towards him. It was

---

[24] Correspondence between Wentworth and Charles I is to be found primarily in Str P 3 and Str P 40, a selection of which is printed in Knowler.

[25] Wentworth to Carlisle, 27 Aug. 1633, Str P 8, p. 12. For other attempts to dampen the expectations of the king and others at court see Wentworth to Arundel, 19 Aug. 1633, Str P 5, p. 11; Wentworth to Windebank, 23 Oct. 1633, Str P 5, p. 21; and Wentworth to Coke, 26 Oct. 1633, Str P 5, pp. 22–4 (Knowler, 1, 138–40).

[26] Carlisle to Wentworth, 14 Sept. 1633, Str P 8, p. 30; Wentworth to Carlisle, 7 Oct. 1633, Str P 8, pp. 31–2 (Knowler, 1, 119).

therefore Carlisle to whom Wentworth turned to interpret the paucity of letters coming from Portland and Cottington, and to evaluate the success of his letters at court.[27]

In the early 1630s, of course, it was William Laud who was Wentworth's most prominent correspondent. Less of a courtier, and therefore less able to guide Wentworth as to the disposition of the court and the temper of the king, he was, however, more informative about the progress of specific policies, and better suited to promote at court those ones particularly favoured by Wentworth. Wentworth's correspondence with Laud testifies to the archbishop's importance as a figure who made Wentworth's absence from court feasible. Laud exploited his ready access to the king, reading aloud Wentworth's letters to Charles promptly – in one case delivering Wentworth's letters to the king within an hour of receiving them. He was often invaluable in ensuring that it was Wentworth's account of events that reached the king first, before the petitions of his opponents. Laud also ensured that the Lord Deputy's views remained effectively 'lodged' in the king's mind, as Wentworth himself put it.[28] Indeed it might be argued that Wentworth wrote two sets of letters to Charles I – one sent directly to the king and the other sent to Laud, to be read or quoted to the king when the opportunity arose.

Laud and Wentworth may well have had similar political aims, but even if they did not share the same political programme, Laud's commanding position at court (at least in the early 1630s) made it vital that Wentworth give the archbishop the *impression* that they had similar political objectives and values. Wentworth's promotion of the interests of the established church in Ireland suited the crown's financial and political needs, but just as importantly, it also gained the Lord Deputy the consistent support of the archbishop. It is not surprising, then, that Wentworth's letters to Laud constantly report his good deeds on behalf of the church in Ireland, often at a higher pitch when he needed Laud's assistance at a time of political crisis. Indeed, one of the attractions of a man such as Laud was the ease with which his preoccupations could be identified and appealed to. Wentworth explained quite frankly in a letter to Cottington his own

---

[27] Sir George Wentworth to Wentworth, 13 March 1633/4, Str P 8, pp. 84–91 (Knowler, 1, 218–22); Wentworth to Carlisle, 8 March 1633/4, Str P 8, p. 81.

[28] Wentworth to Laud, 16 Nov. 1635, Str P 6, p. 279; Wentworth to Laud, 3 June 1634, Str P 6, p. 79.

reading of the archbishop's ambitions: 'he will aspire to be absolute in Church affaires... but in truth I think no further'.[29] Wentworth therefore set out to flatter these ambitions whenever this was necessary. His letters to Laud sometimes include decidedly heavy-handed declarations that he placed himself entirely in Laud's hands in all ecclesiastical affairs, having a complete faith in the archbishop's judgement.[30] Wentworth was also careful, for example, to warn his younger brother George against pushing the suit of a clergyman, one Mr Watts of Trinity College, Cambridge, too far with Laud, stressing the need not to appear an importunate layman in the archbishop's eyes.[31]

In his campaign against the earl of Cork, Wentworth similarly played to Laud's feelings in order to gain much-needed support at an important time.[32] A few years previously he had largely disregarded Laud's wishes over the seating plans affecting members of the Council in the North in York Minster – the need to maintain peace among Yorkshire's fractious and precedence-conscious gentry out-weighed the niceties of religious propriety.[33] Yet in the famous controversy over the earl of Cork's tomb, Wentworth suddenly revealed a sensitivity to lay intrusion and profanity of a most delicate and refined nature. As he laid his plans for a more wide-ranging attack on Cork, Wentworth sought to gain Laud's support for this risky enterprise by focusing on the earl's alleged profanation of St Patrick's Cathedral. While Laud suspended judgement, Wentworth complained that the east-end tomb disrupted his pious devotions. The monument was 'so full in view, that I that desire to do Reverence to God before his Altar (which indeed I see few of them doe) cannot yet frame my selfe to it there, least men might thinke the kings Deputy were crouching to... an earl of Corke... Nay which is worse I protest to God it offendes me extreamly, when I am to say my prayers to have such a landshipp in my eye.'[34] Wentworth's constant promptings finally persuaded Laud to support Wentworth's case against Cork, and he was indebted to the archbishop for assisting his attempts 'so to lock it up with the king, as [Cork's]

29 Wentworth to Cottington, 7 Feb. 1633/4, Str P 3, p. 58.
30 Wentworth to Laud, 14 September 1636, Str P 6, pp. 357–8.
31 Wentworth to Sir George Wentworth, 18 Feb. 1634/5, Str P 8, p. 187.
32 For details of the dispute over Cork's tomb, see Nicholas Canny, *The Upstart Earl* (Cambridge, 1982), pp. 12–13, 43; Wedgwood, pp. 182–3.
33 Wentworth to Laud, 4 June 1633, Str P 8, p. 3.
34 Wentworth to Laud, 18 March 1633/4, Str P 6, pp. 34–5.

earnest pursuits and Guifts underhand be not able to fetch him off'.[35]

But Laud and Carlisle were not Wentworth's only contacts at court, and we need to consider more carefully the nature of the correspondence entered into by Wentworth with other councillors, and its rhetorical (and ultimately political) significance. It is easy to be disarmed by the apparent intimacy and lapses into humour in the letters. Indeed, one recent historian of the 1630s has argued that Wentworth considered the earl of Portland 'the very Principal' of his friends at court merely on the basis that Wentworth told the Lord Treasurer so in a letter.[36] But it needs to be emphasised that the 'personal' nature of these letters was very much contrived.

As this essay has stressed, correspondence represented the only effective way in which Wentworth could be present at court, and his voice heard in discussions. His exchange of letters with prominent Privy Councillors was therefore vital to his position. In this sense, the personal 'asides' had a purpose just as much as the overtly political passages. Wentworth deliberately sought to create an impression of intimacy, the better to convince his correspondent of the closeness of their political alliance. Protestations of personal regard should inevitably be read with a good deal of scepticism; but many descriptions of the relative closeness of a relationship were also standardised and formulaic. Wentworth, for example, would sometimes assure a correspondent that he was his only real friend at court. Historians have been content to accept this verdict of his relationship with Laud, but Wentworth was happy to say the same thing to Carlisle or Cottington, even to Portland (as we have seen), and to be told the same thing at different times by each of these courtiers.[37] Quite simply, given his position, Wentworth could never afford to have only one ally at court – he needed several, each of whom considered themselves to be his particular friend.[38]

---

[35] Wentworth to Laud, 3 June 1634, Str P 6, p. 79.

[36] Kevin Sharpe, *The Personal Rule of Charles I* (1992), p. 148, but contrast with Wentworth's letter to Newcastle, describing Portland as 'the heaviest Adversary I ever had', Knowler, i, 411.

[37] See especially Wentworth to Cottington, 18 Nov. 1634, Str P 3, p. 142 and also Wentworth to Portland, Easter week 1634, Knowler, i, 229–30; Wentworth to Carlisle, 8 March 1633/4, Str P 8, pp. 80–2.

[38] Wentworth explained to Coke that he was always grateful for information, 'albeit I have ever governed my selfe as little by the opinion as any other man yet it is not amisse sometymes to understand how the Market goes and good use to be made of it', 8 Nov. 1633, Str P 5, p. 26 (Knowler, i, 153).

The letters exchanged by councillors also require a more careful reading than they have hitherto received. Letters penned by ministers were by their very nature textually quite complex and a neat division between private and public correspondence cannot easily be made. Letters also had a symbolic importance that existed almost apart from the nature of their contents – a regular correspondence implied intimacy and suggested some degree of reciprocity. Great importance was attached to who received letters, and how regularly. Portland and Cottington, for example, became very concerned at the number of letters being exchanged by Laud and Wentworth, and Cottington made strenuous efforts to gain information as to their contents.[39] During his early days in Ireland, Wentworth himself made the mistake of sending packets of letters for various figures at the English court, but failing to include any for Portland. The Lord Treasurer's annoyance at being so neglected prompted Cottington to warn Wentworth of the need to write to the Lord Treasurer frequently – regardless of whether or not he had anything particular to convey.[40]

It was not solely through letters to leading ministers and courtiers, however, that Wentworth sought to gain information about proceedings at court and to protect his interests there. It was also vital that he employ men who would work for him in the lower, less visible echelons of political life. Among those operating in the less exalted reaches of English political life were the famous newsletter-writer George Garrard, Wentworth's 'man of business' William Raylton, his younger brother Sir George, and his legal representative Thomas Little.

Historians have often exploited George Garrard's newsletters, but little has been said about the nature of his relationship with Wentworth. It is worth emphasising that Wentworth's correspondence with Garrard was not like buying a newspaper. Garrard had his own ties and moved in his own political circles, which enabled him to provide Wentworth with a glimpse of other levels of political activity.[41] He could be a more reliable guide than many in reporting

---

[39] Wentworth to Newcastle, 17 June 1635, Str P 15/112; Wentworth to Laud, 19 Feb. 1634/5, Str P 6, p. 134.

[40] Cottington to Wentworth, 26 Dec. 1633, Str P 3, pp. 52–3.

[41] Garrard frequently stayed with the earl of Northumberland at Petworth and it was at Petworth church that he was made a deacon; see Garrard to Wentworth, 3 Oct. 1635, Knowler, 1 469. Garrard also claimed the friendship of Cottington, whose house he often visited, while Laud reported that Garrard 'never came at me since my living about London till this winter', and then he came first accompanied by Cottington; see Garrard to Wentworth, 12 March 1634/5, Str P 14/323; Laud to Wentworth, 12 May 1635, Laud, VIII, 133.

feelings towards Wentworth at court. As he pointed out to Wentworth in the early 1630s, he was not generally known to be associated with Wentworth.[42] At one point this enabled him to procure an alleged copy of a conversation between Wentworth and the Lord Deputy's great Irish enemy, Mountnorris, simply by chatting to Mountnorris's solicitor. Garrard provides us with fascinating glimpses of the uncharted world of private secretaries and men of business, in which political gossip and information was constantly exchanged and relayed. Of course, it should be remembered that information did not only pass in one direction. Indeed, Wentworth sometimes specifically passed on information to Garrard, clearly with the intention that it would be more widely disseminated. At the same time, Wentworth did not entirely rely on Garrard, and in one of his rare letters to him, he chided the newsletter writer for failing to report on rumours that the Lord Deputy had hounded Clanricard to his death.[43]

William Raylton and Sir George Wentworth were also, in different ways, able to give Wentworth access to networks of official and unofficial information. Raylton was Wentworth's tireless agent in London, constantly active in his master's private and public affairs and he regularly called on ministers, Laud in particular. His formal duties as Clerk of the Council Chamber (and later, Clerk of the Privy Seal) gave Raylton useful access to court information. Indeed, the young Sir George Wentworth explained to his brother how he had asked Raylton to shepherd him about on his first visit to court, being 'altogether ignorant of the Place, the Times and Seasons, that were fittest for me to move about your Lordships Commands'. Raylton's presence at court also made him privy to the useful sort of information only available to insiders. On one occasion, Raylton 'being at the Back-Stairs' was able to report that the king had spent two hours alone with Secretary Coke, dictating a response to Wentworth's own dispatches. Raylton also proved his worth outside the direct confines of Whitehall Palace.[44] Thus, when Garrard showed Cottington a

[42] Garrard to Wentworth, 11 Jan. 1634/5, Str P 14/260 (Knowler, 1 357). Garrard also sought preferment from Wentworth, asking him to intercede with Laud for the reversion to the mastership of Sutton's Hospital, Garrard to Wentworth, 14 Jan. 1635, Str P 14/266.

[43] Garrard to Wentworth, 12 March 1634/5, Str P 14/323; Wentworth to Garrard, 26 Dec. 1635, Str P 8, pp. 331–2.

[44] G. Aylmer, The King's Servants: The Civil Service of Charles I, 1625–1642 (1961, reprint 1974), pp. 178, 514; Wentworth's correspondents frequently mentioned their dealings with Raylton, while at one point Lord Goring reported being in daily contact with him, Goring to Wentworth, 28 Aug. 1635, Str P 15/203; 13 March 1633/4, Sir George Wentworth to Wentworth, Knowler, 1, 217, 219.

letter from an agent of Mountnorris in early 1635, word clearly reached Raylton very rapidly. He actually confronted Garrard in the street the very next day and cross-examined him closely about the manuscript and its circulation.[45]

The case of Sir George Wentworth was somewhat different. Like Raylton, he could report directly to Wentworth on events behind the scenes and among his letters to his influential brother is a very lengthy and minutely detailed account of his first experiences of the court and of the mechanics of court life.[46] But Sir George was also being deliberately groomed by Wentworth for later political service. His relationship to the Lord Deputy meant that he could more properly be presented to the king and ministers, and that his reception could provide a litmus test for the fortunes and status of Wentworth himself at court.[47]

Sir George Wentworth and Raylton were most obviously important in their management of Wentworth's correspondence with the mainland. Raylton was in charge of Wentworth's general correspondence from England: letters were entrusted to his care, and he could also be used to distribute materials in England. For example, on one occasion, Wentworth told Garrard to seek out Raylton, who would show him a copy of the sentence against Mountnorris just so that he would be properly informed as to where 'justice' lay in the case.[48] In delivering and receiving letters, Raylton and Sir George took great care to superintend and report on their reception, and on any courtesies that were accorded them personally as bearers of Wentworth's correspondence. In this way Wentworth could get a clearer sense of the health and general demeanour of the correspondent whose letters might be filled with misleading affirmations of regard. It is impossible to estimate the true extent of the information and assistance which a man such as Raylton was able to provide to

---

[45] Garrard to Wentworth, 12 March 1634/5, Str P 14/323.
[46] Sir George Wentworth to Wentworth, 13 March 1633/4, Str P 8, pp. 84–91 (Knowler, 1 218–22).
[47] *Ibid.*; Windebank, when congratulating Wentworth on his success with the Irish parliament, added that he could attest to the king's pleasure, 'haveing the Happinesse to be present at Bever [Belvoir] Castle when your Brother presented your letters', as the king had exclaimed that it was the best news he had heard in a long time, Windebank to Wentworth, 6 Aug. 1634, Str P 5, p. 250. See also Knowler, 1, 218–19 for Portland's reception of Sir George Wentworth and the latter's remarks on the civility of Lord Weston, who, when Sir George departed, 'would not by any Means leave me till he saw me in my Coach'. For Sir George's use as an intermediary by individuals as various as the earl of Exeter, the earl of Arundel, and Sir William Pennyman, see Str P 15/40, 15/48, 15/50.
[48] Wentworth to Garrard, 16 Dec. 1635, Str P 8, p. 332.

Wentworth. Raylton wrote few letters to Wentworth, instead acting
as a conduit for specific instructions and sensitive information it was
judged imprudent to commit to paper, and occasionally travelling
himself between London and Ireland. It is clear that Raylton was
also expected to be proactive on Wentworth's behalf and he was
often present with ministers during discussions of important business.
He regularly met with Laud and on one occasion the suspicious
archbishop even remarked that 'I am glad that William Raylton
saves us the trouble of a cipher'.[49] Yet, however voluminous the
collection of Wentworth's surviving papers, it is vital to remember
that they do not contain the sum of the information reaching
Wentworth. Indeed, the figure of Raylton lurks in the shadows of the
collection. In conveying sensitive information from others, perhaps
even more as a source of detailed information and astute comment in
his own right, Raylton may well have been Wentworth's most
important single informant.

In January 1635, Viscount Conway ended one letter to Wentworth
with the reflection that either he would send news by Sir George
Wentworth, or that in future he would write in cipher.[50] This brings
us to one recurrent theme of Wentworth's correspondence as a
whole – the fear of intercepted letters. Lord Goring similarly
explained to Wentworth in 1635 that he would convey via Raylton
'some of our dayly passages which I think not soe fitt to trust this and
such like withall especially since the late perusal of papers as they
pass at home and abroad'.[51] Wentworth was therefore forced to
resort to cipher, most commonly in letters to the king and to Laud,
although he occasionally used cipher to Cottington and a number of
others. As 'perusal' was expected, this could lend to the main text of
letters a bland or even deliberately misleading tone. Thus, when
writing to Laud about the earl of Cork, Wentworth, assuming that
the letter might be intercepted and that it would seem suspicious if
nothing in the text referred to Cork directly, inserted a brief, bland
paragraph hoping that all would turn out for the best, finishing
baldly 'and there in present I leave it'. He followed this, of course,
with a lengthy and vitriolic attack on Cork in cipher.[52]

[49] Garrard to Wentworth, 30 July 1635, Str P 15/170; Laud, VII, pp. 217, 293.
[50] Conway to Wentworth, 20 Jan. 1635, Knowler, I, 363.
[51] Goring to Wentworth, 27 July 1635, Str P 15/165.
[52] Wentworth to Laud, 19 Nov. 1634, Str P 6, p. 103; Wentworth to Laud, 3 Jan. 1635/6, Str
      P 6, p. 295.

Fears of a future parliament, and of what might be used against them there, made people constantly wary in their correspondence. While some correspondents, such as Newcastle, urged Wentworth to burn their letters (in vain, it would appear), Wentworth instead regarded it as prudent to keep copies of all his correspondence.[53] Once again, information was power. Such a policy may have been something of a family tradition, for Sir William Wentworth's 'Advice to his son', written by Wentworth's own father, recommended precisely such a course.[54] Wentworth strongly advised his brother-in-law, Lord Clifford, to keep copies of his letters to Cork, noting warily that Cork kept the originals and that 'as for his owne letters, he hath such a Collection as I am persuaded few men in Christendome have besides himselfe'.[55] Nevertheless, there was clearly a tension between the 'burn this letter' culture and those who carefully preserved their correspondence. Laud himself was quite alarmed to hear that Wentworth kept copies of both sides of their correspondence, noting that 'I keepe none of them I send you'. The archbishop particularly feared the use to which enemies might put their letters if either died suddenly – 'I am most confident if either of us fail, our letters will be fingered', he insisted.[56]

Wentworth, however, occasionally found his own collection invaluable. When Lord Coventry reproved Wentworth for having bad-mouthed both him and judges in general, and having referred to them by the scornful term 'Mootmen', Wentworth was able to trace the origins of this back to some ill-advised remarks in a letter to Cottington of some two years before.[57] The 1630s were clearly a time of increasing unease about the circulation of information; not only were letters kept, but conversations were also sometimes carefully recorded (as we have seen in the case of Mountnorris, and as Bishop Williams was also finding to his cost).

Back in Ireland, Wentworth's policies grew in their audacity, as he launched a series of attacks upon the personnel of the Irish council. The earl of Cork, the earl of Clanricard, and the Lord Mountnorris

53 Newcastle to Wentworth, 26 Dec. 1630, Str P 12/182. For Wentworth's justification of this practice, see Wentworth to Laud, 12 Sept. 1634, Str P 6, pp. 244–5.
54 Cooper, p. 18.
55 Wentworth to Clifford, 2 May 1635, Str P 8, pp. 230–2.
56 Laud, vii, 166–7, 211.
57 Coventry to Wentworth, 29 June 1635, Str P 15/132; Wentworth to Coventry, 10 Sept. 1635, Str P 8, pp. 259–61.

all faced humiliation and deprivation in the courts at Wentworth's hands. The narrative of these events is well known, but it is worth focusing again on the role played by Wentworth's networks of information and communication.[58]

Wentworth's opponents were not obscure provincials. They were if anything better provided with court contacts than was Wentworth himself. Wentworth's predecessor as Lord Deputy, Lord Falkland, had learned to his cost how astutely councillors could undermine his position by appealing directly to the court in England.[59] This was serious enough, but Wentworth aimed high, not merely trying to counter the influence of men such as Cork and Clanricard but actively seeking to humiliate them. To do this effectively, he needed to call upon all his court contacts. In the case of the earl of Cork, in particular, Laud played a central role in putting Wentworth's case before the king, and making sure the Lord Deputy's view of events predominated.[60]

But central to Wentworth's communication problem was also the matter of controlling the flow of information to England. He had to ensure, not only that his intelligence got through, but that his opponents' did not. Laud could help here by telling him that Cork's contacts were trying to get to the king, and by ensuring that he got there first. Wentworth's problem in controlling the flow of information into England was a difficult one, and the frequently desperate tone of his correspondence shows just how much of his own career was riding on the successful prosecution of Cork and Clanricard. Wentworth was rarely sure of the king's support, as men such as Cork used a range of colleagues to intervene on his behalf, including the Lord Primate Ussher, the earl of Salisbury, the earl of Pembroke, and even the Lord Treasurer Portland – whose support was successfully solicited by Cork's secretary – though not without Laud getting wind of it.[61]

Sometimes it was a matter less of suppressing alternative points of view, or of controlling the English interpretation of Irish events (in

---

[58]   For Wentworth's pursuit of Cork, see Canny, *Upstart Earl*, pp. 12–17; Kearney, *Strafford*, pp. 70, 127; Clarke, *Old English*, pp. 73–4, 131; Wedgwood, pp. 180–7.

[59]   Kearney, *Strafford*, pp. 10–14, 30–1, 84, 91; Clarke, *Old English*, pp. 38–9.

[60]   Wentworth to Laud, 22 Sept. 1634, Str P 6, p. 97; Wentworth to Laud, 19 Nov. 1634, Str P 6, p. 103. For Wentworth's constant reliance on Laud to ensure that the king received Wentworth's version of events concerning Cork, see Str P 6, pp. 97, 103.

[61]   Wentworth to Laud, 18 March 1633/4, Laud to Wentworth, 11 March 1633/4, Str P 6, pp. 34–8.

the case especially of Mountnorris), than of preventing information getting out at all. Wentworth sought especially to keep some of the rigours of his Irish administration secret from the English court. The wretched Patrick Darcy was not the only person to suffer as a consequence. Darcy complained that it was futile trying to convince people that he was still held prisoner in Dublin Castle when Wentworth reported that he had been released, because the Lord Deputy 'sways all at the fountain'.[62]

Darcy's predicament reminds us that the control of information emanating from Ireland also often meant the physical control of people. Wentworth was always anxious to ensure that his opponents should remain in Ireland, so that he could control them, and control what was reported in England of what he did to them. Suppression of information and limiting the movement of individuals were central to securing his power base. Even before Wentworth moved to Ireland he obtained the right to monitor the movement of individuals and in early 1635, a proclamation was issued which forbade anyone to leave Ireland without the Lord Deputy's consent.[63] Wentworth himself sent a series of letters to the king (and Laud) arguing against Cork's petition that he be granted leave to go to England to clear his name. Indeed the matter was considered serious enough that Laud made a point of also showing the king Wentworth's own letters to Salisbury and Pembroke, which attempted to justify the policy of keeping Cork in Ireland. Wentworth also went to enormous lengths to force the return of the Galway delegates from London to Ireland, telling them that they would be taken to Dublin in the custody of a special messenger if they did not leave instantly.[64]

Wentworth could try to control the movements of specific documents and people, but a major threat to him was that of rumour and misinformation. Specific information could sometimes be suppressed; but misinformation and rumour could never be controlled. Wentworth was far from indifferent to the significance of this and as we have seen, it was slander that he considered his greatest single

---

[62] Clarke, *Old English*, p. 102. In a similar way, Wentworth withheld news from England; for example, failing to mention the check he received in the Irish Commons on 17 November in a letter to Coke dated 19 Nov. 1634, see Kearney, *Strafford*, p. 58.

[63] Kearney, *Strafford*, p. 84; Knowler, I, 362.

[64] Wentworth to Laud, 12 April 1634, Str P 6, p. 46; Wentworth to Laud, 2 Nov. 1635, Str P 6, pp. 271–2; Laud to Wentworth, 16 Nov. 1635, Str P 6, p. 279; Kearney, *Strafford*, pp. 93–4; *NHI*, p. 254.

enemy.[65] Wentworth also had a virtual paranoia about misinformation. He could do nothing about the basic fact that letters between
England and Ireland could take anything between one and four
weeks to arrive. This could be sufficient time to lose the political
initiative. Many weeks might pass before a simple piece of gossip
could be denied. Wentworth's sensitivity to political rumour is
strikingly demonstrated when in late 1634 Cottington off-handedly
asked Wentworth's secretary, Sir Philip Mainwaring, when Wentworth might return to England. When Mainwaring reported this,
Wentworth immediately panicked, demanding to know why Cottington had raised the issue. While he did not doubt Cottington's
friendly intent, he explained that 'understanding the Jealousye of
some, in all, which of late seeme but to relate to me... [and] not
knowing how such rumours, how groundlesse soever, might swimme
in other Mens Fancyes, I did covett there might be as little noyse as
truth in them'.[66]

The impact of rumour and slander is not just incidental to
Wentworth's career. On a more fundamental level, rumour and
misinformation could be and were major political forces. Wentworth
had faced rumours that he had murdered his wife (or at least
contributed to her death) back in 1631 and in 1635 rumour in
England claimed that the Lord Deputy had been assassinated, just as
contenders for the treasurership jostled for position. Wentworth
himself was certainly capable of spreading disinformation and did
not hesitate to encourage Laud to spread false rumours at court.[67]
Recent work by Cust, Cogswell, Bellany and others has emphasised

---

[65]   E.g. Wentworth to Laud, 10 March 1634/5, Str P 6, p. 152, where Wentworth beseeches
      Laud to 'supplicate' the king on behalf of 'this his absent Servant, That whenever any of
      these Calumnies are fastned upon, that they may not yet fasten in his Royall breast, till
      they be proved', asking additionally to know not only the charge but the 'Chardger'.
[66]   Wentworth to Cottington, 18 Nov. 1634, Str P 3, p. 141.
[67]   The rumour of Wentworth's supposed involvement in the death of his wife, Arabella
      Holles, was certainly in circulation at the time of his trial. Robert Baillie describes how
      observers at the trial explained in various ways why Wentworth wept during a speech at
      the mention of his dead wife, including the belief that 'remembrance had stopt his mouth;
      for they say that his first lady, being with child, and finding one of his mistress's letters,
      brought it to him, and chiding him therefore, he struck her on the breast, wherof she
      shortly died', R. Baillie, *Letters and Journals*, ed. David Laing (2 vols., Edinburgh, 1841–2), I,
      291. For reports of Wentworth's supposed assassination, see the account of Sir John
      Okehampton, who claimed to have used the rumour to test the 'hidden affections' of
      Wentworth's friends and enemies alike, Okehampton to Wentworth, 14 March 1634/5, Str
      P 14/330; P. Donald, *An Uncounselled King: Charles I and the Scottish Troubles, 1637–1641*
      (Cambridge, 1990), p. 184. I would like to thank Anthony Milton for drawing this last
      reference to my attention.

the emerging role played by public opinion in the politics of this period and the way in which rumour and slander helped to shape these perceptions.[68] Historians such as Clarke and Canny have also rightly emphasised how Wentworth consistently sought to portray his courtly opponents as raw and lawless chieftains, forcing the English settlers into a stereotyped role of the Irish native. Clarke has emphasised the ludicrousness of this depiction for an accomplished courtier such as Sir Piers Crosby. But Wentworth clearly saw the political value of peddling these extraordinarily distorted views of his opponents, and his success with later generations of historians has been palpable.[69]

It is worth remembering, however, that his opponents were adept at playing the same game, and the more that Wentworth sought to control the flow of informed opinion from Ireland, the more his opponents fabricated their own public image for Wentworth. The shaping of Wentworth's public persona is a rich topic requiring a good deal more research. As rapidly as Wentworth constructed an image of himself as a diligent and selfless royal servant, an alternative image of him as an uncouth, graceless autocrat was served up by his opponents. His deliberate humiliation of a series of Irish earls and lords inevitably drew forth accusations at court that he was a barbarous parvenu bent on undermining the social order. His opponents made great play of the way in which Wentworth had tactlessly held his court of inquiry into the prestigious earl of Clanricard's lands while taking up residence in the earl's own house. Stories circulated of Wentworth's affronts during his stay, grazing his horses in the best meadow, slaughtering deer, and casting 'himself in his riding boots upon very rich beds'.[70] Nor were such images only purveyed in Ireland. As early as 1632, the notion of Wentworth as a rough, northern outsider was gaining currency at the English court and the earl of Pembroke publicly branded him a 'Northern clowne'.[71]

---

[68] T. Cogswell, *The Blessed Revolution: English Politics and the Coming of War, 1621–1624* (Cambridge, 1989); R. Cust, 'News and politics in early seventeenth century England', *Past and Present* 111 (1986); P. Croft, 'The reputation of Robert Cecil: libels, political opinions and popular awareness in the early seventeenth century', *TRHS*, 6th ser. 1 (1991); A. Bellany, ' "Rayling rymes and vaunting verse": libellous politics in early Stuart England, 1603–1628', in K. Sharpe and P. Lake (eds.), *Culture and Politics in Early Stuart England* (1994).

[69] Canny, *Upstart Earl*, p. 11; Aidan Clarke, 'Sir Piers Crosby, 1590–1646: Wentworth's "tawney ribbon" ', *Irish Historical Studies*, 26, no. 102 (Nov. 1988), pp. 142–4, 146, 156–8.

[70] Clarke, *Old English*, p. 97.

[71] PRO, C 115, M35/8406.

Wentworth himself complained of the constant rumours against him at court, of which he was relatively well-informed.[72] These interpreted his policies as being driven entirely by self-interest or personal pique – precisely the qualities which Wentworth himself thought most at work among his opponents. The image of the blunt northerner with a social chip on his shoulder, deliberately setting out to humiliate noblemen, was a formidable weapon against Wentworth's own image of his opponents as uncultured, cynical opportunists. It was all the more effective as it built in part upon Wentworth's own occasional self-portrayal as a blunt, honest Yorkshireman.[73] These rumours would all play their part in the later development in England of the popular image of 'Black Tom'. Pre-1640, however, these hostile images were disseminated among a smaller elite, but their impact was not therefore irrelevant. The image of Wentworth as violent and anti-noble was a potentially powerful one, and was intended to influence those about the court, and ultimately the views of the king himself.[74]

*   *   *

Wentworth returned to England in 1636, to protect his position certainly, but also to trail his Irish successes and gain further status from the king. He had, by this time, proved how remarkably successful government at a distance from the court could be, with a successful parliament completed, royal revenue raised, Cork humiliated, Clanricard dead, and Mountnorris under a death sentence. Once back in London, his former father-in-law, the sharp-tongued Clare, mocked his semi-regal manner, describing how Wentworth

---

[72]   For examples of rumour and common estimation of Wentworth being reported to him from those outside the confines of inner court circles see letters from Sir William Robinson, 2 Nov. 1634, Str P 14/202; Sir John Bingley, 28 Feb. 1634/5, Str P 14/307 and Sir George Butler, 10 June 1635, Str P 15/99.

[73]   Wentworth and Laud frequently joked about the Lord Deputy's greater skill in modern languages and Wentworth enjoyed peppering his letters with French or Spanish expressions (sometimes incomprehensible to the archbishop) as well as Latin tags. Wentworth alternated this learned wordplay, however, with northern expressions and tales from Yorkshire, e.g. Wentworth to Laud, 3 Jan. 1635/6, Str P 6, pp. 294, 297; 9 March 1635/6, Str P 6, p. 334.

[74]   Kearney, *Strafford*, pp. 93, 97. In 1635, Laud warned Wentworth of whispers at court that his proceedings in Ireland were 'overfull of personall prosecutions against men of quality', such as Clanricard and Mountnorris, while in July of the same year he had explained that Pembroke and Salisbury had moved the king to allow Cork to come to England on the basis 'that a nobleman of his rank may not be disgraced there in a public court of justice', see 16 Nov. 1635, Str P 6, p. 280 (Knowler, I, 479); Laud, VII, 150.

was 'muche uppon the stage of town and Court... and so Prince like in every particular he styles himself in the plurall number viz. *we* did thus, and *our* toe was hurt beeing afflicted with the infirmity called the gowt'.[75] Clare may have mocked, but there was no disguising the newly won prestige and status that Wentworth had gained during his absence and the magnitude of his initial impact on his return to England.

His journey to England initially helped to reassure him of his success, but there is a rich irony in the fact that Wentworth felt more despondent about his position precisely when, on returning to court and personal access to the monarch, he should have felt most in control. He felt let down that the king would not grant him an earldom (as usual, Wentworth stressed the need for conspicuous symbolic honours if he were to be a successful royal representative). But he also felt himself to be weak at court, where admission to the king's presence was a far more formal affair than when it had been achieved by letter and where he was the subject of a number of scandalous rumours.[76] Such exclusion was all the more galling for a man used to exercising vice-regal powers and enjoying the concomitant status. He returned to Ireland greatly depressed and in the following years found it increasingly hard to preserve his influence at court.

There may be more than mere matter for irony here. There is a sense in which, initially, at any rate, Wentworth was indeed able to exert control over events more easily when away from court than when he was present there. Wentworth knew that he was no courtier – he lacked the courtly graces of a Holland or an Arundel and the queen scarcely concealed her dislike of him. More importantly, Wentworth at Whitehall lacked the impact that he could make as a distant Deputy, where he was a qualitatively different minister, whose dispatches were often eagerly awaited. If Wentworth's absence from court presented his enemies with many opportunities to disparage him, it also allowed his supporters to put the best

[75] For the reaction to Wentworth's arrival in England see Leicester to Wentworth, 8/18 July 1636, Knowler, II, 9 (an informative, if flattering report) and Wentworth to Wandesford, 25 July 1636, Knowler, II, 16, 21. Clare to Haughton, 1 Feb. 1635/6, P. R. Seddon (ed.), *Letters of John Holles, 1587–1637* (3 vols., Thoroton Society, xxi, xxxv, xxxvi, 1975–86), III, p. 477, italics mine.

[76] Wedgwood, pp. 210–16; Charles I to Wentworth, 13 Jan. 1635/6, Str P 3, p. 244 (Knowler, I, 508–9); Wentworth to Charles I, 23 Aug. 1636, Str P 3, pp. 259–60 (Knowler, II, 26); Wentworth to Charles I, 10 Sept. 1636, Str P 3, p. 262; Clarke, 'Sir Piers Crosby', pp. 143, 146.

possible gloss on the absent Deputy's activities and motives. Indeed, historians may need to qualify some of the *exclusive* importance that they have traditionally attached to physical presence at court. Presence by proxy or by letter – when properly monitored and backed up by an efficient information network – could, at times, play a highly important role in the practice of politics in the seventeenth century.

CHAPTER 6

Thomas Wentworth and the political thought of the Personal Rule

Anthony Milton

The political thought of the government of the Personal Rule is a subject that has not yet found its historian. It was only a minor preoccupation for earlier generations of historians, who were content to trace a polarised ideological world back to the early years of James's reign, in which divine-right monarchy and its adherents were pitted against the zealous upholders of English constitutionalism. In more recent years, however, revisionist historians have evolved a more subtle and persuasive account of English political thought under James I. Rather than the traditional polarised model, they have instead emphasised the degree of ideological consensus that was present before 1625. Seemingly contradictory political theories and languages – ascending and descending theories of the origins of government, divine-right kingship and the 'ancient constitution', the theories of common law and the royal prerogative – were held in an all-consuming embrace. Apparent contradictions remained unexplored due to the operation of agreed linguistic conventions which meant that different principles operated within different contexts. Political conflict therefore had no constitutional dimension: it emerged from a shared set of ideas and ideals. There was thus no distinctive set of 'royalist' or 'absolutist' political ideas.[1]

The question of what was different about the policies and principles of the government of Charles I has therefore become a more urgent one. While the emergence of 'new counsels' in the later 1620s has been discussed in detail in the work of a number of 'post-

I would like to express my grateful appreciation to the editor of this volume for encouraging me to write this chapter, and for providing me with a stream of invaluable references from, and guidance in using, the Strafford Papers.

[1] G. Burgess, *The Politics of the Ancient Constitution: An Introduction to English Political Thought, 1603–1642* (1992); C. S. R. Russell, *The Causes of the English Civil War* (Oxford, 1990), ch. 6; K. Sharpe, *Politics and Ideas in Early Stuart England* (1989), ch. 1.

revisionist' historians, the political philosophy of the Personal Rule
has remained relatively unexplored territory.

Clearly things changed in some way during the 1630s: the Long
Parliament was overwhelmed with complaints and fears of prerogative rule, and the infringement of traditional rights and liberties. But
were these fears justified? If we study the public image erected by the
government of the Personal Rule, there seems to be plentiful
evidence that the regime deliberately eschewed the open public
advocacy of 'absolutist' styles of thought. This was prompted in part
by the fears and rumours endemic at the beginning of the Personal
Rule that an autocratic style of monarchical government was
intended.[2]

This anxiety to dissociate the government from a straightforwardly absolutist complexion is evident from the very beginning of
the Personal Rule. After the dissolution of Parliament in 1629,
Charles was particularly concerned that his actions might be
maliciously misrepresented to the populace. He was therefore
especially alarmed by the circulation of a paper originally composed
in 1614 which urged the king 'to bridle the impertinency of
Parliament' by undertaking a military coup, establishing garrisons
in every town with mercenary troops, and imposing new taxes solely
on the authority of the crown. Charles anxiously set up an investigation to track down those who had distributed the document,
regarding it as a serious smear against the royal government which,
the king explained to the Privy Council, made proposals that were
'fitter to be practised in a Turkish State then amongst Christians'. A
proclamation warned that those raising or nourishing such false
reports would be severely punished.[3] Around the same time, Sir
Robert Filmer's *Patriarcha* seems to have been expressly turned
down for publication by the king. Another 'absolutist' work, Sir
Francis Kynaston's tract on parliaments, which defended the king's
right to tax without them, was certainly read at court, but does not
appear to have been recommended for publication. William Laud
may have had Filmer's and Kynaston's tracts in mind, and possibly
others, when he stated at his trial that several absolutist tracts had
been   written   but   denied   publication   during   the   Personal

---

[2] K. Sharpe, *The Personal Rule of Charles I* (1992), p. 58.
[3] Gardiner, VII, 138–40; L. J. Reeve, *Charles I and the Road to Personal Rule* (Cambridge, 1989),
     pp. 158–62; P. R. Seddon (ed.), *Letters of John Holles, 1587–1637* (3 vols., Thoroton Society,
     xxi, xxxv, xxvi, 1975–86), I, pp. lxix–lxxi.

Rule.[4] Similarly, when John Cowell's notorious *Interpreter* was discovered being surreptitiously reprinted in the late 1630s, those involved were hunted down and prosecuted by Laud, and the government expressly upheld the earlier prohibition on its printing. When one over-eager defender of the king's policies accused Judge Richard Hutton of treason after his decision in favour of Hampden in the case of ship money, the man was fined at the suit of the king and imprisoned.[5]

Clearly, then, the government of the Personal Rule was highly sensitive to any association with outspokenly public 'absolutist' trends of thought. But why did Charles's policies still generate such fears? One answer has been to suggest that it was not Charles's ideas that caused opposition, but his actions. A further refinement of this position has suggested that Charles upheld no new ideas, but that his presentation of ideas and policies was 'unidiomatic'. As Dr Sharpe has suggested, Charles's difficulties emerged, not from the unpopular or radical nature of the policies themselves, but rather from his problems in conveying their conservatism to a worried and sceptical population.[6] Other historians have suggested that Charles's lack of aptitude for personal propaganda was simply one aspect of a more general 'apolitical' temperament – his political problems therefore essentially derived from a personality ill-suited to practical politics, rather than from a novel political programme.[7]

But can we really write of the Personal Rule as lacking any distinctive political philosophy? Part of the problem in testing any arguments concerning the political aims and ideology of the Personal Rule is that it spawned no great ideologues. Kynaston, Filmer and others, while associated in varying degrees with the court, were marginal figures whose ideas did not gain them ostentatious royal

---

[4]   Sir Robert Filmer, *Patriarcha and Other Writings*, ed. J. P. Sommerville (Cambridge, 1991), p. viii; E. S. Cope, *Politics without Parliaments, 1629–1640* (1987), pp. 27–8; Laud, III, 400. It was obviously in Laud's interests to make such a claim in these circumstances, but as a rule Laud does not at any stage seem to have told deliberate untruths at his trial, even if he often withheld incriminating evidence. Moreover, Laud claimed that he had these unpublished tracts by him at that time – a claim unlikely to be made if Laud could not make it good before his accusers.

[5]   D. Freist, 'The formation of opinion and the communication network in London, 1637–*c*.1645' (unpublished Ph.D. thesis, University of Cambridge, 1992), pp. 51–3, 87–8; Knowler, II, 180.

[6]   Burgess, *Politics*, pp. 200–03, 209–10, 213; Sharpe, *Charles I*, p. 197.

[7]   Russell, *Causes*, pp. 198–203; Reeve, *Charles I*, pp. 199–200.

support.[8] But if we look more closely at the ministers of the Personal Rule, Sir Thomas Wentworth stands out in particular as a figure permitting some more detailed study. His correspondence is voluminous, and his natural loquaciousness may possibly provide us with a set of values that can be read off from his words and actions.

At first sight, Strafford would seem to offer more straightforward endorsement for consensual models of early Stuart political discourse. Here is a man who in the 1620s urged a view of the body politic in which King and Parliament worked in harmony; who resisted the Forced Loan and supported the Petition of Right, yet was happy to be co-opted as one of Charles's ministers in the 1630s. At his trial in 1641 he re-emphasised the view that he had held in the 1620s and which he vowed to carry to his grave: 'that the prerogative of the Crown and Liberty of the Subject should be equally looked upon, and served together, but not apart'. A number of witnesses testified at Wentworth's trial to his private insistence that the government should be kept within the law, that the prerogative of the crown and the privilege of the subject should be balanced together, and that parliaments were the happiest way to keep harmony between the king and his people. In his last speech at the scaffold, Wentworth still denied the charge that he was hostile to parliaments, and emphasised that 'I was so farre from being against Parliaments, That I did allwayes think the Parliaments of England were the most happy constitutions that any Kingdome or Nation lived under, and the best means under God to make the king & people happy.'[9] It is small wonder, then, that many historians over the years have suggested that Wentworth and his opponent Pym shared mostly the same body of ideas, and that it was circumstances alone that had pushed them apart.[10]

However, there is a danger that this view of Strafford's political thinking almost entirely leaves out the most important decade of his political career – the 1630s. It is all too tempting to presuppose a continuous strand linking Wentworth's language as an MP in the 1620s with his speeches at his trial in 1641. This temptation is further increased by the tendency of historians of political thought such as

---

[8]   L. Levy Peck, 'Kingship, counsel and law in early Stuart Britain' in J. G. A. Pocock (ed.), *The varieties of British political thought, 1500–1800* (Cambridge, 1993), pp. 107, 111–13.

[9]   J. H. Timmis, *Thine is the kingdom* (Alabama, 1974), pp. 115, 116, 117, 171; *A Briefe and Perfect Relation of the Answeres and Replies of Thomas Earle of Strafford* (1647), p. 105.

[10] Gardiner, IX, 371; C. S. R. Russell, *Unrevolutionary England*, (1990), pp. xvii–xviii; J. P. Kenyon, *The Stuart Constitution, 1603–1688* (Cambridge, 1966), pp. 190–1.

Dr Burgess to concentrate their attention on the arena of public political debate – and most especially in Parliament. This inevitably privileges the 1620s over the 1630s, when Parliament did not sit, and Wentworth felt called upon to make relatively few recorded public speeches, even though he was wielding most political power. To read the principles behind Wentworth's conduct as a minister forward from the 1620s, when he was manoeuvring for position on a local and national level, seems unwise. There are even greater interpretative problems in trying to read Wentworth's 1630s policies back from 1641, and his public declarations at his trial. Wentworth was on trial for his life, and therefore appealing to the ideas and principles of his political enemies, who were sitting in judgement on him. In these circumstances, the last thing that we should expect of him is a candid and objective account of his political beliefs. It is vital, then, to read Wentworth's thoughts during the 1630s in their own right. Moreover, a study of the private as well as the public language of a royal minister may shed different light on the rhetorical foundations of the Personal Rule.

I

This study of Wentworth's political ideas will focus first on his attitudes to law, and then on his views and conduct towards parliaments. It is not difficult to find Wentworth emphasising in the 1620s the need for the king to work within the law, and in 1641 his emphasis, in defending the king's policies, was on the exercise of the king's prerogative in cases of extreme necessity, where the safety of the kingdom was at stake. It has rightly been observed in revisionist work that the common law always allowed for the absolute prerogative of the crown – the only conflicts concerned the extent and nature of its use. Elsewhere – and most notably at his trial – Strafford emphasised the need for a constant balance between law and prerogative. They should be served together, and they naturally worked in harmony, 'hand in hand together'. The question, he opined, should never be raised 'whether the King be above the law or the law above the King'.[11]

However, alongside these commonplace platitudes, we must note Wentworth's regularly voiced conviction that the law had gone much

---

[11]   Timmis, *Thine is the Kingdom*, pp. 80, 114–15, 133–4.

too far, and that the time had come for the prerogative to reassert control – the law invoked in his models of ideal harmony was very different from the law as he saw it currently active in the kingdom. This was the constant emphasis in his correspondence surrounding his roles in the Council in the North and in Ireland, where prerogative courts were championed. If the ultimate end was a harmony, it was to be on the king's terms, and it was for him to decide when a 'balance' had been achieved. Moreover, to redress the balance required a vigorous clawing back of the powers which the law had claimed for itself. This would not look pretty. As Wentworth explained to Laud regarding the situation in Ireland, the rights of the Crown and Church could not be recovered 'unless a little violence and extraordinary means be used for the raising again as there has been for the pulling down'. He reiterated to the Council, in the king's presence, that 'where a Sovereignty... was going down the Hill, the Nature of a Man did so easily slide into the Paths of an uncontrouled Liberty, as it would not be brought back without Strength, not to be forced back up the Hill again, but by Vigour and Force'. If Wentworth were to come across any person not 'intirely set for the Service of my Master... if he came in my Reach... I must knock him soundly over the Knuckles'. When all was properly settled again, Wentworth reassured his hearers, he would change his temper and rule by 'soft and moderate Counsels'. If the end was harmonious, then the means towards it most certainly were not. Viewed in this context, the remark alleged against Wentworth at his trial, that 'the King's little Finger should be heavier than the Loins of the Law', while it may not have been truly spoken by him, does yet have an authentic Wentworthian ring to it.[12]

As his main aim was to undermine the grip of the law as currently constituted, Wentworth was also given in his private correspondence to reserve his sharpest language for lawyers and judges. There was, it is true, a general popular tradition of hostility towards the legal profession which an emphasis on the 'common-law mind' has sometimes minimised.[13] However, this mostly developed a critique of lawyers as exploiters of the common people, whereas Wentworth saw

---

[12] T. Ranger, 'Strafford in Ireland: a revaluation', in T. Aston (ed.), *Crisis in Europe, 1560–1660* (1965), p. 282; Knowler, II, 20–1; Timmis, *Thine is the Kingdom*, pp. 73–4.

[13] W. Prest, 'The English Bar, 1550–1700', in W. Prest (ed.), *Lawyers in Early Modern Europe and America* (1981) pp. 73–4; C. W. Brooks, *Pettyfoggers and Vipers of the Commonwealth* (Cambridge, 1986), pp. 132–8.

the danger as lying more in their trespassing on the rights of the crown. Especially when active as Lord President of the Council in the North, and as head of the prerogative court, Wentworth regularly voiced his contempt for the 'moot men' and 'gownmen'. In 1633, urging the dismissal of one judge – 'a peevish indiscreet piece of Flesh' – Wentworth confessed to Cottington: 'I disdain to see the Gownmen in this sort hang their Noses over the Flowers of the Crown, blow and snuffle upon them, till they take both Scent and Beauty off them.' Frustrated by an attorney in a land dispute in the same year, Wentworth complained that the lawyer had acted 'out of a Popularity and vanity to be therby taken to be a kind of Valenton for the subiectes liberty'. He declared to Archbishop Laud his determination to 'see my master's power set out of wardship and above the expositions of Sir Edward Coke and his Year books'. In this noble work, Wentworth confessed that 'it grieves me to the soul that your lordship should apprehend any so wretched as to tread still so tenderly as it were upon the ice'.[14]

If Wentworth, in attacking 'Sir Edward Coke and his Year books', slaughtered one of the sacred cows of the common-law tradition, he was prepared to aim even higher. For all his defence of Magna Carta in the parliamentary debates on the Petition of Right, Wentworth was not prepared to hear it cited against the king's wishes once he was in the king's service. In December 1633, in a letter to Sir John Coke, he complained of an individual who would not pay the Muster Master or supply his knighthood fine that he was 'in brief as arrant a saucy Magna Charta man as is in all the Country'.[15] A phrase like 'Magna Charta man' should give us pause: while it might be dismissed as a throw-away remark, it surely constitutes a conscious rejection of one of the taboos of the language of the 'common-law mind'. Central to any language or discourse are its shibboleths and heresies, and here Wentworth seemed to be developing his own version of the discourse that Laud and others had created that was powered by a fear of 'popularity'.[16] For Wentworth, however, the crown's enemy was not the many-headed, anti-monarchical multi-

---

[14] Wentworth to Lord Coventry, 10 Sept. 1635, Str P 8, pp. 260–1 (I owe this reference to Julia Merritt); Wentworth to Cottington, 22 Oct. 1633, Knowler, I, 130; Same to same, 15 Sept. 1633, Str P 3, p. 19; Wentworth to Laud, 23 Oct. 1633, Str P 8, pp. 33–4.

[15] Wentworth to Coke, 23 Dec. 1633, Str P 5, p. 36. I am grateful to Julia Merritt for this reference.

[16] On fears of 'popularity' see R. Cust, 'Charles I and a draft Declaration for the 1628 Parliament', *Historical Research* 63 (1990), pp. 143–61.

tude, but rather those who manipulated the law to serve their own private ends rather than the public ends of the monarch. These were all reflections prompted by the state of the law in the North. But in Ireland too, Wentworth saw the law pitted against the prerogative, with the judiciary the most at fault. 'All the judges', he complained to Coke, 'pronounce that for law which makes for the securing of the subject's estate wherein they have so full an interest.'[17]

This should not be taken to imply that Wentworth was simply not interested in following legal process. On the contrary, like other ministers of the Personal Rule, he was confident that the law could be bent to support the royal will. The whole basis of his defence at his trial was an appeal to the letter of the law, and Wentworth was always extremely careful to make sure that he had covered himself. None of his servants in Ireland was more important to Wentworth, or more trusted, than Sir George Radcliffe, his legal expert, whose ingenious legal trickery was vital in enabling the crown to regain the political initiative in Ireland. Strafford's dexterous and duplicitous exploitation of legal loopholes, quibbles and technicalities, and his systematic concentration of judicial power in the hands of the prerogative court of Castle Chamber, over which he directly presided, enabled him to humiliate his enemies and restore the powers of crown and Church alike.[18]

It should be emphasised, however, that these liberties were not being taken solely due to the anomalous constitutional position of Ireland. Wentworth himself emphasised bluntly to Laud that there were lessons here to be learnt for England: 'I know no reason but you may as well use the Common Lawyers in England as I, poor beagle, do here... I am confident that the king... is able by his wisdom and ministers to carry any just and honourable action through all imaginary opposition, for real there can be none; ... *the debts of the crown taken off, you may govern as you please*'.[19]

Wentworth's chief intent was not then to subvert the law, but to bring it more firmly within the powers of the monarch, and this could only be achieved by striking at the 'Magna Charta men' and 'Sir Edward Coke and his Year books'. This is important to bear in mind because the Personal Rule, as recent historians have rightly reminded us, had 'a strong legalistic strain'. It justified itself by

---

[17]   Ranger, 'Strafford', pp. 279–80.
[18]   *Ibid.*, pp. 287–91.
[19]   Knowler, I, p. 173, italics mine.

constant appeal to tradition and custom. This was not a simple smokescreen, but reflected the sincere self-image that Charles cultivated.[20] But if they did not espouse the simple patriarchal language of a Robert Filmer, Charles and his ministers were nevertheless keen to exploit the law in a systematic and unscrupulous fashion. Indeed, the term 'legal tyranny' has been used by one recent historian to describe Charles's persistent abuse of legal formularies and intimidation of the judiciary.[21] If the law could be bent to Charles's will, it made the invocation of new and disconcerting 'absolute' powers unnecessary. The regular claims by Charles and his ministers that the rule of law and the rule of prerogative were intimately related might appear to some as a recognition of the legal restraints on the king's prerogative, but could be read just as easily as an attempt by the prerogative to lay claim to the rhetorical force of the law, and also to make the law dependent on the king. From the king's perspective, if law and prerogative must go together, this surely meant that law must follow wherever he chose to take his prerogative. Any laws which seemed to impede the desires of the crown could therefore be considered illegitimate. A failure to recognise the justice of the king's claims could therefore be deemed to be itself illegal – as revealed most strikingly in the prosecution of the Galway jurors for having decided against the king.[22] Morever, if law was the handmaid of prerogative, it meant that whatever positive laws seemed to impede the desires of the crown could be construed as irregular recent corruptions that must be reversed in the name of 'custom' and 'tradition'. Indeed, even Charles, with all his reverence for custom, was happy to seize on innovatory initiatives when they could help to secure his position. In 1640, when faced with Londoners' recalcitrance over the election of the new Lord Mayor, and the suggestion from the Council that the king should refuse to admit their mayor-elect to office, the king was happy to shrug off the warning that such a policy was unprecedented: 'so that we may get that [the loan of money from London], let inovat, and spare not, it

---

[20] Sharpe, *Charles I*, pp. 194–7.
[21] J. S. Morrill, *The Nature of the English Revolution* (1993), pp. 287–91. While Dr Morrill's point about 'legal tyranny' is well made here, I must however query his suggestion in the same section that the word 'tyranny' was used exclusively to describe the bishops (*ibid.*, pp. 293–4). Anti-Strafford materials are drenched in accusations of tyranny, and the phrase 'arbitrary *and tyrannical* government' recurs like a mantra in the trial proceedings.
[22] Hugh Kearney, *Strafford in Ireland, 1633–41* (Manchester, 1959; 2nd edn, Cambridge, 1989), pp. 95–6.

may be a good example to me, to doe the lyke, upon occasion
hereafter and I see not why ye may not use this occasion so as to
make them lend the willinger'.[23]

II

Wentworth was similarly equivocal in his approach to parliaments.
Echoing the king's declarations, Wentworth was not opposed to
parliaments in principle.[24] Indeed, he had been an active parliamentarian in the 1620s and, as we are constantly reminded, he differed
from many of the advocates of 'new counsels' in the 1620s, and from
his own allies at court (such as Laud and Cottington), in his
continued confidence in the value of parliament. It was Wentworth
who persuaded the king to summon a parliament in Ireland in 1634,
and he was one of the strongest advocates of the calling of the Short
Parliament in 1640, and one of those most obviously disappointed by
the king's dissolution of that assembly. Nevertheless, while Wentworth was clearly a man who believed that parliaments were useful,
and indeed sometimes necessary, and was not therefore a classic
'absolutist' thinker, it is instructive to study quite how he believed
that parliaments should be managed, and the role that they had to
play in national politics.

The parliament called in Ireland in 1634 is an event that has been
surprisingly little discussed by English historians, despite its obvious
value as a guide to government thinking on parliaments during the
years of the Personal Rule.[25] In fact, it was the years of the so-called
'personal rule' that witnessed the only successful parliaments of
Charles's reign – the 'Coronation Parliament' of 1633 in Scotland
and the Irish parliament of 1634–5. Indeed, Wentworth stated frankly
in a letter to his cousin George Butler that the 1634 parliament had
been 'the only ripe Parliament that hath been gathered in my Time,
all the rest have been a green Fruit broken from the Bow, which, as
you know, are never so kindly or pleasant'.[26]

---

[23] J. Malcolm, 'Charles I on innovation: a confidential directive on an explosive issue',
Bulletin of the Institute of Historical Research 53 (1980), pp. 252–5. Charles was here dealing
with the same aldermen whom Wentworth had threatened to hang: C. S. R. Russell, *The
Fall of the British Monarchies, 1637–1642* (Oxford, 1991), p. 141.

[24] See Cust, 'Charles I and a draft Declaration', p. 156; Sharpe, *Charles I*, pp. 702–5.

[25] The parliament is not even mentioned in Cope, *Politics*, and evokes little discussion in
Sharpe, *Charles I*, p. 705.

[26] Knowler, 1 420. On the Coronation Parliament, see A. I. Macinnes, *Charles I and the Making
of the Covenanting Movement, 1625–41* (Edinburgh, 1991), pp. 86–9.

The Irish parliament of 1634 was very much Wentworth's creation, and his correspondence with King Charles and other ministers concerning the project sheds particularly interesting light on the opinions of both men towards such assemblies. Wentworth was convinced from the outset that the calling of a parliament would enable him to strengthen his hand. He explained delightedly to a correspondent how simply playing up the prospect of a parliament to the Privy Council had enabled him to exploit them the more effectively.[27] But when it came to the running of the parliament, Wentworth was determined to lay his plans carefully and well. He reassured the king from the outset that the parliament would do him no harm, and that he would be happy to dissolve it on the slightest pretext. Indeed, in a strikingly frank letter which William Knowler clearly thought it best to omit from his published volumes of Wentworth's correspondence, the Lord Deputy mollified the king in forthright language:

[I] asseure your Ma[jes]tye I have Couradge Sufficient to Advise the breatche of a hundred Parliaments, rather then my Maister should suffer in the least Circumstance of Honour, or Prerogative, and yet serve at after to your Power and Greatnesse, in despite of all popular opinion or opposition, wth ye same strictnesse and Constancy of mind, as if noe such matter had befallen us, as I well trust it never shall.[28]

Clearly, Wentworth was aware that Charles needed a great deal of reassurance and persuasion before he would be happy with a parliament. But Wentworth also forwarded to Charles a detailed plan of action as to how the parliament would be conducted, which reveals a good deal of how Wentworth himself believed that parliaments should behave.

Wentworth needed the parliament in order to grant sufficient supplies as to enable him to keep his army in a state of readiness – it was the army that, as Wentworth explained to the king, was the ultimate foundation of his Irish government, 'that Pillar of your Authority' which was 'of absolute Necessity'. It was also inevitable that an Irish parliament would push for a renewal of the so-called Graces of 1628, some of which Wentworth felt to be potentially 'of great Prejudice to the crown'. Concerned that the parliament 'will press for them all, and uncertain what Humour the denying any of them might move in their Minds', Wentworth therefore proposed

---

[27] Wentworth to Coke, 3 Aug. 1633, Str P 5, pp. 9–10.
[28] Wentworth to Charles, 25 Apr. 1634, Str P 3, p. 68.

that the parliament should occupy two sessions, one in summer and one in winter, 'in the former, to settle your Majesty's Supply, and in the latter to enact so many of those Graces as in Honour and Wisdom should be judged equal, when the putting aside of the rest should be of no ill Consequence to other your royal Purposes'.[29]

The separation of supply and the redress of grievances was of central importance to Wentworth's scheme, and this was not simply a matter of administrative convenience: Wentworth was anxious that a clear conceptual division should be made between the business of the two separate sessions. Speaking to the Irish Privy Council prior to the calling of the parliament, Wentworth made it absolutely clear that there was to be no attempt to bargain in any way, or even to argue for a quid pro quo. The king, he emphasised 'expected to be trusted... he would not in any Case admit of Conditions, or be proceeded withal, as by way of Bargain or Contract'. The key to a successful parliament, Wentworth continued, lay in the parliament's willingness to give the king a completely free hand, and to trust that he would use such a hand graciously:

it was absolutely in their Power to have the happiest Parliament that ever was in this Kingdom; that their Way was most easy, no more than to put an absolute Trust in the king, without offering any Condition or Restraint at all upon his Will, and then let them assure themselves to receive back unasked all that reasonably and fittingly they could expect.

As Wentworth explained, the problems that had occurred in English parliaments had been caused by 'nothing else' but their failure to trust the king.[30]

We should not assume that the promise of redress of grievances was simply a ruse. Although it is true that Wentworth was most concerned to give parliament the impression that the Graces would be granted when he actually intended no such thing, he was however very eager that Charles should provide some unanticipated and gracious rewards to the parliament.[31] But the most important point was that this must not be coerced; there was no sense that redress of

---

[29]   Knowler, I, 185 (cf. p. 61), 184. On the Graces see A. Clarke, *The Old English in Ireland, 1625–42* (1966), pp. 44–59.

[30]   Knowler, I, 237, 239. Wentworth made similar points in his speech to both Houses of Parliament on 15 July 1634: *ibid.*, I, 289–90. See also Charles's comments on the issue of bargaining in his Declaration after the dissolution of the Short Parliament: C. S. R. Russell, *The Causes of the English Civil War* (Oxford, 1990), p. 198.

[31]   See, e.g., Wentworth to Charles, 19 July 1634, Str P 3, p. 103.

grievances was a parliamentary right.[32] It was central to Wentworth's whole position that any such grant must be seen as the free gift of the king.

Moreover, while they might pass laws and raise supply, Wentworth made it clear that he did not consider that parliaments – whether they be in Ireland or in England – had any right to give direction to government policy or to exercise control over state administration. Commenting on Hampden's case in private correspondence with the judge Richard Hutton, Wentworth stated emphatically that private citizens must not ever seek to pry into 'Mysteries of State'. Kings can naturally see further than 'ordinary common Persons' where any past or present 'necessity' might lie, and

> therefore it is a safe Rule for us all in the Fear of God to remit these supreme Watches to that Regal Power, whose Peculiar indeed it is; submit ourselves in these high Considerations to his Ordinance, as being no other than the Ordinance of God itself; and rather attend upon his Will, with Confidence in his Justice, Belief in his Wisdom, [and] Assurance in his parental Affections.[33]

Wentworth was here thinking particularly about Hampden's case, and this should remind us again that we cannot make facile distinctions between Wentworth's behaviour in Ireland and his view of affairs in England. Wentworth had no intention of spending his years tarrying in Ireland – the whole point of his administration was that it should act as a prolonged advertising campaign displaying the abilities that he could put to use in a suitably elevated position back in England. Wentworth was therefore emphatic that the Irish parliament provided significant lessons for the government's future conduct of parliaments in England. He joked with Laud that Cottington should be sent over to 'see and heare that which will make him the wiser and better speaker so long as he lives'. English commentators studied the Irish events with care and ruminated on possible indications that an English parliament might be on the cards. Wentworth did nothing to stifle such suggestions: after securing the first vote of subsidies, he even dared to broach the subject with Charles, suggesting that his success in Ireland 'carryes an Aspect towards England. For Scotland and Ireland haveing thus

---

[32] For some rather different contemporary views on supply and redress of grievances, see T. Cogswell, 'A low road to extinction? Supply and redress of grievances in the parliaments of the 1620s', *HJ* 33 (1990), pp. 283–303.

[33] Knowler, II, 380–1.

fairly begun, wee now sure if there be either Grace or witt left amongst us, shall be thirsty of the Occasion, your Majesty in your owne good tyme, may honour us withall wherin to Expiate our former follyes.' But Wentworth's basic message to Charles in the same letter was not that the time had come to share government. On the contrary, the 'Ground Plott' had now been set 'of the full Accomplishment of all your High Prerogatives and Powers in this Kingdome, where undoubtedly your ma[jes]ty may take your selfe to be as Absolute a Monarke as Christendome can sett forth any'.[34]

If Wentworth was keen to encourage the calling of an English parliament, he was however strongly against the idea of calling one when the king was in urgent need of funds, and therefore vulnerable to bargaining. In early 1637, when war with Spain seemed likely, Wentworth warned Charles of what to expect if the war was prolonged and Charles forced to summon a parliament 'in a Time so conditioned'.[35] As it was, an English parliament would not be called until 1640, and Wentworth was again one of those most insistent in urging it upon the king. We should not be surprised, then, that central to the conduct of the abortive Short Parliament was the attempt to gain supply without redress of grievances, which was to be delayed until a second, winter session. Recent historians have pondered over Charles's inability to recognise that the price of parliamentary supply would have to be immediate redress of religious and political grievances.[36] Rather than being simply a sign of the king's political inadequacies, however, it is surely possible that Charles's expectations were based on the specific advice and strategy of his political 'expert', Wentworth. This, after all, was what had supposedly worked in Ireland in 1634. As in 1634, Wentworth urged the parliament to grant the king their trust. The better to effect this policy, Wentworth did his best to promote a division between the Lords and the increasingly fractious Commons – again, just as he had successfully accomplished in the first session of the Irish parliament of 1634. All the time, Wentworth in the Lords and his secretary Sir Philip Mainwaring in the Commons drew members' attention to

---

[34] Wentworth to Charles, 19 July 1634, Str P 3, p. 102.

[35] Knowler, II, 61. Note also Sir John Melton's distinction between parliaments held at a time of 'tacite Necessity' (and when 'the current of his Majesties Prerogative is strong'), and the danger of summoning parliaments when there was 'an absolute Necessity to impell it': *ibid.*, I, 419.

[36] Russell, *Fall*, p. 93; Russell, *Causes*, p. 194.

the exemplary speed with which subsidies had been granted by the Irish parliament meeting at the same time in Dublin.[37]

The dissolution of the Short Parliament was much to Wentworth's own dismay, but it has hopefully been shown already that while Wentworth viewed parliaments as useful, his view of their role was fundamentally different to that of a man like Pym. They were not there to share in government, to bargain and negotiate, to comment on royal policy. Their summoning was a sign of the king's grace and favour and of the king's readiness 'to tread the ancient paths in public services'; it was not a right of parliaments or the people. And what parliaments most owed the king, Wentworth insisted, was trust. If parliaments had no right to meet, if they had a solemn duty to trust the king's promises, and if there must be no attempt at 'laying clogs or conditions upon the king' because 'Conditions are not to be admitted with any Subjects', it is not surprising that Wentworth was later reported as saying of the Short Parliament that, since supply had been denied by parliament, Charles had a right to raise the money anyway. His reported words, which Lord Conway at least admitted, were that 'if Parliament should not grant the king a sufficient supply, then the king was acquitted before God and man, and might use the authority put into his hands'. That Wentworth also claimed that the king was 'absolved from all rules of government' was more hotly disputed, but that Wentworth held the king to have a right to raise money if parliament did not fulfil its duty in granting supply is surely pertinent.[38] Wentworth was here speaking at a time of military crisis after the dissolution of the Short Parliament. But such language was not merely provoked by such a crisis. Wentworth made it clear to the Irish parliament in 1634 (and in language strikingly similar to the king's opening address to the English parliament of 1628) that the king was not bound in any way to work with them, and parliamentary taxation was not more legal than prerogative taxation: 'The King... desires this great Work may be... settled by Parliament, as the more beaten Path he covets to walk in, yet not more legal than if done by his Prerogative Royal, where the ordinary Way fails him.'[39]

[37] E. S. Cope and W. H. Coates (eds.), *Proceedings of the Short Parliament of 1640* (Camden Society, 4th ser., vol. 19, 1977), pp. 74, 173, 242; J. D. Maltby (ed.), *The Short Parliament (1640) Diary of Sir Thomas Aston* (Camden Society, 4th ser., vol. 35, 1988), p. 42.
[38] Knowler, I, 184, 290; Timmis, *Thine is the Kingdom*, pp. 109, 111, 112, 117.
[39] Knowler, I, 238.

The final emphasis in all of Wentworth's dealings with parliaments was the need for them to trust the king, and to trust Wentworth himself, as the king's representative.[40] In the 1620s, Wentworth had been far from willing to grant such trust, and had urged that it could not be given until the liberties of the subject had been assured. But now that he was in government, trust alone was the duty of citizens. This was enlightened despotism with a vengeance.

If Wentworth reveals a more 'absolutist' style within apparently traditional language, it should be emphasised that he cannot be marginalised from the government of the Personal Rule in the way that Filmer or Kynaston might be. Wentworth assured Charles I in correspondence that he would break a hundred parliaments and make him the most absolute king in Christendom because this was precisely what Charles wanted to hear, and to be reassured by. This was as much, if not more, the language of the Personal Rule than were all the masques and declarations that emphasised harmony, unity and consensus. Moreover, Wentworth's correspondence with Charles over his plans for the 1634 parliament show just how intolerant Charles was. While Charles was happy with the notion that there be two separate sessions, with supply coming first and separately, the king laid down further strict limitations: 'we will admit no Capitulations nor Demands or any Assurance under our Broad Seal, nor of sending over Deputies or Committees to treat here with us, nor of any Restraint in our Bill of Subsidies, nor of any Condition of not maintaining the Army'. If these conditions were not accepted by the members, and if they would not 'be satisfied by our royal Promise for the second Session, or shall deny or delay the passing of our Bills', then Charles insisted that Wentworth should dissolve the parliament forthwith, but continue to fund the army regardless. Any mention of conditions, or reluctance to act as a rubber stamp for Charles's specific desires, would thus result in the immediate dissolution of the parliament, and an Irish Forced Loan.[41]

Wentworth was sensitive enough to the experiences of the 1620s to

---

[40] For Strafford's obsessive, sometimes extravagant demands that councillors and parliaments should give *him* their personal trust, as well as Charles, see, e.g., Knowler, 1, 239. For his emphasis on the importance of trusting the king in the Short Parliament, see Cope and Coates (eds.), *Proceedings*, pp. 71, 73.

[41] Knowler, 1, 184.

know the sort of resistance that a forced loan might bring. In fact, the 1634 session passed a good deal less smoothly than Wentworth intended. He was therefore especially careful to ensure that no word of the proceedings crept back to England except through him. As presented to Charles by Wentworth, the 1634 parliament was indeed one after his own heart, in which subsidies were 'within an howers debate universally yealded unto by your Commons not one voyce dissenting without any offer of Condition or Demande at all on their Part'. Just as the moderate councillors of 1628 had discovered, the best strategy was to control the flow of information to Charles as much as possible, and to ensure that his direct contact with the parliament was minimal.[42] It was a dangerous game: a doubtless anxious Wentworth was informed by Sir George Butler in June 1635 that rumours were being spread and believed by Wentworth's enemies in England that the conclusion to the Irish parliament had not been a success.[43] It may well be that the price for Wentworth's duplicity and his raising of Charles's unrealistic expectations of parliamentary pliability was paid in 1640, when the disorders of the Short Parliament could not be hidden so effectively from Charles's gaze.

What was central to the parliamentary strategy of Wentworth and others, however, was that parliaments should never be held by the king under 'an absolute Necessity'. Parliaments were there to be respectful and submissive, and not to bargain. This sounded all well and good in theory, but in practice this policy was frustrated by the king. The problem was not that Charles was physically incapable of bargaining with his parliaments. But, in the 1620s as in the 1640s, Charles always bargained with the intention of reneging on agreements as soon as he had gained supply.[44] Charles's problem was that he had a natural aversion to parliaments. Wentworth was convinced that parliaments would only work effectively when the king was not desperate for supply. But unless he was desperate for supply, Charles would not call parliaments in the first place. This simply guaranteed that Charles only met parliaments when he was most likely to fall out with them.

[42] Wentworth to Charles, 19 July 1634, Str P 3, p. 102. Cf. R. Cust, 'Charles I, the Privy Council and the Parliament of 1628', *TRHS*, 6th ser., 2 (1992), pp. 33–4, 47.

[43] Sir George Butler to Wentworth, 10 June 1635, Str P 15/99. I am grateful to Julia Merritt for this reference. See also Kearney, *Strafford*, p. 58.

[44] Cust, 'Charles I... and the Parliament of 1628', pp. 44–5, 49; Cust, 'Charles I and a draft Declaration', pp. 156–7.

III

Can we talk of a political philosophy behind these actions, and indeed behind the Personal Rule in general? In the view of a number of recent historians, we cannot. The struggle to isolate a particular idea as being distinctive to Caroline political thinking has been mostly fruitless. The divine right of kings, for example, was a commonplace of early Stuart political thought – Charles's friends and enemies alike were happy to recognise it. The appeal of Wentworth and Charles to 'necessity' and 'reason of state' is again far from distinctive: both the supporters and the opponents of the Petition of Right, and of Charles's policies in the 1630s, made systematic recourse to these notions.[45] Moreover, if we take 'absolutism' to have as its basis a clearly stated and vigorously defended belief that the king can make law by himself, and that he has no need to call parliaments, then neither Charles nor his ministers can be made to subscribe to it.[46] As a number of historians have recently noted, Charles's policy of rule without parliament developed 'by default rather than from any positive, deliberate action'.[47]

Clearly, there is no simple pigeon-hole into which Wentworth and his master's political views can be placed. However, the suggestions either that this means that Charles had no distinctive political convictions, but was simply 'apolitical', or that it was merely Charles's actions rather than his ideas that caused conflict, are not solutions – they beg rather more questions than they answer. Most seriously, they imply a false antithesis between ideas and actions. The suggestion that it was the actions rather than the theories of Charles that created fear is not particularly helpful: theories cause widespread fear only if they are taken as holding the potential to be translated into action. Similarly, if people's actions are vastly different from what is expected of them by their contemporaries, then we may assume that they do not share the same ideas as their opponents as to what is right or wrong. Similarly, to suggest that disputes only occurred due to disagreements over the king's misuse of agreed powers is to identify the specific legal case made against the

[45] Russell, *Causes*, pp. 145–9; G. Burgess, 'The divine right of kings reconsidered', *English Historical Review* 425 (1992), pp. 837–61; R. Tuck, *Philosophy and Government, 1572–1651* (Cambridge, 1993), pp. 118–19.
[46] Russell, *Causes*, pp. 150–2.
[47] Cust, 'Charles I. . . and the Parliament of 1628', p. 49.

king, but does not help to answer the question of *why* the king felt justified in 'misusing' such powers. Again, to suggest that Charles was 'apolitical' is to imply that there is only one way of doing politics, and that if Charles was not following this approach then it was due to purely personal failings or a lack of imagination, rather than because he had a different idea of the way that politics should be carried out.[48]

Moreover, it is particularly unfortunate if historians of political thought resort to an antithesis between ideas and actions at a time when cultural historians are increasingly looking for political ideas in a whole range of cultural forms and actions, from masques, processions and household ordinances to architecture, music, paintings, and popular verses. Indeed, a rounded portrait of Wentworth's political views would have to include discussion of his taste in portraiture, architecture and court ceremonial. It would particularly impoverish views of the period if we were to grant a political philosophy only to those who express their views in the formal political treatises beloved of more recent political thinkers.

We need to begin by addressing rather more searchingly the fact that the outward face of the Personal Rule stressed law, custom and tradition. These were important themes in court culture and public debate alike. But our study of political thought cannot end there, and attention merely to public rhetoric may severely attenuate our understanding of the period. This is particularly true of the suggestion that Charles was not so much novel in his thinking as unidiomatic in the expression of his ideas. If, like Dr Burgess, we limit our attention to 'the rules governing the conduct of political debate in the public arena' we are pre-selecting our evidence: we should hardly be surprised that in the process we uncover a consensual set of political languages, and that political conflict emerges as a conflict over use of language and idiom. This is not to suggest that a study of the 'languages of political debate' is not a useful one – but it is a limited one, and should not be confused with the study of political ideas. Moreover, it could surely be argued that a study of 'the rules governing public debate' is seriously incomplete without a study of the things that were written or spoken but were considered to be inappropriate for public debate. This deficiency is compounded in Dr Burgess's work, as he explains that he is writing a study of 'the

[48] See references in notes 6 and 7 above. See also K. Sharpe and P. Lake (eds.), *Culture and Politics in Early Stuart England* (1994), introduction, p. 4.

structure of public discourse' which deliberately does not choose to
address 'what people said in the privacy of their families, or wrote in
the privacy of their studies... Whether people thought things that
they were unable to express publicly is a separate issue.'[49] It is
arguable whether this is indeed a separate issue; it is certainly not a
less important one. Moreover, when we examine private discourse
we need not simply move to what is discussed in the family home –
correspondence of ministers with the king is surely of some use to the
historian who seeks to evaluate the thinking behind public declarations of intent and legitimation.

Again, attention to 'the rules governing public discourse', as
analysed by recent historians, has done little to illuminate the views
of the king, as 'the rules' are taken as normative and behaviour that
breaks them is presented as being due to simple ignorance. For
example, one recent historian has suggested that Charles lacked 'any
sense of when it was appropriate to use the languages of absolute
prerogative'.[50] But Charles surely had a sense of when it was
appropriate; it was simply not the same sense as that held by some of
his subjects. If Charles did not always use accepted political
'languages' in the proper manner, it is more than likely that he was
not comfortable doing so. If he used the language of the royal
prerogative in a 'common-law' setting, it was presumably because he
felt that it belonged there, and also because he feared that some of
the traditional language of the 'common-law mind' at least potentially threatened his prerogative.

In fact, it is not impossible to divine some elements of a political
philosophy behind the policies of Wentworth and the king. In part it
is useful to remember that we are dealing, not with a single simple
language, but with a novel combination of elements from the
languages of law, custom, and prerogative. But there are also surely
elements of absolutism, too.[51] We need to be careful here. As a
number of historians have rightly emphasised, 'absolutism' is a
woolly term, and there are great contrasts in the thinking of a
number of 'absolutist' thinkers.[52] However, there is a danger that
absolutism is at times approached from the standpoint of thinkers

---

[49] Burgess, *Politics*, p. xi.   [50] *Ibid.*, p. 202.

[51] C. Holmes, 'Parliament, liberty, taxation and property' in J. H. Hexter (ed.), *Parliament and Liberty from the Reign of Elizabeth to the English Civil War* (Stanford, 1992), pp. 136–7.

[52] C. S. R. Russell, 'The theory of treason in the trial of Strafford', *English Historical Review* 80 (1965), pp. 35–6; J. W. Daly, 'The idea of absolute monarchy in seventeenth-century England', *HJ* 21 (1978), pp. 227–50.

such as Filmer, and that historians are employing an unrealistic yardstick for measuring 'absolutism'. If we assume that 'absolutism' necessarily insisted that a king must always be the maker of laws, and that parliaments were an irrelevance, then the ideas of Wentworth and the king inevitably appear moderate and traditional, if a little incoherent. However, if we look at an archetypal absolutist such as Bodin, we can find a similar incoherence. Bodin was most concerned to emphasise that sovereignty must be indivisible, and that mixed government was impossible. But he did not therefore believe that parliaments were unnecessary: on the contrary, he urged that they should be regularly called, and that taxation should always be levied through parliaments except in a case of absolute emergency. Bodin's concern was to emphasise that there were no *enforceable* limitations on the king's authority. But there were moral restrictions: absolute kings were subject to the law of nature, and must not infringe upon their subjects' liberty and property. Monarchs were also 'bound' by customary fundamental law, but not in a way that could be enforced by their subjects.[53]

If we look behind the rhetoric used by Wentworth and Charles, and concentrate instead on the presuppositions that underlay their treatment of the law and parliaments: their conceptual distinction between a parliamentary provision of supply which must be automatic and unconditional, and a redress of grievances, which must not be requested but made entirely dependent upon the wishes of the king; their insistence that 'Conditions are not to be admitted with any Subjects'; their emphasis on the king's power to redress the balance of law and prerogative as he saw fit; their conviction that the king alone has the right to identify a condition of 'necessity'; we find, behind these assumptions, there surely lurks more than a whiff of the absolutist notion that sovereignty was indivisible, and truly mixed government impossible.

Tracing parallels between the ideas of Wentworth and of Bodin is not entirely fanciful. To begin with, it should be emphasised that Wentworth was not averse to reading works of political philosophy. Among works that we know him to have read, we may list Raleigh's *Prerogative of Parliaments* and Buchanan's *De Jure Regni apud Scotos*. For all his self-representation as the simple parochial northern squire,

[53] Jean Bodin, *On Sovereignty. Four Chapters from The Six Books of the Commonwealth*, ed. J. H. Franklin (Cambridge, 1992), introduction; J. H. Franklin, *Jean Bodin and the Rise of Absolutist Theory* (Cambridge, 1973), ch. 5.

Wentworth had travelled to France in the years 1612–13, and had had plenty of opportunity to study the effects of the civil wars which had prompted Bodin's thinking. We know from his travel diary that he purchased and made copious notes from a number of political treatises, including works by Tacitus, Lipsius, Duplessis-Mornay, several histories of the French Wars of Religion, and Bodin's *Republic*.[54] Bodin was also a major influence behind a work which constituted perhaps the most sophisticated defence of the policies of the Personal Rule to be written during Wentworth's lifetime – *The Elements of Law Natural and Politic* by Thomas Hobbes. Completed in 1640, Hobbes's work was apparently intended as a philosophical defence of the policies of the Personal Rule, and his dedicatory epistle to the earl of Newcastle suggests that the earl might pass the book on to 'those whom the matter it containeth most nearly concerneth'. Clearly the king and his ministers were intended here, and quite possibly Wentworth himself, as he and Hobbes shared two close acquaintances in Newcastle and Sir Gervase Clifton. Hobbes's anxious flight from England in November 1640 may well have been prompted by Strafford's impeachment, and the fear that the *Elements* might become part of the Commons' investigations into Strafford's machinations against the liberties of the subject. Hobbes's work contains (among other things) an emphatic denial of the idea of 'mixed monarchy', a rejection of the notion that subjects had absolute property rights, and a firm affirmation that subjects had no right to exercise private judgement when the security of the realm was held to be at stake. Mixed constitutions simply did not exist, and as parliament possessed no right to punish the king they could not be said to partake of sovereignty in any meaningful sense: 'he that cannot of right be punished, cannot of right be resisted; and he that cannot of right be resisted, hath coercive power over all the rest, and thereby can frame and govern their actions at his pleasure'.[55]

There is no need to assert any direct link between the ideas of Wentworth and his sovereign, and those of Bodin or Hobbes. But to notice these parallels should at least serve to remind us that ideas of absolute royal sovereignty need not take the extreme forms created

[54] Cooper, pp. 176, 266; Str P 30 (Wentworth's travel diary), *passim*.
[55] Thomas Hobbes, *The Elements of Law Natural and Politic*, ed. F. Tonnies (2nd edn, 1969), pt 2 ch. 1; Tuck, *Philosophy*, pp. 313, 314; R. Tuck, *Hobbes* (Oxford, 1989), p. 24; J. P. Sommerville, *Thomas Hobbes: Political Ideas in Historical Context* (1992), pp. 18–19.

by Filmer, but could easily dress themselves in the raiment of tradition and regular parliaments.

If the king or Wentworth might have shrunk from the specific theories being enunciated by Hobbes, this should not make them an irrelevance. Dr Burgess has recently suggested that the 1630s and beyond might be typified as the time of 'the crisis of the common law', in which Charles's 'legal tyranny' prompted a confused anxiety that the law might not be a sufficiently strong or unambiguous guardian of peoples' liberties and interests.[56] This is surely true, but we must not neglect that there were other developments, too. The events of the 1620s also created fears in several quarters of the threat of 'popularity', and a concern that parliaments were exceeding the bounds of their legitimate authority. In the writings of Filmer, Kynaston, Hobbes, Heylyn and others one may discern one set of answers to a 'crisis of the mixed constitution' – a crisis that is just as evident in the anxieties and presuppositions behind the thoughts and actions of Charles, Wentworth, Laud, Finch and others.

Undoubtedly, the Personal Rule is not best approached through a study of the thinking of Filmer and Hobbes. They represented a small constituency, and indeed even the less rigorously philosophical assertions of Wentworth cannot be taken as simply representative of the Personal Rule – there were a range of factions within the Council, with their own views of what government policy should be. Nevertheless, if the number of 'pure absolutists' was small and marginal, this does not make them an irrelevance. We may compare this situation *vis-à-vis* 'absolutism' with the role of 'Arminianism' in the Laudian Church. Very few Laudian churchmen can be clearly accused of 'Arminianism', still fewer of outright 'popery'. Indeed, the regime made a point of distancing itself from forthright and self-declared 'Arminian' thinkers, prevented publication of their views, and prosecuted them wherever possible as publicly as possible. Unambiguously 'Arminian' divines such as Samuel Hoard are the ecclesiastical equivalents of pure 'absolutists' such as Sir Robert Filmer and Sir Francis Kynaston. But if the Laudian regime was not formally guilty of Arminianism or of crypto-popery, and made a point of trying to avoid these charges where it could, it is nevertheless true that Laudians had a very different perception of Arminianism and popery than did their Calvinist critics. Moreover, while they

---

[56] Burgess, *Politics*, pp. 210–11, 214–30.

sought most of all to emphasise custom, tradition and legality in their reforms, and in their own terms were merely restoring the Church 'to the rules of her first reformation', they were blatantly disregarding it in practice, distorting laws, exhuming precedents, using an appeal to earlier, abandoned 'custom' in order to revile and discount more recent customs as merely corrupt. Moreover, the fact that Laudians stressed laws, custom, and reverence rather than doctrinal change does not mean that a set of innovatory doctrinal positions cannot be discerned behind their positions. Many of their presuppositions may also have been entirely compatible with Arminianism, even if they did all they could to avoid making such a direct association.[57]

It has been the argument of this essay that the political thought of the Personal Rule can be seen in a similar light. For all its stress on law, tradition and custom, more innovatory and radical ideas can be seen behind the policies of the Personal Rule. Self-conscious, public, and theoretically sophisticated absolutist doctrine was as inimical to Charles – and its propagators as marginal to his government – as were the doctrinaire Arminians in the Laudian church of the 1630s. To portray the 1630s as a simple clash between absolutist and constitutionalist dogmatists would be as erroneous as presenting them as a straightforward conflict between Arminians and Calvinists. This approach simply duplicates the binary opposites by which each side misrepresented the other. But this does not mean that there were not significantly different ideological forces at work. Thomas Wentworth provides us with an object lesson that absolutist notions and innovatory policies can lurk behind, and arguably be inseparable from, the public rhetoric of harmony, balance and tradition that were the public face of the government of the Personal Rule.

[57] For this interpretation of Laudianism see my *Catholic and Reformed: The Roman and Protestant Churches in English Protestant Thought, 1600–1640* (Cambridge, 1995), esp. ch. 8 and conclusion. See also P. Lake, 'The Laudians and the argument from authority', in B. Y. Kunze and D. D. Brautigam (eds.), *Court, Country and Culture* (Rochester, N.Y., 1992) pp. 149–76; P. Lake, 'The Laudian style: order, uniformity and the pursuit of the beauty of holiness in the 1630s', and P. Lake and K. Fincham, 'The ecclesiastical policies of James I and Charles I', in K. Fincham (ed.), *The Early Stuart Church, 1603–1642* (1993), pp. 23–49, 161–85.

CHAPTER 7

The attempted Anglicisation of Ireland in the seventeenth century: An exemplar of 'British History'

Nicholas Canny

Several calls have been made in recent years for a 'New British History' which will treat of developments within the three kingdoms of England, Scotland and Ireland as but parts of a single process.[1] The exponents of this cause insist that they have more in mind than comparative history, and like all crusaders for a new cause they tend to disregard the writings of previous scholars which clearly meet with their specifications of what this 'New British History' should be.[2] Those who come to the subject from a conventional training in English history also display a certain insensitivity towards Scottish and Irish affairs, and this is especially evident from their employment

This essay first appeared in Ronald Asch (ed.), *Three Nations – A Common History? England, Scotland, Ireland and British History c.1600–1920* (Bochum, 1993). An expanded version will appear in *Ireland in the English Colonial System*, under contract with Clarendon Press.

[1] J. G. A. Pocock, 'British History: a plea for a new subject', *Journal of Modern History* 47 (1975), pp. 601–28; J. G. A. Pocock, 'The limits and divisions of British history: in search of the unknown subject', *American Historical Review* 87 (1982), pp. 311–36; J. C. D. Clark, 'English history's forgotten context: Scotland, Ireland and Wales', *HJ* 32 (1989), pp. 211–28; H. Kearney, 'The problem of perspective in the history of colonial America', in K. R. Andrews *et al.* (eds.), *The Westward Enterprise: English Activities in Ireland, the Atlantic and America, 1480–1650* (Liverpool, 1978), pp. 290–302; H. Kearney, *The British Isles: A History of Four Nations* (Cambridge, 1989); S. G. Ellis, ' "Not Mere English": the British perspective', *History Today* 28 (Dec. 1988), pp. 41–8.

[2] As far as Ireland is concerned, the attempt to present the history of Ireland in a British context dates back at least to W. E. H. Lecky. During the past generation, several effective works on Ireland have been presented in a British context, for example, H. F. Kearney, *Strafford in Ireland, 1633–41: A Study in Absolutism* (Manchester, 1959; 2nd edn, Cambridge, 1989); D. Stevenson, *Scottish Covenanters and Irish Confederates: Scottish–Irish Relations in the Mid-Seventeenth Century* (Belfast, 1981); T. C. Barnard, *Cromwellian Ireland: English Government and Reform in Ireland, 1649–1660* (Oxford, 1975); cf. further M. Perceval-Maxwell, 'Ireland and the monarchy in the early Stuart multiple kingdom', *HJ* 34 (1991), pp. 279–95. I would contend that my own first book, especially where it discussed provincial councils and revolt, contained a decided 'British' dimension: N. Canny, *The Elizabethan Conquest of Ireland: A Pattern Established, 1565–1576* (Brighton, 1976). To my mind, the finest example of 'British' History in practice, and one that I have never seen referred to by the champions of the new cause, is O. Macdonagh, *The Inspector General: Sir Jeremiah Fitzpatrick and the Politics of Social Reform, 1783–1802* (1981).

of the terms 'Britain' or 'British Isles' to describe the geographic entity that they propose to study, even when this area includes Ireland. To me it appears that one real shortcoming of the 'New British History', at least where the early modern period is concerned, is that it is political history in the narrow sense which proceeds from the assumption that the course of political events can be explained independently of social and economic considerations. As a consequence of this assumption, historians, such as Conrad Russell, imply that social and economic conditions in the three kingdoms were similar if not identical, and they ignore the fact that developments in one kingdom could have had entirely different consequences in the other two because of the different circumstances which obtained there.[3]

Another and perhaps greater weakness of the 'New British History' that has so far been written on the seventeenth century is that it presumes the central importance of those events which have featured prominently in conventional English history, and alludes to developments in Ireland and Scotland only in so far as these assist our understanding of such key episodes as the English Civil War. Two distortions have resulted from this. First, many historians of Scotland and Ireland, presented with the opportunity to have a moment in the sun, have concentrated upon those aspects of their subject that can be seen to have exerted an impact upon these episodes of accepted importance, and they have consequently neglected developments that might be considered of mere local or national significance. And the second distortion has occurred because historians, having been encouraged to explain how events in Scotland and Ireland exerted an influence over the course of English affairs, tend to ignore how developments in England shaped the course of events in Scotland and in Ireland.[4] This second distortion, I would contend, is the more serious of the two because it is my considered opinion that the influence which England exerted upon Scotland and Ireland was altogether more potent than the influence

---

[3] C. S. R. Russell, *The Fall of the British Monarchies, 1637–1642* (Oxford, 1991).

[4] It might be argued that Scotland during the early modern period was never subjected to the same thrust of Anglicisation as Ireland. However, the attempts by those who dominated the Scottish Lowlands to extend their influence over the Highlands might be considered in the same light; see the old-fashioned D. H. Willson, *King James VI and I* (1956) and the more recent J. Wormald, *Court, Kirk and Community: Scotland, 1470–16141*. (1981). The assignment by Oliver Cromwell of Roger Boyle, Baron Broghill, to reorganise Scottish affairs might be considered as the most significant attempt to treat the three kingdoms as a single unit under English control.

which operated in the opposite direction. Indeed, I would go so far as to suggest that the attempted Anglicisation of Ireland (and also of Scotland) must become the central theme of any subject called British History if this subject, as it has been defined by its advocates, is to have any credibility.

The whole question of the English government employing its resources to achieve the Anglicisation of Ireland is one that came forward, almost by accident, during the course of the sixteenth century. For several centuries previous to then the English crown had abandoned the ambition of the twelfth-century Anglo-Norman monarchs to achieve political domination over Ireland, and had satisfied itself with retaining its interest in that part of the country which remained under the control of the descendants of the Anglo-Norman lords. This area, which lay mostly in the east and the south-east of the country, was known politically as the Lordship of Ireland. The more stable areas of the Lordship (in the valleys of the rivers Liffey and Boyne in the east of the country, and in the valley of the Nore to the south-east) were inhabited principally by an English-speaking population who followed English legal and tenurial practices, and who owed allegiance to the English crown through the administration and parliament that had been established in Dublin. The low-lying fertile terrain in the valleys of these three rivers lent itself to tillage farming, which was supplemented by pastoral agriculture on the uplands. The service needs of the farming community were met by a series of inland towns which maintained commercial connections with the port towns of Dublin, Waterford and Drogheda where some manufacturing was conducted. All of these factors of language, lineage, occupation, allegiance and human settlement suggest that society in this more stable area of the Lordship of Ireland was strikingly similar in appearance to English society, and to lowland English society at that. What made it different, however, was that the community in these low-lying areas lived in close proximity to the Gaelic population in the mountainous and boggy parts of the country who constantly threatened them with raiding parties seeking to seize their moveable property and to destroy their crops. This ever-present threat forced the English community in Ireland to expend much of its resources on providing for its own defence. Their predicament was symbolised by the Pale, that series of fortified positions which they were forced to erect in the outlying reaches of the Boyne and Liffey river valleys. A further continuous outlay of resources was associated with maintaining a viable passageway between the English community in this area and that in the River Nore basin. Again, because of the ever-present military threat, the farming and gentry population in these Anglicised areas were forced increasingly to rely upon their lords to provide for their protection. Such reliance involved them in paying military exactions to their overlords, and as the lords became more militarised, they, in turn, became a threat to the liberties and prosperity of the farming and commercial community. Some lords, in their effort to increase their power and social standing, took to employing Gaelic methods for raising and maintaining armed followers, and this trend, which is referred to by historians as Gaelicisation, was decried by the settled English community in Ireland as degeneration.[5]

The use of this term degeneration makes it clear that people in the settled English community in Ireland at the close of the Middle Ages had come to think of themselves as the sole upholders of civil standards in a country which was generally barbaric. The depiction of the Gaelic population as barbarians had been executed most graphically by the Anglo-Norman writer Giraldus Cambrensis who had accompanied King Henry II to Ireland in 1172, and who described his exploits and those of the first Anglo-Norman lords in Ireland in florid detail. For Giraldus, the Anglo-Norman involvement with Ireland was justified on Christian as well as political grounds because, as he portrayed it, life in Gaelic Ireland was incompatible with Christian principles.[6] This axiom was adhered to and further elaborated upon by the descendants of the Anglo-Normans in succeeding centuries, and writers from the English-speaking community in Ireland, even into the sixteenth century, contended that they were not only the sole civil but the sole Christian people in Ireland. By then, however, they had come to accept that the government in England was no longer interested in completing the conquest of Ireland that had been undertaken by the Anglo-Normans, and their calls upon the crown were for

---

[5]   These themes are outlined in such general accounts as R. Frame, *Colonial Ireland, 1169–1369* (Dublin, 1981) and A. Cosgrove, *Late Medieval Ireland, 1370–1541* (Dublin, 1951). The phenomenon of Pale society is discussed in more detail in N. Canny, *The Formation of the Old English Elite in Ireland* (National University of Ireland, O'Donnell Lecture) (Dublin, 1975); and S. G. Ellis, *The Pale and the Far North* (National University of Ireland, O'Donnell Lecture) (Galway, 1986). An altogether more detailed treatment is presented in a sequence of essays in F. H. A. Aalen and K. Whelan (eds.), *Dublin, City and Country from Prehistory to Present* (Dublin, 1992).

[6]   Giraldus Cambrensis, *Expugnatio Hibernica: The Conquest of Ireland*, ed. and trans. A. B. Scott and F. X. Martin (Dublin, 1978).

assistance in their effort to preserve themselves from the dual threat of overthrow by the Gaelic population from without and degeneration from within their own community.[7]

This description makes it clear that all that remained securely in English hands in Ireland at the close of the Middle Ages was an outpost whose very survival as a recognisable English community was seriously in doubt. As such, as we learn from the writings of Steven Ellis, it was not exceptional, and he contends that we must study this community, together with the other outposts of English influence in Britain and on the continent, if we are to have a true understanding of the nature of the English state and society at that time.

If this was the reality of the power of the English state at the close of the fifteenth century, it was to change rapidly as the sixteenth century progressed, and nowhere more decisively than in Ireland. These changes were possible because the Tudor monarchs were altogether more secure on the English throne than their immediate predecessors had been, and were able to engage upon a consolidation of their power in Ireland such as previously would have been unthinkable. The consolidation that King Henry VIII and his advisors had in mind, soon involved the government in an effort to expand the area of English influence in Ireland beyond its traditional boundaries, sometimes by military force, and at other times by persuasive methods backed by force. The advances made into previously Gaelic or Gaelicised areas were taken initially to promote the security of the Anglicised community in Ireland, and the strategy begun in Henry's reign was persisted with during the reigns of his two immediate successors, Edward VI and Mary I. Efforts were made at the same time to procure the allegiance of the loyal community in Ireland to the form of church doctrine favoured by each of these monarchs, but the fact that the forward political thrust persisted regardless of the religion of the monarch makes it clear that it was independent of religious considerations.[8]

---

[7] Canny, *Old English Elite*; C. Lennon, *Richard Stanihurst, the Dubliner, 1547–1618* (Dublin, 1981); C. Brady, 'Conservative subversives: the community of the Pale and the Dublin administration, 1556–1586', in P. J. Corish (ed.), *Radicals, Rebels and Establishments* (Belfast, 1985), pp. 11–32; B. Bradshaw, *The Irish Constitutional Revolution of the Sixteenth Century* (Cambridge, 1979). Steven Ellis has argued in his publications that the Pale community was far more enduring than was protested in their jeremiads: S. G. Ellis, *Tudor Ireland: Crown, Community and the Conflict of Cultures, 1470–1603* (1985), esp. pp. 53–107; S. G. Ellis, *Reform and Revival: English Government in Ireland, 1470–1534* (Woodbridge and New York, 1986).

[8] Ellis, *Tudor Ireland*, pp. 85–110, 183–277.

While the purpose behind the government's actions was to stabilise the position of the English community in Ireland, each new advance produced an unforeseen outcome or complication. This occurred because the monarchs, and the English-born people they appointed in control of Irish affairs, knew little about the country or its society. Ignorance was no bar to initiative however, and when repeated efforts failed to insulate the traditionally loyal areas from Gaelic assault by surrounding them with a chain of fortified garrisons, the officials in Dublin became increasingly fixed upon the view that the only solution to the continuing instability was to establish English government authority everywhere in Ireland.[9]

This statement of purpose was consistent with what the English-speaking population in the country had always been seeking. Yet when it was advocated by the officials, it did not elicit any enthusiastic response from the leaders of that community. This coldness or even hostility towards the new aggressive forward policy can be explained by a variety of factors. First, the loyal community resented the fact that most senior positions in the government and also in the church were now being assigned to people born in England rather than, as previously, to candidates from within the English community of Ireland. Another development which alienated the loyal community from crown policy was the increasing reliance of the governors upon the royal army and its officers rather than upon the Irish Council and Parliament. Wages for the crown troops were paid in England, but governors were devising ever more complex strategies to compel the loyal community to meet the principal costs of maintaining the troops once they had arrived in Ireland.[10] There was thus also a fiscal issue which divided the loyal community in Ireland from its government, but the issue which ultimately polarised the two English elements in Ireland was religious in nature.

The government, as we saw, did expect the English community in Ireland to follow its wishes in matters of religion, but its preoccupation with political matters left it with little opportunity to promote a sustained evangelisation drive among the English population in the country. This neglect meant that this population, despite the occasional conformity of some of its leaders, remained essentially Catholic at a time when society in England was

---

[9]   R. Loeber, *The Geography and Practice of English Colonisation in Ireland from 1534 to 1609* (Athlone, 1991); Canny, *Elizabethan Conquest.*
[10] Brady, 'Conservative subversives'.

becoming increasingly Protestant in its commitment. The consequences of this divergence in religious allegiance became more
evident from the mid-1560s forward, and already by the late 1570s it
was being stated openly by English Protestant officials in Ireland
that the presumed loyal population was neither English nor loyal. A
distinction was increasingly drawn by the officials between the
English-by-birth and the English-by-blood, and they soon moved to
cast doubt on the Englishness of the English Irish.[11] Such distinctions were made with the purpose of accentuating their point that
the only true subjects of the crown were those who were both
committed Protestants and born in England. All others, whatever
their professions of loyalty, it was alleged, had degenerated from
the civility of their progenitors, and were a threat to the security of
the English crown and its position in Ireland because of their
persistent attachment to Catholicism.[12] This argument which was
designed by English-born officials and soldiers in Ireland to discredit their principal critics and rivals for patronage, received a
sympathetic hearing from senior officials in London. They, like
their subordinates in Ireland, had come to equate civility with
Englishness, but had also come to identify allegiance to Protestantism as one of the essential conditions of being English and civil.
The initial hope of the officials in London was to advance the
Englishness of Ireland, in the same way as had been done in
England and Wales, through the establishment of provincial councils that would promote and uphold the authority of the central
government in the outlying regions.[13] Such instruments seemed
inadequate to the purpose however as tension mounted between
England and Spain, and when first the Papacy and then the
Spanish monarchy provided moral encouragement and military
support to those in Ireland who would challenge the queen's
authority on the grounds that she was a heretic to whom no
Catholic subject should owe allegiance. And a further reason for
associating Catholicism with disloyalty emerged at this time,
because many of the more Anglicised families in Ireland began to
send their sons to continental Europe for education as priests in

---

[11] Canny, *Old English Elite*; Ellis, *Tudor Ireland*, pp. 245–8.
[12] N. Canny, 'Identity formation in Ireland: the emergence of the Anglo-Irish', in N. Canny
and A. Pagden (eds.), *Colonial Identity in the Atlantic World, 1500–1800* (Princeton, 1987),
pp. 159–212, esp. 161–75.
[13] Canny, *Elizabethan Conquest*, pp. 93–116.

Catholic seminaries that were closely identified with the more
extreme political pronouncements of the Counter-Reformation.[14]
Queen Elizabeth herself was alarmed by these developments and
incensed by all challenges to her authority that were justified on
religious grounds. This moved her to approve military intervention
in Ireland which escalated to the point where it became the most
expensive undertaking of the Tudor state. When doing so, however,
she never acknowledged that what she was about was the comprehensive conquest of the country, but her officials in Ireland and her
officers in the field believed that the achievement of such a conquest
should become their objective.[15]

Those who thought in this way and who worked towards this
objective were clearly inspired by such authors as Edmund Spenser
and Sir John Davies, who were themselves officials in Ireland and
who set down coherently argued statements in favour of the
Anglicisation of Ireland.[16] Such statements, in so far as they
recommended a conquest of the country which would ultimately
open the way for the introduction of English legal procedures and
land tenure into the previously Gaelic areas of the country, were
consistent with traditional medieval policy of the Anglo-Normans.
Significantly also, these writers drew heavily upon what Giraldus
Cambrensis had to say about Gaelic society as a justification for
their recommendations.

However, these authors departed significantly from Giraldus and
those who followed in his tradition in several respects, and it is these
differences which made their contributions original. Their first major
departure from the medieval writers is that they rejected the supposi-
tion that the existing English population in the country should serve
as the instruments of reform and Anglicisation. This was now utterly
rejected because it was argued that the Anglo-Normans had not
themselves been a fully civil people at the point of the original
conquest, and that their descendants had further degenerated
through their association with the Gaelic population. The issue of

---

[14] H. Hammerstein, 'Aspects of the Continental education of Irish students in the reign of
      Queen Elizabeth I', in T. D. Williams (ed.), *Historical Studies. Papers read before the Irish
      Conference of Historians*, no. 8 (Dublin, 1971), pp. 137–53; N. Canny, *From Reformation to
      Restoration: Ireland 1534–1660* (Dublin, 1987), esp. pp. 152–9.

[15] Canny, *Reformation*, pp. 108–67.

[16] E. Spenser, *A view of the present state of Ireland, 1596*, ed. W. L. Renwick (Oxford, 1970); Sir
      John Davies, *A Discovery of the True Causes why Ireland was Never entirely Subdued... until the
      Beginning of His Majesty's Happy Reign* (1612).

degeneration which had been of such concern to the Anglicised community was now being turned against themselves, and in two respects. Now it was being argued that degeneration from civil standards was inevitable whenever a civil people were placed in close proximity to a barbaric order, and it was being further stated that a civil people who thus degenerated made more formidable enemies than pristine barbarians such as the Gaelic Irish. Following upon this the English-born writers questioned the possibility of recalling those who had lapsed from civil standards or preventing further degeneration through statutory law. Whenever this was done, contended Spenser, English law became a weapon in the hands of those who were inveterate enemies of the crown, and was used to counter the interests of the crown. What was required, he said (and most of his English contemporaries in Ireland agreed with him), was a conquest of the country which would displace all who held power and influence in Ireland, whether Old English who had become tainted by their associations with barbarism or Gaelic Irish who, it was contended, were Scythian in origin.[17]

This overthrow of the existing political and social order which was recommended by the theorists was with the purpose of erecting a new one which would meet with the highest standards of civility. These standards were clearly to be English ones, and the instruments of promoting them were to be zealous English Protestants who were to be placed in charge of the government of Ireland, and who were to be established as landowners and leaders of their localities in all parts of the country. Aided by the soldiers, who would remain in the country after the conquest had been accomplished, these officials and proprietors would break up and disperse the existing kinship networks in the country, and resettle the indigenous population on lands which they would hold from themselves. There they would reside in close proximity to the farming and artisan population from England, who were regarded as an essential element of each plantation that was to be established. The role of these settlers was to provide an example to the native population on how the land could be improved, and on how to make best use of the resources of the country. To this extent they were to have an educational as well as an economic function, but the formal educational role was to be left to the schoolmasters in the series of parochial and grammar schools

---

[17]   Spenser, *View*, pp. 21–37.

that were to be endowed out of confiscated property and to the Protestant clergy who were to be similarly supported.[18] The only consistent issue in contention between those who advocated such comprehensive schemes of reform was the extent to which use should be made of the Irish language in this educational and evangelisation drive. Some, such as Sir William Herbert, suggested that the educators should learn the Irish language and compose suitable instruction manuals and hymns in that language for the schooling of the Irish population. Spenser, on the other hand, contended that the formal educational and evangelisation effort would have to wait until the Irish population had become conversant in the English language through their interaction with the settler population.[19] All were agreed, however, that the end purpose was to draw the Irish to a civil condition and to the Protestant faith, and they looked forward with Sir John Davies to the prospect that the next generation of the Irish would 'in tongue, and heart and every way else become English so there would be no difference or distinction but the Irish sea betwixt us'.[20]

While Davies, when writing this in 1612, was optimistic that this objective was attainable, he was so only because a programme for promoting a large plantation in Ulster had just been put in place. Moreover, he believed that this would serve as a preliminary to further plantations which would result in the gradual, but, not the less, systematic dispossession of Catholic proprietors in the other three provinces. This, he felt certain, was now attainable because of the comprehensive nature of the military victory that had been achieved by the forces of the crown, over all opponents, in 1603. Furthermore, Davies was satisfied that a massive reallocation of property in Ireland could be given full legal sanction because he proposed to achieve a Protestant majority in the Irish parliament by reducing the level of representation from the Old English areas while increasing that from the parts of Ireland that had recently been planted. The concern of Davies with legal niceties suggests that he was more moderate than Spenser, but we now know, from the study by Hans Pawlisch of Davies's career in Ireland, that Davies was seeking to employ the civil and common law in the same way that Spenser would have used the

---

[18]   *Ibid.*, pp. 161–3.
[19]   Sir William Herbert, *Croftus Sive de Hibernia Liber*, ed. and trans. A. Keaveney and J. A. Madden (Dublin, 1922), pp. 105–17.
[20]   Davies, *Discovery*, p. 272.

weapons of war to achieve the same objective, which was to make society in Ireland a replica of that in England.[21]

The advancement of such a policy, if it had been pursued, would certainly constitute a major theme of any 'New British History' that might be written. The subject would have every claim to be described as British because the objective of the reformers was to impose the standards and religion of the dominant kingdom, England, upon one of the lesser ones, Ireland, and because they, or at least Davies, could countenance the idea of enlisting the support of Scottish Protestants in the fulfilment of this task. The subject would also meet any definition of Britishness because the method of promoting change through plantation in Ireland was quite similar to that favoured by King James VI of Scotland, before he became king also of England and Ireland, for bringing the more remote regions of his Scottish kingdom under the control of his government at Edinburgh. And the strongest claim of the subject to be included within any agenda for British History is because authors such as Spenser and Davies contended that the security of England (and implicitly that of Scotland also) was reliant upon the implementation of the reform programmes which they elaborated in such detail. Such authors advanced theological and strategic arguments to support this proposition, but their essential argument was that any attempt by a single monarch to sustain religious diversity within a plurality of kingdoms was certain to end in calamity. In so far as there was a high-minded motive behind the composition of reform literature on Ireland it was to draw attention to this anomaly and to advance the case for the Anglicisation of Ireland which the various authors believed was the only measure to prevent catastrophe descending upon all three kingdoms.

The logic of the position adopted by those English officials who advocated the promotion of the Anglicisation of Ireland through a process of colonisation was, for the most part, ignored by senior officials of the London administration, and was officially endorsed only at moments of political crisis. This, as I have previously argued, was because officials in London could never bring themselves to give a high priority to Irish affairs other than when the collapse of authority there threatened the security of England itself.[22] Because

---

[21] H. S. Pawlisch, *Sir John Davies and the Conquest of Ireland: A Study in Legal Imperialism* (Cambridge, 1985).

[22] Canny, *Reformation*, pp. 108–87.

of the short-sightedness of these senior officials many historians have also come to believe that resort to colonisation was exceptional in England's dealings with Ireland during the seventeenth century. Such historians, with Hiram Morgan as the most recent recruit to their ranks, seem to think that simply because a continuing process of colonisation for Ireland was not endorsed by the London government, this policy was abandoned. In support of their claim for its abandonment, they point to the establishment of English-style legal institutions and procedures throughout Ireland from the beginning of the seventeenth century forward, and to the extension of parliamentary representation in Ireland to include all elements of the population. Here, in this similarity of institutions and procedures, they claim, is the reason why the two jurisdictions of England and Ireland should be considered part of the same British polity. Furthermore, these historians seem convinced that the Irish Catholic elite who endured into the seventeenth century were so conscious of the benefits to themselves of English constitutional procedures that they became discontented, and even resorted to revolt, whenever their rights and liberties as subjects of the crown were threatened or infringed upon. According to this definition, British History is constitutional history, and Ireland's place within a British polity is justified by the involvement of the population there with English-style constitutional procedures.[23]

Those historians who are attached to this view have been especially attracted to the politics of the Old English in Ireland during the first half of the seventeenth century, and to the confrontation that developed between them and Thomas Wentworth who served as governor in Ireland 1633–41. The Old English, according to this interpretation of events, were strict constitutionalists, while Wentworth represented the absolutist trend in English monarchical government, which threatened the liberties of subjects in England no less than in Ireland. What Wentworth was about in Ireland, it is said, was a preliminary to what he would have had the king attempt in England, and, on this basis, developments in Ireland are invoked as a major contributory factor to the heightening of tensions between the supporters of King and Parliament in England itself.[24]

The work of those historians who perceive the years that Wentworth spent in Ireland as an interruption upon a prolonged period of

---

[23]   H. Morgan, 'Mid-Atlantic Blues', *The Irish Review* 11 (1991–2), pp. 50–5.
[24]   A. Clarke, *The Old English in Ireland, 1625–1642* (1966); Kearney, *Strafford*.

constitutional rule has been disturbed somewhat by the recent work of Hans Pawlisch.[25] This demonstrates how English legal forms and procedures could be used to promote what was in effect a policy of exploitation aimed at the dispossession of all Catholic proprietors in Ireland. If we accept what Pawlisch has to say about the service of Sir John Davies and his master, Sir Arthur Chichester, in Ireland then we are forced to conclude that normal constitutional relations between the English monarch and his Irish Catholic subjects were developed only during the years 1622–29, when the deputyship was held by Henry Cary, Viscount Falkland. Even then it emerges that the concessions and assurances to the Irish Catholic elite that were made first by King James I and later by King Charles I were wrung from them, first because they wished to improve their own relations with Catholic monarchs on the continent, and second because the government was fearful that Irish Catholics would engage in disturbances at a time when England was at war with Spain. These promises made by the monarchs to their Catholic subjects were, however, stridently resisted by all Protestant interests in Ireland, including most members of the administration, and were regarded with suspicion by many members of the English political nation. This suggests that it was factors of expediency rather than any change of heart which explains why Irish Catholics were able to participate more openly in the constitutional process during the late 1620s and why they could look forward to being treated as equals with any other of the king's subjects. While the expectation of Irish Catholics were thus raised it was never accepted by the king's Protestant subjects in any of the three kingdoms that Catholics should be treated equally with Protestants, and a great number of Protestants believed fervently that the very existence of Catholic landowners constituted a threat to the security of the state.[26]

When account is taken of this reality it appears that any measures taken by Wentworth to counter the promises made by the monarchy to Irish Catholics would have been welcomed by Protestants in the three kingdoms. Wentworth's offence in the eyes of Protestants was not that of curtailing the liberties of Catholics, but in his moving at the same time to reduce the power and influence of Protestant landowners in Ireland. And his greatest offence of all was in organising an army in Ireland, which included Catholic officers and

[25]   Pawlisch, *Davies and the Conquest.*
[26]   Clarke, *Old English,* pp. 28–59.

men, to assist the king in his effort to bring his recalcitrant subjects in Scotland to heel. It was only at this point that Protestants of the three kingdoms began to express sympathy for the way in which Irish Catholics had been treated by him, but then only for the purely cynical purpose of broadening the spread of opposition to Wentworth so that he could be more easily destroyed.[27]

These developments, which have been studied in detail by a succession of historians, only came to the fore, however, towards the end of Wentworth's service in Ireland, and they served to draw him away from an agenda that he had set himself almost from the moment that he had taken up office in the country. During these years, Wentworth had been working assiduously to re-fashion Irish society in a manner that would have pleased the theorists who, long before then, had advocated the Anglicisation of Ireland through a process of colonisation. These endeavours of Wentworth have, however, escaped the attention of historians and for two reasons: first because historians have become obsessed with discerning the causes of the English Civil War and the Irish contribution to that disturbance, and second because Wentworth proceeded with such stealth that even his senior officials in government (and the king) did not know the objectives to which he was working. While Wentworth was careful to conceal his purpose when he spoke and acted on the public stage, he could be very explicit about his objectives when corresponding with his confidants in England such as Archbishop Laud and Secretary Coke. A close study of Wentworth's papers also reveals what might have inspired him to strive after the particular set of objectives he set before himself. One point that emerges clearly from his private correspondence is that he saw himself as a reforming governor with a specific reform agenda to fulfill in a relatively short space of time. How long he gave himself to implement his programme is not clear, but he did insist on several occasions that he intended to return to England after his work in Ireland was accomplished. As early as 1633, in the course of advising Laud on why young rather than elderly clergymen should be encouraged to take up positions in the church in Ireland, he pointed out that settled clergymen 'of parts' would be 'loath to come to bury themselves here in Ireland in their old age' whereas young, vigorous men, aged between thirty-five and forty-five, would willingly 'bestow part of

---

27   N. Canny, *The Upstart Earl: The Social and Mental World of Richard Boyle, First Earl of Cork* (Cambridge, 1982), pp. 1–40; Canny, *Reformation*, pp. 188–206.

their travail and watches upon us... if in the hope to be then called back'. In this respect, wrote Wentworth, 'I judge the clergy by the laity for this is, in my own walk, my own desire'. There could be no clearer statement that Wentworth saw himself (if we might use the phrase of Ciaran Brady) as a 'programmatic governor' and the programme which he set before himself was that of assisting the clergy in their effort to achieve 'the reformation of this church'. This objective, as Wentworth himself stated, was a 'vast... work', but he was confident that it was attainable 'in good time' with the assistance of God, the king and Archbishop Laud.[28]

By the reformation of the church, as we shall see, Wentworth meant the conversion of all elements of the population, Catholic as well as Protestant, to the form of Protestant worship that was favoured by the king and Archbishop Laud. Before he could proceed with this ultimate objective, Wentworth had to ensure that the church was adequately endowed to provide livings for the Protestant clergy that he wished to have appointed, and that sufficient controls were in place to ensure that these clergy would observe the theological and liturgical rulings that were decreed by the king. On the question of endowment Wentworth discovered that an enormous amount of land that should have rightfully belonged to the church had fallen into the control and use of landed proprietors, Protestant as well as Catholic. To remedy this situation Wentworth, operating through an executive tribunal, had these landowners called to account and divested of this property.[29]

Then, once these first steps had been taken to improve the endowment of the church, Wentworth could give thought to the recruitment of clergy in England to serve in the various Irish dioceses. Some of these were to be appointed to positions that had previously lain vacant because of the inadequacy of the livings attached to the parishes. More, however, were to take the places of serving Protestant clergy who were to be dismissed from their positions either because of scandalous behaviour or because they were not of sound doctrine. To facilitate these removals Wentworth commissioned an investigation into the condition of the various Irish

[28] Wentworth to Laud, 9 Sept. 1633, Str P 8, f. 17. On programmatic governors see C. Brady, 'Court, castle and country: the framework of government in Tudor Ireland', in C. Brady and R. Gillespie (eds.), *Natives and Newcomers: The Making of Irish Colonial Society, 1534–1641* (Dublin, 1986), pp. 22–49.

[29] Kearney, *Strafford*, esp. pp. 69–84.

dioceses. Those investigations which were of principal concern to him were the Ulster dioceses where he discovered that, not only many of the clergy, but the church-wardens and 'preaching scoolmasters' were 'desperate non conformists' from Scotland.[30] Such people, who favoured Calvinist doctrine and a Presbyterian mode of church organisation, were as offensive to Wentworth in Ireland as they were to Laud in England, and he complained to Laud, in words that would have been familiar to the archbishop, of how troubled he was 'to see all government, order and decency in this our church trodden down to dirt and nothing appearing but a half face of something like an Annanias'.[31] The aesthetic offence was compounded with a political one when the leaders of this Calvinist group began to identify with the Covenanters who stood against the king's effort to impose an Anglican form of Protestant worship upon Scotland. Wentworth sought to forestall the spread of such defiance into Ireland by obliging Scottish settlers in Ulster to take an oath that they would not make common cause with the Scottish Covenanters. This measure, which earned Wentworth the enduring hatred of godly Protestants in the three kingdoms, was consistent with his endeavour to promote a revision in the official doctrine of the Church of Ireland. The existing formulation of doctrine did not satisfy Wentworth because it made too many concessions to Calvinism, and he proceeded to bring Irish church doctrine into line with that recently recommended by Archbishop Laud for the church in England.[32]

This effort by Wentworth to consolidate the position of the Protestant church and to establish it on sound doctrinal basis was seen by his contemporaries, and by most historians since then, as no more than extending to Ireland the kind of Arminian church settlement that was being imposed by Laud and King Charles upon England and Scotland. It was certainly that, but the consolidation of the position of the church in Ireland was considered by Wentworth as the essential pre-requisite to his moving to win, or force, the compliance of the Catholic population in Ireland with the Church established by law. While this preliminary work was underway, Wentworth saw little point in disturbing or harassing Catholics, and he saw considerable merit in conceding a *de facto* right of worship to

---

30 Henry, Bishop of Down to Wentworth, 18 Oct. 1638, Str P 20B/134.
31 Wentworth to Laud, 28 Aug. 1633, Str P 8, f. 13.
32 A. Ford, *The Protestant Reformation in Ireland, 1590–1641* (Frankfurt a.M., 1985), pp. 243–76.

Catholics so that they would never suspect his greater purpose. While thus concealing his hand from public view, Wentworth made clear his detestation of Catholicism to his correspondents in England, while in Ireland he moved gradually but systematically to undermine the position of Catholic landowners who were the bulwark of the Catholic clergy. Because of the stealth with which he moved, neither Catholics nor Protestants recognised the full sweep of what he intended, nor for that matter have historians who have studied Wentworth's career in Ireland.

On those occasions when Wentworth revealed his true feelings about Catholicism he did so in a virulent fashion. The claim being made by the Old English for favourable treatment, out of consideration for their long record of loyalty to the crown, made no impression upon Wentworth. 'They set forth', he said, 'how they and their ancestors have at all times been faithful subjects, and yet in a manner the whole country hath been within memory in actual rebellion.'[33] And, as he looked to the future, he expected no better. Writing in 1636, Wentworth warned that until the Old English were 'brought to a conformity in religion, the Crown of England may not in wisdom repose any confidence in them'. In that same letter he inferred that the political endeavours of the Old English were acting as an obstacle to the efforts being made to bring 'the natives... into the paths of civility', with the result that these natives might still 'be accounted animals, mean betwixt rationals and brutes, than men'. The way in which the Old English were impeding the civilising process was by providing protection and patronage for friars and Jesuits. It was Wentworth's ultimate intention to have such clergy expelled from the country, and while, in 1636, he did not consider it opportune to remove them, he gave an assurance that when the time was right he would 'take all speed and courage in the execution'.[34]

The reason why Wentworth wished, in 1636, to delay his proposed onslaught against the Catholic clergy was because he was then pushing ahead with a plantation in the province of Connacht and County Clare. The vast bulk of the land in this area west of the river Shannon was in the possession of Catholics, most of whom could not produce titles which were good in law for the estates which they occupied. Spokesmen for the Protestant interest in Ireland had repeatedly called upon the government to remove these proprietors

[33] Wentworth to Coke, n.d., Str P 9, f. 177.
[34] Wentworth to Coke, 6 July 1636, Str P 9, f. 53.

and to establish a plantation along the lines of what had been implemented in the provinces of Munster and Ulster. However, the lobbying of Irish Catholics during that critical juncture of the mid-1620s had earned the proprietors in Connacht a reprieve from plantation under the terms of the Graces conceded to them in 1628 by King Charles I. In return for a series of substantial payments to the king, the landowners were assured that they would be granted full legal title to their properties under an act to be processed through the Irish parliament. The promised parliament was never convened and the act never passed, and when Wentworth did assemble the first of his Irish parliaments in 1634, he made it clear that he intended both to disregard the promises made by the king and to proceed with a plantation. When doing so he was warned that his 'severity may disaffect that people and dispose them to call the Irish regiments forth of Flanders to their assistance'.[35]

This reminder of the dangers associated with his work may have further convinced Wentworth that he should refrain from taking action against Catholic priests until he had first brought their patrons under firm government control. This, as he saw it, could best be done through plantation, and the kind of plantation which he visualised for Connacht was similar to that which had been implemented in North County Wexford during the 1610s. Under such a scheme the occupants who did not have good title to their estates would forfeit everything to the crown but would receive back the equivalent of three-quarters of their property with a secure title. This, however, would be on the tenure of knight service which would provide a regular income to the crown, and would make it possible for the government to require the grantees and their heirs to take the Oath of Supremacy. If applied rigidly this would ensure that all native proprietors in Connacht would be forced to conform in religion. Even more important for Wentworth was the fact that one-quarter of the land in Connacht would become available to English-born Protestant proprietors who would become the basis for government support in the province. When this final element was in place Wentworth was satisfied that he would have a scheme which would advance 'the service of the Crown, the increase of religion and the future peace and safety of the kingdom'.[36]

What Wentworth meant by the service of the crown was obviously

---

[35] Wentworth to King Charles, 10 Sept. 1636, Str P 3, f. 262.
[36] *NHI*, pp. 219–22; Wentworth to Coke, 7 Apr. 1635, Str P 9, f. 6.

the enhancement to the revenue and patronage of the crown that would follow from the plantation, and he advised specifically that the king should apply 'the benefit of those plantations to the Crown' and not leave 'them open as a prey to every pretender'.[37] The increase in religion would follow because, as he described County Galway which was to be included within the scheme, 'the people there' were 'in a manner wholly popish and Irish, not a Protestant and Englishman of note in the whole county [and] extremely addicted in their affections to Spain'.[38] Plantation would thus be beneficial to true religion because it would both weaken those who were 'unsound and rotten at the heart' and provide the government with the opportunity to 'line them thoroughly with English and Protestants'.[39] The enhancement of the security of the realm that would derive from plantation was implicit in Wentworth's condemnation of the Catholicism of the Irish in Connacht. However, besides being 'the likeliest and most open [area] to an invasion', Connacht was also a region where the subjects were greatly dependent on their lords. Such dependency would obviously be shattered by the plantation scheme which Wentworth envisaged, because the socially dominant group in the province would now be the freshly established English Protestant proprietors. Their influence would also bring an end to 'the power which the popish clergy have with the people there'.[40]

These arguments advanced by Wentworth to justify a plantation in Connacht suggest that his policies were being shaped by the theorists who had argued how Ireland could best be Anglicised. Like the theorists, Wentworth believed that with the policy of plantation 'lay a principal means of the security and flourishing of this kingdom in religion, peace, civility and trades'. Civil improvement would accrue because the Irish, as well as being papist (or perhaps because of it), were addicted to 'idleness and want of manufacture'.[41] The settlement of English in their midst would obviously provide an immediate remedy for this social deficiency, but Wentworth also apparently accepted the notion that the Irish would be reformed by the example of the civil living of the settlers once plantation had taken place. And, in a passage reminiscent of the most blatant special

---

[37] Wentworth to Windebank, 27 Nov. 1637, Str P IIA, f. 22.
[38] Wentworth and Council to Coke, 9 July 1639, Str P IIA, f. 249.
[39] Wentworth to King Charles, 10 Sept. 1636, Str P 3, f. 262.
[40] Considerations if King Charles declared war on Austria, n.d., Str P 3, f. 283; Wentworth and Council to Coke, n.d., Str P IIA, f. 249.
[41] Wentworth and Council to Coke, n.d., Str P IIA, f. 249.

pleadings of the theorists, Wentworth explained how the loss of one-quarter of their lands would be to the long-term material benefit of the Connacht landowners because 'these three parts remaining will after this settlement be better and more valuable to them than the former four parts... as well in regard of the benefit they shall have by the plantation as of the security and settlement they shall gain in their estates'.[42]

Almost as if to show that such arguments about the civil benefits that would derive from plantation were not mere rhetoric, Wentworth went into considerable detail in describing his own efforts to establish a plantation in the O'Byrnes' country in County Wicklow at the same time that the larger plantation in the west of Ireland was being negotiated. His intention was to make his own endeavours in Wicklow 'an example for those of the other plantation now on foot', and 'a perfect work... for posterity'. Earlier efforts by the English at building in Wicklow, such as the construction of Cary's Fort, were to be superseded by his own fort and lodge at Cosha, and those English who had already settled in Wicklow were to be compelled to invest in similar buildings.[43] Then, on the more specifically material side, Wentworth commissioned detailed 'Directions for Establishing a Plantation in Ireland'. This document, sixty pages in length, outlines projects for the processing of timber and the erection of an ironworks at Arklow. To this purpose, skilled workers were to be recruited from England, and the document showed how 'men of mystery' such as bellows-makers, founders, furnace-men, and hammer-men could be attracted to Ireland for half the wages they could command in England because they would be assigned farms of land on Wentworth's estate in Wicklow. Their efforts would, in time, leave ground open to arable farming, after trees and roots had been removed, and the document explained that masons and millers would then be required to facilitate the establishment of a permanent civil society.[44]

While thus providing a practical insight into what he himself believed could be achieved through plantation, Wentworth also alluded to what had already been accomplished in Ireland. In passing through the planted lands in Munster, between Clonmel and Limerick, Wentworth described it as 'a country upon my faith . . . as

[42] Report of Wentworth and the Connacht Commissioners, 30 Nov. 1637, Str P IIA, ff. 30–31.
[43] Wentworth to Coke, 29 Aug. 1636, Str P IIA, f. 125.
[44] Directions for Establishing a Plantation in Ireland, n.d., Str P 34.

well husbanded, built, and peopled as you are in England'. The 'industrious and well-conditioned' appearance was, he contended, due directly to plantation and he warned that 'unless by this means we be able to invite the English, flatter not yourselves with the hope of any lasting good from this kingdom'.[45] Wentworth had similar favourable comments to make about Ulster, despite his reservations about the religious leanings of the Scots. Writing in 1639, he expressed concern that there were 'one hundred thousand at least of the Scottish nation' settled in Ireland, but he still believed that they could be made useful if 'a good hand' was held over them to prevent them from joining the Covenanters.[46] Because of their potential, Scots were considered by Wentworth to be better subjects than Irish Catholics. However, his favourable impressions on the plantation in Ulster were formed because many of the grantees had been English, and he was concerned that none of the English grantees should be deprived of their estates simply because they had not fulfilled their plantation conditions. In this respect he moved to halt a possible re-plantation in the one county in Ulster that had been planted by the London merchant companies. To do so, he asserted, would have been altogether out of keeping with the 'crime' they had committed and would take no account of the more important consideration that they had 'settled themselves there *bona fides* upon valuable considera-tions, and by their charge and industry exceedingly improved those lands above what they were at their entry'. Any move to dispossess the Londoners, he said, would discourage 'all other planters through the whole realm' and would 'so dishearten the English from bestowing themselves on this side as will be to the prejudice of the Crown many thousands in the future plantations'.[47]

On this occasion Wentworth significantly referred to his plantation plans in the plural, and the contrasts which he developed between those areas which had been planted and those which remained in Catholic possession were designed to strengthen his case for a comprehensive plantation of all property remaining in Catholic possession. Even as the juries were proving crown title to lands in Connacht and Clare, Wentworth was secretly setting the wheels in

---

[45] Wentworth to Conway, 21 Aug. 1637, Str P 10A, f. 44; Wentworth to Laud, 16 Aug. 1637, Str P 7, ff. 40–1.

[46] Wentworth to Vane, 14 May 1639, Str P 10B, ff. 76–7.

[47] Wentworth to Cottington, 8 Dec. 1638, Str P 10B, ff. 22–4; Wentworth to Laud, 3 Nov. 1638, Str P 7, f. 134.

motion for a plantation of the Lordship of Ormond in counties
Tipperary and Kilkenny. And as the Connacht jurors clinched the
case for the crown by proving that the province could be claimed as
the 'ancient inheritance of the Crown' Wentworth concluded that
the Old English lawyers 'within the Pale' who had contested the
crown title would 'begin now to find his Majesty hath the same title
to a great part of Meath which he hath to Connacht, and that many
other pieces amongst them also are upon older, fair and just claims
subject to plantation'.[48] The private investigations which Wentworth
set afoot showed that where crown title to Connacht could be proven
by tracing ownership backwards to the original conquest of the
province by the de Burgos, crown title to much of Munster could
similarly be proven by tracing lineages backwards to the Norman
conquest of Robert FitzStephen. Thus, in his opinion, most of the
lands of Munster that had not been included within the Elizabethan
plantation in that province and that still remained in Catholic
possession were now liable to confiscation. Similarly for the province
of Ulster, Wentworth was able to justify the seizure of Upper and
Lower Iveagh in County Monaghan by making reference to the Irish
parliamentary act of 11 Elizabeth which had declared the entire
Lordship of Tyrone confiscate to the crown. And, more generally,
Wentworth's agents compiled a 'book' of minor holdings in Catholic
possession in various parts of the country which could now be seized
either because previous owners had once committed treason or
because the lands had been ecclesiastical property.[49]

It is only when these various references are pieced together that
we come to appreciate that what Wentworth referred to as 'the great
work of Plantations' was not the plantation of Connacht alone but
the resettlement of almost all land in Ireland that remained in
Catholic possession. He did not divulge his full scheme publicly
because plantations were 'not to be gone about but in time of peace'
and a general scheme was likely to arouse unrest. Even what he was
attempting in Connacht was, he acknowledged, the cause of 'dis-
contentments and grumblings', and we also know from Wentworth
that he realised that what he hoped to implement in Ireland was a
revolutionary scheme such as would not have been contemplated for
England. Writing to Sir Henry Vane and alerting him to distur-

[48] Report of Wentworth and the Connacht commissioners, 30 Nov. 1637, Str P 11A, ff. 30–1;
      Wentworth to [Coke?], 9 Nov. 1635, Str P 9, f. 103.
[49] Str P 24–25/275, 280, 281, 284, 295.

bances which might result from the plantation in Connacht, he asked
him to imagine the effect that a similar 'operation', which would
deprive every landowner of a 'a full fourth of all his lands . . . would
have with your people in England'.[50]

Besides his fear of the tumult that would result from an
announcement of a general plantation, there were also practical
reasons why Wentworth proceeded cautiously. It was, he said,
'impossible to do all at once', and he stated further that 'we hold it
not fit to embrace more having so much already in our hands'.[51]
Another reason which dictated caution was the intense lobbying of
the Catholic party at court to counter the plantation in Connacht.
The most persistent of the lobbyists was the earl of Clanricard (or
St Albans as Wentworth referred to him, using his English title),
and Wentworth used all the resources at his command to prevent
Clanricard having his estates in Galway declared exempt from the
plantation. Wentworth's real objection, as he made clear to such
confidants as Sir Henry Vane and Archbishop Laud, was that the
exemption of Clanricard's estates would create a precedent that
would be followed in subsequent plantations, thereby defeating his
principal purpose of undermining the authority of the Catholic
proprietors. He was not able to state this objection to the king
because this would have revealed that what he had in mind for
Ireland was a general confiscation of Catholic estates. Instead he
sought to hold the king to his schemes by promising – quite
implausibly – that the plantation of Connacht alone would
'shortly... pay the debts of the Crown of England' while also
making the government of Ireland free of charge to the English
exchequer.[52] When, in due course, the king hearkened to Clanricard's appeal and declared his estates exempt from the proposed
plantation, Wentworth remonstrated with Treasurer Vane that a
gift by the king of £100,000 in ready money to Clanricard would
have been preferable to the exemption because of the way in which
it had prejudiced 'the future plantations'.[53]

As it transpired none of the plantations, not even that in Connacht,
were proceeded with because, at the moment when Wentworth was

[50] Wentworth to ?, n.d., Str P 9, f. 206; Wentworth to Vane, 30 May 1639, Str P 10B, f. 77.
[51] *Ibid.*
[52] Wentworth to Laud, 9 March 1636, Str P 6, f. 331; Wentworth to Vane, 9 July 1639, Str P 10B, f. 121; Wentworth to Laud, 9 March 1636, Str P 6, f. 328.
[53] Wentworth to Vane, 9 July 1639, Str P 10B, f. 120.

about to launch his scheme in Connacht, his energies were suddenly
diverted to assist the king with his political difficulties in Scotland
and England. What is important, however, is the evidence that,
before this distraction occurred, Wentworth had decided upon a
programme of plantation for Ireland that was as extensive if not as
comprehensive as that later implemented by Oliver Cromwell. The
differences between the two is that Cromwell and his associates
aimed to deprive Catholic landowners of all their estates, where
Wentworth believed that Catholics could be permitted to retain
three-quarters of their property provided they were closely super-
intended and their lives monitored by the English proprietors he
intended to settle on the quarter of the land surface that would
become crown property. Wentworth was more lenient because he
believed that Catholic landowners who were placed within this
reformed social framework would be compelled, over the course of
time, to abandon their religion in favour of Protestantism. The
purpose behind his scheme is clear from his willingness to exempt the
Connacht estates of both Lord Ranelagh and Sir Charles Coote,
who were of English planter stock, from the proposed plantation,
and also the estates of the Gaelic, but Protestant, earl of Thomond in
County Clare. Not even Thomond was to be exempt from the
supervision of English Protestant proprietors however. On the death
of the fourth earl in 1639, Wentworth immediately recommended
that his heir should not continue to enjoy government over County
Clare because this had made 'them in the nature of count Palatines
[and] gave unto them a greater dependency than in reason of state
ought to be afforded to any of the natives of this kingdom'.[54] It seems
to have been his wish that the existing English settlers in Ireland, and
certainly the Scots, should also be made subject to the government of
these new proprietors. The Scots required such supervision because
of their Calvinist leanings, but Wentworth left no doubt that he
lacked confidence in all existing Protestant planters and officials in
Ireland and believed that they had become corrupt and degenerate

---

[54] Wentworth to ?, 22 April 1639, Str P IIA, f. 227. Dr Mary O'Dowd, in discussing the issue
of plantation in Connacht, believes that Wentworth wished to grant no exemptions, either
to Protestant or Catholic proprietors. It is true that he made such statements, especially
when dealing with Clanricard's claims, but the weight of evidence in his own
correspondence suggests that he did intend to exempt lands already in Protestant
ownership from confiscation. M. O'Dowd, *Power, Politics and Land: Early Modern Sligo, 1568–
1688* (Belfast, 1991), p. 54.

because of the lack of proper order and discipline in both Church and State before his own arrival in Ireland.[55]

All of this indicates that Wentworth believed that his series of plantations would mark a new beginning in the social and religious reform of the country. The religious reform would have become possible because the plantations and the political reordering of the country would have reduced the ability of Catholic landowners to provide patronage and protection to Catholic clergy. The weakening of the authority and independence of Catholic proprietors would also have made it impossible for them to oppose the withdrawal of toleration from the Catholic clergy; and we know from Wentworth himself that he did intend to expel priests from the country at the appropriate time. This time would obviously have been after the plantations had been put into effect, and after the Church of Ireland had been given renewed strength with the recovery of whatever property had been lost to it through lay improprietorship, and with the appointment of more clergymen and the establishment of firm discipline. The persecution of the Catholic clergy was therefore to coincide with an active missionary effort on the part of Protestant ministers and there seemed good reason to expect that this would succeed because the ministers would have direct access to the common people who previously had been shielded from outside influence by their Catholic lords.

The one element of Wentworth's scheme that was not revealed was the identity of the new proprietors who would be so crucial to the scheme's success. There are several hints in Wentworth's correspondence with his confidants that associates of theirs were pressing for grants of Irish land, and Wentworth on a few occasions made reference to proprietors who he thought would not be suitable. One of these was the duke of Lennox whose secretary, one Mr Webb, was active in Ireland seeking a grant 'for the whole plantation of Connacht'. Lennox, together with the earls of Arundel and Nithsdale, were recommended to Wentworth by the king without response, but Wentworth seemed more enthusiastic about a brother of Lord Chief Justice Finch who was recommended to him by Cottington. Besides these hints, there are indications that Wentworth had intended to take for himself a large section of the Connacht lands.[56] From these various pieces of information it

[55] Canny, *Upstart Earl*, pp. 9–19, 155–9.
[56] Wentworth to Cottington, 4 Nov. 1633, Str P 3, f. 32; King Charles to Wentworth, 20 Oct.

appears that Wentworth would have preferred as proprietors, English over Scots, and Protestants over Catholics, and that he would have wanted all new landowners to be strong supporters of crown and church. Where these proprietors were to find appropriate settlers for their estates was an issue to which Wentworth had not given much thought but which he obviously believed would be problematic as we can gather from his sneering observation to Archbishop Laud. 'Indeed I have sometimes thought those that go to New England and the other plantations in America might better, by order of the state there, be directed hither where we do in very truth want men exceedingly. But then again when I considered how far most of those people are run out of their wits already I was very well content they should run far.'[57]

Even where the details were not worked out, it is clear that Wentworth was working to a plan, and the plan seems to have been based on the theories that had been formulated in Ireland both before and immediately after the Elizabethan conquest of the country. While it is possible to point to parallels between this plan and the schemes formulated by the advocates of aggressive Anglicisation it is less easy to establish direct influences. It would, for example, be tempting to suggest that his endeavours in Ireland had been inspired by Spenser's *View of the Present State of Ireland* (1596), but Wentworth never referred to the Spenser text in his writings. However, we can be certain that Wentworth was familiar with Spenser's *View* because the first published edition of the text appeared only in 1633 and was dedicated to Wentworth by Sir James Ware who had edited this version. Moreover, the text was recommended by Ware as superior to all other works, 'a few passages excepted', that treated of the reformation of Ireland.[58] While we can consider Spenser's *View* as a possible influence on Wentworth's thinking, we do know that he set about educating himself on how to proceed with the reform of the country from the moment of his appointment. Already in 1633, he remarked that he was 'yet in gathering with all possible circumspection my observations whereupon, what and when to advise a reformation'.[59] Part of what he had

---

1633, Str P 3, f. 39; Cottington to Wentworth, 28 June 1635, Str P 3, f. 214; O'Dowd, *Power*, esp. pp. 115–19.

[57] Wentworth to Laud, 8 June 1638, Str P 7, f. 104.

[58] Preface by Sir James Ware to E. Spenser, *A View of the State of Ireland. Written Dialogue Wise between Eudoxus and Irenaeus* (Dublin, 1633).

[59] Wentworth to Carlisle, 7 Oct. 1633, Str P 8, ff. 30–1.

gathered was a document described as *A Survey of the Government of Ireland 1 January 1631/2*, which was an historical sketch of England's involvement with Ireland similar to that provided in Davies's *Discovery*.[60] Another item that has survived among Wentworth's papers is one entitled *The Heads of all Such Matters as I conceive do conduce for Advancement of the Crown's revenues and the Certainty and Security of the Better subjects of Ireland*. This anonymous text, like the previous one, devoted much space to an historical narrative but employed it to demonstrate the onset of degeneracy first of the Anglo-Norman settlers and more recently of the Elizabethan settlers in Munster. In both instances degeneracy was attributed to 'the immoderate greatness' of those who acquired land in Ireland and who consequently enjoyed excessive authority over 'the earth tillers'. The most recent in this catalogue of neglect were the undertakers in Munster, many of whom had acquired holdings far in excess of the recommended 12,000 acres, with the result that 'some of the heirs of such undertakers are so degenerate as they have renounced their religion and gone to popery'.[61] And a third text surviving among Wentworth's papers, *Butt's Discourse on the State of Ireland*, was also consistent in its arguments with the earlier theorists and pointed to three reasons why the kingdom of Ireland remained in a 'most deformed, desolate and miserable estate'. These were, first, 'the intolerable, malicious instigations of... the Roman clergymen', second, 'the common envy and hatred of most all this country nobility, gentry and farmers freeholders (of the Roman succession) against all strangers in general, but more especially against them that are not of their society', and third, 'the privileges in all or most of the cities or towns corporate in this kingdom' whereby foreign merchants and tradesmen were excluded. The continuation of the *Discourse*, which recommended that Ireland be organised on Protestant lines after the example of the United Provinces, would certainly not have met with the approval of Wentworth, because of his strong monarchical preference.[62] However, the general diagnosis would have confirmed him in his opinion that the security of the three kingdoms would only be achieved when Ireland had been thoroughly Anglicised through the process of plantation and resettlement.

Once account is taken of this direction of Wentworth's policy and

---

60 'A Survey of the Government of Ireland...', Str P 34.
61 'The Heads of all Such Matters...', Str P 24–25/142.
62 'Butt's Discourse on the State of Ireland', Str P 24–25/141.

its inspiration we can conclude that the government in Ireland during the entire period 1603–42 was firmly set upon a radical course of Anglicisation except for the brief interlude during the 1620s when this was abandoned for tactical reasons. This establishes that those English officials who served in Ireland had come to perceive Irish social conditions as essentially different from those which obtained in England, and had come to see their primary function as that of reshaping Irish society so that it would conform with English standards. These officials had therefore departed totally from the political philosophy that had obtained up to the first half of the sixteenth century when the purpose of government was considered to be the protection of those in Ireland who owed allegiance to the English crown. It seems clear from Wentworth's correspondence that many senior officials in London were ready to endorse this newly defined function of government, and it appears from the early years of the seventeenth century that even the monarch, in that case King James, recognised the logic of the drastic course being recommended to him by his representatives in Ireland. However, that monarch's primary concern was with establishing himself firmly on the throne of England while maintaining his influence in Scotland, and his occasional enthusiasm for innovation in Ireland was dampened by his concern to make progress in areas of government that were important to him. Queen Elizabeth, who had preceded him on the English throne, was equally reluctant to give a high priority to Irish affairs, although she had steeled herself to see the war against Tyrone through to the bitter end. Financial considerations go a long way to explaining the queen's general hesitation to give her approval to extreme measures, but she was also held back by her belief that her primary obligation was to uphold the position of those who professed loyalty to her, even when these refused to be included within the religion of the state. King Charles I shared this same conservatism with Queen Elizabeth, and his officials, including even Wentworth, had to work around him when it came to determining a policy for Ireland. As a consequence, the English government had no official policy where Ireland was concerned, and the absence of such a policy was an essential source of weakness for the monarchy. It was such because it left Charles seeking to uphold a status quo in Ireland at a time when this status quo was considered anomalous and threatening by his Protestant subjects in all of the three kingdoms. This leads us to the conclusion that the collapse of the British monarchy occurred not because of the policies that were pursued by Charles, but because he failed to endorse a scheme of government for Ireland that was considered just and reasonable by the vast majority of the more influential subjects in the three kingdoms. Had he taken the advice that was proferred so liberally by the theorists, and had he given a free hand to Wentworth, it is likely that he would have encountered armed opposition from the Catholic landowners in Ireland, possibly supported by Irish soldiers returned from service in continental Europe. Such an operation would have been formidable but not insuperable because the king, and Wentworth, in opposing it would have enjoyed the fulsome support of Protestants in England, Scotland and Ireland. A war, the ultimate objective of which was the Anglicisation (and the Protestantisation) of Ireland, would thus also have contributed to the formation of a coherent British monarchy, the previous existence of which was no more than putative.

The fact that the king failed to accept the advice that was offered him meant that he was left with the problem of governing three kingdoms, each of which (and especially Ireland) had a society and a polity that was different from the other two. His attempts (and those of his successors, including Oliver Cromwell) to grapple with this problem have been the subject of fruitful investigation by historians, but of equal merit is the historical work which seeks to describe and explain the distinctiveness of each of the three kingdoms. Such work is important because, as will be evident from this chapter, the policy-makers of successive British monarchs frequently proceeded as if each kingdom was a self-contained entity, and only occasionally treated the three monarchies as a single political jurisdiction. Further work on the particular is also necessary because the social context was distinctive within each of the kingdoms, and also because those who dominated local society within the kingdoms functioned on at least three levels – within the locality, in national politics and at court – almost as if each level of power and influence was independent of the others. Continued investigation of the separate jurisdictions is also called for so that we can better understand the very different continental contacts that were maintained by the several communities in each of the three kingdoms. These contacts with the continent contributed to and helped sustain the diversity of the three kingdoms, and inspired individuals to engage upon undertakings that would have been beyond their ken had they limited their horizons to the kingdoms of the British monarchy. While thus encouraging further investigation of the particular, I should also emphasise that I am not disparaging what has already been written and what, hopefully, will continue to be written within a broader British context. My concern rather is that excessive emphasis on the British dimension to the history of the three kingdoms will result in people forgetting that the best history is that which addresses problems to which solutions must be pursued in complete disregard of any geographic frontiers.

CHAPTER 8

'God bless your free Church of Ireland':
Wentworth, Laud, Bramhall and the Irish Convocation of 1634

John McCafferty

I

In November 1638, Wentworth was directed by Laud to answer those Scots in Ireland looking for the same concessions as their countrymen had been granted that 'whatsoever he [the king] hath indulged to Scotland, is because they have had there sometime a church government, such as it was, confused enough without bishops; but for Ireland, it hath ever been reformed by and to the Church of England'.[1]

Was this so? Was the Church of Ireland merely a branch grown out of the Church of England? The Henrician statutes seem to confirm Laud's view giving the overall impression that the Church of Ireland was to follow, to the letter, such changes as were made in the Church of England. However, Ireland was not England and *cuius regio* was not to be *eius religio*. In the reconstruction of the established church after Mary's reign we can detect the beginnings of a Church of Ireland which had a distinct identity, moulded on the one hand by the religious environment of Ireland and on the other by the effects of that environment on Reformation attitudes.

The Irish Act of Uniformity of 1560 permitted the use of Latin and in stark contrast to England most of the Marian episcopate stayed on.[2] While the subsequent failure to bring in the Thirty-nine Articles might have originally been a feature of Catholic survivalism it created the basis of a reformed Church of Ireland which sought, much more than in England, to define itself against the Catholic Church.

Also significant for the future was the opening of Trinity College

---

[1] Laud to Wentworth, 2 Nov. 1638 , Laud, VI, 543–4.
[2] H. A. Jeffries, 'The Irish parliament of 1560: the Anglican reforms authorized', *Irish Historical Studies* 26 (1988), pp. 128–41.

Dublin to students in early 1594. Trinity was modelled on Emmanuel
and the 'puritan' ethos was reflected not only in its constitution but
in the choice of heads – the first acting Provost was Walter Travers.
He was succeeded by Henry Alvey and William Temple which
reinforced the Cambridge link and the godly aspect of the college.

James I re-endowed the university in a bid to attract native Irish
students who would play a crucial role in converting the Irish to
Protestantism. In this respect, the college was not successful. Only a
small number of the students, even in the late 1610s were of native or
of Old English extraction.[3] Trinity's performance as a seminary was
also disappointing – in 1622 there were only thirteen of its graduates
throughout all eight of the Ulster dioceses despite generous endowment from the plantation lands.[4]

It has been argued that what is important to mark in Trinity's
failure as an instrument of Anglicisation is not that it became 'a
puritan bastion', but that there was an increasing predestinarian
emphasis in theological thought. Yet it is equally important to see in
Trinity the development of the Church of Ireland being steered in a
more Reformed direction.[5] In doing so, it was to become an example
to be emulated by some elements in the Church of England.

It would be wrong to suggest that the Protestant Church turned its
back entirely on the Gaelic Irish. In 1608, William Daniel (a product
of Emmanuel and Trinity College Dublin) published his *Leabhar Na
nUrnaightheadh gComhchoidchiond*. This was more than a translation of
the Book of Common Prayer into Irish, it was an expression of the
identity of the Church of Ireland. The preface contrasted the
'ancient flourishing state of religion in Ireland' with a country which
now 'doth generally sit in darkness', a decline caused by the
corruptions of the papacy.[6] Daniel's purpose in translating the
Prayer Book was polemical – to undeceive the Irish but to undeceive
them with a certain bias in that translation.[7] Throughout, 'minisdir'
is used instead of 'sagart' (priest). Furthermore, while he uses native
phrases for various saint's days (e.g., *lá fheile Muire na féile Brigdhe* for

3   A. Ford, *The Protestant Reformation in Ireland, 1560–1641* (Frankfurt, 1987), p. 105.
4   *Ibid.*, p. 78.
5   *Ibid.*, p. 199; A. Clarke, 'Varieties of uniformity', in W. J. Shiels and D. Wood, (eds.), *The
     Churches, Ireland and the Irish* (Oxford, 1989), p. 118.
6   *Leabhar Na nUrnaightheadh gComhchoidchiond* (Dublin, 1608), sig A2; F. R. Bolton, *The Caroline
     Tradition of the Church of Ireland* (1958), p. 8; Ford, *Protestant Reformation*, pp. 125–6.
7   W. Reeves, *The Book of Common Prayer according to the use of the Irish Church, Its History and
     Sanction* (Dublin, 1871), pp. 35–6; N. Williams, *I bPrionta I Leabhar: Na Protastúin agus Prós na
     Gaeilge, 1567–1724* (Baile Átha Cliath, 1986), chs. 3, 9, *passim*.

the Purification of Mary) the almanac has nowhere near the same number of saint's days as the English book of 1604, and mentions no Irish saints, not even Patrick. Clearly, the Church of Ireland was not going to make any attempt to inculturate. The same desire to define Protestantism in opposition to Catholicism is to be found in the use of 'comhchoidhchiond' (common) throughout rather than 'catoili-ceach' wherever the word 'catholic' occurred. Not surprisingly, the Act of Uniformity translated is the English one of 1559, rather than the Irish one.

As an expression of identity, two points should be noted. The first is the veneration of the early Irish church. This gave the Church of Ireland a historical pedigree, allowing ancient disputes such as the dating of Easter to be interpreted as proof of the Celtic church's original independence from Rome. The second feature of this Prayer Book is the quiet but significant alteration of parts of the English liturgy and the silent omission of the form of ordering bishops and priests while following the 1604 book in all other respects. This was the practical expression of Irish autonomy.

The Irish Articles of 1615 were a veritable declaration of the independence of the Church of Ireland.[8] The Irish Articles contained all but one of the Thirty-nine Articles; they also condensed some of the English Homilies and incorporated eight of the Lambeth Articles.[9] While it is true that the Irish Articles were 'unmistakably to the theological left', how far did they reflect the identity of the Church of Ireland beyond articulating a predestinarian theology in the face of the 'obduracy' of the Gaelic Irish?[10]

An immediate connection can be made with Daniel's Book of Common Prayer in the omission of English Article 36 on the consecration of bishops and ministers. This was an important lacuna in that it broadened the base of the Church of Ireland in order to preserve a united Protestant front in the face of Catholicism. Article 80 was the very cornerstone of this Protestant unity: 'The Bishop of Rome is. . . that man of sin foretold in the Holy Scriptures.'[11]

But the Irish Articles were more than reactive: Peter Heylyn correctly maintained that subscription to the Irish Articles meant

[8]   It is interesting to note that no Irish translation of the 1615 Articles was made.
[9]   R. B. Knox, *James Ussher, Archbishop of Armagh* (Cardiff, 1967), p. 17.
[10]   Clarke, 'Varieties of uniformity', p. 118.
[11]   The edition of the Irish Articles in *The Whole Works of James Ussher*, ed. C. R. Elrington and J. R. Todd, (17 vols., Dublin, 1847–64), I, appendix iv, was used as a working text.

easy subscription to the 'articles of all the reformed (or Calvinian) churches' but subscription to the English Articles allowed no such continental drift.[12] Heylyn saw that the Church of Ireland in 1615 was proceeding in its own direction and the Articles were the product of its independence. The constitutional arrangements of the kingdom of Ireland were crucial to this development of the church's identity as they left room for the articulation of the experiences of the Irish church in articles of religion. When the clergy of Dublin declared in 1647 that 'the reformed Church of Ireland under the government of our dread sovereign the King is and ever was reputed a free national church', they were not just fighting a rearguard action for the preservation of the Prayer Book, they were arguing for a distinct tradition and identity.[13]

However, Irish independence was not absolute, nor was there any real indigenous or autocephalic Protestant tradition emerging. The Irish Articles of 1615 were a gloss on, or an elaboration of, the 1562 and 1566 Articles, Daniel's Prayer Book was a translation, not a new composition, and the omission of English Article 36 was offset by the fact that there was episcopacy (and with a vengeance, there being twenty-five dioceses!) with full hierarchical government. The Church of Ireland might have been constitutionally independent and it might even have been moving down a more 'continental' road but the truth was that any such development was coming out of a recognisably English context, and could easily be placed on an English spectrum. As the balance of ecclesiastical power and, indeed, of ecclesiology itself shifted after the death of James, the qualified independence of the Church of Ireland came up for review.

II

It was precisely because the Irish Articles had a resonance in England that attention was focused on them by Wentworth's ecclesiastical factotum, John Bramhall, shortly after his arrival. In 1626 and 1628 bills had been introduced in the English parliament aiming to give joint statutory authority to the Thirty-nine Articles and the

---

[12] P. Heylyn, *Respondet Petrus* (1658), p. 128.
[13] E. Borlase, *History of the Execrable Irish Rebellion* (1680), p. 96. 'The Articles of the Church of England were not held or reputed the Articles of the Church of Ireland, and when they were received, they were not received in any acknowledged subordination to the Church of England.'

Irish Articles.[14] Thus, the problem of preserving the peace of the Church of England and the question of the autonomy of the Church of Ireland were linked.

Bramhall first suggested establishing the English Articles: 'I doubt much whether the clergy be very orthodox and could wish both the Articles and Canons of the Church of England were established here by Act of Parliament or State; yet as we live all under one kingdom, so we might both in doctrine and discipline deserve an uniformity.'[15] Bramhall's wish to conform Ireland to the Church of England was actuated as much by an ambition to create internal unity in the Church of Ireland through applying the ban on contentious debates as it was by a desire to create outward conformity. Wentworth, writing to Laud some months later, explicitly alluded not to the lack of uniformity but to the expression of autonomy: 'It is true indeed these Articles were changed here, which are such the Primate disavows and myself rest amazed that they ever slipped themselves in amongst us.'[16] The imposition of the Thirty-nine Articles would solve an English problem and an Irish problem simultaneously.

Accounts of the 1634 convocation have tended to focus on the English Articles as the main event and relegate the drive to canonical uniformity to the position of an epilogue or, at best, a mildly successful counter-attack on the part of Ussher and the Church of Ireland. This is mistaken – the canons and a canonically inspired set of church reforms were an essential and significant counterpart to the Articles, and to the drive for temporal reform: 'the repair of the material and spiritual church together', as Laud put it.[17]

In a key letter in which, as he put it, Wentworth 'anatomised' the 'Irish ecclesiastical disease', the Lord Deputy proposed that High Commission should be re-established in Ireland but of the six reasons given for re-establishing the Commission, only one related to the problem of recusancy. This was a radical break with past policy which had used High Commission as a key instrument in the presentment and fining of recusants. Under Wentworth, however, it was to be used as a means of securing the uniformity required by the canons (once they had been passed) and of overhauling the internal judicial

---

[14] N. Tyacke, *Anti-Calvinists* (Oxford, 1991), pp. 154–5.
[15] Bramhall to Laud, 10 Aug. 1633, *The Works of the Most Reverend John Bramhall*, ed. A. W. H. (5 vols., Oxford, 1842–5), I, lxxx–lxxxii.
[16] Wentworth to Laud, 5 May 1634 , Str P 6, p. 56.
[17] Laud to Wentworth, 11 March 1634, Laud,VI, 354.

mechanisms of the Church. Laud's response to this proposal added a
further twist: 'I hope your lordship will be content we shall leave
power to the Commission here to call over such causes as may appear
too strong for that court, or in any great respect be fit to be heard
here.'[18] This provision marks another important departure – Ireland
was not only being brought into line with England but through a
supervisory role for the English High Commission there was the
means to ensure that it stayed in line. Under Laud and Wentworth,
haphazard and incidental attention to Ireland was transformed into
sustained attention and unprecedented interference.[19]

The great difficulty about discussing the Irish convocation of 1634
is that the journals are missing.[20] I have attempted to reconstruct the
exact sequence of events in Convocation, but as this is too long and
complex for the present purposes, I will instead mention only a
number of key events and themes.[21] There are two main facts to
bear in mind. The first is that Wentworth wanted, as he put it, to
'carry it so as to have the Articles of England received in *ipsissimis
verbis* leaving the other as no ways concerned in the state they now
are, either affirmed or disaffirmed'; that is, to see the English Articles
accepted without any reference at all to the Irish Articles. The
second is that Ussher was intent on preserving the Irish Articles in
some form or other but had given Wentworth the impression that he
was for their suppression.

While the first session of Convocation in July and August got off to
an amicable start by voting eight subsidies, it ended in a near miss
for Wentworth as an attempt was made on the last day of the first
session (2 August) to have the Irish Articles confirmed along with the
English just two hours after they had been proposed, 'without
consulting his majesty or his deputy'.[22] What we might call the Irish

---

18   Laud to Wentworth, 12 April 1634, Laud, VII, 67.
19   Wentworth agreed: Wentworth to Laud, 5 May 1634, Str P 6, pp. 56–7. In fact Laud
     already used English High Commission to deal with Irish matters in acting against a Jew
     running a school in Derry, Laud, VI, 308–9.
20   They were extant amongst Clarendon's Irish manuscripts but dropped out of sight after
     the sale of the Chandos library and did not reappear in the British Museum or the
     Rawlinson collection. Trinity College Dublin, MS 1062, p. 65; R. Nicholson, *The Irish
     Historical Library* (Dublin, 1724) p. 28; Bolton, *Caroline Tradition*, p. 11.
21   A narrative drawing on the full range of Wentworth and Bramhall correspondence has
     never been attempted before. I am attempting to do so in my forthcoming Cambridge
     University Ph. D. dissertation. The closest, so far, to a full narrative in print is in Bolton,
     Caroline Tradition , pp. 11–18.
22   Bramhall's agent in the lower house was James Croxton, who had been recommended to
     Mountnorris as a chaplain by Laud.

'church party' had, for its part, accepted that the English Articles would be authorised for Ireland but sought to give their own confession equal status. The first session, then, can be characterised as a period of skirmishing in which Ussher gradually dropped his pretence of acquiescence but avoided open conflict by continuing to work with Bramhall. Wentworth's almost casual allusion to 'some little trouble there had been in it, and we are all bound not to advertise it over' evokes an image of opposing sides with strong views endeavouring to avoid a major incident. Given the delicate state of the Commons, none wished this more fervently than Wentworth.[23]

Laud, too, was concerned to keep all quiet and especially to conceal Ussher's involvement from Charles who would react very poorly to any apparent disobedience. Laud did tell Charles about the plan to have the English Articles received without either affirmation or denial of the Irish confession. This met with the king's approval.[24] On the wider plane, public knowledge of events which could be construed as unjustified interference in the affairs of the Church of Ireland (or even, as it later was, an act of tyranny) would be a godsend to his opponents. This concern with damage limitation persisted even when any semblance of a quiet passage was lost. By the middle of December, the action had shifted to the lower house in an effort to push the Irish Articles through by pressure from below.[25] This move also offered Ussher the chance to use the intransigence of the clergy as an excuse while refraining from expressing his personal opposition to the proposed settlement.

Wentworth expressed his determination to go ahead as planned, even raising the possibility of imposing the English Articles and Canons 'by the King's immediate pleasure' without the assent of Convocation, but only as a last resort after every effort to secure assent had been exhausted.

On 10 December, Wentworth's patience broke. As he explained later, it was Ussher's profession of his doubts about getting the English Articles through the lower house which alerted him.[26]

23 For this session of the Irish House of Commons, see Hugh Kearney, *Strafford in Ireland*, *1633-41* (Manchester, 1959; 2nd edn, Cambridge, 1989) chs. 5, 6; A. Clarke, 'The government of Wentworth', in *NHI*, III, ch. ix.
24 Laud to Wentworth, 20 Oct. 1634, Laud, VI, 397.
25 Wentworth identified the opposition in Convocation as a group filled with 'a contradicting spirit of puritanism', Str P 6, p. 123.
26 Wentworth to Laud, 16 Dec. 1634, Knowler, I, 342: 'I rested secure upon the Primate, who all this while said not a word to me of the matter. At length I got a little time, and that most happily too, informed myself of the state of affairs.'

Preoccupation with the intricate game he had been playing in Parliament, he claimed, had led him to rely on Ussher. In fact, Wentworth had completed his last manoeuvre against the Old English on 27 November so his energies were not as fully engaged during the final days of the session. Bramhall claimed that it was he who had alerted Wentworth to the danger in Convocation, and given the speed with which the latter acted on 9 and 10 December this is probably true.[27] Therefore, in his letter to Laud, Wentworth was magnifying his own part and placing the blame on Ussher whose tactics in Convocation had been very like his own in Parliament.

What had happened? The lower house of Convocation had formed a select committee which proceeded to examine the English Canons 'without conferring at all with their bishops'.[28] In the margins of the book they marked those they allowed with an 'A' and others with a 'D' which stood for *deliberandum*. They had also composed an Irish Canon 5 which established the 1615 Articles on pain of excommunication.[29] For Wentworth, the draft canon was the worst of both worlds – an authorisation of the Irish Articles and a broadening of the base of the established church.

Wentworth hauled George Andrews (the chairman of the committee) before him and proceeded to examine the annotated canons with growing anger: 'I told him certainly not a dean of Limerick but an Ananias had been there in spirit, if not in body, with all the fraternities and conventicles of Amsterdam.' Andrews was not permitted to report back to the committee. Next, Ussher, Anthony Martin of Meath, Bedell of Kilmore, John Leslie of Raphoe, Bramhall and Henry Lesley (as Prolocutor of the lower house) and the members of the committee were summoned to appear before the Lord Deputy the next morning. Another angry speech ensued in which Wentworth represented the actions of the committee as an attack on the hierarchy of the church. A series of orders followed: Andrews was not to report anything from the committee to the lower house, Lesley was to 'break up' the house if any member of the committee attempted a question, and only the reception of the English Articles was to be put to the house. The votes, 'content' or 'not content', were to be recorded by name 'without admitting any other discourse at all, for I would not endure that the Articles of the Church of England should be disputed'. Finally Ussher was deputed to frame a canon which, when checked by the Lord Deputy, could then be sent on to the Prolocutor.[30]

Wentworth's actions obliterated any prospect of independent action on the part of Convocation. They could accept or reject the English Articles – no more and no less. It is striking that no formal powers had been invoked; Wentworth had acted simply in person as viceroy. He was conscious that he might have acted *ultra vires* and, while he tried to trivialise his anxieties,[31] he repeatedly pressed Laud for a letter from the king 'either of allowance of what I have done or for my absolution'.[32] Constitutionally, it was a tricky point. The Irish Act of Uniformity extended the authority to 'ordain and publish' ceremonies and rites to the Lord Deputy, but it is unlikely it could have been stretched to cover these actions. Royal approbation or absolution was the only sure defence.

Ussher's canon represented a last ditch effort to salvage something from the wreckage.[33] He began with a 'manifestation of our agreement', an attempt to soften the blow by portraying the acceptance of the English Articles as the agreement of one free church with another. He went further and tried in the final clause to sneak in a form of the 'Decree of the Synod' attached to the end of the 1615 Articles. Deprivation of benefices (not always possible to enforce, especially in parts of Ulster) was a far cry from excommunication and public revocation. It was this last clause which spurred Wentworth, disliking both the sanction and evocation of 1615, to draw up his version 'more after the words of the canon in England'. This new draft brought Ussher rushing to Wentworth to press for his own canon as 'he feared the canon would never pass in such form, as I had made it'.[34]

Wentworth persisted, as he explained to Laud, because he felt he could no longer trust the primate to be frank with him.[35] Once again, Wentworth avoided openly personalising the conflict. Ussher,

---

[30]   Wentworth told Laud he was sending him a list of those on the committee; this too, is no longer extant. Wentworth to Laud, 16 Dec. 1634, Knowler, I, 343.

[31]   'I am not ignorant that my stirring herein will be strangely reported and censured on that side, and how I shall be able to sustain myself against your Prynnes Pims and Bens, with the rest of that generation of odd names and natures, the Lord knows,' Knowler, I, 344.

[32]   Wentworth to Laud, 16 Dec. 1634, Knowler, I, 344. For pressure on Laud to have his letter: Knowler, II, 381; Laud, VII, 118, 122, 280.

[33]   Str P 20/172.   [34]   Knowler, I, 344.

[35]   'Having taken a little jealousy that his proceedings were not open and free to those ends I had my eye on', Wentworth to Laud, 16 Dec. 1634, Knowler, I, 344.

like the earl of Cork, was not to become a focus for opposition. His standing in England meant any controversy would have more than domestic implications. At the same time, Laud and Wentworth could be confident that if no overt offence was given, the primate would hold his peace.

A letter to the Prolocutor was dispatched enjoining a straight vote without debate and a record of the 'voices consenting or dissenting'.[36] That afternoon the canon was passed unanimously by the bishops and the rest of the clergy with only one dissentient.[37] Strategically, this was a comprehensive defeat for the Irish 'church party'. The only resort now was to argue that since the Irish Articles had not been touched on, one way or another, double subscription was a valid option. Yet by avoiding the disaster of dissolution, Convocation remained sitting and capable of affecting the shape of the canonical settlement. Overall, then, it was a qualified defeat for the Church of Ireland.

III

The third session of Parliament began on 26 January 1635 but there was to be no easy passage in Convocation. By the middle of February Bramhall found himself embroiled once again. A new book of canons composed 'of the English and Irish Canons never yet allowed and the Injunctions' was being offered to Convocation 'upon a pretence that the English canons will not pass freely unless they be brought in by a wile'. He admitted, grudgingly, that some special canons might be needed 'for this meridian' but expressed his opposition to some of those now on offer.[38] Here was an important difference in perception between Wentworth and Bramhall and the Irish clergy. For the Lord Deputy and bishop, any discrete Irish canons would merely allow for the specifics of the Irish situation, but the overall thrust of legislation would establish and even improve on the English standard – this was their principle of congruence. For the rump of the Church of Ireland the goal was to preserve something of autonomy and peculiarity by more widespread modifications.

---

[36] Wentworth to the Prolocutor, 10 Dec. 1634, Trinity College Dublin, MS 1038, f. 111v; Str P 20/173.

[37] Knowler, I, 344.

[38] Bramhall to Laud, 18 Feb. 1635, Huntington Library (San Marino, California), MS HA 14048.

Skirmishing started again. Bramhall had persuaded Ussher to send the drafts to Laud for his 'advice' but was still confident of the English Canons in full.[39] Laud duly reviewed the canons, treating the question of Ussher gingerly: 'I have pressed the English Canons to be received *formaliter*, a little softer to my Lord Primate... I leave the further care of this business to you.'[40] The primate was now in a stronger position than before, as Wentworth had stretched his powers to the limit to secure the English Articles. His needling actions – attacking Laud's protégé Croxton, backing Dean Andrews, giving spiky sermons – were all hushed, but still audible notes, of discontent. Behind them lay, as ever, the spectre of a public breach. Wentworth got the message. In his next letter to Laud he acknowledged the desirability of a full set of English canons but laid great emphasis on Ussher's opposition: 'the Primate is hugely against it... lest Ireland might become subject to the Church of England, as the province of York is to that of Canterbury'.[41] Wentworth failed to understand Ussher: the primate's objections were a matter of 'punctilio', a mere 'crotchet', he had been put up to it by 'puritan correspondents of his' who took advantage of his desire to please everybody. Wentworth also referred Ussher to Laud's judgement. The invocation of Canterbury on top of total incomprehension only added oil to Ussher's fire. Laud was hardly better, his only comment to Wentworth being that these objections were proof that Armagh had been behind the opposition to the Articles.[42]

With such misunderstanding, the session ended on 21 March. The final session of Parliament began on 24 March.[43] By 13 April Wentworth was able to inform Laud that a book of canons had been passed even though Ussher had gone to the point of threatening to resign 'least forsooth, the Church of Ireland should be held subordinate to the Church of England'.[44] This had happened not because

---

[39] Though Bramhall was beginning to appreciate the opportunities – a chance to make up canonically for some of the losses in Parliament such as the failed bills on simony and for residence of beneficed persons, Bramhall to Laud, 20 Dec. 1634 , Shirley, *Papers*, p. 44.

[40] Laud to Bramhall, 4 March 1635, Huntington Library, Hastings MSS HA 15172, no. vi.

[41] Wentworth to Laud, 10 March 1635, Knowler, 1 381.

[42] Laud to Wentworth, 27 March 1635, Laud, vi, 118. Laud's further comment: 'what hurt were it more that the canons of the Church should be the same, than it is that the Laws are the same?' indicates that he had completely missed the tenor of Ussher's previous letters to him.

[43] Parliament was dissolved on 18 April 1635.

[44] Wentworth to Laud, 18 April 1635, Str P 6, p. 162.

Wentworth had arrived at an understanding of Ussher's fears but because he had come to accept that some concessions had to be made. The new book of canons was a compromise. Wentworth and Bramhall could be jubilant about altars at the east end, or auricular confession but they had to concede defeat on bowing to the name of Jesus for, as Wentworth remarked, 'They have no more joints in their knees for that than an elephant.'[45]

Ussher expressed his desire to extend the 'right hand of fellowship' and give 'due honour' to the Church of England but cautioned against giving up the right to an Irish Church, lest in time there should come into existence the canonical equivalent of Poynings's Act.[46] Some discrepancy must continue as an expression of *autezia*, 'that there is no necessity of the same in all churches that are independent, as these are, of one another; that Rome and Milan might have different canons and modes and yet the same faith and charity and communion'. Laud's response to the outcome was sarcastic: 'God bless your free Church of Ireland, though for my part I do not think the canons of the Church of England would have shot any of the freedom of it.'[47]

IV

If the Irish Canons were a compromise, who composed them and how much did they differ from the English Canons of 1604? Andrews's committee formulated modified versions of English Canons 5 , 13, 14, 15 and 17.[48] Canon 5 was altered, as we have seen, to include subscription of the Irish Articles, while each of the others was rewritten in such a way as to lessen its impact or make it less specific. Twenty-eight other canons were 'doubted of'.[49] Out of the thirty-three English canons touched upon by the committee of convocation, ten were omitted from the final version, eight were

---

[45] Wentworth to Laud, 18 April 1635, Str P 6, p. 164. See also Nicolas Bernard, *Judgment of the Archbishop of Armagh* (1657), p. 147.

[46] J. Vesey, *Athanasius Hibernicus* (1676), p. xix: 'that nothing shall be law here that were not first allowed there, and afterward, that we must refuse nothing here, that there had obtained a confirmation'.

[47] Laud to Bramhall, 11 May 1635, Huntington Library, Hastings MSS HA 15172, no. vii.

[48] 5 (on subscription), 13 (celebration of Sundays and holydays) 14 (Book of Common Prayer to be said reverently and distinctly on Sundays), 15 (the liturgy to be said or sung in cathedral churches) and 17 (Masters and fellows of Colleges to wear surplices).

[49] Eleven of the twenty-nine English Canons eventually omitted were in the range English Canons 72–141.

modified in some way[50] and fifteen were reproduced verbatim. A total of 141 English canons became 100 Irish – 29 English canons were dropped entirely and there were 11 uniquely Irish canons. The canons, as a whole, betray some signs of haste – while the English Canons and the Scottish Canons of 1636 are divided into thematic sections, the Irish Canons follow no discernible thematic order and there are a number of non-sequiturs and small contradictions throughout.

The alterations made to the English Canons were much more than the raggedness of a deal worked out in a hurry. In their final form the Irish Canons were the product of a clash between Bramhall, trying not only to ensure the greatest conformity with England but also to target specific Irish abuses and 'improve' on the English Canons, and Ussher, who was seeking to preserve the broader more godly base of the Irish church and trying to ensure that some marks of independence were included in the canons. In the event, Bramhall went far beyond a grudging acceptance of some canons necessary for 'that meridian' and Ussher secured something other than total defeat.

In itself, Irish Canon 7 reproduces many of the features of the wider canonical settlement.[51] It was an amalgam of three English canons – 14, 18 and 25. A close reading of this canon is highly revealing. The first thing to note is the alterations to the canons it encompasses. English Canon 14 begins: 'the Common Prayer shall be said or sung distinctly and reverently upon such days as are appointed to be kept holy by the Book of Common Prayer'. Irish Canon 7 specifies that 'parsons, vicars and curates shall celebrate divine service at convenient and usual times'. So while the Irish Canons do not enjoin the use of the litany (English Canon 15), the rules for timing of litanies are transferred to the celebration of Divine Service. The Irish Canons specify 'Sundays and holydays', again corresponding to English Canon 15 rather than English Canon 14, which merely specifies the days appointed by the Prayer Book. English Canons 14 and 15 were on the list of those 'doubted' by the Irish committee, but while the litanies of English Canon 15 have been dropped, its provisions have been imported to strengthen English Canon 14.

English Canon 18, again one of those 'doubted of', has been

---

50   That is, beyond minor changes, such as replacing 'England' with 'Ireland', etc.
51   *Constitutions and Canons Ecclesiastical* (Dublin, 1635).

heavily cut. It omits the ·English preamble 'let all things be done decently and according to order' but keeps the provisions for behaviour during services. But it then proceeds to omit completely the directions on kneeling and standing and, of course, bowing at the name of Jesus. English Canons 16 and 17 regulating behaviour in university chapels were omitted from the Irish Canons; this looked very much like a victory for Trinity College.[52] English Canon 24, on the use of copes, was bound to fall if ritual gestures had been pushed out, but English Canon 25 managed to survive.

The omission of English Canons 16, 17, and 24, as well as the mutilation of English Canon 18, looked very much like a victory for Ussher. But it was not clear-cut, because Bramhall had contrived to alter one line of English Canon 14 which now read: 'All ministers likewise shall use and observe the orders, rites, *ornaments* and ceremonies prescribed in the Book of Common Prayer and in the *Act for Uniformity printed therewith.*'[53] By inserting the references to 'ornaments' and the Act of Uniformity, Bramhall had clawed back considerable ground. The standard of vestments as well as the orders, rites and ceremonies were to be those of 2 Edward VI.[54] Only a royal command (or under the Irish Act of Uniformity, that of the Lord Deputy and Council) could now make any alteration, which was not about to happen. Ussher and his supporters were permitted to pare away the English Canons only to the degree which Bramhall and Wentworth were willing to countenance in the interests of peace. In return, they had to accept clauses written by Bramhall which limited their success. Irish Canon 7 was not an unqualified Laudian victory but neither was it an Irish triumph. It was a compromise which allowed both sides to believe that they had won the argument.

In canons dealing with the sacraments the Irish code was most distinct. Irish Canons 19 and 94 (confession and altars) have always been singled out as indicating a Laudian high-tide mark in the Irish Church. The directions for 'the special ministry of reconciliation' were tacked on to English Canon 22.[55] The canon exhorted people, on hearing the bell, to examine their consciences, and if then 'finding themselves extreme dull or much troubled in mind, they do resort

52 But a short-lived one, as the new Laudian statutes would regulate on these matters.
53 This phrase (italics mine) is to be found in Irish Canon 13, 'Preachers and Lecturers to read divine service and administer the sacraments twice a year at least'.
54 This meant that he also saved the use of the sign of the cross in baptism, so ostentatiously missing from the Irish Canons.
55 English Canon 22, 'Warning to be given beforehand for the communion'.

unto God's ministers' to receive advice and counsel 'as the benefit of absolution likewise for the quieting of their consciences, by the power of the keys which Christ hath committed to his ministers for that purpose'.[56]

Irish Canon 94 was composed of English Canons 80, 81, 82 and 83 but with a number of key changes. It shifted the communion table from the chancel (English Canon 82) to the east end and it also stipulated 'a cup of silver for the celebration of holy communion'. As the status of the altar was improved, the Word took a blow – Irish Canon 94 omits the direction to place the Ten Commandments on the east wall.[57]

To these we must add a unique Irish Canon, 43, which provided for the consecration of new churches. This was more than just a preparation for the construction of new churches in the course of plantation. All three canons, 19, 94 and 43 reflect a special emphasis on the eucharist and the church as a place set apart. Within the church, the altar was to be the focus of attention and, in the hearts of the communicants, absolution provided a way up to the altar – an altar at which the priest administered the sacramental wine in a precious cup. There might be no mandatory bowing, but Irish Canon 18 extended the kneeling required of members of the universities (English Canon 23) to all communicants.

The new provisions were an assault on the practices of the Irish church. In his own chapel, Ussher had no table[58] and in St Peter's, Drogheda, where he preached on Sundays, the communion table 'was placed lengthwise in the aisle'.[59] Wentworth was quick to emphasise the canons on the altar and confession to Laud who was pleased enough to comment that the refusal to receive the English Canons unchanged had had some advantages.[60] Once again, Ireland proved to be a place where the Church of England could be improved on.

Laud exhibited more enthusiasm for the canon on confession than for that on the altar.[61] Why confession? If the provisions made in the

---

[56] See Scottish Canons (1636), ch. xvii, 9.
[57] Also, perhaps reflecting the high numbers of graduate clergy, parishes did not have to provide the Book of Homilies but they did have to procure the King James Bible.
[58] 'No bowing here I awarrant you!', Wentworth to Laud, 27 Nov. 1638, Knowler, ii, 249.
[59] W. Brereton, *Travels in Holland and... Ireland*, ed. E. Hawkins (Manchester, 1844), p. 135.
[60] Laud to Wentworth, 12 May 1635, Laud, vii, 132: 'And one passing good thing we have got by it, besides the placing of the altar at the east end, and that is a passing good canon about confession'. See also Wentworth to Laud, 13 April 1635 and 14 July 1635, Str P 6, pp. 164, 201.
[61] Laud to Bramhall, 11 May 1635, Huntington Library, Hastings MSS HA 15172, no. vii.

Irish Canons placed renewed emphasis on the sacraments, they also gave, in this canon above all, more attention to the role of the priest in the administration of the sacraments.[62] Bramhall, like Neile, acknowledged the usefulness and antiquity of confession but was always careful to castigate Roman abuses of it.[63] Since 'God absolves by the priest', the dignity of the clerical estate was a necessary adjunct to the dignity of the priest, which these canons emphasised.[64] This has nothing to do with Dutch or 'English' Arminianism. This clericalism, resurgent in England during the 1630s, was capable, in Ireland, of expression not just through a vigorous temporalities campaign or through sermons but in the formulation of a code of canons.[65]

A clue to the foundation of this Laudian clericalism is to be found in a letter to Ussher of 1636.[66] In it, Laud expressed the king's concern at the failure of bishops to wear rochets and episcopal attire at prayers and preaching 'as if they were ashamed of their calling'.[67] To propitiate Ussher he explained: 'His Majesty's meaning is not conformity to the Church of England, but with the whole catholic church of Christ.'[68] As the temporal rights of the church were conceived of and claimed in historical terms, so were the customs and order of the church.[69] Laud's programme was not Romanisation but re-catholicisation. Now that the Church of England had been 'weeded' of the abuses of Rome the customs of the early church could be rediscovered through careful study of the Fathers and reused without fear of superstitious contamination. Ussher, too, sought historical warrant but in the identification of the 'remnant' of the true church. Laud and Bramhall (in his works of the 1640s and 1650s) were not concerned with Waldensians, Cathars and Celtic monks but with discerning the nature of the 'true' catholic church. Ireland's previous peculiarity was to be replaced with a settlement better representing the historical catholic church.

---

[62] See Tyacke, *Anti-Calvinists*, pp. 221–2. Laymen have no power of absolution, *Works of Bramhall*, II, 167.

[63] *Works of Bramhall*, V, 160, 190–1, 223; Tyacke, *Anti-Calvinists*, p. 110.

[64] *Works of Bramhall*, V, 213.

[65] A. Foster, 'The clerical estate revitalised', in K. Fincham (ed.), *The Early Stuart Church* (1993), p. 139; Tyacke, *Anti-Calvinists*, pp. 221–2.

[66] Laud to Ussher, 5 Nov. 1636, Laud, VII, 291–3.

[67] Laud, VII, 293.

[68] 'Which ever since her times of peace and settlement (if not before also) has distinguished the habit of a bishop from an inferior priest'. Laud, VII, 292–3.

[69] For temporal reform, see J. McCafferty, 'John Bramhall and the Church of Ireland, 1633–41' in A. Ford, K. Milne and J. McGuire (eds.), *As By Law Established* (Dublin, 1995), pp. 100–11.

But, as has been stressed, there was no outright victory for Bramhall. The canons relating to the ordination and quality of ministers presented something of an admonition to any project of uncovering the true historical universal church. Irish Canons 29, 30 and 42 are based on English Canons 31, 32, 33, 74 and 75. These English canons refer to 'the ancient fathers of the church, led by the examples of the apostles',[70] 'the practice of the primitive church'[71] and 'the true ancient and flourishing churches of Christ'.[72] All of these phrases were silently dropped from the Irish Canons which copy these particular English canons in every other respect. This was most likely the handiwork of Ussher who although devoted to the study of patristics was part of a growing band of scholars pushing the point of 'corruption' further and further back.[73]

Irish Canon 31 set out to prevent the reopening of old wounds by making an ambiguous reference to 'the Articles of religion generally received in the churches of England and Ireland' which could be interpreted satisfactorily by either party. Yet Irish Canon 32, in rewriting English Canon 36 on ministerial subscription, shifted the balance considerably. It enjoined subscription to the first four Irish canons as opposed to the three articles contained in English Canon 36. An Irish minister subscribed not only to the king's supremacy but to a *duty* to declare it four times a year while his English counterpart was only enjoined to do so by canon. But it is in Irish Canons 3 and 4 that the real difference lies. English ministers were to subscribe that the ordinal and Prayer Book contained 'nothing contrary to the word of God, and that it may be lawfully so be used'. The Irish Canons went much further, excommunicating those who preached or declared 'anything in the derogation or despising of the said book, or of anything therein contained'.[74] Irish ministers *subscribed* to Irish Canon 4, suffering excommunication for any attack on the Church order and hierarchy. The Prayer Book was at the very centre of Irish subscription. The Irish Canons, then, elevated not only the priest, but the priest

---

[70] English Canon 31.   [71] English Canon 32.   [72] English Canon 74.
[73] The collegiate suffrage of the British delegates at Dort (of whom Samuel Ward was one) was extremely selective in its use of the Fathers. I owe this point to Seán Hughes with whom I have had many illuminating conversations. Bramhall did manage to slip in a reference to the 'solemn ancient and laudable custom' in Irish Canon 17 (English Canons 60 and 61) on confirmation.
[74] Irish Canon 3.

holding the Prayer Book, and the Prayer Book as the symbol and test of uniformity.[75]

Despite Bramhall's initial reluctance the Irish Canons ended by making numerous allowances for Ireland. These are most obvious in the canons relating to the use of the Irish language, but also in those relating to ecclesiastical jurisdiction, recusants, schools, temporalities and a number of other matters, such as the allowance in Irish Canon 41 on the visitation of the sick for those 'who have not formerly resorted to the church'.

Canonical formulation was one thing, but observance and enforcement were another. The code of canons was a qualified triumph for Bramhall and Wentworth, though they liked to present the convocation to Laud as a signal victory. The reality of the following years was continued difficulty in securing conformity. In November 1636, Laud wrote to Ussher in the name of the king, commanding bishops to wear episcopal attire, especially rochets. In a postscript, he also sought that 'all priests and ministers throughout that kingdom read public prayers and administer the Sacraments duly in their surplices', a sign that Irish Canon 7 was not being complied with.

Bedell of Kilmore continued to place the communion table in the body of the church (an infringement of Irish Canon 94), he preferred to use psalms directly from the Bible rather than the Prayer Book (a possible violation of Irish Canon 3) and 'he came often to church in his episcopal habiliments, but oftener without'.[76]

Again, in late 1636 Laud found occasion to complain of the 'general neglect of the keeping of all holydays' (contravening Irish Canon 6), a sign that the attitude to holydays found in Daniel's Prayer Book was still alive and well in the Church of Ireland. Wentworth praised the reliability of the clergy he had imported in contrast to the others who 'are more affected with the service of Mr Calvin than with our English liturgy'.[77] It was one of his imports, the unfortunate James Croxton, who drew criticism in the diocese of Ossory by hearing the confessions of some of his congregation to prepare them for the sacrament. Croxton appealed to Laud, justifying himself on the basis of Irish Canon 19.[78] It seems, then, that while confession was allowed for in the canons it was not possible to

---

[75]   Note also the omission of English Canon 38, 'Revolters after subscription censured'.
[76]   *Two Biographies of William Bedell*, ed. E. S. Shuckburgh (Cambridge, 1902), pp. 152–3.
[77]   Wentworth to Laud, 23 April 1638, Str P 7, p. 92.
[78]   Croxton to Laud, 18 April 1638, PRO, SP 63/256/84; *CSPIre, 1633–47*, p. 84.

act upon it without causing controversy. The change of penalty from *ipso facto* excommunication to 'let him be excommunicated' in several canons[79] blunted the edge of the Irish Canons in print, but non-compliance blunted them, ambitious as they were, in practice. Some bishops, like Bedell, were prepared to go their own way and probably turn a blind eye to the activities of their clergy. High Commission could not prosecute every recalcitrant clergyman. In the canons, the Irish church had preserved something of its autonomy, and in the parishes it preserved something of its more austere customs.

V

Where did the convocation of 1634 leave the Church of Ireland? This is an important question because the Convocation was a key moment in the history of the Church of Ireland and its outcome helped determine its future and the future of the Protestant Reformation in Ireland.

Another way of posing the same question is to ask what the real status of the Irish Articles was after 1634. Ussher, as we know, insisted that the 1615 Articles 'stand as they did before'.[80] During Convocation, Wentworth, Bramhall and Laud had been at great pains to prevent any debate on this matter, preferring to let Ussher believe what he would.[81] Wentworth's true aspirations were revealed in a letter to Wandesford from London in 1636: 'The Church was improved in her patrimony, and become altogether conformable to this of England in doctrine and government, by the acceptance of the Articles and Canons of England, so as now they were become one, which properly they could not be said to have been before.'[82] This, of course, was typical of Wentworth's tendency to overstate, but it still represents his general perception.

In all the polemical writing produced in the 1650s and after, only one fact is accepted by all sides: it is that Ussher and some other bishops required subscription to both sets of Articles.[83] Bramhall

---

[79] Irish Canons 1–5 and 22.
[80] Ussher to Laud, 15 Sept. 1635, *Works of Ussher*, XVI, 9.
[81] See especially Laud to Wentworth, 20 Oct. 1634, Laud, VI, 386–7.
[82] Wentworth to Wandesford, 25 July 1636, T. Carte, *The Life of James, Duke of Ormond* (5 vols., Oxford, 1851), V, 209.
[83] See R. Parr, *The Life of the most reverend Father in God, James Ussher* (1686), p. 42; N. Bernard, *The Judgement of the Late Archbishop of Armagh* (1657), pp. 113, 120; J. Vesey, *Athanasius Hibernicus* (1676), p. xvii; P. Heylyn, *Cyprianus Anglicus* (1668), p. 272; H. L'Estrange, *The*

chose to talk tough on double subscription years later: 'if any bishop had been known to have required any man to subscribe to the Irish Articles, after the English were received and authorised under the great seal of Ireland, he would have been called to account for it'.[84] This is not strictly true – only an overt refusal or denunciation of the English Articles could have been proceeded against. Furthermore, the chances are that Wentworth and Bramhall turned a blind eye to any double subscription in the hope that as new bishops were appointed, the practice would die out.

The other certain fact is that after the Restoration the Irish Articles did not re-emerge. The petition of Dublin clergy in 1647 defended the status of the Irish Articles and the autonomy of the Church but the Irish convocation beginning in 1661 (presided over by Bramhall) made no mention of the 1615 Articles. What caused the total eclipse of the Irish Articles?[85] Much of the energy of the Restoration convocation went into addressing the problem of presbyterianism as it had now emerged. The Solemn League and Covenant was duly censured and reproved and the 1662 Prayer Book enthusiastically accepted for Ireland.[86] The striking resemblance between the Westminster Confession and the Irish Articles was not lost on them either. In a Church of Ireland in which Bramhall had triumphantly carried out a mass consecration of bishops, there was no question of returning to, or defending, the 1615 Articles. Tainted with Westminster they would never be revived.

This was more momentous than the loss of a distinctive Irish confession, it was the end of a 'free' Church of Ireland. Statesmen and bishops now used the terms Church of England and Church of Ireland interchangeably.[87] The nervous emergent Protestant ascendancy sought to define itself against Irish Catholics and Scottish Dissenters alike and it was, after all, in this period that the notion of an 'Anglican' church as a judicious *via media* began to emerge. Irish Anglicans professed that English faith in an English Church in

---

Reign of King Charles (1656), p. 137; N. Bernard, *The Judgment of the Late Archbishop of Armagh* (1659), p. 352.

[84] *Works of Bramhall*, v, 81, c. 1658/9.

[85] An important article on this question by John Morrill appeared too late to be considered here, but see J. Morrill, 'A British patriarchy? Ecclesiastical imperialism under the early Stuarts', in A. Fletcher and P. Roberts (eds.), *Religion, Culture and Society in Early Modern Britain* (Cambridge, 1994).

[86] Although they duly went through the motions of appointing a committee to scrutinise it. Trinity College Dublin, MS 1038, ff. 19–79, contain the journals of this convocation.

[87] I owe this point to James McGuire.

Ireland. Ussher's nightmare had come true – the identification with the Church of England became increasingly complete, culminating in the complete obliteration of all but the faintest marks of autonomy in the Act of Union of 1800.

There is a final question to be asked about the 1630s and that is whether there was an attempt at a Canterburian primacy over all three churches? As far as Ireland was concerned, Laud's degree of involvement was certainly unprecedented. In July 1634, Laud joked with Wentworth about his deep engagement in both Scottish and Irish church affairs: 'I think you have a plot, to see whether I will be *universalis episcopus*, that you and your brethren may take occasion to call me Antichrist.'[88] But what was Laud's own wish for the Church of Ireland? He placed Wentworth's first report of Irish church improvements in the registry at Lambeth, so as to offer 'some encouragement to my successors to take some care of Ireland till all be settled there'.[89] This shows that Laud still conceived of his involvement in the work in Ireland in the way in which Ussher had originally seen it – as aid. Laud accepted Wentworth's device of temporal improvement as a prelude to further reformation and, on this level, his interest in the Church of Ireland was paternalistic rather than hegemonic.

Why then, the imposition of the English Articles and attempted imposition of the English Canons? Laud stressed the need, as we know, for 'spiritual' as well as material repair. English doctrine and discipline was precisely that: a means of repairing what was viewed as the shabby and badly built edifice which was the Church of Ireland. Laud, as much as Ussher, would have regarded any revival of the twelfth-century claims of Canterbury to be 'Brittanicarum Primas' or 'Totius Britanniae Primas' as chimerical.[90] He did, however, think in terms of three kingdoms, but this was a different matter as it centred on royal, not Canterburian, supremacy. Laud wished to repair both Scotland and Ireland and bring them into closer congruence with the Church of England. This did not mean that the Church of England was the standard. It, too, was in need of some restoration work. The opportunities to make settlements in Scotland and Ireland provided room for setting standards to which

---

[88] Laud to Wentworth, 3 July 1634, Laud, VI, 385.
[89] Laud to Wentworth, 23 Jan. 1636, Laud, VII, 230.
[90] Marie Therese Flanagan, *Irish Society, Anglo-Norman Settlers, Angevin Kingship* (Oxford, 1989), pp. 7–55.

the Church of England could aspire. After 1636, the Scottish, Irish and English codes had forty-one canons in common, notably those regulating the quality, discipline and behaviour of ministers, marriage regulations, the furniture and layout of churches and conduct and gestures during services. Yet, the Scottish and Irish Canons both allowed for quasi-sacramental confession and absolution, albeit in slightly different contexts.[91] Here was a sign of the beginnings of a new standard, to which all three churches might conform while still observing peculiarities of custom, discipline and organisation. After 1636, the churches of all three kingdoms had a Prayer Book, a set of canons and a High Commission. Each had a minimum of worship and discipline and each had, under the crown, a means of enforcing it.

The convocation of 1634, then, was not a victory of the Church of England over the autonomy of the Church of Ireland (though the turbulent decades that followed made it so) but a realignment of the Church of Ireland within the three kingdoms. As it turned out, Ireland proved to be a deceptively easy exercise in realignment.

[91] Irish Canon 19 and Scottish Canons, ch. XVIII, 9.

CHAPTER 9

Strafford, the 'Londonderry Business' and the 'New British History'

Jane H. Ohlmeyer

In May 1635, after a humiliating, fourteen-day trial in Star Chamber, Derry, Coleraine and over 40,000 acres of land belonging to the City of London reverted to the crown. To add insult to injury the City was fined £70,000 for, among other things, failing to plant a sufficient number of British tenants, for inadequately fortifying the settlement, for depleting the woods, and for allegedly depriving the king of an estimated £60,000 in revenue. In the months immediately following the trial the City attempted to recover its forfeited acres. Even though Strafford suggested that the crown should retain the customs of Coleraine and Derry, together with the fishings, he urged Charles to reach a settlement with the City which, smarting after the verdict, refused to collect ship money (allegedly to the ditty 'Hey-down-Derry'). 'It could not be denied', Strafford reminded Laud in August 1636, 'but the Londoners were out great sums upon the Plantation, and that it were not only very strict in their case, but would discourage all other Plantations, if the uttermost advantage were taken'. Moreover the Lord Deputy prophesied that the alienation of the City 'might produce sad effects; whereas in my poor judgment they were rather to be as tenderly... dealt with, if not favoured and kept in life and spirit'.[1]

However, increasingly desperate for cash and genuinely believing the Londonderry plantation could yield a small fortune, Charles I finally resolved in June 1637 to evict the Londoners permanently and to put their lands on the market. Hardly surprisingly the City felt furious and even though Charles later reinstated them, as Clarendon noted in his *History of the Rebellion*, the Londoners 'rather remembered how it had been taken from them than by whom it was restored: so

I am grateful to Professors Aidan Clarke and Geoffrey Parker for their comments on an earlier draft of this chapter and to Dr John Scally for sharing his views on Robert Barr with me.
[1]   Wentworth to Laud, 17 Aug. 1636, Knowler, II, 25.

that at the beginning of the Parliament the City was as ill affected to the Court as the country was'.[2]

Despite the obvious importance of the 'Londonderry Business', as contemporaries dubbed it, the fate of the plantation in the months after May 1635 has attracted little attention. T. W. Moody in his masterly study focused on the plantation prior to 1635, devoting a mere 25 pages, of a total of 415, to the years between 1635 and 1641;[3] while Hugh Kearney in his fascinating account of Strafford's administration in Ireland attached little significance to the 'Londonderry Business'.[4] Part of the problem stems from the enormity of Strafford's own archive and the absence, until relatively recently, of an effective 'antidote' to the Lord Deputy's poisonous pen. For as Aidan Clarke has reminded us on a number of occasions one of Strafford's greatest 'accomplishments was a prose style of compelling authority and plausibility, and that this, combined with the paucity of other evidence, was responsible for one of his major successes – that of imposing his own version of the events of his deputyship upon generations of historians, approving and disapproving alike'.[5] But the Hamilton archive, now in the Scottish Record Office in Edinburgh, together with some other courtiers' correspondence helps to correct the biases of Strafford's papers and, in addition, contains a wealth of information on the proposed settlement of Londonderry after 1637.

Moreover the tussles over the 'Londonderry Business' between some of the leading figures at the Caroline court, when fully documented, also shed much light on the nature of government in early Stuart Ireland and, in particular, on Strafford's triple goals of making Ireland financially self-sufficient, enforcing religious confor-

---

[2]   Edward Hyde, earl of Clarendon, *The History of the Rebellion and Civil Wars in England...*, ed. W. D. Macray (6 vols., Oxford, 1888; re-issued, 1992), I, 500.

[3]   T. W. Moody, *The Londonderry Plantation 1609–41. The City of London and the Plantation in Ulster* (Belfast, 1939), chs. 16, 17. See also Raymond Gillespie, 'Historical revisit: T. W. Moody, *The Londonderry Plantation, 1609–41*', *Irish Historical Studies*, 29 (1994), pp. 109–13.

[4]   Hugh Kearney, *Strafford in Ireland, 1633–41. A Study in Absolutism* (Manchester, 1959; 2nd edn, Cambridge, 1989), pp. 186–7. Michael Perceval-Maxwell, in an important article on the strained relationship between Strafford and the Ulster Scots, avoids delving into the 'reorganization of the Londonderry plantation' and accepts Wentworth's account of it. Michael Perceval-Maxwell, 'Strafford, the Ulster-Scots and the covenanter', *Irish Historical Studies* 18 (1973), pp. 524–51, at p. 530 and Perceval-Maxwell, 'Ireland and Scotland, 1638 to 1648', in John Morrill (ed.), *The Scottish National Covenant in its British Context 1638–51* (Edinburgh, 1990), pp. 195–7.

[5]   Aidan Clarke, '28 November 1634: a detail of Strafford's administration', *Journal of the Royal Society of Antiquaries of Ireland* 93 (1963), p. 161.

mity and further 'civilising' the Irish. Equally importantly it high-lights the fluid, intimate relationship between the core and the periphery of the Stuart monarchy during the pre-war years and demonstrates how a desire to control lands in one of the 'darkest', most remote corners of Charles I's patrimony contributed signifi-cantly to the outbreak of the 'Wars of the Three Kingdoms'.

*   *   *

In 1609 Sir John Davies confessed that Ulster was 'heretofore as unknown to the English here as the most inland part of Virginia [is] as yet unknown to our English Colony there'.[6] That same year in an attempt to introduce 'civility, order and government amongst a barbarous and unsubdued people',[7] James I and VI gifted a little over 40,000 acres of north Ulster, formerly belonging to the O'Ca-hans, to the citizens of London to create a Protestant colony and to introduce to the region English language, dress, customs, legal practices, architectural styles and, equally important, to promote English agricultural methods and develop a market economy in an otherwise commercial backwater.

Despite attracting reasonable numbers of English and Scottish colonists (1,800 in all), the plantation nevertheless became a financial liability for the London investors who received extremely low annual rentals (of only £2,300) and were obliged to spend any profits which they made from the lucrative fishings and their private customs monopoly on maintaining and improving their colony.[8] Thus, according to Moody's calculations, over a period of twenty-one years the Londoners' gross receipts totalled only (at most) £37,500 or nearly £1,800 per annum; while expenditure, especially on building – which according to their own account amounted to £100,000 – meant that by 1635 the City had contracted net losses of around £40,000.[9]

Instead of the City creaming off substantial dividends, as the king unfairly maintained, individual farmers and chief tenants enriched themselves. Colonists such as John Rowley, initially chief agent for

---

6   Davies to Salisbury, 24 Aug. 1609, HMC, *Salisbury MSS*, xxi, 121.
7   James I and VI to Chichester, 21 Dec. 1612, *CSPIre, 1611–14*, p. 310.
8   The town of Coleraine (and its liberties of 3,000 acres) paid £400 to the city of London; the city of Derry (and its liberties of 3,000 acres) paid £450 and the twelve proportions paid £1,440, Scottish Record Office, Gifts and Deposits (hereafter SRO, GD) 406/M 1/33.
9   Moody, *Londonderry Plantation*, p. 339.

the Londoners, or Tristram Beresford, another agent and mayor of Coleraine, illegally exported timber, illicitly felled trees for pipe-staves which they then sold, set up breweries, mills and tanneries without licence, alienated church lands and rented holdings at extortionate rates to native Irish tenants. Over a three-year period Rowley alone embezzled £30,000 of City money; while Beresford accumulated a small fortune and carved out a considerable empire for himself in and around Coleraine.[10]

Aware of the potential profits, four very different offers (see the appendix to this chapter) were made for the Londoners' lands once the king's decision to take them over became known. In December 1636 Strafford made his own bid for a twenty-one-year lease to the plantation (appendix, offer IV). He proposed paying an annual rent of £8,000 and an additional £32,000 for the customs farm of Derry and Coleraine, which was to remain in the king's hands. Strafford's preoccupation with making money and acquiring property has been well documented: he controlled the extremely lucrative Irish customs farm (which Kearney estimated made him a personal profit of slightly over £35,000); he dominated the ill-fated tobacco monopoly; and he speculated in thousands of acres of land in Counties Wicklow, Wexford, Kildare and Sligo. Thus his annual income from Irish sources totalled around £13,000 and this, combined with a rental of £6,000 from his Yorkshire lands, made him – together with the earls of Cork and Worcester – one of the richest men in the three kingdoms.[11] Given that he also coveted large tracts of confiscated land in Connacht and had already profited from acquiring planted lands in Wicklow, the Lord Deputy no doubt realised the potential returns from County Londonderry.[12] However, his long absences in Ireland ensured that, apart from a brief spell after 1639, he never exercised 'a major influence on the government of the personal rule',[13] which left him feeling insecure and dependent

[10] Moody, *Londonderry Plantation*, pp. 144–50, 169, 263, 273–4, 344.
[11] Kearney, *Strafford*, pp. 179–83, 178–9; J. P. Cooper, 'Strafford and the Byrnes' Country', *Irish Historical Studies*, 15 (1966), pp. 16–17; Terence Ranger, 'Strafford in Ireland: a revaluation', in Trevor Aston (ed.), *Crisis in Europe 1560–1660. Essays from Past and Present* (1965), p. 275.
[12] Cooper, 'Strafford and the Byrnes' Country', pp. 16–19; Nicholas Canny, 'The attempted Anglicisation of Ireland in the seventeenth century: an exemplar of "British History"', this volume, pp. 157–186.
[13] Kevin Sharpe, *The Personal Rule of Charles I* (New Haven, 1992), p. 139.

primarily on Archbishop Laud to further his suits at court, including his designs on the Londoners' lands.[14]

Others also had their eyes on the plantation. Late in March 1637, Charles gleefully notified Strafford of another offer for a twenty-one-year lease to the Londoners' lands (appendix, offer I). This anonymous entrepreneur proposed paying an annual rental of £8,000 and a £20,000 entry fine.[15] Then, in December 1637, James Hamilton, third marquis and later duke of Hamilton, who, as one of the Star Chamber judges, had ruled against the City in 1635, made a further bid (appendix, offer II). He offered a rental of £12,000 for a forty-one-year lease, payable to the English exchequer in instalments every May and November, together with an entry fine of £10,000 on condition that he received the lands by May 1638, that he be exempt from paying rent for the first six months, that he should have liberty to cut timber from the king's woods for building and firewood, and that fish worth under 100 marks should be exported without charge.[16]

Next in line to the Scottish throne after the royal Stuarts, Hamilton had replaced Buckingham as Charles's favourite and trusted advisor. Clarendon later noted that even though Hamilton 'had more enemies and fewer friends in court or country... His interest in the king's affections was equal, and thought superior, to any man's'.[17] A consummate courtier and a skilful speculator, with extensive estates in both England and the central lowlands of Scotland, Hamilton also endeavoured, together with Henry Rich, earl of Holland, to discredit Strafford's handling of the Irish customs and to acquire his own lease for the farm and for land in Ireland, especially in Ulster, where many of his kinsmen had settled. However Strafford, who loathed the marquis,[18] skilfully frustrated Hamilton's repeated

---

[14] Laud raised the issue with the king on numerous occasions. See Laud, VII, 342, 420, 483–5, 488.

[15] Charles I to Wentworth, 27 March 1637, Str P 3, p. 274. In all, this offer was worth a capital sum to the crown of £140,000, but included the customs of Derry and Coleraine. Wentworth to Charles I, 3 April 1637, Str P 3, pp. 275–6 (Knowler, II, 65). I still have not discovered the identity of this speculator.

[16] Valuation of several propositions made to the king for the lands and customs belonging to the Londoners, sent to Laud, 30 Oct. 1638, BL, Add. MSS 21,125 ff. 1–4v. See also details of an offer for Londonderry made to the king, Dec. 1637, Str P 3, p. 309. Moody, *Londonderry Plantation*, pp. 394–6, discussed this offer but failed to link it to Antrim and Hamilton (p. 394). Initially Hamilton, confident that 'the deputy nor none for him will give so much', thought in terms of proposing an annual rent of £9,200.

[17] Clarendon, *History*, I, 199.

[18] Wentworth, as Antrim reminded Hamilton, 'does not love you'. Antrim to Hamilton, 13 Oct. 1638, SRO, GD 406/1/653.

attempts to gain acres in the proposed plantation of Connacht, in County Down (near Lord Clandeboy's estate) and later in Leinster as well.[19] As the 1630s progressed and the Lord Deputy became increasingly suspicious of Hamilton's dealings with the Covenanters, relations between the two deteriorated to the point where Charles urged them to reconcile their differences 'seeing they were persons that he meant to trust with most of his business'.[20]

Given his poor relationship with Strafford, Hamilton tried to maintain anonymity regarding his intentions in Londonderry, as did his principal partner in the venture, the earl of Antrim (and with some success – it took nine months, till August 1638, for Strafford to realise that the offer came from them). The earl owned a vast estate of nearly 340,000 acres in County Antrim which made him the largest land-owner in Ulster and one of the greatest in Ireland. As the grandson of the infamous earl of Tyrone, he enjoyed extensive kinship ties to the leading Gaelic families in Ireland; while the marriage of his siblings linked him to prominent Old English dynasties, especially in the Pale. Of Scottish descent, he continued to be recognised by Clan Donald as 'lord of the isles' and remained closely allied to the great Scottish houses of Gordon, Ogilvie and Hamilton. Finally, thanks to his marriage to the royal favourite, the duchess of Buckingham, he owned innumerable English properties, including York, Wallingford and Walsingham houses in London and gained easy access to the king and queen, together with other leading figures at the Caroline court, especially Hamilton, the duke of Lennox and Laud.[21]

Relations between Antrim and Strafford had deteriorated steadily since the earl's visit to Ireland in the spring of 1637 during which, according to Strafford, he passed 'his judgment upon me privately that he liked me not, and that I was proud'.[22] No doubt Antrim – perhaps like Hamilton – regarded Strafford as a jumped up gentleman who had been raised by administrative service to the king far beyond his social status and who had little right to interfere with

[19] He had already made tentative enquiries about acquiring lands in Connacht and in County Down. Hamilton to 'Lord Depute Sibolds', 7 Oct. 1635, SRO, GD 406/1/246; Hamilton to Wentworth [1636], SRO, GD 406/1/8381; Hamilton to Thomas Lord Cromwell [1636], SRO, GD 406/1/8377. For his attempts to acquire land in Connacht, see SRO, GD 406/1/246 (Knowler, II, 3); and for Leinster see *CSPIre, 1633–47*, p. 242.

[20] Quoted in Sharpe, *Charles I*, p. 842. See also Laud, VII, 534–5.

[21] Jane H. Ohlmeyer, *Civil War and Restoration in the Three Stuart Kingdoms. The Career of Randal MacDonnell, Marquis of Antrim, 1609–1683* (Cambridge, 1993), pp. 12–13, 18–19, 33–9, 42–54.

[22] Wentworth to Laud, 10 July 1637, Str P 7, p. 35v.

the prerogatives of a great aristocrat.[23] For his part, Antrim ran foul of Strafford by failing to pay his dues to the Court of Wards and Liveries, by quibbling over the terms of the duchess of Buckingham's substantial holdings in the Irish customs, by promoting the interests of his Catholic kin and friends at court and by endeavouring, with the aid of Queen Henrietta Maria, to restore St Patrick's Purgatory, County Donegal.[24]

Hardly surprisingly then, Strafford rejected in September 1637 Antrim's offer to buy 3,000 acres around Coleraine (2,000 of which his father had sold to the plantation).[25] Little did Strafford realise that at this time Antrim, together with Hamilton, was also finalising the details of a combined offer for all of the City of London's lands in County Londonderry. In 1637 Archibald Stewart, Antrim's factor, prepared for Hamilton a detailed valuation of Londonderry's assets. Despite being the smallest county in Ireland, with few natural assets and 'not much arable [land]',[26] Stewart believed that the land, fishings and customs were worth £18,000 if well managed.[27] Stewart urged Hamilton to make a bid for the region 'and to suffer noe others, to come betwixt your lo[rdshi]p and it; for if it doe not prove better, then this my estimat, I am confident, it will prove noe worse'. Stewart added 'I doe no[t] send your lo[rdshi]p this information by way of conjectur but by diligent inquiries made by me... and of my own knowledge.'[28]

While Stewart provided Hamilton with facts and figures, Antrim offered advice on how his patent should be drawn up, in the event that the king accepted their proposal.[29] According to the earl, Hamilton should request the rights to all ferries and to salmon and eel fishing on the River Bann and Loughs Foyle and Neagh; to distil whiskey; to erect tanneries; to hold and be clerk of the region's fairs and markets; to export local grain without a licence; to elect all

---

23 See for example Wentworth to Laud, 10 July 1637, Str P 7, p. 35v. I am grateful to Professor David Stevenson for this observation.

24 Ohlmeyer, *Civil War and Restoration*, pp. 68–72.

25 Antrim to Wentworth, 19 Sept. 1637, Str P, 17/191.

26 List of revenues available from lands in Londonderry (probably drawn up late in 1637), SRO, GD 406/1/501. For detailed descriptions of the region's natural resources, see George Hill, *An Historical Account of the Plantation in Ulster at the Commencement of the Seventeenth Century* (Belfast, 1877; reprint, Shannon, 1980), pp. 362–3, 374–6.

27 Details of the offer made by Hamilton for County Londonderry, SRO, GD 406/M 1/33.

28 Archibald Stewart to Hamilton, 1 Feb. 1637[-8], SRO, GD 406/1/359.

29 Memorandum (presumably prepared by Antrim late in 1637) for Hamilton of what was to be asked of the king regarding his patent for County Londonderry, SRO, GD 406/M 1/37.

parochial officials – customs officers, mayors and sheriffs; to appoint the captain of the strategically important castle of Culmore; to establish twelve manor courts, similar to those on Antrim's own estate; to punish poachers; and, finally, to enjoy any other privileges granted to the City in its patents. In other words Antrim's carefully prepared memo pressed Hamilton to negotiate for total control over Londonderry's economy, judiciary and administration, something which Strafford, determined to undermine the power of regional magnates rather than enhance it, would never have even considered.[30]

During Hamilton's long absences in Scotland after June 1638 Antrim, who resided in London until late August, together with Will Murray, a groom of the bedchamber who enjoyed a close relationship with both the king and queen and strong connections with the Scots, furthered the 'Londonderry Business' at court. Back in Ulster, Stewart, Lord Clandeboy – Hamilton's presbyterian kinsman, who owned a sizable estate in north Down – and Robert Barr, a Scottish merchant with a smallholding near Glasgow, took charge of the venture. Barr, in particular, had crossed swords with Strafford when, acting on Hamilton's instructions, he made a bid for the Irish customs farm and petitioned to serve as governor of Culmore Castle which overlooked Derry's harbour.[31] He further infuriated Strafford in September 1637 by acquiring 'a speciall license under the signet and signature royal of going and coming over without my comptrol' – presumably to liaise with Hamilton's Irish contacts. In a letter to Laud, the Lord Deputy lambasted Barr 'as a petty chapman', 'such a broken pedlar, a man of no credit or parts' who held 'on this side very inward intelligence with some here, which wish me ill' and spread 'untruths' about him to the king.[32]

The fourth and final offer for the Londoners' investment came from Sir John Clotworthy, who together with the other colonists financially committed to the plantation, offered a fee farm rent of £9,000 and £32,000 for the customs, which were to remain in the king's hands (appendix, offer III).[33] The son of an English soldier-

---

30 Antrim's advice on what was worth bargaining for (probably drawn up late in 1637), SRO, GD 406/M 1/324. Stewart repeated this advice, Archibald Stewart to Hamilton, 1 Feb. 1637[-8], SRO, GD 406/1/359. Antrim also urged him to double the rent to be offered for the town of Coleraine (which the earl coveted) 'rather than go without it'.

31 Laud, VII, 118, 142. See also Hugh O'Grady, *Strafford and Ireland. The History of His Vice-Royalty with an Account of his Trial* (Dublin, 1923), pp. 298, 380–2.

32 Wentworth to Laud, 27 Sept. 1637, Knowler, II, 107.

33 Though the names of his partners are never mentioned they presumably included his kinsmen, Beresford and Rowley, and other prominent English settlers such as George

adventurer, Sir Hugh Clotworthy, who had served as one of the agents of the London corporation, Sir John held a sixty-one-year lease of the Drapers' proportion and owned an extensive estate in County Antrim (he sat as MP for the county in 1634).[34] His mother had been a Loftus, daughter of the archbishop of Dublin, and he was also related by marriage to other prominent English settlers such as Tristram Beresford and Edward Rowley.[35] Though of English provenance, Clotworthy's presbyterianism, his friendship with leading Scottish preachers and planters, and his refusal to relinquish the private monopoly he held of licensing taverns, wines and whiskey in Counties Down and Antrim did not endear him to the Lord Deputy, who, for his part, refused to grant him a commission to the company of horse commanded by his father. Moreover Clotworthy's close alliance with the anti-Strafford faction (he had married a daughter of Lord Ranelagh, president of Connacht and one of Richard Boyle, earl of Cork's leading political allies) created further tensions between the two.[36] Though Clarendon asserted that he was 'utterly unknown in England',[37] Clotworthy nevertheless enjoyed influential connections there as well for he was related by marriage to the parliamentary leader, John Pym, became a client of the earl of Warwick and enjoyed a close relationship with the earl of Holland.[38]

Significantly all of these potential investors also had a direct interest in the 'Scottish troubles' which had reached a head following riots in St Giles's church, Edinburgh, against the introduction of Laud's new English service book. In May 1638 Charles dispatched Hamilton north, on the first of three missions, to persuade the recalcitrant Scots to abandon their covenant. Though Hamilton made two further visits (in August and again in September), all attempts to find a middle ground failed and it quickly became apparent that force remained the only alternative. On 11 June 1638 Antrim, still at court, reminded the king that 'the small remnant of

---

Canning, farmer of the Ironmongers' proportion, John Freeman, farmer of the Goldsmiths' proportion, and Ralph Wall, farmer of the Merchants' proportion.

[34] For further details see George Hill, *The Montgomery Manuscripts (1603–1706) Compiled from the Family Papers...* (Belfast, 1869), p. 156.

[35] One of Rowley's sisters married Beresford; the other married Clotworthy's brother. Hill, *Plantation in Ulster*, pp. 404–5.

[36] Raymond Gillespie, *Colonial Ulster. The Settlement of East Ulster 1600–1641* (Cork, 1985), p. 146.

[37] Clarendon, *History*, I, 224.

[38] Perceval-Maxwell, 'Ireland and Scotland', pp. 201–3. In February/March 1641 Clotworthy lobbied for Holland to be appointed as Lord Deputy of Ireland, p. 202.

my name in Scotland have refused to sign the covenant' and offered himself and his men for royal service.[39] From Edinburgh, Hamilton urged Charles to employ the earl, suggesting that an army levied and paid for by Antrim, and supplemented where possible by Strafford, should be the first line of royalist offence in the west of Scotland.

Sir John Clotworthy soon learned of the design. He had left Ireland in June 1638 on the pretext of furthering his interest in the 'Londonderry Business' at court and had spent a number of days in Edinburgh conferring with leading Covenanters before continuing his journey south,[40] where he immediately heard that 'Antrim was recommended by the marquis [of Hamilton] to the king, as a man that might contribute largely to his service in this business'.[41] In addition to keeping the Covenanters well informed of developments at court, Clotworthy, on behalf of his English patrons, urged the Scots not to accept a settlement until Charles called a parliament in England.[42]

This the king resolutely refused to do and instead relied on extra-parliamentary sources of revenue to finance his struggle against the Covenanters. These included the income Charles hoped to receive from the Londonderry plantation and in the autumn of 1638 he asked Strafford to evaluate the bids made for the investment. In a detailed assessment, sent to Charles in October, the Lord Deputy poured scorn on all of the offers, save his own. He argued that the anonymous bid of March 1637 must have come from 'some inferior mean minded person' intent on turning out the present tenants.[43] He expressed similar concerns about Antrim and Hamilton's proposal.[44] Even though they offered a high rental of £12,000, according to Strafford's estimate, the bid was worth a capital sum to the crown of

---

[39] Antrim to Hamilton, 11 June 1638, (SRO, GD 406/1/1156. See also Ohlmeyer, *Civil War and Restoration*, ch. 3 and Mark Charles Fissel, *The Bishops' Wars. Charles I Campaigns against Scotland, 1638–1640* (Cambridge, 1994), pp. 167–70.

[40] Wentworth alerted Laud that 'the puppy is so much for the common cause of their bretheran that he is gone to Edinburgh to see what becomes of the kirk'. Quoted in Peter Donald, *An Uncounselled King. Charles I and the Scottish Troubles, 1637–1641* (Cambridge, 1990), p. 191. Presumably he presented the petition from the 500 individuals interested in County Londonderry, *CSPIre, 1633–47*, pp. 194–5.

[41] [Clotworthy?] to John Flemming, 21 June 1638, *CSPD, 1637–8*, pp. 524–5. For details on Clotworthy's mission to London, see Donald, *An Uncounselled King*, pp. 191–6.

[42] Allan Macinness, *Charles I and the Making of the Covenanting Movement 1625–41* (Edinburgh, 1991), pp. 192–6. He was in Dublin in August 1639. J. S. Reid, *History of the Presbyterian Church in Ireland*, ed. W. D. Killen (3 vols., Belfast, 1867), I, 264.

[43] Wentworth to Charles I, 3 April 1637, Str P 3, pp. 275–6 (Knowler, II, 65). See also *CSPIre, 1633–47*, pp. 202–3. Wentworth sent Laud a copy on 30 October.

[44] Wentworth to Laud, 11 Aug. 1638, Str P 7, pp. 124–5.

only £136,000 – 10 per cent less than his own proposal – largely because it kept the customs in private hands and because of the length of the lease.[45] More seriously, according to Strafford, their offer made no provision for the future security of the present tenants; on the contrary the 'main drift' was 'to turn out all the now occupants without any consideration', which would ruin the English plantation in Ulster so that the province would become 'totally possessed by the Scottish'.[46] Finally, he objected to selling the county to an individual and argued that the state should control it.[47] '198 [Hamilton] must not, will not' have the lands, he ranted to Laud in August 1638, especially 'at this time when such a cloud hangs over them by reason of the mighty Scottish plantations' in east Ulster.[48] Laud enthusiastically endorsed Strafford's objections adding 'you have all the reason in the world to fear, if the Scottishmen should multiply too much in those parts, they may break into the same distempers there, which now trouble their own country'.[49] The anxious archbishop even feared that if Hamilton were granted the lands and they ceased to be 'independent upon the state... that example will go on like a canker and that government be lost... and perhaps that kingdom too'.[50]

Extant documents relating to the 'Londonderry Business' in the Hamilton papers suggest that, while entirely understandable given the increasingly tense situation in Scotland, these anxieties regarding Antrim and Hamilton had little foundation and that one must be cautious about uncritically accepting Strafford's assessment of the offers. Certainly his claim that Hamilton and Antrim would overthrow the existing settlement and restore the former, native proprietors to their old farms appears to be suspect; as does his assertion that 'the poor English planters in Coleraine might be sacrificed to his lordship's [Antrim's] greedy appetites and vain ambition'.[51] To begin with, Hamilton and Antrim, as their correspondence and memos on the venture demonstrate, remained sensitive to the plight of the 'ancient possessors' who had settled the land 'when it was wayst and haveing spent so much time and charge in improving the

---

45 Hamilton agreed to relinquish the customs if his rent was reduced by £3,000.
46 Wentworth to Charles I, 27 Feb. 1638, Str P 3, p. 310.
47 Wentworth to Charles I, 7 May 1638, Str P 3, pp. 319–20.
48 Wentworth to Laud, 11 Aug. 1638, Str P 7, pp. 124–5.
49 Laud to Wentworth, 30 May 1638, Laud, VII, 439.
50 Laud to Wentworth, [10 Sept.] 1638, Laud, VII, 484.
51 Wentworth to [?], 8 Dec. 1638, Str P 10B, p. 22.

same'.[52] Moreover the earl, in particular, qualified in the eyes of his contemporaries (and subsequent historians) as an 'improving' landlord who, like his father, had encouraged English and Scottish Protestants to settle on his neighbouring County Antrim estates and worked hard to run his vast patrimony, as the earl himself noted, according 'to the general good and settlement... [and] so near as may be to the manner of England'.[53] No evidence, save for Strafford's waspish tirades, suggests that he would have behaved otherwise in Londonderry. Moreover there appears to have been some local enthusiasm, especially from the inhabitants of Coleraine, for Antrim and Hamilton's proposal.[54] Even Laud thought the Lord Deputy 'utterly deceived in your fears about Mr Barr; for if I understand the king aright, he hath no purpose to displace any of the tenants there. And whatever it is that is in project (for I confess I know not), it will not reach to the under tenants, but only to those greater tenants that took it immediately from the City, and were certainly more delinquents ... than either the companies, or the City itself.'[55] In short, in his assessment of Antrim and Hamilton's offer, Strafford's partisanship on his own behalf is apparent.

The Lord Deputy was slightly less scathing of Clotworthy's proposition because it provided for the continuity of the plantation. However he opposed granting the land in fee farm and for so little return.[56] He therefore urged the king to accept his own proposal. Even though he offered no entry fine and the annual rent he proposed was significantly less than Hamilton's (by £4,000), he claimed that the overall value of his bid was worth 10 per cent more than Hamilton's and 20 per cent more than Clotworthy's and enjoyed the added bonus of encouraging further English settlement and of tempering the 'Scottish or natives in those parts'.[57]

It quickly became apparent that the king, still determined to extract the greatest possible gains, did not see eye to eye with Strafford over the 'Londonderry Business'; and even though Charles tried to reassure his suspicious Lord Deputy and equally nervous

---

[52] Details of the offer made by Hamilton for County Londonderry, SRO, GD 406/M 1/33.

[53] Antrim to Ormond[?], 2 Aug. 1637, Str P 17/151.

[54] Memorandum for Hamilton from inhabitants of Coleraine, [c. mid 1637–c. spring 1638], SRO, GD 406/M 1/324.

[55] Laud to Wentworth, 30 July 1638, Laud, VII, 465.

[56] Strafford estimated its capital value was £14,000 less than Hamilton's and £30,000 less than his own.

[57] Valuation of several propositions made to the king for the lands and customs belonging to the Londoners, sent to Laud, 30 Oct. 1638, BL, Add. MSS 21,125, ff. 1–4v.

archbishop that he had no intention of overturning the plantation, Laud feared in March 1638 that since 'profit is grown to be such a prevailing argument' the king might accept Hamilton's offer.[58] Again in October he fretted about the fate of the business 'considering how many things are cunningly put upon his majesty, quite contrary to the fair face that is put upon them'.[59] Laud's concerns appear entirely justified since later the same month Antrim, who had just moved to Ulster, informed Hamilton that providing the situation in Scotland remained stable, there 'will be no loss in [the] Londonderry business, but a visible gaine, therefore your lo[rdshi]p may confidentlie goe on w[i]th the bargen, and I beseech you when you are next at court conclude it if it be possible'. He added: 'I am certain the deputy gives noe assistance to your adversaries, so I thinke your opposition will be but slight.'[60] Antrim's 'outflanking' tactics, similar to those used by generations of Irishmen who hoped that by manipulating the anti-Lord Deputy faction at court they might further their personal goals in Ireland, infuriated Strafford – who had tried hard to prevent Irish issues being raised with the king without his knowledge and approbation. At the same time Charles's apparent willingness to heed the counsel and claims of Irish courtiers such as Antrim or, more spectacularly, the earl of Clanricard, who skilfully torpedoed the entire plantation of Connacht by persuading the king to exclude County Galway from the settlement, increased Strafford's sense of isolation, insecurity and paranoia and undermined his authority in Ireland.

Moreover the king's handling of the affair jeopardised one of the central goals of Strafford's lord deputyship. For if overhauling Ireland's finances was one objective of his administration, his 'thorough' policies also aimed at extending royal control through the policy of plantation. The Lord Deputy believed that the settlement of English colonists remained the best means of enriching Charles and for 'civilizing... this people, or securing this kingdom under the dominion of your imperial crown'. He continued that 'plantations must be the only means under God and your majesty to reform this subject as well in religion as manners'.[61] To this end Strafford challenged the legitimacy of land titles wherever he could so that the

---

58 Laud to Wentworth, 27 March 1638, Laud, VII, 420.
59 Laud to Wentworth, 8 Oct. 1638, Laud, VII, 488.
60 Antrim to Hamilton, 13 Oct. 1638, SRO, GD 406/1/653.
61 Wentworth to Charles I, 24 Aug. 1635, Knowler, I, 450.

crown could regain control of land and redistribute it at a greater
profit to Protestant, English colonists.[62]

Unlike his predecessors, Strafford remained determined to
exclude the Scots from this 'civilising' process on the grounds that
further Scottish expansion in Ulster, or, for that matter, in Connacht,
would alienate central control and destabilise the more sensitive
areas of the Stuart dominions.[63] For instead of reinforcing English
authority, as James VI had originally intended, continued Scottish
intervention in Ireland, especially in Ulster, served to undermine
royal authority and offer an alternative focus of loyalty for the British
settlers. Thus Strafford and Laud remained convinced that the
passage of the Londonderry lands to any Scot – whether he be a
Protestant lowlander, like Hamilton, or a Catholic highland chief,
like Antrim – jeopardised the well-being of future English settlements
throughout Ireland. In other words the Londonderry plantation had
become a struggle for control of the region's trade, inhabitants,
fortifications and churches between Scots colonists and English
administrators, rather than Catholic Gaels and Protestant planters.

In November 1638, much to Laud's relief, Charles informed
Strafford that 'I have rejected all offers, and have appointed a
commission for settling of [the Londoners' lands] for my best
advantage both in honour and profits.'[64] Instead of vesting control of
the plantation in Strafford or the Irish executive, he appointed
Bishop John Bramhall, Sir William Parsons (whose candidacy Strafford later vetoed) and two Englishmen with no Irish connections, Sir
Ralph Whitfield and Thomas Fotherly. Much to Strafford's horror,
Charles also insisted that since the lands now formed part of his
personal estate the income arising from them should be paid in cash,
rather than in bills of exchange, directly to the English exchequer
thereby further depleting Ireland's already scant reserves of specie
and enfeebling Strafford's valiant attempts to make the Irish
economy self-sufficient. The fact that it had taken Charles over two
years to reach a decision over the fate of the plantation also

---

[62] The most spectacular of his plantation schemes was Connacht, but he also had designs on
the O'Brennan lands in County Kilkenny, the O'Toole and O'Byrne lands in County
Wicklow, the baronies of Upper and Lower Ormond in County Tipperary and County
Clare. In these areas Strafford hoped to root out those who were 'unsound and rotten at
the h[e]art' and replace them with English Protestants, Wentworth to Charles I, 10
September 1636, Str P 3, p. 262.

[63] Knowler, II, 195–6.

[64] Charles I to Wentworth, 5 Nov. 1638, Knowler, II, 232.

frustrated Strafford, for it meant that the crown had already lost at least £16,000 in rents,[65] while the value of the lands had plummeted due to the tense political climate in Ulster and Scotland, making it increasingly hard to find colonists willing to settle such a 'high risk' area. Predictably Strafford blamed Antrim and Hamilton for 'distracting the Business thorough [*sic*] their mighty, yet vain Assurances of greater profit and service'.[66]

Just as Charles decided to keep the Londoners' lands for himself, the prospect of war with Scotland became a reality. The royalist grand strategy envisaged a fourfold attack: Charles I and the main English army were to assault Scotland from the Borders; Hamilton and the Royal Navy were to land 5,000 troops at Aberdeen; Antrim was to invade the Western Isles and join forces with the men mobilised by his kinsmen; and finally, Strafford was to send an Irish expeditionary force to Dumbarton. Largely because the control of the Scottish conflict at this point lay in the hands of his rivals at court – Hamilton, Holland and Thomas Howard, earl of Arundel – Strafford's contribution to the war-effort remained limited: much to his disgust, he played second fiddle to Antrim and Hamilton. However by spring 1639 the king's elaborate plans for the recovery of Scotland were in a shambles, and ultimately lack of money and the poor working relationship between Antrim and Strafford, combined with Charles's inability to co-ordinate the operation effectively, ensured that Irish aid for the king in the First Bishops' War never materialised. Undaunted by this debacle, Strafford began, the following spring, to levy a fresh Irish army of 8,000 foot and 1,000 horse – partly financed by rents from Londonderry – which he intended to send against the Scots.[67] However, on 20 August, the Covenanters invaded England, defeating the king's forces eight days later near Newcastle-upon-Tyne.

The Bishops' Wars proved to be military and political catastrophes for Charles. The Short Parliament summoned to finance the king's army against the Scots had refused to do so until its grievances were redressed, and so was dissolved. Military defeat in 1640 forced the king to call the Long Parliament which met on 3 November and,

[65] Wentworth to [?], 8 Dec. 1638, Str P 10B, p. 22.
[66] Wentworth to Charles I, 17 Oct. 1638, Knowler, II, 225.
[67] Knowler, II, 399, 400. The cost of levying, arming and paying 8,000 foot and 1,000 horse between April and September 1640 amounted to £50,000, PRO, E 405/285 f. 143; *CSPIre, 1633–47*, p. 244.

rather than supporting the continuation of the war-effort as Charles
had naively hoped, instead resolved, at the insistence of the Scots, to
impeach his Irish lord lieutenant. For by this point the bulk of the
king's subjects, whatever their ethnic and religious backgrounds, held
Strafford, who from the summer of 1639 had effectively replaced
Hamilton as Charles's leading advisor, personally responsible for the
disastrous Second Bishops' War and the misfortunes which had
befallen the king during the final months of his personal rule. Those
whom Strafford had alienated included Hamilton who, together with
Sir Henry Vane, Ranelagh, Parsons and Clotworthy, effectively
facilitated the Lord Deputy's ruin by dispatching Barr to Ireland to
co-ordinate the anti-Strafford faction there.[68]

Mobilising anti-Strafford sentiment in the Irish parliament, which
had been summoned in March 1640 to pay for the 'new army',
proved easy and it ringingly endorsed the Scottish call for a trial,
providing, as Michael Perceval-Maxwell put it, 'enough political
ammunition for its English counterpart to fire the ultimate weapon
of impeachment'.[69] On 7 November the Irish House of Commons
adopted a petition of remonstrance which condemned every aspect
of Strafford's government in Ireland, including 'The extream and
cruel usage of certain late commissioners and others [towards] the
inhabitants of the City and county of Londonderry, by means wherof
the worthy plantation of that county is almost destroyed, and the said
inhabitants are reduced to great poverty, and many of them forced
to forsake the country,... to the great weakening of the kingdome in
this time of danger, the said plantation being the principal strength
of those parts' (article 8).[70] Three Ulster MPs, including Edward
Rowley (who as a patentee for the customs of Antrim and Down had
lost heavily when Strafford incorporated them into the general
customs farm) served as members of the committee which presented
the Irish grievances to the English House of Commons, which, on 28
November, also accused Strafford of 'The destroying of the plantation of London-Derry'.[71]

How justified was this charge? Certainly, after November 1638, the

---

[68] O'Grady, *Strafford*, pp. 647–8. For details see M. Perceval-Maxwell, 'Protestant faction,
      the impeachment of Strafford and the origins of the Irish civil war', *Canadian Journal of
      History* 17 (1982), pp. 237–9.

[69] Perceval-Maxwell, 'Protestant faction', p. 249.

[70] *Journals of the House of Commons of the kingdom of Ireland... (1613–1791)* (28 vols., Dublin, 1753–
      91), I, 230.

[71] J. Rushworth (ed.), *The trial of Thomas, earl of Strafford* (1680), p. 12.

commissioners appointed by the king, intent on securing immediate returns, had raised rents two- or threefold (to the levels advocated by Antrim, Hamilton and Stewart in 1637).[72] Thus the rents charged between 1640 and 1641 exceeded £9,000.[73] Whitfield and Fotherly also rearranged the boundaries of the original plantation and called in the leases of the greater tenants. For instance, they stripped Clotworthy of his title to the Drapers' lands; while Tristram Beresford, who owned the Haberdashers' allotment with two others, lost his entire estate, which was divided among thirty individuals. Other farmers relinquished one-half or two-thirds of their holdings but continued to pay the full amount of their old rent for the residue, while those who refused to co-operate or infringed the crown's prerogatives were severely dealt with.[74] According to one memorandum prepared by the Irish parliament early in 1640 the commissioners dispossessed some inhabitants of Derry and Coleraine 'and let their houses unto strangers, because they would give most for them, without any consideration to the owner; and those that they dealt kindliest withal was to let them have their own houses at full value that a stranger would give for them'.[75] Thereby Antrim, despite violent opposition from Strafford, finally acquired a twenty-one-year lease of '300 acres in the liberties of Coleraine about Mountsandle'.[76]

In short, Strafford's worst fears had been realised. But it was the king's most trusted servants, and not Antrim and Hamilton, who rode roughshod over the Londonderry plantation and turned out 'all the now occupants without any consideration'. In addition the commissioners' apparent eagerness to interfere with land titles 'for his majesty's best profit'[77] added to the general sense of tenurial insecurity created by Strafford's plantation schemes elsewhere and the rigorous policies pursued throughout Ireland by the 'commission of defective titles'. Though Strafford cannot be held directly respon-

---

[72] *CSPIre, 1647–60*, p. 230. Hamilton proposed increasing Derry's rent to £800, Coleraine's to £700 and the proportions to £3,600, SRO, GD 406/M 1/33.

[73] On account of dire economic circumstances, the exodus of many pro-covenanting settlers to Scotland and the quartering of the 'new army' in Ulster, only a little over £5,000 ever reached the exchequer, Moody, *Londonderry Plantation*, pp. 400–1.

[74] *CSPIre, 1647–60*, pp. 229–30.

[75] *CSPIre, 1647–60*, p. 230.

[76] Antrim to [Hamilton], 13 July 1639, SRO, GD 406/1/1164. See also Wentworth to Vane, 7 July 1639, Knowler, II, 422–4; Antrim to Hamilton, 26 Sept. 1639, SRO, GD 406/1/1166.

[77] T. W. Moody and J. G. Simms (eds.), *The Bishopric of Derry and the Irish Society of London* (2 vols., Irish Manuscripts Commission, Dublin, 1968), I, 226.

sible for the actions of the commissioners – and indeed he complained to Laud about the high-handed manner in which Whitfield
and Fotherly conducted affairs – the local populace nevertheless
blamed him for threatening their livelihoods together with their
political and economic power in the local and national arenas –
hence the inclusion of a clause dealing directly with the fate of the
plantation in the remonstrances of both the Irish and English Houses
of Commons and the presence at the impeachment proceedings of
Beresford and Rowley.[78] In addition Clotworthy, who sat in the
Long Parliament for Maldon in Essex, became the principal intermediary between the English, Scottish and Irish malcontents and
seconded Pym's motion for the appointment of a committee of the
whole House to consider Irish affairs.[79]

Had it not become clear that the commissioners, especially Whitfield and Fotherly, together with Charles himself, were directly
responsible for bungling the 'Londonderry Business', the destruction
of the plantation and the hardships suffered by the inhabitants would
undoubtedly have featured at Strafford's trial which began on 22
March 1641. As it was, the Lord Deputy's alleged mishandling of the
customs of Coleraine and Derry came under close scrutiny and
involved witnesses with close ties to the Londoners' plantation;[80]
while Clotworthy orchestrated the case against Strafford and testified
against him on a number of occasions. Little wonder Laud damned
him in his diary as 'not otherwise worthy to be named but as a
firebrand brought from Ireland to inflame this kingdom'.[81]

More important, the City, still sulking over its treatment in Ulster,
allied closely to Pym and played a key role in Strafford's downfall.[82]
The citizens of London were among the first to call for the earl's
execution and pressured the House of Lords to pass the bill of
attainder by threatening to withhold a loan of £120,000 unless
Strafford 'pays the penalty for his alleged crimes with his life'.[83]
When Parliament had asked the City for a loan the previous year

[78] *LJ, 1578–1714* (vols. II–XIX, London, 1767+), IV, 117.
[79] Conrad Russell, *The Fall of the British Monarchies 1637–1642* (Oxford, 1991), pp. 383–4.
[80] Thus Robert Goodwin, who after training as a lawyer became a freeman of the Drapers'
      Company, Town Clerk and Collector of Customs for Derry, asserted that Wentworth had
      been creaming off substantial profits from the customs of Derry and Coleraine. Moody,
      Londonderry Plantation, pp. 350, 450.
[81] Laud, IV, 437–8.
[82] Robert Ashton, *The City and the Court 1603–1643* (Cambridge, 1979), pp. 203–4 and C. H.
      Firth, 'London during the civil war', *History* 11 (1926), pp. 25–8.
[83] *CSP Venetian 1640–42*, p. 141.

Samuel Vassall, one of the London MPs, reminded the house that the 'Londonderry Business' 'sticks heavy upon them'.[84] It was not until November 1641, the month after the outbreak of the Irish rebellion, that Charles promised to restore the City to their Londonderry estates, which he admitted formed 'no great gift. But I intend first to recover it and then to give it to you whole and entirely.'[85] Charles's attempts to conciliate the City came too late and ultimately his greed and his insensitive treatment of the 'Londonderry Business' helped to alienate his primary source of credit, forcing the merchant community permanently into the parliamentary camp.

The 'Londonderry Business' thereby highlights very clearly the complex interrelationships of the Stuart monarchies. For by sequestering the City's plantation in the first place and by then trying to extract whatever profit he could from it, Charles dragged issues, previously confined to the periphery, into the central arena and in so doing inadvertently helped to destabilise royal government in Dublin, in Edinburgh and in London at a critical point in his reign.

Therefore the only way of fully understanding the 'Londonderry Business' is by setting it in the multi-dimensional context of the three Caroline states. To begin with, the individuals involved, especially Clotworthy, Hamilton and Antrim, were all 'men of the three kingdoms' with vested interests throughout the Stuart archipelago who served as vital human conduits disseminating intelligence and nurturing an increasingly complex web of allegiances. Second, the geographical location of County Londonderry, virtually within sight of Scotland, and the English flavour of the original plantation with its close ties to the commercial centre of London, highlight the extent to which Ulster had become a 'melting pot' – a frontier society where the Presbyterian and Anglican planter together with the Catholic Gael struggled to further their respective ethnic interests, to promote their national religions and to forge a distinctive identity. Finally, Strafford's racial prejudices against the Scots, whatever their ethnicity and religious beliefs, destabilised the uneasy *modus vivendi* of the Celtic 'periphery' and created a powerful interdenominational, multi-racial faction determined to make him pay for his 'thorough' policies and endless provocations. However, this uneasy British and

---

[84] Quoted in Valerie Pearl, *London and the Outbreak of the Puritan Revolution* (Oxford, 1961), p. 87.
[85] Quoted in Pearl, *London*, pp. 127–8. As it turned out Oliver Cromwell, not Charles I, returned the City to their Londonderry lands; yet throughout the 1640s both Antrim and the Scottish commissioners repeatedly vied for control of the region.

Irish alliance, which rested almost exclusively on a common hatred of Strafford, by successfully securing the Lord Deputy's execution also paved the way for the outbreak of the Ulster rebellion and thereby, ultimately, contributed to the onset of the 'Wars of the Three Kingdoms'.

Caroline politics during the later 1630s resembled an orrery – a clockwork mechanism devised to represent the motions of the planets about the sun. The 'Londonderry Business' then becomes merely one of the planets which revolved around the British monarchies, regularly crossing paths with and casting shadows over other issues and eventually joining with them to cause an eclipse. For as Clarendon perceptively noted in his *History*:

if this sottish [*sic*] people had not, without any provocation, but of their own folly and barbarity, with that bloody prologue engaged again the three kingdoms in a raging and devouring war; so that though Scotland blew the first trumpet, it was Ireland that drew the first blood; and if they had not at that time rebelled, and in that manner, it is very probable all the miseries which afterwards befell the King and his dominions had been prevented.[86]

[86] Clarendon, *History*, VI, 2–3.

APPENDIX: An assessment by Strafford in October 1638 of four offers made to the king for County Londonderry

Offer I: Made in a letter of 27 March 1637 by an anonymous individual

£8,000 present rent @ 10 years' purchase	£ 80,000
£8,000 improvement on expiration of the term @ 5 years' purchase	£ 40,000
Fine	£ 20,000
	£140,000

Offer II: Made by Hamilton (and Antrim) in December 1637/ January 1638. This included customs revenues

£12,000 present rent @ 10 years' purchase	£120,000
Improvement of £8,000 p.a. on expiration of the term, viz. 41 year's, @ 1 years purchase and 1/2	£ 12,000
Fine (deducting £6,000 allowed for first 6 months rent)	£ 4,000
	£136,000

Offer III: Made by Sir John Clotworthy and the rest of the 'now occupants'

£9,000 fee farm rent @ 10 years' purchase	£ 90,000
Customs, £2,000 p.a. @ 10 years' purchase	£ 20,000
Estimate that customs within 10 years will be worth £1,000 p.a. more @ 7 years' purchase	£ 7,000
Estimate that customs within 20 years will be £1,000 p.a. more @ 5 years' purchase	£ 5,000
	£122,000

Offer IV: Presented to the king by 'the writer' [Wentworth] for a 21 year lease

£8,000 @ 10 years' purchase	£ 80,000
£8,000 for improvement @ 5 years' purchase	£ 40,000
Customs rated as in offer III	£ 32,000
	£152,000

Source: Valuation of several propositions made to the king for the lands and customs belonging to the Londoners, sent to Laud, 30 October 1638 (BL, Add. MSS 21,125, ff. 1–4v).

CHAPTER 10

The public context of the trial and execution of Strafford

Terence Kilburn and Anthony Milton

The trial and subsequent execution of Thomas Wentworth, earl of Strafford, constitutes one of the great set-piece dramas of English history: an intensely theatrical confrontation of one of Charles I's ministers with some of his most determined critics, as well as a curtain-raiser for the confrontations of the Civil War. While it has always fascinated generations of early Stuart historians, it is only in recent years that the complex high politics surrounding these events have been fully reconstructed, thanks to the painstaking and meticulous research of scholars such as Conrad Russell. New manuscript sources have been discovered and exploited, and the events in Parliament have now received a possibly definitive account. And yet, as Professor Russell has rightly observed, MPs' behaviour was often directed to an audience beyond the confines of the House. When a tiny minority of the Lords in the Short Parliament can be observed forcing an apparently futile division against overwhelming odds, we may well suspect that this is done for the consumption of an outside audience. Similarly, the proceedings against Strafford in the Long Parliament were being very consciously played out before a wide and intrigued public audience – either assembled in the public galleries, or petitioning outside Westminster Hall, or conversing in the streets and squares of London, or sitting at home in the provinces, anxiously devouring news of events at the centre of the kingdom.[1]

This was a time when, as a number of scholars have pointed out, an active and informed public opinion was emerging to exercise an important voice in the affairs of the realm. As Professor Lake has explained, the circulation of political news and rumour, in the form

We are grateful to the editor for her very helpful comments on an earlier draft of this chapter.

[1] A. Fletcher, *The Outbreak of the English Civil War* (1981), esp. introduction and ch. 1; C. S. R. Russell, *The Fall of the British Monarchies, 1637–1642* (Oxford, 1991), pp. 274–302, 107n and *passim*.

of religious, parliamentary and literary materials of varying sophistication, was feeding 'the growth of something like a public sphere, or
spheres'. The popular political consciousness that emerged was one
prone to polarised views of the political process, and often preoccupied with meditations upon the corruption of the court. But this
consciousness did not constitute a single unified 'public opinion'.
Rather, a number of inchoate public opinions were generated,
capable of construing authority in a variety of ways, and therefore
enticingly open to being courted or seduced by a variety of political
actors, by the crown or its critics alike.[2]

The publicity given to Strafford's prosecution brought the trial
and its issues very dramatically into the public sphere. The crowds
that squeezed into Westminster Hall during the trial itself, or massed
threateningly outside the same building while the bill of attainder
was debated, remind us forcibly that events inside Parliament were
not hermetically sealed from those outside. There is a very real sense
in which the trial of the earl of Strafford was carried out as much in
the public domain as in Parliament. This was a public trial that ran
alongside the formal judicial proceedings in Parliament, sometimes
appropriating materials for its own judgement, sometimes being
sedulously courted by those inside Westminster Hall.

The public trial of Strafford, as it was carried out in printed and
scribal copies of genuine and fabricated parliamentary speeches,
pamphlets, satires, and verse libels, is a rich but unresearched aspect
of the politics of 1641. It will be impossible to cover all aspects of the
public trial of Strafford in this brief essay. Recent research by
Pauline Croft, Thomas Cogswell and Alastair Bellany on earlier
Stuart decades has demonstrated the riches that may be unearthed
by an examination of the surviving manuscript collections of separates and verse libels, and an analysis of the circumstances of their
circulation and distribution.[3] Here, however, our attention will be
restricted simply to some of the pamphlets printed before, during

---

[2] P. Lake, review article on C.S.R. Russell in *Huntington Library Quarterly* 57 (1994), pp. 193–4;
T. Cogswell, 'The politics of propaganda: Charles and the people in the 1620s', *Journal of
British Studies* 29 (1990), pp. 187–215; R. Cust, 'News and politics in early 17th century
England', *Past and Present* 112 (1986), pp. 60–90.

[3] T. Cogswell, *The Blessed Revolution: English Politics and the Coming of War, 1621–1624*
(Cambridge, 1989); P. Croft, 'The reputation of Robert Cecil: libels, political opinion and
popular awareness in the early seventeenth century', *TRHS*, 6th ser., 1 (1991), pp. 43–69;
A. Bellany, '"Raylinge rymes and vaunting verse": libellous politics in early Stuart
England, 1603–1628', in K. Sharpe and P. Lake (eds.), *Culture and Politics in Early Stuart
England* (1994) pp. 285–310.

and after the trial of Strafford in order to trace some aspects of the extraordinary unofficial public trial of Strafford that was conducted alongside, and often in close dialogue with, the formal trial in the Palace of Westminster. Even a study of this type can only be tentative in its conclusions, however: discussion of much of the relevant pamphlet literature is bedevilled by problems of dating, which makes it often possible only to speculate on the precise timing of a particular publication, and the specific intention which might therefore lie behind its appearance.[4]

I

In the first months of the Long Parliament, public opinion on Strafford would seem to have been shaped and inflamed chiefly by the dispersal, in printed and scribal form, of the Commons' articles of impeachment against him. The original set of nine articles against Strafford was circulated widely: Lady Brilliana Harley, for example, was sent a copy by her husband (then a sitting member) in December, and quickly dispatched a copy to her son. She had to wait longer for the later set of twenty-two articles, writing on 15 February that she had heard that 'my Lord Straford is aquesused of most abominabel maters, but I have not hard any particulars'. She did not have much longer to wait, however, as the charges were soon printed, more than three weeks before the date set for the trial. The Lords reacted angrily by appointing a committee to examine the whole business of licensing and printing, and soon brought charges against one printer for publishing the articles against Strafford. Their efforts were to no avail, however: Sir Thomas Knyvett sent on

---

[4]   The dating of tracts by the bookseller George Thomason offers little assistance here. Thomason often dates tracts according to the date of the event to which they refer (thus parliamentary speeches are dated according to the day that they were delivered, which is most unlikely to be the date of publication). Wherever possible, therefore, contemporary observations of a tract have been used to help in dating its emergence, although even here care needs to be used as these remarks may sometimes be referring to the circulation of scribal copies rather than printed editions. Allusions to specific points in the trial, or later execution, allow certain pamphlets to be dated more precisely, although their exact proximity to the event described may be difficult to determine: aspects of Strafford's trial were being fought over well after he had been executed, as the proceedings over Digby's speech make clear (see below). Similarly, some of the many editions of the conclusion of Strafford's defence against his impeachment may well date from after his execution. One edition of speeches made by Pym and St John during Strafford's trial was entered in the Stationers' Register the day before Strafford was executed: G. E. B. Eyre and C. R. Rivington, *A Transcript of the Registers of the Company of Stationers of London, 1640–1708* (3 vols., 1915), I, 23.

to John Buxton 'all the Articles against the Earl of Strafford' on 2 March, the day after the House of Lords had sought to counter the publication.[5]

If the dispersal of these articles helped to feed public interest in Strafford and his forthcoming trial, it also doubtless encouraged readers to prejudge the issues raised against him. Among the articles were the charges that Strafford had worked to overthrow the laws and government of England and Ireland with the aim of bringing in arbitrary and tyrannical government, that he had assumed 'regall power' in Ireland and the North, that he had encouraged papists and stirred up war between England and Scotland, and that he had plotted against parliaments and deliberately sought to create enmity between Charles and his people. The specific charge that he had advised the king to use an Irish army to subdue the English was present in the earliest version of the impeachment articles. The articles, and much of the following parliamentary discussion of Strafford's case, were therefore pitched at an alarmist and inflammatory level, and their circulation rapidly ensured that the fate of Strafford became a matter of national concern and polarised debate.[6]

The circulation of parliamentary speeches bearing on the trial also served to spread the views of Strafford's prosecutors further. The regular traffic in news and information between London and the provinces that was already active in the 1620s had for some time included scribal copies of parliamentary speeches. While these undoubtedly continued to be distributed, the early months of the Long Parliament were distinctive for the way in which this scribal publication became extended into print, with an extraordinary explosion of printed parliamentary speeches. Some of these may have been basically authentic in content, albeit heavily edited and expanded versions of what had actually been delivered, but others were wild fabrications. This was an expansion which partly reflected publishers responding to market demand and the relative leniency of

---

[5] *Letters of Lady Brilliana Harley*, ed. T. T. Lewis (Camden Society, 1st ser., vol. 58, 1854), pp. 104, 114; J. H. Timmis, *Thine is the Kingdom* (Alabama, 1974), p. 61; D. Freist, 'The formation of opinion and the communication network in London, 1637–c.1645' (unpublished Ph.D. thesis, University of Cambridge, 1992), pp. 42–3, 121; *LJ*, IV, 174, 175; HMC, *Var. Coll.* II, p. 261. Several editions of the articles were published: see STC 25247, 25247.5, 25248, 25248.3, 25248.5, 25248.7.

[6] *The Journal of Sir Simonds D'Ewes*, ed. W. Notestein (New Haven, 1923), pp. 60–63n; Timmis, *Thine is the Kingdom*, pp. 56–9.

restrictions on publication at this time, but some of the speeches were undoubtedly published at the active behest of the members themselves. There was an increasing tendency for members to speak from scripts, and this may often indicate a readiness to address a wider public audience than the parliament house.[7]

A number of parliamentary speeches relating to Strafford's impeachment certainly found their way into print during this time. Typically, they sought to attack Strafford as the cause of all the miseries into which the kingdom had fallen. Strafford provided a useful scapegoat for a broad swathe of political opinion. Even before the impeachment of Strafford, early speeches by the likes of the earl of Bristol, Lord Digby, Lord Falkland and Sir John Holland all spoke of the king's evil ministers and pernicious councillors. In Lord Falkland's speech in particular, Strafford was repeatedly identified as the cause of all the ills of the three kingdoms, and as the one who had sought to divide the king from his people. As winter turned to spring, these published versions of parliamentary speeches were helping to shape and harness popular political opinion against Strafford, while at the same time counties were incited to petition Parliament for the removal of such evil councillors. Condemnation of Strafford, in particular, became synonymous with the pursuit of justice. Strafford had become the emblem (and in many ways the explanation) of the Personal Rule: kill Strafford, and the Personal Rule died with him. Not only was this a representation of the issues which could make ready sense to a broader political nation, but it also served a valuable purpose for many of those politicians who had been associated to a varying extent on a local or national level with the abuses of the Personal Rule. By locating all the iniquities of that time in the person of Strafford, they helped to defend themselves and also the general integrity of the country's governors. Moreover, as Peter Lake has already noted, the value of simplistic conspiracy theories of the sort that attached to Strafford was that they could explain political malpractice and conflict without impugning the basic political structure of the realm, and without doing any damage to the fundamental conviction that, left to itself, the political system naturally worked towards unity and consensus, and was not in need of any radical surgery.[8]

[7] A. D. T. Cromartie, 'The printing of parliamentary speeches, November 1640–July 1642', *HJ* 33 (1990), pp. 23–44; Russell, *Fall*, p. 107n.

[8] *A Speech made to the House of Commons concerning Episcopy. By the Lord Viscount Faulkeland* (1641),

These speeches may have helped to establish a hostile climate for Strafford. It is interesting to note, however, that many of the speeches most closely concerned with the early moves to impeach Strafford only seem to have been published several months later around the time of the trial itself. For example, Pym's speeches following the reading of the articles against Strafford and Sir George Radcliffe (made on 25 November and 31 December respectively) were apparently not published until after 25 March, when the trial was well under way, and may not even have appeared until the bill of attainder was under discussion.[9]

Once it was underway, the trial attracted keen public interest, but did not proceed in the manner in which the trial managers had hoped. Strafford's defence was careful and effective, and the prosecution was reduced to abandoning some articles, and resorting to increasingly tenuous legal arguments. It was becoming all too clear that the Lords were unlikely to vote for Strafford's impeachment. Before the Lords could reach their judgement, therefore, there were moves in the Commons to replace the impeachment for treason with the more straightforward act of attainder, whereby Strafford would simply be declared to be guilty.[10]

II

It is the move to a bill of attainder that seems to have prompted a new surge in publications relating to Strafford. It was a move by the Commons which accepted that the legal case against Strafford was unlikely to convince a majority in the Lords. An act of attainder, of course, was hardly likely to be more amenable to the Lords in these circumstances. It is a move that can only be explained by the assumption that other forms of persuasion, beyond those of simple jurisprudence, were required. If Strafford's opponents felt that it would be necessary to have recourse to non-parliamentary means, this was a conviction that seemed to be felt with equal strength by Charles I. Throughout the preamble to the trial, and the legal proceedings themselves, there had been fears and threats that other

p. 10; C. Roberts, *The Growth of Responsible Government in Stuart England* (Cambridge, 1966), pp. 111–12; P. Lake, 'Anti-popery: the structure of a prejudice', in R. Cust and A. Hughes (eds.), *Conflict in Early Stuart England* (1989) pp. 72–106.

[9] *Two Speeches made by John Pymm Esquire...* (Wing P4302: 1641).

[10] Timmis, *Thine is the Kingdom*, chs. 4–5.

means might be employed by the different parties. The initial impeachment of Strafford may well have been impelled by fears that he was about to accuse Pym and his allies of treason, and the decision to commence the trial seems to have been prompted in part by the failure of the projected settlement of early 1641 that was based upon the 'bridging appointments' of Saye, Pym and others. The move to attainder was made at a time when there were already strong rumours of the existence of what would later be revealed as the First Army Plot.[11]

As fears of the king's possible actions grew, so the determination to bring outside force to bear on the deliberations in Westminster seems to have increased. Back in November, Pym had delivered a message to the House of Lords from the Commons urging that the proceedings against Strafford be speedy and secret: witnesses should be 'speedily examined', and the names of parties and nature of questions kept private until they were used in the trial 'whereby subtile Practices and Combinations may be prevented, and the Truth secured from Corruption and Concealment'.[12] If the same anxiety in the treatment of witnesses was plainly present in March, there yet seems to have been a new willingness to secure as wide a publicity for the trial as possible. The more that the parliamentary leaders were starting to move out of the normal sphere of political manoeuvre, the more important it became to mobilise broader public support. As the trial progressed, there appears to have been a greater keenness to court public opinion more directly. There was a clear need, not just to outmanoeuvre Strafford, but to get as many people aware of the charges against him as soon as possible.[13]

One of Strafford's prosecutors, John Glyn, had already given a foretaste of where popular pressure might be brought to bear, in his extraordinary remarks at the trial on 5 April. Confronting the objection that the evidence for Strafford's intention to use the Irish army against England rested on the sole testimony of Sir Henry Vane, for which a further witness was necessary, this experienced lawyer invoked as the second witness 'vox populi' – the voice of the people – which testified to the truth of this charge. This was scarcely legal language, but it also drew attention to the fact that, if the 'voice

---

[11] Russell, *Fall*, pp. 274, 292–3; Roberts, *Growth*, p. 82.
[12] *LJ*, IV, 94.
[13] For examples of trial speeches by Strafford's prosecutors published around this time, see those by Glyn and Maynard in Thomason Tract (hereafter Th.) E.196 (45), E.207 (10).

of the people' was crucial to the case against Strafford, then it was a voice that needed to be properly instructed.[14]

As the bill of attainder worked its way through the Commons in April and was then submitted to the Lords, the polemical pressure palpably increased. 'By order of the Common house', the speech with which Oliver St John introduced and vindicated the bill to the Lords was published together with Pym's speech from the closing stages of Strafford's trial justifying the general charge of treason. This was one of the very rare 'official' publications of parliamentary speeches.[15] This publication was clearly aimed at pressurising the Lords rather than whipping up a popular frenzy. St John's laboured thirty-eight–page contribution was a careful legal case aimed at educated legal opinion. But St John's arguments were repeated by Pym and Glyn in a shorter and more user-friendly form, and with a more political slant, in a way that made them accessible to a wider audience. Pym's *Declaration* before the Lords underwent further popularisation, presumably with his consent. While in the official publication the *Declaration* was twenty-eight pages long, a slimmed-down eight-page version which concentrated on pithy turns of phrase rather than the more laboured and discursive passages went through several impressions.[16]

With the move to attainder, and the increasing evidence of problems in the Lords, there was a great expansion in the number of pamphlets which sought to make the case explicitly for Strafford's execution. These were mostly very brief works, seldom more than six or seven pages in length, sharper and punchier than some of the more laboured legal expositions of St John and Glyn. There can be little doubt that such publications had at least tacit official backing, and may have been part of a carefully orchestrated campaign designed not only to manipulate and inflame popular political opinion, but also to counter any attempt to secure Strafford's release.

A number of polemical strategies were adopted, in a number of different formats, including dialogues and supposedly intercepted letters to friends in the country. One particularly prominent element was the charge of political apostasy, which was raised by MPs and

---

[14] Timmis, *Thine is the Kingdom*, p. 119.
[15] *The Declaration of John Pym Esquire, upon the Whole Matter of the Charge of High Treason, against Thomas, Earle of Strafford, April 12 1641 with An Argument of Law, concerning the Bill of Attainder of high Treason of the said Earle of Strafford, before a Committee of both houses of Parliament... by Mr St John... on April 29.1641* (1641); Cromartie, 'Printing', p. 28.
[16] *Master Pimmes Speech to the Lords* (Th.E.196 (47)); cf. E.207 (9) and E.208 (8).

anonymous pamphleteers alike. While the earl of Bedford pointedly copied out Wentworth's 1628 speeches in defence of the Petition of Right into his commonplace book, other readers were helped out by the publication of these speeches in printed form at this time: no commentary was provided, but the message was unmistakable.[17]

A more radical tone was adopted by the anonymous author of *A Declaration Shewing the Necessity of the Earle of Straffords Suffering*, who urged the Lords to follow the Commons in condemning Strafford before it was too late. This is a curious piece: it draws upon the medieval legal precedents, reviews of Strafford's Irish policies and arguments over definitions of treason that were prominent in parliamentary speeches, but combines them with the more fantastical fears and preoccupations of popular rumour. Thus it claimed that Wentworth 'aimes at Monarchy', and 'whereas it is observed that all Papists speake well of him and his actions, it is very likely in recompence thereof he would bring in Popery vi & armis, having power under his Majesty to raise armes, and all for a Bulwarke to support his greatnesse'. Along with his political faults, it was claimed that Strafford manifested all the moral infirmities as well: he was 'libidinous as Tiberius, cruell as Nero, covetous as rich Cressus, as terrible as Phalaris, as mischievous as Sejanus'. The author sought to dwell in particular on the forbidding personal appearance of Strafford: 'his pallid colour sheweth revenge, his sower face, cruelty; his stooping and looking to the earth, avarice; his gate, pride; his demeanour, insolency'.[18]

An anonymous pamphleteer in a brief seven–page tract appears to have aimed particularly at moderate opinion that had not been convinced by the case against Strafford, and which was perhaps somewhat alarmed by the tone of Strafford's prosecutors. Emphasising that 'whether his Lordship be guilty of high treason, I cannot determine', although 'many foule things stick upon him by manifest proofs', the author explicitly distanced himself from both the pro- and anti-Strafford camps, and delineated instead a *via media* which stressed the purely pragmatic grounds for getting rid of Strafford. Where some authors sought to convict Strafford of apostasy and hypocrisy by referring to his speeches in the 1628 parliament, this

---

[17] Russell, *Fall*, p. 283; *Two Speeches made by Sir Thomas Wentworth, now Earle of Strafford, in the Parliament holden at Westminster 1628. The one concerning the liberty of the Subject. The other the Priviledge of the Houses of Parliament* (Wing s5802: 1641).

[18] Th. E.158 (2).

anonymous author intriguingly sought to court moderate royalist opinion by attacking Strafford's 1620s' behaviour in stirring up early parliaments against the king: he had done more harm in causing division in the 1620s than in any of the later charges brought against him.[19]

An extra edge was given to this campaign in favour of the attainder by the fact that the case against it was also reaching the public stage. There had hitherto been little attempt to court public opinion in Strafford's defence. This was partly because Strafford was constructing a tightly argued legal defence which eschewed vigorous rhetoric or appeals to the broader political nation.[20] There was also undoubtedly a great deal of pressure to avoid adopting a pro-Strafford line in print. The compiler of a tract published in 1647 condemned 'the faint-heartednesse of the Presse, which durst not speake freely, for fear of Arbitrary Treason' at the time of Strafford's trial.[21] Admittedly, this comes from one of the few post-execution pro-Strafford tracts produced by royalists, but the suggestion that tacitly understood official censorship and fears of parliamentary censure and reprisal tied the hands of printers during the period of the prosecution of Strafford – just as fears of popular tumult were to intimidate various members of both Houses of Parliament – cannot be lightly dismissed.

Nevertheless, the text of Strafford's final summing-up at his trial went through no less than seven editions in 1641. In contrast to the other parts of his defence, this is a pithy and user-friendly summary of his position, providing a cogent rehearsal of the case against cumulative treason, combined with an account of the touching moment when his self-composure deserted him as he appealed on behalf of his children by his second wife, Arabella Holles. This piece was swiftly answered by two short works: the *Answere to the Earle of Strafford's Oration* (apparently lifted from the trial proceedings) reiterated the case for cumulative treason, while *Annotations upon the Earle of Straffords Conclusion* reprinted the speech in full, with rebuttals of every point in intemperate marginal annotations.[22] The publication of the *Conclusion* drew surprisingly little comment from Parliament,

[19] *The Earle of Strafford Characterized in a letter sent to a friend in the Countrey* (1641).
[20] Timmis, *Thine is the Kingdom*, pp. 184, 186, 189.
[21] *A Briefe and Perfect Relation of the Answeres and Replies of Thomas Earle of Strafford* (1647), p. 96 [97].
[22] For editions of *The Conclusion of the Earle of Straffords Defence*, see Wing s784, s784A, s784B, s784C, s784D, s784E and s784F.

however – possibly because many of the editions post-date Strafford's later execution, but certainly not because they were insensitive to the publication of pro-Strafford opinions, as the controversy caused by George Digby's speech made clear.

On the occasion of the critical third reading of the bill of attainder in the Commons – 21 April – Digby gave a speech in which he stated that although he believed Strafford to be guilty of treason, he doubted that Strafford could be found guilty of treason for a set of offences not yet deemed in law to be treason. Digby also expressed grave reservations about Vane's testimony that Strafford had advised the king to use the Irish army to subdue royal opponents in England. For Digby, the lack of proof on this matter in particular meant that all notions of Strafford's treason had 'quite vanished away'. Digby's speech struck at the very heart of the case against Strafford.[23]

In the face of a violent parliamentary reaction to his speech, it is especially significant to note that Digby would appear to have chosen to go public with it in order to vindicate himself before a wider public audience. The speech was rapidly published in both printed and manuscript form. This was the first pro-Strafford piece to be published, although the title, *The Lord Digby His Last Speech Against the Earle of Strafford*, is an interesting and revealing one. Digby's speech does indeed include a violent attack upon Strafford, condemning his tyranny, pride and passion. To Digby, Strafford was 'the most dangerous Minister' and 'that grand Apostate of the Commonwealth', and 'a name of hatred in the present ages by his practices, and fit to be made a terrour to future ages by his punishment'.[24] This partly seems to reflect the hegemony of anti-Strafford rhetoric in the public domain: even a defence of him had to ape the terminology of Strafford's opponents. Digby's use of such rhetoric may conceivably have been prompted by the fact that a public campaign against his speech had already swung into action. If, on the other hand, it was a pre-emptive attempt to disarm opposition then it signally failed, as we will see.

There was an all-too-obvious need to counter the publication of Digby's speech. This came in the form of an anonymous tract entitled *An Answer* which Thomason dated to 21 April. The intention of the *Answer* was clear enough – a damage limitation exercise meant to question Digby's motives, dismiss his arguments as the products of

---

23   Timmis, *Thine is the Kingdom*, pp. 148–50.
24   Th. E.198 (1).

mere scruple and, in so doing, to undermine the credibility of his objections to the charge of treason.[25]

The publication of such printed anti-Strafford propaganda urging his execution, combined doubtless with a vastly larger underground trade in manuscript materials and rumours, does much to explain the well-known public tumult surrounding the trial and execution of Strafford. There was plenty here to fuel the anger of the mob and dissuade the king from any notion of trying to save Strafford's life. The campaign to undermine Digby's challenge to the charge of treason served to incite a popular clamour for Strafford's head. On 24 April the Londoners' Petition, signed by 20,000 'men of good ranke and qualitie' and instantly sold as a broadsheet, complained that until Strafford was executed 'neither Religion nor their lives, liberties or estates can be secured', as they feared that 'there may be practices now in hand to hinder the birth of your [Parliament's] great endeavours, and that we lye under some more dangerous plot than we can discover'. The anonymous pamphleteer who urged that Strafford must on pragmatic grounds be executed 'as a just sacrifice to appease the people' was alluding to a popular pressure that was palpably increasing.[26]

Perhaps the most famous and direct appeal to this increasing popular outrage by those pursuing Strafford's attainder in parliament was the posting up at the Exchange and 'in many places in London and Westminster' of the names of those MPs who had voted against the bill of attainder, under the heading 'Enemies of Justice, and Straffordians'. The crowds which massed around the Palace of Westminster as the Lords debated the bill of attainder were undoubtedly encouraged and partly directed by Strafford's opponents in Parliament. Those involved in the popular protests of 1640/1 included members of the educated ranks, the well-to-do, freemen, liverymen, shop-keepers, as well as artisans and labourers.[27] Their presence may have been orchestrated to some extent, but their hatred of Strafford was doubtless genuine, and bore witness to the effectiveness with which the charges and arguments against him had been disseminated.

[25] *An Answer to the Lord Digbies Speech in the House of Commons to the Bill of Attainder of the Earle of Strafford* (Th. E.198 (3)). This may be an example of an edited speech given in Parliament on 21 April in reply to that given by Digby.

[26] *The Petition of the Citizens of London to both Houses of Parliament, 1641* (Th. 699, f4, 13); *The Earle of Strafford Characterized*, pp. 6–7.

[27] B. Manning, *The English People and the English Revolution, 1640–1649* (1976), pp. 10–18.

III

Strafford's execution was one of the great showpieces of English history. Hollar's famous print shows the vast crowds that swarmed to see his death, and contemporary accounts testify to the public rejoicing at his death. One observer commented how people who had travelled to London to see the execution 'rode in triumph back, waving their hatts, and with all expressions of joy, thro' every Town they went crying, His head is off, his head is off!... and breaking the windowes of those persons, who would not solemnize this Festival with a bonfire'.[28] His death released a flood of popular anti-Strafford pamphlets. These utilised a range of weapons earlier witnessed in the posthumous abuse of Robert Cecil and the duke of Buckingham. Anagrams of his various titles were circulated – 'o what wit, treason, harmes' and 'worser rul'd not traytors head must off' being among the more inspired. His name was punningly rendered as 'want worth'. One satirical pamphlet conducted him across the river Styx in the company of a complaining Charon. Another bizarre tract described how immediately before Strafford's execution a young gentleman had a vision of Strafford as a 'tall blacke man' in a dream. Another pamphlet depicted him falling out with his old ally Laud and bitterly reproaching him for his fate – this was a pamphlet which by some malicious means found its way into Laud's hands in the Tower, to his great distress.[29]

Amid all these popular burlesques, however, many verses took Strafford's fall as the opportunity for more conventional musings on the vanity of earthly glories, urging their readers to 'take an example from Lord Wentworth all/ Lest by high climbing you do chance to fall'. Where Laud had been the handmaiden of a diabolical popish plot, Strafford had fallen due to weaknesses to which most men were

---

[28] Sir Philip Warwick, *Memoires* (1701), p. 164. We are grateful to Julia Merritt for this reference.

[29] *The Divine Dreamer: or, A short treatise discovering the true effect & power of dreames... Whereunto is annexed The Dreame of a young Gentleman, immediately before the death of the late Earle of Strafford* (Th. E.157 (6): 1641); *The Downfall of Greatnesse for the Losse of Goodnesse. A Poem; Or, A short Survey of Thomas Lord Wentworth... His History and Tragedy* (Th. E.157 (1): 1641); *A Description of the Passage of Thomas late Earle of Strafford, over the River of Styx, with the conference betwixt him, Charon, and William Noy* (Th. E.156 (21): 1641); *The Discontented Conference betwixt the two great Associates, William, Archbishop of Canterbury, and Thomas, late Earle of Strafford* (Th. E.157 (3)); Laud, III, 444. Laud later complained that 'bitter and fierce libels' came out *before* Strafford's death, 'to keep up and increase the people's hate against him', but they seem in fact to have mostly dated from after Strafford's execution (*ibid.*, 444–5).

all too susceptible. Thus in the case of even a fiercely anti-Strafford satirical verse-tract like *Newes from Rome*, while it featured the Pope lamenting that 'My Irish King is dead', it also included a lengthier and more ponderous 'Elegaicall Confabulation betweene Death and Honour' which presented Strafford in a more sympathetic light, noting only his valour and wisdom, but reflecting that Death conquers all. Other verses, including some that were posthumously fathered upon Strafford himself, depicted him as a flawed hero, who had deserted his earlier virtues, and whose greatest fault had been overweaning ambition rather than popish plotting.[30]

These were not irrelevant musings on the public stage, however – there was a broader political dimension to this activity. After his death, the political struggle over Strafford's legacy continued. In the politics of later 1641 and 1642, the reputation of Strafford and the manner of his death became an important ground of political controversy. In May 1641, a number of verses and other papers under the name of Strafford were referred to the Committee for Printing of Books.[31] This was a concern prompted, not just by alarm at public debate, but because very basic issues regarding the trial had been opened up with the printing of Digby's speech against the attainder *after* the Commons had voted in favour of the bill.

Digby's speech rapidly went into a second edition, and provoked a strong reaction from Parliament. A committee was established, chaired by Sir John Evelyn, which concluded that the speech contained 'matters untrue, and scandalous'. The committee's report of 13 July condemned the printing of the speech as a criminal act. Those responsible were castigated as delinquents for having printed and published the speech, which was ordered to be burnt publicly by the hangmen at Westminster, Cheapside and Smithfield. All stationers and others possessing copies of the tract were ordered to hand them over to the Company of Stationers for burning.[32]

---

[30] Thomas Herbert, *An Elegie upon the Death of Thomas Earle of Strafford* (Wing H1528); *Newes from Rome* (Th. E.158 (18)); *Verses: Lately written by Thomas Earle of Strafford* (Th. 669 f4 (11)); *A Short and true Relation, of the life and death of the Earle of Strafford* (Wing S3557A); *Downfall of Greatnesse*. We are grateful to Julia Merritt for drawing our attention to this point. See also her introduction to this volume.

[31] *CJ*, II, 146 (cf. 148, 160).

[32] *Sir John Evelyn. His Report from the Committee, Appointed to consider of the Printing of the Lord Digbyes Speech concerning the Bill of Attainder of the Earl of Strafford* (Th. E.163 (6)); *CJ*, II, 208, 209. It is not entirely clear whether this reaction was partly prompted by the reprinting of Digby's speech at around this time, alluded to in the title of Th. E.198 (3).

The printing of Digby's speech re-opened the whole question of Strafford's guilt and forced Parliament into the necessity of justifying the earl's execution by publishing a revised edition of *An Answer*. This was republished 'in regard of the reprinting of that speech' with the stated intention of thwarting 'the Lord Straffords hopes, that hee may hereafter appeare lesse guilty of the death hee died'.[33] The reprinting of Digby's speech additionally led to the publication of *An Aproved Answer* by 'a worthy gentleman' which described the offending speech as 'Partiall and Unlikt', and complained in particular of how it aimed at 'stealing away the affection, not convincing the Iudgment'.[34]

If these pamphlets represented a semi-official campaign to clear Parliament of the accusation of having committed judicial murder, they were soon taken up and exploited by a popular market for Strafford material that had clearly developed its own momentum. An interesting example here is a pamphlet dated by Thomason as being published in June 1641, entitled *A Printed Paper Cald the Lord Digbies Speech to the Bill of Attainder of the Earle of Strafford, Torn in Pieces and Blowne Away*. This is in fact simply another edition, in tattier format and with a more colourful title, of the more official *Aproved Answer* against Digby's defence. The *Printed Paper* is almost certainly a pirated edition, produced by an unscrupulous printer prompted by an identifiable market for justifications of Strafford's execution among the broader populace.[35] Again, the question of where parliamentary influence ended is a moot one: it may well be that, having incited a popular clamour for Strafford's execution, the parliamentary managers had little option but to sit back and let popular enthusiasm for the discussion and ridiculing of the earl continue until it finally ran out of steam.

The extraordinary outpouring of pamphlets concerned with Strafford's last speeches and execution show even more clearly the complex interactions of rigid party affiliations with a broader sphere of public opinion. Last dying speeches were an important genre of publication in early modern England. As Dr J. A. Sharpe has

---

[33] Th. E.198 (3).   [34] Th. E.198 (2).

[35] Th. E.160 (16). The poor print quality, tatty format and anonymous printer are telling. Ironically, this pirated edition went through two printings while the original only seems to have managed one. For a similar example of a book's sales being usurped by a pirated copy with a more appealing title, see the example of Peter Heylyn's *Survey of the Estate of France*, supplanted by a pirated edition entitled *France Painted to the Life*. DNB, s.n. 'Peter Heylyn'.

argued, the last dying speech was a carefully regulated mechanism by which those found guilty and sentenced to death, at the last publicly confessed their guilt and repentance. Public executions thereby allowed the state to proclaim to the people its power and authority in a public and highly theatrical fashion. If these public executions of criminals were important public occasions, then political executions were potentially a great deal more significant. It was in the conduct of the execution itself that the state hoped to justify its actions against its opponents. Nevertheless, public executions were not necessarily the smooth operation that their managers hoped for. In the case of recusant priests, for example, Peter Lake and Michael Questier have recently demonstrated the ways in which the condemned man might be able to turn the public event to his own advantage, refusing to confess his guilt and instead seizing on the opportunity to propagate his faith more widely by a public martyrdom. In these cases, the condemned man manipulated the theatrical possibilities of the occasion in order to vindicate himself and his faith in the most public manner possible. The public mutilation of Burton, Bastwick and Prynne on the scaffold in 1637, in which their intended humiliation became instead a powerfully stage-managed public martyrdom, had already revealed the dangers for the government in allowing such events to slip out of their control.[36]

Despite the popular enthusiasm for Strafford's death, the manner of his final execution and the popular pamphlet debate that followed it arguably provides us with another example of a struggle for control of the scaffold as an important public stage. Strafford's conduct on the scaffold was high theatre in which he essentially took over control of the event. Instead of confessing his guilt, Strafford took the opportunity to emphasise his innocence of religious or political heterodoxy. While magnanimous in his good wishes to all, he yet warned the country of what they should expect of an intended reformation that was begun with the shedding of innocent blood. If he was penitent for his sins, he yet made it clear that these did not include the charges for which he was being executed. This was a

---

[36] J. A. Sharpe, '"Last dying speeches": religion, ideology and public execution in seventeenth century England', *Past and Present* 107 (1985), pp. 144–67; P. Lake and M. Questier, 'Agency and appropriation at the foot of the gallows' (forthcoming); K. Sharpe, *The Personal Rule of Charles I* (1992), pp. 762–5. We are grateful to Professor Lake and Dr Questier for allowing us to see a draft of their paper in advance of publication.

superb performance, and even Strafford's enemies had to admit the impressiveness of Strafford's playing. One of the sets of anti-Strafford verses published in the wake of the execution, while damning Strafford's policies unreservedly, had to admit that his demeanour on the scaffold had been exemplary, and lectured the 'headless multitude' that they should not 'censure and condemne this great man, as one utterly lost' but should judge charitably of his end. His latter days were his bad days, but his last day was his best.[37] One report of his execution – by no means a straightforwardly pro-Strafford account – observed how Strafford spoke with 'such a grace and deliberation' that 'many that before reioyced at the newes of his sentence, did now testifie their compassion by their teares'.[38]

The expected 'last dying speech' had thus failed to materialise, and this represented a serious reverse for the anti-Strafford campaign – there was a sense in which Pym's junto had lost at the very hour of their victory. Could a man who had borne himself so nobly on the scaffold really be the Machiavellian figure that they had depicted? The problem was resolved in a remarkably straightforward fashion. Since Strafford had not obliged his opponents with a last dying speech in the traditional form, they seem to have composed a more appropriate one for him instead. Shortly after Strafford's execution, a printed version of his last speech was in circulation which fully met the traditional criteria. The speech that he had delivered from the scaffold had been too public, and too widely heard, for another one to be plausibly substituted. Instead, the public were presented with a speech allegedly made by Wentworth *before* he reached the scaffold – when he was about to leave the Tower, and addressed to the Lords who had come to accompany him thence.

In this speech, Wentworth behaves in the more accepted fashion. He punctiliously assures the Lords that he is satisfied with every aspect of the conduct of the trial: 'never any subject, or Peere of my rank had ever that help of Counsell, that benefit of time, or a more free and legall tryall then I have had'. He accepts entirely the justice of the case against him, and enthusiastically approves of the benefits that will be gained by his execution:

for to the Law I submit my selfe, and confesse that I receive nothing but justice: for he that politickly intendeth good to a Commonweale, may be

[37] *Downfall of Greatnesse*, p. 6.
[38] *A True Relation of the Manner of the Execution of Thomas Earle of Strafford* (Wing T3002A), p. 8 (cf. p. 1).

called a just man, but he that practiseth either for his owne profit, or any other sinister ends, may bee well termed a delinquent person... And moreover I ingenuously confesse with Cicero, That the death of the bad is the safety of the good that be alive.

He was explicit about the reasons for his misconduct. He had been arrogant and ambitious, aspiring to be 'a God amongst men'. All ambitious men 'to possesse their ends, care not to violate the Lawes of Religion, and Reason, and to breake the bonds of Modesty and Equity... of which as I have beene guilty, so I crave at Gods hands forgivenesse'.[39]

Here was a speech that confirmed his accusers' charges and fears, and vindicated the managers of the trial and execution from any suggestions that they might have strained or even overturned the law in order to secure Strafford's death. The care with which the speech specifically approves the conduct of the trial leads one to suspect that the trial managers might well have had some hand in its production.

The Tower speech seems to have gone through at least two editions, but was then confronted by an angry refutation, published as *A Protestation against a foolish, ridiculous and scandalous Speech, pretended to be spoken by Thomas Wentworth, late Earle of Strafford, to certaine Lords before his comming out of the Tower*. This was possibly the work of Strafford's family, and claimed the testimonials of a number of the Lords who had been present when Strafford was fetched from the Tower, who denied that Strafford had ever delivered the speech attributed to him. The pamphlet also provided the text of the self-vindicating speech which Strafford had delivered on the scaffold. To boost its appearance of authenticity still further, the pamphlet provided a copy of the paper allegedly left by Strafford on the scaffold, containing the heads of his last speech in his own hand.[40]

Here, then, was a pro-Strafford reading of his last thoughts, presenting a Strafford who was not penitent, but steadfastly resolute, defying convention by protesting his innocence and loyalty to the king, and refusing to accept any notion of guilt. There seem to have been no further pamphlet exchanges over the authenticity of this scaffold speech – contemporaries and later historians would seem to have accepted it as genuine.

The further history of the treatment of Strafford's last dying

---

[39] *The Earle of Strafford, his speech in the Tower* (Wing s5785). Cf. s5785A.
[40] Th. E 208 (17). See also 'J. B.', *The Poets Knavery Discovered, in all their lying Pamphlets* (Th. E.135 (11)), sig.A2v.

speech is however even more intriguing. The nearest thing to an anti-Strafford response came in the form of a pamphlet with the unambiguous title *Great Satisfaction concerning the Death of the Earle of Strafford... With a serious consideration of certaine Conclusions observed from his last Speech upon the Scaffold*. The pamphlet takes the form of a dialogue between a Scotsman and a Jesuit about Strafford's scaffold speech. While the Jesuit is enthusiastic, the Scotsman expresses his concern that Strafford did not fulfil the traditional requirement that he be fully penitent, and 'would not acknowledge that he was justly executed for his sins'. The two disputants move through each section of the speech, the Jesuit approving each sentiment expressed and the Scot putting the worst possible gloss on every heading. Where the suggestion is made that the charge of cumulative treason made against Strafford was unjust, the Scot obligingly provides a detailed list of legal precedents, apparently lifted directly from the printed speeches of Glyn and St John. Here, and elsewhere in the tract, the aim seems more to educate than to entertain, and the greatest worry appears to be that the public might respond favourably to the printed versions of Strafford's scaffold speech. By putting such a favourable response in the mouth of a Jesuit, and making the Scotsman the mouthpiece for all the arguments in defence of the execution, the tract can be sufficiently confident that it has conveyed the necessary message that it allows itself to end on a charitable note, hence avoiding an appearance of simple malice. Having made it plain that Strafford was guilty as charged and deserved to die, the Scotsman concedes that Strafford ended his speech by asking for forgiveness for his sins in the more conventional manner, and the Scot therefore concludes the pamphlet with the reflection that people should 'judge charitably of him' and assume that his final repentance may have won him God's forgiveness.[41]

The publication of this dialogue shows the contemporary significance and concern attached to the matter of Strafford's last speech, and the perceived need to guide public opinion in the matter. But if there was a clash of opinion between pro- and anti-Strafford groups, the public sphere would appear to have found its own bizarre way of dealing with this conflict. The scaffold speech clearly found an enthusiastic audience: no less then seven editions of it were published in 1641. But this print run was exceeded by that of

[41] Wing G175 (1641).

another publication, entitled *The Two Last Speeches of Thomas Went-worth*. This work sought to cash in on the popular appetite for material surrounding Strafford's execution by publishing both the Tower speech *and* the scaffold speech, with the extraordinary result that Strafford is made both to confess his guilt and to maintain his innocence in successive speeches. This composite publication appears to have gone through no less than nine editions in 1641. Various marketing strategies may have been at work here, and some of the variant copies of the *Two Last Speeches* with erratic foliation numbers may well represent attempts to sell excess stock of the single speeches by creating a composite work.[42] Nevertheless, a number of the editions include woodcuts of the trial unique to this publication, so that the *Two Last Speeches* must be granted to be a separate work in its own right.

The popularity of the *Two Last Speeches* reminds us that the public sphere might be influenced by both pro- and anti-Strafford camps, but could not be secured by either. We have already seen how the poets' response to the execution was decidedly ambiguous – their muse was often stirred more by contemplating the action of fate in humbling the great, than by discussing Strafford's crimes and the justice of the execution. Other publications have an even more ambiguous nature. What are we to make, for example, of the four editions published in 1641 of Strafford's last letter to the king? This is the letter, written on 4 May 1641, in which Strafford released the king from his promise to protect Strafford's life, and urged him to agree to the bill of attainder. Strafford's son later claimed (erro-neously) that this letter was a forgery, presumably because it could be read as both justifying the execution and hinting at Strafford's acceptance of some form of guilt. But it could also be read as evidence of Strafford's nobility of character, prepared to sacrifice himself for the good of the country.[43] We may assume, perhaps, that the letter was read in both ways.

Similarly, the copies of Strafford's supposed last letter to his wife –

---

[42] Editions of the scaffold speech: Wing s794, s794A, s794B, s794C, s795, s795A, s795B; editions of the *Two Last Speeches*: s799, s799A, s799B, s799C, s5800, s5800AA, s5800A, s5800B, s5800C (all in 1641). S5800 includes the woodcuts. The scaffold speech was also reproduced in several other works: e.g., *A True Relation of the Manner of the Execution of Thomas Earle of Strafford* (Wing T3002A).

[43] C. H. Firth (ed.), 'Papers relating to Thomas Wentworth, First Earl of Strafford', *Camden Miscellany*, IX (1895), p. ix n. (we owe this reference to Julia Merritt). For editions of the letter see Wing s5789, s5789A, s5790, s5790A (all 1641).

another very popular publication in the months following Strafford's execution – may have been designed to elicit sympathy. It is a fabrication (even contemporaries soon identified this piece as simply a reworked version of Raleigh's last letter to *his* wife) but there was clearly a healthy market for sentimental final letters. It is not surprising that the Raleigh letter was chosen: this is a letter that Robert Browning regarded as 'the most pathetic, probably, in the language'. However, its impact in this case was greatly problematised by the fact that it was several times printed in conjunction with another fabricated brief letter to 'a great lady' which sounds a far more sinister note, making cryptic references to the need to secure £2,000 secretly 'for we shall slay the Beast with many heads, and destroy the Devils brood before they dreame or mistrust'.[44]

Clearly, then, the popular appetite for Strafford material after the execution was catholic in its taste, presumably being fed by publishers who were happy to print whatever they thought would sell, and by writers and poets who, as one commentator complained, 'for a little mercenary gaine, and profit, infused plenty of Gall, and Wormewood into their lying, and Satyricall lines'.[45] But even these more popular, flexible genres were susceptible to exploitation by more polarised political elements.

Particularly intriguing in this regard is one of the editions of the fabricated last letter of Strafford to his wife which prints it together with a parliamentary speech given by William Pleydell in defence of episcopacy. This could conceivably be an example of a printer trying to make an unpopular parliamentary speech a more saleable commodity by combining it with a more popular item. But it is at least possible that it may represent an early attempt to exploit Wentworth's status as a royalist martyr in its most popular and sentimental form in order to direct readers towards the defence of other aspects of the more moderate 'constitutional royalist' programme – in this case the defence of episcopacy.[46]

---

[44] See *Two letters sent from the Earle of Strafford* (Wing s5801): cf. s5784G, s5786, s5788; Robert Browning, *Prose Life of Strafford* (1892), p. 260n. *The true Copies of the three last Letters* (Th. E.170(6); Wing s5797) combines these two letters with Strafford's last letter to the king and his final petition to the House of Lords, in which he pleads for them to have compassion on his children after his death. Also included in this publication is an elegy supposedly written by Strafford before his death in which he conventionally deplores earthly vanities and laments his fate.

[45] J. B., *The Poets*, sig.A3v.

[46] *A Letter Sent from the Earle of Strafford to his Lady in Ireland, a little before his death...Together with a Speech of Mr Plydell Esquire Concerning the Church* (Wing s5787).

The gradual emergence of the royalist party, along with the mass circulation of the details of Strafford's final hours, ensured that there was a great deal more competition over the public image of Wentworth than has often been granted, and that the image that did emerge was a good deal more complicated than the 'Black Tom' of popular memory. But while it is tempting to portray the avalanche of the more popular tracts relating to Strafford as the propaganda work of duelling political parties, the reality appears to have been different, and a good deal more interesting. The continuing public trial of Strafford was one that both sides were happy to encourage, but was also one in which neither the parliamentary managers nor Strafford's defenders had control over the final verdict. They were competing advocates in the court of a public opinion that seems, within limits, to have been capable of a certain autonomy of judgement.

Retrospective: Wentworth's political world in revisionist and post-revisionist perspective

Peter Lake

As Julia Merritt observes in her introduction, many of the central issues in the recent historiography on early Stuart politics can be summed up in and through variant readings of the career and opinions of Thomas Wentworth. Thus, a good deal of the initial thrust of revisionist writing can be encapsulated in the question: did Strafford change sides? Much recent writing (most notably by Kevin Sharpe and Glenn Burgess) on the political culture of the period, and of the Personal Rule in particular, comes together nicely around variant readings of Strafford's behaviour and opinions during the 1630s.[1] The recent accounts (produced by Professor Russell and Dr David Smith) of the emergence of 'constitutional' royalism – the coalescence around Charles I of distinctively 'moderate' strands of opinion in 1641/2 – centre on questions raised by Strafford's impeachment.[2] And, of course, many of the tensions and contradictions inherent in recent invocations of the British problem as an explanation for the outbreak of the English Civil War are thrown into relief by Strafford's career in Ireland. This essay will attempt to set these issues in a wider historiographical context and to use many of the essays in this book as a way into what I will describe as a distinctively post-revisionist mode of historical writing. In so doing I do not want to make inflated claims for the methodological or conceptual novelty of a certain school or group of writers. Claims to historiographical significance set in a methodological key too often turn out to be claims to have reinvented the wheel. On the contrary, what follows is intended merely to provide some account of the current state of historiographical play in the interpretative aftermath

[1] K. Sharpe, *The Personal Rule of Charles I* (1992); G. Burgess, *The Politics of the Ancient Constitution* (1992).

[2] C. S. R. Russell, *The Fall of the British Monarchies* (Oxford, 1991); D. L. Smith, *Constitutional Royalism and the Search for Settlement c. 1640–1649* (Cambridge, 1994).

of what has come to be called revisionism and to use the figure of Wentworth to do so.

I

'WHIGGERY' AND THE MODERNISATION MOTIF

The historiography of early modern England produced during the post-war period could arguably be said to have been dominated by various forms of modernisation theory. All the most influential accounts of the period centred on claims about its signal importance as the breeding ground or birthplace of various of the central aspects of modernity. Capitalism; the rise of the gentry and/or the capitalist middle class or middling sort; the emergence of individualism, whether economic or affective; the rise of the modern state, parliament; the rise of modern science, and the disenchantment of the world and the advent of classificatory systems and forms of knowledge of the natural world based not on their relationship or use to human society but on other more objectively verifiable characteristics – all these were processes that were held to have taken place in the period between roughly 1500 and 1800. Whatever their ideological orientation most of the leading historians of early modern England in the immediate post-war period – R. H. Tawney, Sir John Neale, Christopher Hill, Lawrence Stone, Sir Keith Thomas, and even in a partial and somewhat eccentric way, Sir Geoffrey Elton – all made their reputations playing off, applying and developing some variant of modernisation theory. Here was a developmental schema in which the early modern period played the role of midwife to modernity, a crucial transition period between some sort of feudal, pre-capitalist, lineage-based, magically organised *before*, and a recognisably modern – capitalist, individualist, bureaucratised, 'rational' – *after*.[3]

Here was the master narrative, the interpretational key, that both gave coherence to the various stories these historians told

---

[3] R. H. Tawney, 'The rise of the gentry, 1558–1640' first published in 1941, and reprinted in J. M. Winter (ed.), *History and Society: Essays by R. H. Tawney* (1978), pp. 85–128; J. E. Neale, *Elizabeth and Her Parliaments, 1559–1581* (1953); J. E. Neale, *Elizabeth and Her Parliaments, 1584–1601* (1957); C. Hill, *Society and Puritanism in Pre-Revolutionary England* (1964); L. Stone, *The Crisis of the Aristocracy, 1558–1641* (Oxford, 1965); L. Stone, *The Family, Sex and Marriage in England, 1500–1800* (1977); K. V. Thomas, *Religion and the Decline of Magic* (1970); K. V. Thomas, *Man and the Natural World* (1983); G. R. Elton, *The Tudor Revolution in Government* (Cambridge, 1953).

about early modern England, and lent significance to their findings. It did so in part by linking those findings to crucial characteristics and concerns in the present, thus making their assumption that this was an important period which had something crucial to tell the present about what it was and where it came from, seem obvious, indeed self-evident. Of course, behind these assumptions lurked the major social theorists of the late nineteenth and early twentieth centuries – Marx and, in particular, Weber – insights and nostrums from whose thought were now applied and mapped onto the assumptions and achievements of late nineteenth-century English ('whig') historiography, summed up in the dominating figure of S. R. Gardiner.[4]

Here a central linking factor was provided by 'puritanism' – a religious force central to Gardiner's political/constitutional narrative which, in the hands of these later historians, was transformed into perhaps the crucial standard-bearer for modernity. Puritanism was an ideological solvent central to their accounts of the ways in which medieval, feudal, pre-capitalist, pre-revolutionary, traditional, lineage societies were transformed into something else (often, of course, in spite of, rather than because of, the best intentions of the puritans themselves). The stories told by Hill, Thomas and Stone were all linked by the parallel role played within their different versions of the modernisation story by hot protestantism/puritanism. Thus for Hill puritanism was the bearer of attitudes and ideological stances centrally important for mercantile and artisanal capitalism and the self- and labour-discipline that went with it. For Stone it was a crucial individualising agent that helped disrupt and replace older lineage- and honour-based social codes, and served, with its odd mixture of an austere patriarchalism and a stress on the affective joys of companionate marriage, as a bridge between the lineage-based society that preceded it and the recognisably modern world of affective individualism that came after it. For Keith Thomas hot protestantism was a major actor in a whole series of modernising processes of which the most important was

---

[4]   For perhaps the most explicit invocation of modernisation theory, see L. Stone, *The Causes of the English Revolution, 1529–1642* (1972), esp. ch. 1; see also the autobiographical remarks in L. Beier, D. Cannadine and J. Rosenheim, *The First Modern Society* (Oxford, 1989), pp. 575–95, esp. p. 585 for the centrality of Weber. For a sense in which much of Hill's work was conceived as a struggle to appropriate the whig political narrative for a very different (marxist) notion of English exceptionalism, see C. Hill, *The English Revolution, 1640* (1979), first published in 1940 and much reprinted since.

that disenchantment of the world, that plays so crucial a role in both his major books.[5]

Much, but obviously not all, of the work done in this mode sought, by taking the political narrative produced by Gardiner more or less as read, to penetrate beneath the surface of political history to the real causal motors of historical change and conflict in the society and economy of the day. Assuming the centrality of the English revolution as both a sign and effect of major social and economic change and then, indeed, as a further cause of such change, these 'modernising' historians sought to broaden the range of historical inquiry from the doings of the political elite to encompass the seismic shifts of the society upon which that elite rested.[6] In the process they greatly broadened the range of questions it was proper for historians to ask, the range of sources they should seek to consult in answering them, and the range of social classes or groups whose history they should attempt to write. These developments, of course, represented pure gain for the discipline, and they retain a significance and impact far wider and more lasting than the initial paradigms that helped to produce and legitimate them.

The result was a powerful rhetoric justifying not only a certain 'take' on the period but also a certain 'take' on the discipline of historical research itself. This rhetoric and the assumptions that underpinned it never achieved anything like dominance in the field but it did lay claim, for some decades, to hegemony. For here was both the 'cutting edge' of scholarly research and the source of some of the most widely read and commonly regurgitated narrative histories of the period. Nor was this mode of analysis remotely like an interpretational, let alone an ideological, monolith. Even from within the modernisation paradigm itself dissenting voices were raised against some of the broader claims and contentions based upon it. Elton's relations with this nexus of concerns were always ambiguous; his was a process of modernisation limited to the workings and ideology of the central state and all but complete by 1540.

---

[5] Hill, *Society and Puritanism, passim*; Stone, *Family, Sex and Marriage*, parts 3, 4; Thomas, *Religion and the Decline of Magic, passim*, and esp. chs. 3, 4. See also Thomas's recent article 'Cleanliness and godliness in early modern England', in A. Fletcher and P. Roberts (eds.), *Religion, Culture and Society in Early Modern Britain* (Cambridge, 1994), pp. 56–83, where, having played with a positive correlation between various sorts of protestant zeal and changing levels and notions of personal cleanliness, he undercuts the argument with a sustained invocation of the proverbial filthiness of the Scots.

[6] See Stone, *Causes of the English Revolution* and the essays by Hill and Stone in J. G. A. Pocock (ed.), *Three British Revolutions, 1641, 1688, 1776* (Princeton, 1980).

Modernity having conferred significance on the central findings of his own research, he was free to take a sceptical, and indeed frankly hostile, attitude to many of the assumptions and projects of his great contemporaries. A moderniser, arguably even something of a whig in his attitude to the Cromwellian reformation in church and state, Elton could be a revisionist everywhere else and played with gusto the revisionist *enfant terrible* in the period after that in which his own career was made.[7] Similarly, the relationship of Professor Trevor-Roper to this nexus of concerns was always ambivalent, as he brought a sort of high Tory whig scepticism to bear on the interpretations of Hill, Tawney and Stone. The result, however, was more like a series of ironic inversions and appropriations of the modernisation story rather than any direct assault on the paradigm itself.[8] The point here, of course, is that for all the differences of political and intellectual inflection and ideological orientation contained within the modernisation motif as it is here defined, there was a common bedrock of assumption and argument, a common rhetoric of significance attached to notions of the rise of 'the modern'. The pervasiveness of these attitudes was all the more impressive for the range of different ideological positions and political predilections contained within it.

Here one is tempted to indulge with David Cannadine in an exercise in the amateur sociology, if not of knowledge, then at least of historiographical style. For here, in Cannadine's excessively dismissive phrase, was 'the old Whig history of Britain's unique and privileged development dressed up in Butskellite guise'.[9] The sense conferred by this historiographical mode on the national past as containing a knowable direction towards 'modernity', defined institutionally in terms of the secular state and parliament (Elton), culturally in terms of the emergence of a recognisably modern, rational

---

[7] Indeed, Elton has a good claim to be viewed as the first revisionist. See his famous essay of 1965 'A high road to civil war?' reprinted in his *Studies in Tudor and Stuart Politics and Government* (Cambridge, 1974), vol. II, pp. 164–82. See also his contrasting reviews of Stone, *Causes of the English Revolution* and C. S. R. Russell (ed.), *The Origins of the English Civil War* (1973) in *HJ* 16 (1973), pp. 205–8 and 17 (1974), pp. 213–16 respectively. The review of Russell makes it clear how far Elton was also an early sceptic on the subject of 'puritanism'.

[8] See the astute remarks of Nicholas Tyacke, 'The ambiguities of early-modern English protestantism', *HJ* 34 (1991), pp. 743–54, esp. pp. 743–9. See also P. Lake, 'Protestants, puritans and Laudians', *Journal of Ecclesiastical History* 42 (1991), pp. 618–28, esp. pp. 625–8.

[9] D. Cannadine, 'British history: past, present – and future?', *Past and Present* 116 (1987), pp. 169–91, at p. 173.

and thoroughly individualist and disenchanted view of the world (Thomas and Stone) and socio-economically in terms of the emergence of capitalism and of a socio-political world organised around the means of production and divisions between classes recognisable to present-day observers (Hill), fitted very well with many of the fundamental assumptions of the post-war period.

The benefits of modernity, the controllability of the historical process, the benign capacity of the state to intervene and shape the economic and social development of the nation, all seemed confirmed by these narratives. In the worlds of punditry, alternative policy-making, and finally mainstream politics, many of these statist, melioristic assumptions were called into question under the impact of seemingly intractable national decline and economic crisis in the 1970s. It may, indeed, be no accident that, in the realm of historical thought, the same decade produced a major rethink of the great shifts and transitions of the early modern period. Moreover, as we shall see, these revisionist accounts emphasised the tight fiscal limits on the state, and the incapacity of contemporary institutional arrangements and conceptual tools to understand or control change, and dwelt on, indeed arguably romanticised, the intractable conservatism, the relative changelessness of the real provincial England as against the interfering, polarising and ultimately destructive activities of ambitious politicians, metropolitan elites and interventionist intellectuals.[10] This is not to claim that revisionism was a Thatcherite or even necessarily a conservative or reactionary phenomenon, but it is to observe that it was recognisably a product of the same politico-ideological conjuncture that produced Thatcherism.

II

REVISIONISM AND ITS DISCONTENTS

The relationship between the modernisation paradigm (particularly the search for the social causes of the Civil War that was that paradigm's most immediate effect on empirical research) and the

---

[10] C. Haigh, 'Puritan evangelism in the reign of Elizabeth I', *English Historical Review* 92 (1977), pp. 30–58; C. Haigh, 'The Church of England, the Catholics and the people', in C. Haigh (ed.), *The Reign of Elizabeth I* (1984), pp. 195–219; C. Haigh, 'From monopoly to minority: Catholicism in early modern England', *TRHS* 5th ser., 31 (1981), pp. 129–47; A. Everitt, *The Community of Kent and the Great Rebellion* (Leicester, 1966); J. S. Morrill, *The Revolt of the Provinces* (1976).

subsequent course of historiographical development was complex, even dialectical. The various investigations into the role of the gentry in the events leading to revolution produced some extraordinarily distinguished empirical research, ranging from Professor Aylmer's study of the *King's Servants* (in part a testing of various generalisations about the impact of court office on the fortunes and allegiances of crucial elements in the ruling class) to Professor Underdown's *Pride's Purge* and beyond to Lawrence Stone's *Crisis of the Aristocracy*. At a less heroically conceived level, the gentry controversy generated a whole slew of local studies designed, at least initially, to test out in detail generalisations about the rise of the gentry.[11] Under the impact of the torrent of empirical information thus assembled the various attempts to produce social causes for the Civil War proved, if not simply unsuccessful, then at least terminally inconclusive. *En route*, however, crucial elements in what would emerge as the next stage/s of the historiography emerged. In the pursuit of the gentry into their 'countries' the linked notions of the county community and of localism were coined and herein lay the germs of a very different account of Civil War allegiance and side-taking. But not all the straws in the wind were being blown in the same direction. Take for instance David Underdown's *Pride's Purge* or Patrick Collinson's *Elizabethan Puritan Movement*. Underdown's book at one level was an attempt to identify the real revolutionaries, the enthusiastic regicides, in order sociologically to categorise them and thus to test various claims about the social origins of the revolution. But, taking on board Alan Everritt's insistence that politics in the localities looked a good deal different from politics at the centre, Underdown's book turned into a multi-layered and multi-centred analytical narrative of a short but crucial period in the crisis of the 1640s. In short, starting within one interpretational mode, it ended in another.

So too did Collinson's *Puritan Movement*. Here was a book conceived within one of the most ferociously whiggish portions of the whig politico-religious narrative as it was produced and reproduced after the war – Sir John Neale's account of the relations between Queen

---

[11] G. E. Aylmer, *The King's Servants: The Civil Service of Charles I, 1625–42* (1961); D. Underdown, *Pride's Purge* (Oxford, 1971); for the local studies see, for instance, M. E. Finch, *The Wealth of Five Northamptonshire Families, 1540–1640* (Northamptonshire Record Society, 1956); A. Simpson, *The Wealth of the Gentry* (Cambridge, 1961); J. T. Cliffe, *The Yorkshire Gentry from the Reformation to the Civil War* (1969); Everitt, *Community of Kent*.

Elizabeth and her parliaments, and in particular of the central role played in that dialogue by an oppositionist puritan movement. Collinson's book took that movement as its starting point, but the consequent narrative was set in so carefully constructed a political and ideological context that many of the central assumptions of the whig account were undermined and rearranged. Without adopting anything resembling a polemical tone or adversarial stance towards the interpretative mode within which his argument appeared to operate, Collinson in effect took that mode apart. In the terms used in this essay, the book leapfrogged the revisionist segment of the dialectic and went straight into what I will describe below as post-revisionism. It did so, moreover, through a version of 'puritanism' that by the end of the book had become thoroughly narrativised and politicised. And in a series of subsequent studies Collinson in effect redefined 'puritanism'. Rather than the espousal of a body of distinctively and coherently 'puritan' beliefs, the process of being or becoming a puritan emerged as the result of a labelling process. It was presented as a form of identity formation, in which images and self-images were constructed and deployed in a number of inherently changing and dynamic political, ideological and social contexts. As such it rendered an hypostatised 'puritanism', conceived as some sort of modernising ideological monolith, increasingly unavailable as a catch-all explanatory factor and/or transitional phase in modernising narratives of the sort described above. At a number of levels, therefore, Collinson's work of the late 1950s and early 1960s was profoundly subversive of the modernisation model outlined above.[12]

We are not, therefore, dealing here with simple monoliths but with a series of dialogues and dialectical discussions between interpretative modes and organising assumptions, on the one hand, and the results of particular empirical research strategies, on the other. Of course those strategies were at the outset very often shaped or framed by questions drawn from some larger mode or model, but their results were certainly not determined by those models. Historical research of the highest quality can in this sense, if not transcend,

[12] P. Collinson, *The Elizabethan Puritan Movement* (1967), based on his 'The puritan classical movement in the reign of Elizabeth I' (unpublished Ph.D. thesis, University of London, 1957). See also a number of succeeding essays collected in Collinson's *Godly People* (1983). I have expanded on these points in my introduction to G. Nuttall, *The Holy Spirit in Puritan Faith and Experience* (Chicago, 1992), pp. ix–xxv and in 'Defining puritanism – again?', in F. Bremer (ed.), *Puritanism: Transatlantic Perspectives on a Seventeenth-Century Anglo-American Faith* (Massachusetts Historical Society, 1993), pp. 3–29.

then certainly lead beyond the particular interpretative conjuncture that first prompted it. But for all that, it remains the case that it was not until the 1970s and the rise of the so-called revisionist position that the modernisation story, and the whig political narrative which that story both assumed and in some sense confirmed, was subjected to a full-scale critique.[13]

The initial effect of the revisionist assault was a massive reappropriation of the realm of the political as a fit subject for historical study. For it cannot be emphasised enough that while the modernisation narratives outlined above were nearly all in some sense predicated upon, or at least conceived as being entirely compatible with, Gardiner's political narrative, none of the modernisers themselves was in the business of writing or even of thinking much about political narrative. In challenging the assumptions that underpinned their approach, the importance and originality of the work of a number of revisionist scholars, and in particular of Conrad Russell, can scarcely be overestimated. Starting with Russell's introduction to the 1973 collection of essays on the *Origins of the English Civil War*, which was echoed in Kevin Sharpe's introduction to *Faction and Parliament*, revisionists pointed out that the nature of the events the social or cultural origins of which were being sought was unclear. We needed to return to the construction and construal of the political narrative itself if any sense were to be made of the causes either of the English Civil War or of the revolution that followed it. Russell and Mark Kishlansky (in the brilliant introductory chapter to Russell's *Parliaments and English Politics*, and in Kishlansky's article on the emergence of adversary politics) began to sketch an alternative view of how early Stuart political culture and the political system operated. Then, in the later sections of Russell's book on the 1620s and in Kishlansky's book on the rise of the New Model Army, revisionists produced narratives that illustrated just what the new political history would look like.[14]

The responses to Russell's work were deeply revealing of the depth

---

[13] Here I am attempting to ape the style of argument advanced for the historiography of the Industrial Revolution by David Cannadine in his article 'The present and the past in the English industrial revolution, 1880–1980', *Past and Present* 103 (1984), pp. 131–72.

[14] Russell (ed.), *Origins of the English Civil War*, esp. the introduction; C. S. R. Russell, *Parliaments and English Politics, 1621–9* (Oxford, 1979), esp. ch. 1; K. Sharpe (ed.), *Faction and Parliament* (Oxford, 1978), introduction; M. Kishlansky, 'The emergence of adversary politics in the Long Parliament', *Journal of Modern History* 49 (1977), pp. 617–40; M. Kishlansky, *The Rise of the New Model Army* (Cambridge, 1979).

of the interpretational break that he proposed. On the one hand, he was accused of denying the role of principle or ideology in contemporary politics, of rendering the subject meaningless by reducing the political process to a shapeless narrative of manoeuvre and counter-manoeuvre, of reneging on any search for long-term causes for the high political events and interactions that constituted his main object of study, of relapsing into a sort of nihilist empiricism that rendered the subject both uninteresting and unteachable. All of these criticisms seem to me inappropriate and inaccurate, telling us far more about the assumptions and sensibilities of Russell's critics than anything that was to be found between the covers of Russell's books. It is not true that Russell eschewed the search for long-term causes or structural analysis. Rather his analyses of the 1620s and latterly of the early 1640s have turned on a number of such long-term structural problems. These have been identified as: first, the relations between centre and localities and the long-term impact of inflation on the fixed revenues of the English state that produced what Russell calls the functional breakdown; second, the impact, after the Reformation, of religious division on a society where religious consensus was assumed to be a *sine qua non* for political stability and social peace; third, the impact of those same confessional conflicts on a European states system in which the confessional identity of protestant England had continually to be squared with the diplomatic and dynastic interests of the English monarchy; and finally, the so-called British problem, the impact of the realities of what was after 1603 a tripartite multiple monarchy on a still insular and parochial English ruling class and political system. Moreover, all this was conceived in an explicitly comparative framework with generalisations about the insights into the course of contemporary state-building on the continent, culled in particular from Sir John Elliot's work on Spain, being integrated into Russell's analysis of English and latterly of British developments. Again, Russell and the revisionists did not expel ideology from their account of the way in which politics worked. Rather, Russell radically redescribed the ideological and cultural context within which early Stuart politics happened. He stressed (to translate his findings into somewhat more modish language) the presence and power, in both church and state, of certain dominant discourses all of which emphasised the need for agreement and consensus, and which tended to construe the presence of disagreement and division as evidence not of politics as normal but of deep and corrupting dysfunctions in the political system or body politic. If anything, these cultural aspects of revisionism were rendered more explicit and taken further by Kishlansky's work on adversary and consensus politics, and in a number of studies by Kevin Sharpe.[15]

That the revisionist projects (and in particular Russell's work) have been at times misread may in part be the revisionists' own fault. Russell himself has not always dwelt on the long-term structural elements in his argument (although of late he has devoted the whole of his recent *Causes of the English Civil War* to such issues). Moreover the densest of his narrative passages, together with a mode of presentation and argument that often seeks to make wider interpretational questions turn on some crucial detail or narrative passage (a tendency nicely exemplified in his contribution to this volume), have allowed the accusation that his work is characterised by an unreflective and narrow empiricism. Of the available ways of asserting historiographical significance, revisionists have always shown a fatal attraction to the rhetoric of the obscure manuscript source, rather than, for instance, the impulse towards the last French theorist but one, favoured in more 'advanced' historiographical circles. These propensities have helped to contribute to what remain serious misreadings of Russell's work and a serious underestimate of the significance of the entire revisionist project, lapses that are best explained not only by the revisionists' self-image and self-presentation but also by the extent to which the holistic assumptions of the various modernisation paradigms sketched above had become synonymous, in certain circles at least, with a whole

[15] These concerns can be traced throughout Russell's corpus from the early articles on 'Arguments for religious unity in England, 1530–1650' (first published in 1967 and reprinted in Russell's *Unrevolutionary England* (1990), pp. 179–204) and in his piece on 'Parliament and the King's finances' in *Origins of the English Civil War*, pp. 91–116. The crucial treatments of ideology and consensus are to be found in 'Parliamentary history in perspective, 1604–29' (first published in 1976 and reprinted in *Unrevolutionary England*, pp. 31–57) and at greater length in chapters 1 and 6 of *Parliaments*. The comparative aspects are implicit in the afterword to *Origins of the English Civil War* by J. H. Elliot (pp. 246–57) and are made explicit in 'Monarchies, wars and estates in England, France and Spain, *c.*1580–*c.*1640' (first published in 1982 and reprinted in *Unrevolutionary England*, pp. 121–36). The application of some of these comparative insights, organised now under the rubric of multiple monarchy, to 'the British problem' started with 'The British problem and the English civil war' and 'The British background to the Irish rebellion of 1641' published in 1987 and 1988 respectively and reprinted in *Unrevolutionary England*, pp. 231–51 and 263–79 respectively, and reached fruition in *The Causes of the English Civil War* (Oxford, 1990) and *The Fall of the British Monarchies*. Similar tendencies can also be traced in the essays reprinted in J. S. Morrill, *The Nature of the English Revolution* (1993).

range of claims to historiographical significance and conceptual breadth.[16]

But while this sort of reflexive nay-saying represented one response to Russell, the other common reaction was a simple acceptance of his major claims about the central political narrative, many of which swiftly became enshrined as the current text-book orthodoxy.[17] The rapidity with which Russell's major conclusions were incorporated into the canon might ironically be construed as a function of the success with which the more holistically conceived and broadly construed versions of the modernisation story had distracted scholarly attention away from politics. In England at least (although less so in America, where versions of the old whig story still played a central role in sustaining national myths and self-images – it was perhaps easier to be an Anglophile in America than in England during the 1970s and early 1980s)[18] there were relatively few scholars either actively engaged in the political history of the period or with a determinedly whiggish interpretational stake in the existing political narrative.

But whatever the reason for it, such an easy acceptance of what were clearly intended to be provocative, even tendentious, claims may not have been the best response to early revisionism. The negative impact of Russell's assault on the whig narrative was very considerable and the significance of his achievement in defamiliarising the politics of the period, reminding us of how little we knew about the central political narrative and rendering that narrative available for fresh analysis and new research, is hard to overestimate.

---

[16] For examples of the early response to Russell see L. Stone, 'The revival of narrative: reflections on a new old history', *Past and Present* 85 (1979), pp. 3–24, esp. pp. 20–1, where Russell is described as one of a number of 'antiquarian empiricists'. For a more recent example of the same dismissive approach, see D. Cannadine's characterisation of a school of 'new high-political archive grubbers, whose accounts of brief episodes in the history of seventeenth-, eighteenth- and nineteenth-century England are so myopic as to be almost devoid of any meaning at all' in Cannadine, 'British history: past, present – and future?', p. 189; see also T. K. Rabb, 'Revisionism revised: the role of the Commons', *Past and Present* 92 (1981), pp. 55–78.

[17] See, for instance, Russell's contentions about the capacity of the House of Commons to bargain supply for the redress of grievances; now called into radical question by Tom Cogswell. See Cogswell's article 'A low road to extinction? Supply and redress of grievances in the parliaments of the 1620s', *HJ* 33 (1990), pp. 283–303.

[18] J. H. Hexter, 'The early Stuarts and Parliament: old hat and the nouvelle vague', *Parliamentary History* 1 (1982), pp. 181–215. Also see the introduction to J. H. Hexter (ed.), *Parliament and Liberty from the Reign of Elizabeth to the Civil War* (Stanford, 1992), part of a larger series on 'the making of modern freedom'. On which, see J. H. Hexter, 'The birth of modern freedom', *Times Literary Supplement*, 21 Jan. 1983.

However, the destructive, inversionary force of the initial texts in which these claims were made rendered many of Russell's findings more appropriate objects for argument and debate than immediate synthesis and acceptance.

Because of both the structure of the texts of early revisionism and of the nature of the reception of those texts, historians who wanted to engage in debate with revisionism faced rather a stark choice: should they opt to write under the sign of the status quo, 'the whig narrative', 'what we had always thought' and assert that Gardiner was right, or should they take seriously the impact of the revisionist challenge to the old whig master narrative and start to root about in the interpretational rubble created by the revisionism? To take the latter option was, of course, to operate in an interpretational terrain largely devoid of signposts and fixed positions. In short, both revisionist and post-revisionist historians of early Stuart England have had, for rather a long time now, to go about their business without the security blanket of the old established master narrative/s of modernisation that had dominated their field for decades.

III

LIVING WITH THE DEATH OF WHIGGERY

This state of affairs came about with none of the self-proclaimed theoretical sophistication that has attended similar moves in other periods of English history. But lacking its Patrick Joyce, the period could at least lay claim to its own high Tory prophet of anti-modernism. Attempting to hitch together two traditionally distinct historiographies, J. C. D. Clark sought to present his own rendition of eighteenth-century English society as an *ancien régime* as a necessary coda to, and working out of, earlier revisionist writing on the seventeenth century. For Clark, at least, here was a paradigm shift of considerable import. Others not enamoured of Clark's brand of high Tory idealism could see only chaos and cacophony at the end of the revisionist rainbow. David Cannadine, for one, bewailed the process of balkanisation consequent upon the ditching of the master narratives that had hitherto organised the field into an intelligible story. Cannadine could discern only an intellectual wasteland of academic sub-disciplines and sub-specialisms unable to talk effectively to each other let alone to a wider public.[19]

Most revisionists, however, while remaining aloof from Clark and Joyce's alternately high Tory and post-modernist triumphalism admitted, at least by implication, that there was a problem. For, rather than enjoying the chaotic indeterminacies and interpretational instabilities that their initial assault had created, they clung instead to the shadow of the whig narrative they had set out to destroy. Continuing to characterise the interpretational field as a choice between whig recidivism and revisionist purity, they justified their own interpretations – their insistence on the absence of ideological conflict, on the primacy of religious passion as the sole or at least the dominant cause of political conflict and violence, on the disruptive effect of the Scots and of Scots ideology and propaganda on an otherwise inherently moderate and unified English political culture, and on the personal peculiarities and rigidities of Charles I as an exogenous and inexplicable destabilising force – as the only ways to explain conflict without reverting to the discredited polarities and assumptions of whiggery.[20] Indeed, it may be a necessary feature of all such dialectically defined revisionist manoeuvres, at least in their first stages, to remain tied inextricably to the categories and stories they set out to undermine. Only thus can they retain the coherence and hard-edged novelty with which they entered the debate and stave off entry into the interpretational cacophony that their own initial negative impetus has set off.

I have argued at length elsewhere that this is a marked feature of Professor Russell's more recent work and it figures prominently in the self-presentation of the work of other revisionists in other fields, most notably in that of Patrick Joyce, who continually confronts the reader with a choice between the purity of his own post-modern

[19] See, for instance, P. Joyce, 'The end of social history?', *Social History* 20 (1995), pp. 73–91 or the introduction to Joyce's *Democratic Subjects* (Cambridge, 1994); J. C. D. Clark, *Revolution and Rebellion: State and Society in England in the Seventeenth and Eighteenth Centuries* (Cambridge, 1986); Cannadine, 'British history: past, present – and future?'.

[20] See, for instance, Russell, *Causes* and *The Fall*; on religion as an exogenous cause of conflict, see the articles reprinted in part 1 of Morrill, *Nature of the English Revolution* (1993); on the incompetence, even irrationality, of Charles as a politician, see in addition L. J. Reeve, *Charles I and the Road to Personal Rule* (Cambridge, 1989) and P. Donald, *An Uncounselled King: Charles I and the Scottish Troubles, 1637–41* (Cambridge, 1990). Kevin Sharpe has reshuffled the pack of revisionist arguments, rehabilitating Charles – indeed rendering the Caroline view of the world normative for the period – and playing up the fatal alliance between a small minority of genuinely subversive English puritans and the Scots as the explanation for political conflict. See Sharpe, *Charles I*, esp. chs. 12, 13.

indeterminacy and a whig-marxist narrative to which nearly all other commentators on the period are assimilated. As a legitimating manoeuvre, of course, this has a limited shelf-life, since once the dragon of whiggery is slain other structures of interpretation and categories of analysis will have to be developed and used in an interpretational terrain where the simple assertion of their identity as non-whig cannot be deployed to demonstrate their coherence or use.[21] In other words, the usual processes of historical research and argument will have to be resumed with the trump card of opposition to a benighted whig or marxist paradigm no longer in play. In this sense, revisionist scholars need to confront more directly the con-sequences of the success of their own early iconoclasm.

IV

REVISIONISM AND THE RETURN OF THE MASTER NARRATIVE

In the early modern period, at least, attempts have been made to do that. Russell in particular has, from the outset, sought to replace one set of modernising master narratives (the rise of the gentry, of Parliament, of puritanism/protestantism) with a series of long-term trends and tendencies. These have often remained implicit, their consequences left unstated, as Russell invoked long-term structural forces to explain short-term political crises and conjunctures. But the outlines of these structural forces and narratives could always be discerned in the background of Russell's narrative. Thus Russell emphasises the tensions between the local and the national, the attendant functional breakdown, and the relative incapacity of the crown to wage successful continental land war, all forming part of an implicit problematic stretching from Agincourt to Blenheim. His emphasis on the need for religious unity in an age of confessional conflict is the start of a longer-term narrative, if not of secularisation, then at least of realignment between the secular and the spiritual, the church and the state, the religious and the political. Similarly, the

---

[21] See Joyce, 'End of social history' and *Visions of the People: Industrial England and the Question of Class, 1840–1914* (Cambridge, 1991), *passim*. For this view of Russell's relationship to a continually reconstituted vision of a whig 'other', see my review article of Russell's recent work in *Huntington Library Quarterly* 57 (1994), pp. 167–97. As ever Kevin Sharpe fearlessly follows the basic tendencies of the revisionist position to their logical conclusions and his account of *The Personal Rule of Charles I* provides perhaps the clearest example of this propensity.

revisionist emphasis on consensus politics as the dominant ideological and institutional mode in the early period leads inexorably towards a narrative about, if not the rise of adversary politics, then at least about another realignment between the rhetorics of faction, party and interest, on the one hand, and those of unity, political virtue and the common good on the other. It is, of course, precisely this nexus of concerns that has been at the centre of Professor Kishlansky's more recent work, which stands out amongst revisionist scholarship for its willingness to tackle head-on the long-term consequences of the revisionists' short-term explanations for revolutionary events.

If one were to follow these implicit narratives where they lead one would end up in the late seventeenth or even in the early eighteenth century where, of course, they threaten terminal damage to Professor Clark's version of eighteenth-century England as an *ancien régime*. And here we are confronted by one of the ironies of a good deal of revisionist writing. For as revisionist historians in each period remove the 'positive', 'forward-looking' causes that underpinned the older modernising accounts of, say, the Reformation or the Revolution, they render those events even more cataclysmic in their conse-quences for the succeeding period.[22] Thus Dr Haigh's short-term, high political account of the English Reformation renders that event far more contingent and contested than, say, Professor Dickens's account would allow. But Haigh's version also ensures that since no one much wanted it, once the Reformation finally happened (as Haigh now admits that it did) it must have had deeply disturbing, culturally, politically and socially disruptive effects. Thus, a Refor-mation for which there are few long-term causes logically must and does provide Professor Russell and Dr Morrill with some of their crucial long-term causes for the disturbance of the mid-seventeenth century. The English Civil War as a war of religion stems directly from the incomplete, partial and heavily contested course of the English, Scottish and Irish reformations.[23] Similarly the political convulsions of the seventeenth century, visited upon a society devoid

---

22 Compare the accounts of the Reformation in C. Haigh (ed.), *The English Reformation Revised* (Cambridge, 1987) and C. Haigh, *English Reformations* (Oxford, 1993) with that in A. G. Dickens, *The English Reformation* (1964). Also compare Haigh's remark of 1990 that 'there might have been no Reformation: indeed there barely was one' (C. Haigh, 'The English Reformation: a premature birth, a difficult labour and a sickly child', *HJ* 33 (1990), pp. 449–59, at p. 459) with Haigh's more recent claim that 'in the 1580s England was fast becoming a Protestant nation' (Haigh, *English Reformations*, p. 279).
23 Russell, *Causes*, chs. 3, 4.

of deep social or ideological divisions, a society in which consensus politics and religious and wider ideological unity were held to be normative and indeed normal, must have had effects in the succeeding period likely to call any stable version of England as an *ancien régime* into radical question. Indeed, one might be tempted to essay the generalisation that it is a characteristic of much self-consciously revisionist writing in a number of periods not so much fundamentally to challenge the established narratives of change and conflict as to postpone them to the next period, i.e. to the period about which the revisionist writer is not actually writing.

All these tendencies towards the long-term, the structural and the totalising account remain largely implicit, only half worked out or expressed in much revisionist writing. But of late, revisionist writers themselves have had recourse to an interpretational key that restores to the period many of the benefits conferred upon it by the old modernisation narratives. It confers a degree of interpretational coherence, appears to link the period to current political and moral concerns, and provides a legitimating rhetoric of conceptual innovation and a broadening of historical perspective. I refer of course to the so-called British problem. Here is a perspective that enables John Morrill to open a paper on the English Revolution with comparisons with contemporary events in the Balkans, current British politics and the European Community.[24] Here, indeed, at least *in potentia*, is a coherent story of nation and identity building, of partial integrations and disintegrations, of differing versions of the British state capable of linking the early modern period to the present.

We have here therefore one possible way out of the interpretative impasse created by the original destructive impact of revisionism in the extrapolation and development of a new set of structural narratives and trends from within the writings of the revisionist themselves. Ironically, while it has been an axiom of much revisionist writing that – following Russell's insight of 1973 – the Civil War was a separable event from the Revolution and thus that both 1642/3 and 1649 were natural *caesurae* in the political and ideological history of the period,[25] many of these implicit long-term structural narratives suggest a chronological unit of

---

[24] J. S. Morrill, 'The Britishness of the English Revolution', in R. Asch (ed.), *Three Nations – A Common History?* (Bochum, 1993), pp. 83–115.
[25] Russell, *Origins of the English Civil War*, pp. 1–5.

interpretation starting in the period immediately after the Reformation and stretching into the decades after 1688. Here at least seems a natural resting place for the problematic of the functional breakdown, stretching as it were from *The Tudor Revolution in Government* to the *Sinews of Power*.[26] Here too, with the Toleration Act, is a natural end to the dialectic between religious division and the search for unity and orthodoxy set in train by the Reformation, and here too, perhaps, a natural resting place in Mark Kishlansky's pursuit of adversary politics. If the various long-term problematics posited by Russell's account are to provide an agenda for further research, this seems to be the appropriate period within which to conceptualise the questions and to look for the answers. There are signs, indeed, that such researches are under way, with a number of scholars seeking to cross the great divide of 1660. Kishlansky's case study of the breakdown of adversary politics in the conduct of parliamentary s/elections is perhaps the best-known example of this trend.[27] It has been followed more recently by Victor Stater's study of the changing roles of the Lord-Lieutenancy and the emergence of the Lords-Lieutenant in the late seventeenth century as political bosses. Mike Braddick's magisterial survey of *Parliamentary Taxation in Seventeenth-Century England* provides another fascinating exercise in the same mode. Perhaps Jonathan Scott's attempt to import wholesale his own version of the problematics of the first half of the century into the second is a little over-enthusiastic, but the impulse to follow the themes and forces underlying earlier revisionist accounts of the early part of the century through the revolutionary decades and beyond is a sound one. While Scott's attempt to do so privileges continuity over change to a sometimes ludicrous extent, Steve Pincus's pursuit of the protestant cause and of the notions of universal monarchy that went with it from the end of the sixteenth century to the 1690s seems an exemplary model of the sort of tightly focused yet chronologically wide-ranging project which might yield the most fruitful results.[28]

[26]   J. Brewer, *The Sinews of Power: War, Money and the English State, 1688–1783* (New York, 1989).
[27]   M. A. Kishlansky, *Parliamentary Selection* (Cambridge, 1986).
[28]   V. Stater, *Noble Government: The Stuart Lord Lieutenancy and the Transformation of English Politics* (Athens, Ga., 1994); M. J. Braddick, *Parliamentary Taxation in Seventeenth Century England* (Royal Historical Society Studies in History, 1995); J. Scott, 'Radicalism and Restoration: the shape of the Stuart experience', *HJ* 31 (1988) pp. 453–67 and J. Scott, *Algernon Sidney and the Restoration Crisis, 1677–1683* (Cambridge, 1991), esp. part 1.

V

NARROWNESS VINDICATED: POST-REVISIONISM AND LIFE AFTER
THE DEATH OF MASTER NARRATIVES

There are, however, other ways to respond to the challenge of
revisionism: to the relative absence of master narratives (totalising
teleological accounts of the period) that the process of revisionism
has created. Here I want to identify, with perhaps a touch of
overstatement, a distinctively post-revisionist approach to the period.
What, in this context, does post-revisionism involve? At the most
general level, it involves taking seriously many of the basic claims
and assertions of early revisionism. In particular, it involves accepting
the relative autonomy and indeterminacy of the political and viewing
this as an opportunity to interpret and reintegrate the central
political narrative into a number of different religious, cultural and
social contexts.

To approach this task without relying on the priorities and
assumptions either of the old whig narrative or of the revisionist
inversion or rejection of that narrative was, of course, difficult, and
in meeting those difficulties something like a genre or sub-genre was
developed. This happened not through the pursuit of theoretical or
methodological novelty so much, as in response to the exigencies of
doing focused and historiographically effective research after and in
dialogue with revisionism. This genre is best exemplified by Richard
Cust's book on the Forced Loan, Tom Cogswell's book on the
Spanish Match and the parliament of 1624, Alastair Bellany's Ph.D.
dissertation on news culture and the Overbury murder, and Cynthia
Herrup's forthcoming work on the Castlehaven event.[29]

All four take discrete events, relatively easy in themselves to
delimit and define, and pursue their causes and ramifications at a
number of social, cultural and institutional levels. Here they are
entirely the progeny of the revisionist project as Professor Russell

---

[29] T. Cogswell, *The Blessed Revolution: English Politics and the Coming of War, 1621–1624*
(Cambridge, 1989); R. P. Cust, *The Forced Loan and English Politics, 1626–1628* (Oxford,
1987); Alastair Bellany, 'The poisoning of legitimacy? Court scandal, news culture and
politics in England, 1603–1660' (unpublished Ph.D. thesis, Princeton University, 1995). See
in particular parts 1 and 2 for the discussions of the Overbury murder summarised here.
Professor Herrup's study of the construction and reconstruction of the Castlehaven affair
in the course of the seventeenth century will be an important contribution to this style of
writing. I should like to thank her for letting me read various drafts of her work in
progress.

and others have delineated it. For these studies are not centred on Parliament; they look instead at a number of centres of power: in Cust's case the court and the Privy Council, and in Cogswell's case the court, the Privy Council, the Parliament and a variety of foreign powers. Both Cust and Cogswell also move the focus away from Westminster and Whitehall into the localities; Cust in a study of enforcement and the politics of local compliance and resistance, and Cogswell in a genuinely innovative attempt to get at movements of public opinion as they can be reconstructed from a whole range of sermon, tract and newsletter materials (both printed and manuscript). Both are aware of the extent to which politics at court, in the Council and in Parliament was played out before wider audiences. Cust's study of the loan refusers and some of Cogswell's subsequent essays on the legitimation and criticism of official policy before wider audiences show conclusively how major political players and relatively marginal local operators and aspirants like Wentworth were acutely aware of the arenas and audiences in and before which they played out their political hands and shaped their political images.[30]

Bellany's treatment of the Overbury murder is similar in its approaches and ambitions. An event with a fairly obvious beginning and end is taken and retold. We start with the highest of high politics, the manoeuvres of court factions and individuals in the murkiest of intra-court manoeuvres. The lacunae in the evidence, the historian's necessary lack of certainty about who precisely is doing what to whom, are freely admitted as Bellany tells his story. For the point of this exercise is not so much precisely what happened (although that as far as it can be known does matter) but on the ways in which contemporaries told and retold that story, how they interpreted and glossed it and the networks through which those tellings and retellings were transmitted. Bellany moves rapidly from the court to the country, from high politics, state trials, royal proclamations and legal position papers to newsletters, verse libels and cheap print. Cynthia Herrup's forthcoming study of the Castlehaven trial makes use of a similar range of genres to read off the wider cultural and ideological resonances of a scandal involving buggery, rape, popery and the flagrant abuse of patriarchal power. In this sort of work, we

---

[30] Cust, *Forced Loan*, chs. 3, 4; T. Cogswell, 'England and the Spanish Match', in R. P. Cust and A. L. Hughes (eds.), *Conflict in Early Stuart England* (1989); T. Cogswell, 'Politics and propaganda: Charles I and the people in the 1620s', *Journal of British Studies* 29 (1990), pp. 187–215.

are being presented with the opportunity to integrate the highest of high political narratives – court scandals and factional manoeuvres, the precise course and nature of which remained murky even to contemporaries – into wider cultural and ideological contexts. Here the tendency is not to write off high politics as elitist and retrograde but to see it as the ground for and occasion of a whole series of cultural and political interactions. If brought to fruition, such work may well serve to redefine the boundaries of the political in this period, and to change the way political history is written.

These studies are revisionist in their rejection of the pieties and polarities of the traditional whig narrative and in their research agenda, looking at a number of centres of power and political manoeuvre, at Westminister and Whitehall as well as in the localities and, in Cogswell's case, in the chancellories of Europe. The result (to appropriate a phrase that cannot remain unambiguous to a native of London) is a species of thick description. That is, an event whose beginning and end is relatively self-evident and whose prominence (if not whose meaning) is clear both in the established canon of historical writing and indeed in the concerns of contemporaries, is taken and analysed at a number of different social, cultural and institutional levels. There is a narrative structure provided by the event itself – this is *histoire événementielle* with a vengeance and quite right too – but the analysis could in principle proceed without direct reference to any of the big questions posed by the whig/modernisation narrative or by the revisionist inversions of the same.

However, while the post-revisionist mode as I am defining it may owe much to revisionist precept, it goes beyond revisionist practice in a number of ways. Firstly, it does genuinely free the political narrative from a whiggish obsession with Parliament in a way that Professor Russell for one has never done. Secondly, it also frees the period before 1640 from that obsession with teasing out the causes of the Civil War that revisionism took over wholesale from its whig 'other'. Thirdly, by breaking off event-sized bits it becomes possible, indeed necessary, to reintegrate many of the other narratives embedded in the socio-cultural history of the period, many of which were at least initially prompted by the modernisation narrative, although they are now just as often written against it. Thus Cust's account of the popular response to the Loan turns on recent accounts of the social structure of Essex and, more generally, on various renditions of the emergence of the middling sort and the processes of social and cultural differentiation that went with it. Cogswell's and particularly Bellany's accounts of news culture and the wider audiences before whom politics was increasingly played out are inexplicable outside a wider socio-cultural context concerned with the role of gossip, libel and popular ceremony in structuring and policing certain moral and gender economies and hierarchies. Ann Hughes's account of the basis of the parliamentary cause and of Lord Brooke's local power-base in Warwickshire is similarly founded on recent work on the connections between different patterns of agrarian structure, local patterns of power and alternative models of 'social order'.[31] But lastly, and perhaps most importantly, post-revisionism refuses the false choice between whiggery or revisionism. The choices between conflict and consensus, secular and religious conflict, between the essentially ideologically defined court/country division and the structurally and/or socially constructed local/central dichotomy, with which revisionist writing has tended to confront the reader, are all refused.

To make the point more clearly, let us take the post-revisionist treatment of localism as a test case. Arguably, early revisionism sought to replace what had become the conventional division between court and country – all but synonyms, on the revisionist reading at least, for government and opposition – with the dichotomy between a local gentry living their social and practical lives in local (county) communities largely untouched by the passions and ambitions of court politics, and the business of a central state whose financial and administrative exactions tended to provoke only resistance and resentment in the localities. These localist impulses operated, in the standard revisionist accounts, in an uneasy middle ground located somewhere between conscious ideology and an instinctive defence of the material and social interests of the local ruling class. These impulses were often, however, discussed under the rubric of 'localism' – a term which implied a rather more self-conscious and aggressively ideological stance. This was a stance which, revisionists claimed, came to full expression in a variety of neutrality pacts and movements for settlement in the localities as the parties at Westminster drifted towards war in 1642.[32] Subsequent

---

[31] Cust, *Forced Loan*, ch. 5; A. Hughes, 'Warwickshire on the eve of the civil war: a county community?', *Midland History* 7 (1982), pp. 42–72; A. Hughes, 'Local history and the origins of the civil war' in Cust and Hughes (eds.), *Conflict in Early Stuart England*, pp. 107–33.

[32] Everitt, *Community of Kent*; Morrill, *Revolt of the Provinces*.

research called these claims into question, with Dr Holmes and Dr Hughes emphasising the relatively centralised nature of the English state and legal system, and the cultural and intellectual homogeneity of the gentry. This cast considerable doubt on the foundational status of the county community in the lives even of the greater (let alone the parish) gentry. Thus, on the one hand, the unit of the county community was broken down into a number of overlapping networks and arenas, some much smaller than and others stretching far outside the county.[33] On the other hand, other scholars emphasised the complex interactions between a number of local interest groups and entities and a variegated central authority created whenever any large-scale initiative (fiscal or administrative) emanated from the centre.[34] Other historians, like Dr Cust and latterly Dr Bellany, showed through their study of the circulation of news and rumour how often far-flung areas of the country were integrated into something like an emergent public opinion.[35] But this was not necessarily to revert to an insistence on the supremacy of the national and the political over the local and the particular, of the overtly ideological over the unselfconscious parochialism and particularism of the ruling class. In a number of case studies Ann Hughes has shown how the local could be differently construed and constructed against different notions of the national. On her view the local took on very different meanings and inflections depending on the political and institutional circumstances in which it was constructed and deployed. 'Localism' could, therefore – with widely differing degrees of difficulty, according to the political, ideological and institutional context – be integrated into variant readings and constructions of the nation state and the common good.[36]

Such findings ought to open up rather than close down the field of local history, allowing scholars to see the local and the national as integrally linked, continually being constructed and reconstructed in

[33] Hughes, 'Warwickshire'; C. Holmes, 'The county community in Stuart historiography', *Journal of British Studies* 19 (1980), pp. 54–73.

[34] P. Lake, 'The collection of ship money in Cheshire during the 1630s: a case study of relations between central and local government', *Northern History* 17 (1981), pp. 44–71.

[35] R. P. Cust, 'News and politics in early seventeenth-century England', *Past and Present* 111 (1986), pp. 60–90; A. Bellany, ' "Raylinge rymes and vaunting verse": libellous politics in early Stuart England', in K. Sharpe and P. Lake (eds.), *Culture and Politics in Early Stuart England* (1993), pp. 285–310.

[36] A. L. Hughes, 'Militancy and localism: Warwickshire politics and Westminster politics', *TRHS* 5th ser., 31 (1981), pp. 51–68; A. L. Hughes, 'The King, parliament and the localities during the English civil war', *Journal of British Studies* 24 (1985), pp. 236–63.

relation to one another. While the conventional county study, generated by the exigencies of the debate over the gentry and sustained by the organising notions of the county community and of localism, might have had its day, other ways of construing and studying a newly politicised and narrativised notion of the relations between the local and the national have emerged. Studies based on networks that transcend the individual county, on families and their connections in a number of social and cultural arenas, on certain central institutions, on certain intense periods of interaction between the centre and the localities, all open up different ways both to reconceptualise and study local/central relations. The result, then, of all this critical attention should be not to render local history a dead end, but rather a fresh field for study.[37]

Here a forthcoming book by Tom Cogswell on Leicestershire serves as a model. Taking as its subject the interaction between the fiscal demands of the state during the 1620s and the local power and aspirations of a nobleman in financial difficulties, the earl of Huntingdon, Cogswell's narrative integrates national and local politics, while addressing agendas drawn from a number of historiographical debates, ranging from issues raised by Lawrence Stone's *Crisis of the Aristocracy* to arguments about the fiscal capacities of the state in the 1620s, the balance between local and national taxation and the nature of the relationship between central and local government. Here that relationship is seen as a process, part of larger political narratives rather than simply as an administrative or fiscal problem. Structural analysis is elided into political narrative and the gap between the short term and the long term, the structural and the political significantly narrowed.

Strafford's career lends itself beautifully to many of these approaches and in many of the essays collected in this volume we can see some of the central features of the post-revisionist mode as it has been characterised here. The refusal to accept the false polarity between conflict and consensus, the rejection of a simple two sides model of the politics of the period can be seen clearly in both Dr Cust's and Dr Milton's chapters. Cust's analysis of the way in which Wentworth constructed his persona through the deployment of a

---

[37] For example, see J. Eales, *Puritans and Roundheads: the Harleys of Brampton Bryan and the Outbreak of the English Civil War* (Cambridge, 1990); Slater, *Noble Government*; Cust, *Forced Loan*; Lake, 'Collection of ship money in Cheshire'; and now A. Gill, 'Ship money during the Personal Rule of Charles I' (unpublished Ph.D. thesis, University of Sheffield, 1990).

number of images and stereotyped claims to virtue and independence while still pursuing office at court is an exemplary reading of
an increasingly common career path – that of the ambitious public
man, anxious to retain support in his locality and in the arena of
public opinion while using the standing thus achieved to further a
career at court. Such careers have much to tell us about the
dynamics of the political system and the complex manoeuvres and
manipulations through which contemporaries made their way to
office, profit and political virtue. Anthony Milton's essay shows us
Strafford's later use, in the very different circumstances of the 1630s,
of what remained in many ways recognisably the same stock of
assumptions and images, now inflected in a distinctly Caroline and
indeed absolutist mode. Thus revisionist claims about the common
languages in which the political was described, organised and
manipulated are confirmed, while revisionist conclusions about the
extent and nature of ideological division and disagreement in this
period are falsified. There could scarcely be a clearer demonstration
of the ways in which Wentworth/Strafford both did and did not
change sides. This clearly was a question *mal posé* on both the
revisionist and whig sides of the equation. We return to the insight of
Firth quoted in the introduction by Dr Merritt, but we do so with a
considerably enriched sense of the process whereby careers were
made in court and country during this period.

Again, Dr Quintrell's article shows how a carefully reconstructed account of even the smallest event (or in the case of
Laud's failure to be appointed Lord Treasurer a non-event) can
throw light on larger issues. Here the narrative mode, deployed
through a microstudy, throws into stark relief the nature of politics
at the Caroline court, with the major players shadow-boxing
around the uncertain, indeed masked, intentions of a gnomic
monarch, and William Laud showing both the nature and the
limitations of his career as a court politician. Again John McCafferty's piece is a tribute to the importance of telling a political
story, played out not merely in the manoeuvres of the court and
convocation house but before wider bodies of opinion, in this
instance in Ireland and England. Here is a masterly demonstration
of the way in which a real sense of ideological difference and
division can be brought to bear on an ostensibly consensual
process of decision-making, made up of often implicit gesture and
counter-gesture, threat and counter-threat.

In their return to politics, their emphasis on the importance of process and the narrative mode, their concern with looking at a number of centres of power at once, with broadening the focus from the centre into the localities, with stressing the interactions between those arenas and with looking behind assumed ideological polarities and labels to analyse the use made by individuals and fractions of particular arguments and claims – all of the authors discussed here are in many ways operating in a recognisably post-revisionist world. But while the agenda and some of the procedures of post-revisionism may stem directly from revisionist precept, the substantive conclusions of much of the resultant research fit neither within the structures of the received wisdom against which revisionism was a reaction, nor within the staunchly anti-whig, inversionary straitjacket of revisionist interpretation. On the one hand, it is clearly not enough to conclude that Gardiner was right and that we can all therefore go about our business safe in the knowledge that the revisionist dragon has been slain. On the other, it is unclear how to arrange and narrate all this new research.

As we have seen, one reaction to the resulting interpretational cacophony is, echoing David Cannadine's and Patrick Joyce's responses to similar changes in a later period, to throw up one's hands at the balkanisation of the field, alternately lamenting the pedantic specialisation of the modern academic scene and/or excoriating the unreflective, fact-grubbing empiricism of English historiography. Such responses are surely misguided. The field is in transition: an old master narrative has been disrupted and displaced and the result is not (yet) a new dominant paradigm but a number of new undertakings and approaches.[38]

There are, as I have argued above, a number of different long-term problematics and periodisations implicit in revisionism itself and emerging out of the thick description of post-revisionist scholarship. These can be pursued, perhaps with the notion not only of multi-centred political narratives, but also through the notion of particular conjunctures linking different social, political, ideological and religious narratives in analyses of different sorts of events or crises. Here, for instance, narratives of social differentiation and cultural development, the emergence of a number of public spheres or arenas for the formation and canvassing of differently constituted

---

[38] Cannadine, 'British history: past, present – and future?'; Joyce, 'End of social history?'; Joyce, *Democratic Subjects*, introduction.

bodies of public opinion, narratives of state formation and fiscal, institutional and military change, shifts in the balance of European power, differently constituted religious orthodoxies, might all interact in particular conjunctures. Each of these levels of change, these ways of thematising and delineating the object of research, might demand very different periodisations and modes of research but all might be seen to be in play in the course of the account of any given conjuncture or event.

A great deal has been written of late about the dead hand of the master narrative in historical writing. But it is arguably impossible to write history without some implicit sense of before, during and after. Historians who make the loudest claims on this subject too often become the subject of their own work. Here the point at issue becomes as much the self-reflexive epistemological and rhetorical sophistication and self-consciousness of the author as any wider, recognisably historical project. Moreover, as Amanda Vickery has recently pointed out, even those who talk loudest of the need to avoid totalising master narratives, who deny the existence of any reality or context outside 'the text', habitually reproduce certain of those narratives in the course of their own attempts to read the texts in front of them. They do so, as we have seen, either by simply postponing the changes conventionally supposed to have occurred during their period to a later one, or through the use of general terms and categories (e.g. capitalism, consumer society, the public sphere) that carry with them implicit schemas of development, often all the more mechanical and teleological for their being left implicit and unexamined.[39] But if historiographical life without at least implicit master narratives is unattainable, life with a multiplicity of such narratives, the relations between which are held to be contingent and not ordered in some obvious and pre-ordained way, might be thought to represent some sort of advance. It is here that the impact of revisionism, rightly understood, is most valuable and that the genres and procedures inherent in post-revisionist practice have the most to offer.

[39] For a recent debate in which these issues are discussed and some of these tendencies displayed, see the exchanges between Gyan Prakash, Rosalind O'Hanlon and David Washbrook in *Comparative Studies in Society and History* 32 (1990), pp. 383–408, *ibid.*, 34 (1992), pp. 141–67 and *ibid.*, pp. 168–84. See also A. Vickery, 'Golden age to separate spheres? A review of the categories and chronology of English women's history', *HJ* 36 (1993), pp. 383–414, esp. pp. 413–14, note III.

THE BRITISH PROBLEM PROBLEMATISED

It is as one such instance of conjuncture, of the intersection through political crisis of a whole series of different narratives in three very different societies, that the so-called British problem is probably best conceived. This is to prefer the billiard ball version of the subject to the long-term, almost Braudellian, structuralism that some writers bring to the topic of British history and the British problem as an explanatory device in seventeenth-century English/British/Archipelagian history. It is also to resist the temptation, proffered by some revisionist writers, to use the British problem as some sort of new master narrative, resolving many of the interpretational problems inherent in the revisionist approach to the causes of the English Civil War, and linking the events of the mid-seventeenth century to a number of pressing contemporary concerns in a way reminiscent of the old whig narratives of the emergence of English liberty and the rise of Parliament.

Used thus, the British problem represents the continuation of revisionism by other means. As with localism, the impulse towards division and conflict is displaced from England elsewhere. In the most extreme formulation of the localist model, conflict was 'artifically inseminated' into the English localities from a polarised centre. Now, through the British problem, rebellion, resistance theory and the more extreme forms of religious passion are imported into a relatively stable England from Scotland and Ireland. The complex interactions between events, ideological fragments and political factions in all three kingdoms are then invoked to explain both the outbreak of civil war in England and indeed the subsequent course of conflict, the failure to achieve settlement and the ultimate recourse to regicide. As Nicholas Canny observes in this volume, it is not clear that much more is involved here than an enriched account of English politics and the English state, with events in the three kingdoms being invoked no longer simply as exogenous variables, bolts from the blue, to explain English events, but with a more systematic view of the nature and locus of their intention being used to play up their interconnections from the very outset. There is of course nothing wrong with an enriched version of English politics and the operations of the English state. Indeed, that is a project in which historians of the political crises of the 1640s and 1650s in England, Scotland and Ireland all have a considerable stake. But as Canny observes, it is less than clear that this involves the emergence of a new British history.

Moreover, the importation of Scotland and Ireland as major causal factors in explaining the Civil War does not so much solve as displace the revisionist problem. For the Irish and Scottish narratives and historiographies being invoked to explain 1640–2 contain many of the same tensions and controversies that they are being invoked to solve or expel from the revisionist account of English history. Thus the extent to which the Scottish rebellion had long-term causes stretching back well before 1637, through Charles I's reign or even earlier, is surely as controversial among Scottish historians as the same question about the roots of the English crisis of 1640 is among their English colleagues.[40] Similarly, is the Irish rebellion best explained as a result of short-term crisis generated by the rabidly anti-papal nexus between the dominant faction/s in the English Long Parliament and their Scottish allies? How far was it conditioned and produced by the reaction against Strafford's regime? How, in turn, should we conceive of that regime? Was it but one aspect of Caroline absolutism in three kingdoms or rather a natural product of longer-term trends in English policy towards Ireland? These are all real and unresolved questions in Irish historiography, or so Nicholas Canny's essay suggests. The relationship between the long and the short term, the systemic and the interactive, are all therefore up for grabs in any number of the available English, Scottish and Irish (and Anglo-Scottish and Anglo-Irish) narratives. And so a great deal turns on what versions of Irish and Scottish history are being invoked and integrated into the English narrative, and of course vice versa. In the case of Scotland at least, we have English revisionists like Professor Russell invoking Scottish narratives that root the covenanting movement in elements in Caroline policy that were evident almost from 1625 on. Here then is a high road to revolt with the like of which revisionists would have no truck at all in England.[41]

Following Canny, what we may be seeing here is not so much a genuinely British history, but rather a tracing out of the effects of

---

[40] For the most recent treatment of these issues, see A. Macinnes, *Charles I and the Making of the Covenanting Movement, 1625–1641* (Edinburgh, 1991).

[41] See C. S. R. Russell's review of Macinnes, *Charles I* in *The Times Literary Supplement,* 26 July, 1991.

English policies in Scotland and Ireland. Again, this is a perfectly legitimate and sensible subject for study with important things to tell historians of all three kingdoms. As the essays in this volume by Anthony Milton and Julia Merritt both argue, Strafford for one was governing Ireland with one eye on his royal master in England and with the hope of a return to higher office at home. His attitude to the Irish parliament of 1634–5 may well parallel the management of the Coronation Parliament in Scotland. In both, the precise nature of what Charles regarded as a parliament *à sa mode* may have been revealed rather more starkly than in anything that happened in England during the 1620s. Dr McCafferty's claim that the refurbished and Laudianised Church of Ireland was not so much the end of a process of Anglicisation as a part of a process of reform in three kingdoms in which the Church of Ireland, in all its newly polished patristic and catholic purity, could serve as a model for the further reform of the Church of England, makes the same point.[42]

It is now surely clear that the temper of the Caroline regime cannot properly be judged from its policies in England alone. More extreme and radical versions of policies and assumptions at work in England may well be observed in Scotland and Ireland during the Personal Rule, and it may well be that we can best judge which way the wind was blowing by collating and comparing Caroline policy in three kingdoms. Thus while royal concern with crown and church lands was pushed far further in Ireland and Scotland than in England, there clearly were schemes in England involving, for instance, royal forests and London tithes, just as there may be (as Dr Milton suggests) significant similarities between Charles's handling of the Short Parliament and Wentworth's of the Irish parliament of 1634–5. Moreover, as Jane Ohlmeyer's chapter on the Londonderry plantation shows, English interests as central as the City of London could not have been oblivious to these parallels.

This, however, is not so much a new subject – British history – as a more integrated reading of English, Scottish and Irish *histories*. Moreover in pursuing this process of integration there is, or should be, no stably 'British' archimedian point from which to view these events. To assume that there is, as Nicholas Canny and Keith Brown have both argued, comes perilously close to the introduction of a covertly

---

[42] On this subject see also J. S. Morrill, 'A British patriarchy? Ecclesiastical imperialism under the early Stuarts', in Fletcher and Roberts (eds.), *Religion, Culture and Society*, pp. 209–37.

Anglocentric, English master narrative through the back door. For English historians, of course, this is less than a capital offence – in this period we are surely still dealing with distinct if interrelated national histories, and in that context Anglocentricity seems a natural enough viewpoint for historians of England, just as Hiberno- or Scotto- centricity seem equally natural and sensible perspectives for historians of Ireland or Scotland. However, such necessary differences in perspective are not best hidden under an elaborately 'British' rhetoric. To both paraphrase and disagree with Jane Ohlmeyer, we should *not* seek to view the 'crisis of the mid-seventeenth century' 'as an *equilateral* triangle of conflict involving all three of the Stuart kingdoms' but rather as involving a series of interactions between those kingdoms and (as Ohlmeyer's own account of Antrim's continental contacts and schemes shows) a still more generalised 'abroad'.[43] Moreover, those instructions will always look different according to both the particular kingdom and the particular part of the crisis from which the overall process of interaction is being viewed. In short, there is nothing equilaterally or stably 'British' about this process at all. For certain events, certain segments of the crisis (either taking place in or being viewed from England, Scotland or Ireland) such a tripartite reading is clearly essential; for others it is less so. To quote Keith Brown, at times the Britishness of the British problem may stem from little more than the fact that the events under discussion took place in the geographical space conventionally called Great Britain and Ireland.[44] Moreover, over the seventeenth century as a whole, those looking for a structural geopolitical key to unlock the process of state formation and political development in England might look as much to the triangle linking England to the Low Countries and a dominating and threateningly popish continental power (at differing times Spain or France) than to the problematic of 'Britain' and her multiple monarchy.[45] Put another way, are many of the long-term trends mobilised by Russell and others to discuss early Stuart politics best

---

[43] J. Ohlmeyer, *Civil War and Restoration in the Three Stuart Kingdoms: The Career of Randall MacDonnell, Marquis of Antrim, 1609–1683* (Cambridge, 1992), p. 279.

[44] K. Brown, 'British history: a skeptical comment', in Asch (ed.), *Three Nations – A Common History?*, pp. 117–27, at p. 126.

[45] The point, of course, is not to pose this question as an either/or choice between mutually exclusive paradigms or frameworks, but, on the contrary, to stress that the period can be chopped up in a number of different ways depending on how the problematic at hand is conceived, and what the appropriate period is judged to be for the discussion of that problematic.

viewed from the perspective of 1642 and the 1640s and 1650s or from those provided by the 1580s and 90s, on the one hand, and by 1688 and the regime that emerged during the 1690s, on the other?

Whether therefore we should go from the undoubted significance of interactions between England, Scotland and Ireland for any understanding of the crises of the 1640s and 1650s to a new master narrative, a dominant legitimating discourse about British history, national identity and multiple monarchy, linking this period directly to contemporary concerns about Northern Ireland, the union with Scotland and the European Union, seems at least questionable. Having freed ourselves from one present-minded paradigm, it seems a shame to lock ourselves so quickly into another. Better, perhaps, to prolong the luxurious and rather rare indeterminacy and multi-vocality of the post-revisionist moment.

Index

Printed in Great Britain by
Amazon.co.uk, Ltd.,
Marston Gate.